Amazon

Amazon

At the Intersection of Culture and Capital

Edited by Paul Smith, Alexander Monea,
and Maillim Santiago

ROWMAN & LITTLEFIELD
Lanham • Boulder • New York • London

Published by Rowman & Littlefield
An imprint of The Rowman & Littlefield Publishing Group, Inc.
4501 Forbes Boulevard, Suite 200, Lanham, Maryland 20706
www.rowman.com

86-90 Paul Street, London EC2A 4NE

British Library Cataloguing in Publication Information Available

Library of Congress Cataloging-in-Publication Data

Names: Smith, Paul, 1954 November 23- editor. | Monea, Alexander, editor. | Santiago, Maillim, editor.
Title: Amazon : at the intersection of culture and capital / edited by Paul Smith, Alexander Monea, and Maillim Santiago.
Description: Lanham : Rowman & Littlefield, [2023] | Includes bibliographical references and index.
Identifiers: LCCN 2022035773 (print) | LCCN 2022035774 (ebook) | ISBN 9781538165225 (cloth) | ISBN 9781538175583 (paper) | ISBN 9781538165232 (ebook)
Subjects: LCSH: Amazon.com (Firm) | Amazon.com (Firm)--Influence. | Amazon.com (Firm)--Corrupt practices. | Electronic commerce. | Teleshopping.
Classification: LCC HF5548.32 .A456 2023 (print) | LCC HF5548.32 (ebook) | DDC 381/.142--dc23/eng/20220811
LC record available at https://lccn.loc.gov/2022035773
LC ebook record available at https://lccn.loc.gov/2022035774

™ The paper used in this publication meets the minimum requirements of American National Standard for Information Sciences—Permanence of Paper for Printed Library Materials, ANSI/NISO Z39.48-1992.

~

Contents

Acknowledgments vii

Introduction ix
Paul Smith, Alexander Monea, and Maillim Santiago

Part I. The Political Economy of Amazon

Chapter 1 Amazon's Anti-Trust Paradox 3
Lina Khan

Chapter 2 Amazon 1-Click and the Value of Broken Infrastructure 101
Ulysses Pascal

Chapter 3 Logistics of Probability: Anticipatory Shipping and the Production of Markets 115
Nikolaus Poechhacker and Eva-Maria Nyckel

Chapter 4 Amazon Warehouse Work: Machinic Dispossession and Augmented Despotism 131
Alessandro Delfanti

Part II. Practices of Resistance

Chapter 5 Platforms, Resistance, Organizing 149
Jamie Woodcock and Callum Cant

Chapter 6 Disrupting Work with Play on Mturk.com: A Visual Essay 165
xtine burrough

Chapter 7 Difference and Dependence among Digital Workers: The Case of Amazon Mechanical Turk 183
Lilly Irani

Part III. Amazon and Culture

Chapter 8 Unending Consumption: A Prime Example 195
David Arditi

Chapter 9 Amazon Eats Whole Foods: Empire-Building and the Acquisition of Conscious Capitalism™ 211
Lisa Daily

Chapter 10 Virtuous Viewing and Amazon Studios 227
Maillim Santiago

Part IV. Environmental Impact

Chapter 11 Quick and Slow Violence: The Age of Billionaire Biodiversity 247
Brett Hutchins, Libby Lester, Richard Maxwell, Toby Miller, and Whitney Monaghan

Chapter 12 Decoding Amazon's Climate Pledge: Public Relations and the Platformization of Governance 269
Emily West

Chapter 13 Confronting the Regionalism of Amazon Web Services 287
Patrick Brodie and Paul O'Neill

Part V. Appendix

Appendix Art and Action 307
Hiba Ali and Nina Sarnelle

Index 323

List of Contributors 341

About the Editors 345

Acknowledgments

Like any book, this one would not have been possible without a lot of support from institutions, colleagues, and friends. We'd like to thank our editors at Rowman & Littlefield: Rebecca Anastasi who signed the project and provided initial support and Charles Harmon who took over for her and helped see us to completion. We'd also like to thank our enthusiastic contributors, including those represented here in the final project, those who agreed to participate in the conference but whose ability to contribute to the volume was upset by the pandemic, and those who submitted materials for our call for contributions. It was a pleasure working with them, and we are very excited to see the finalized version of their efforts here in print. Last but not least, we want to acknowledge and thank and encourage the work of all those who count themselves as against Amazon. But particularly, in our local context, we thank Marley Pulido Vargas and Danny Cendejas, community activists who were so helpful and enthusiastic about this project from the start. They are among the many thousands of activists around the world whose opposition to Amazon we share.

Introduction

Paul Smith, Alexander Monea, and Maillim Santiago

> "If you are doing anything interesting in the world, you're going to have critics."
>
> —Jeff Bezos (Recode, 2016)

In 1994, Jeff Bezos and his then wife MacKenzie Scott took a road trip across the United States to move to Seattle and to start an online bookstore called "Cadabra" out of their garage, or so the myth goes. Prior to the move, Jeff Bezos had been working as a senior vice president at the tech-oriented hedge fund D.E. Shaw, drawing a lucrative salary. He used the connections he made there to hire initial talent for the company and to put together a small group of angel investors, including his Wall Street friends, friends of his parents, friends from Princeton University, his alma mater, and local investors, who seeded the company with a million dollars (Bayers, 1999). Bezos parlayed this into an eight-million-dollar Series A from Kleiner Perkins in June 1996 (Rosoff, 2016). Bezos played the part of the scrappy tech founder to a tee, specifically purchasing a house with a garage so he could enact the archetypal Silicon Valley mythos (Press, 2021). Within a few years, he was the subject of numerous glowing interviews highlighting his rags-to-riches tech founder story and by 1998 had cracked the Forbes 400 Richest People in America list with a net worth of over a billion dollars ("The Richest People in America," 1998).

Since its founding in 1994, Amazon has steadily and inexorably become probably the most visible and easily recognized e-commerce platform in the world. Bezos' obsession with growth and disruption—deeply indebted to the "California ideology" of libertarian technologists (Turner, 2006)—has led to marked expansion as the online bookstore has increasingly become the "everything store." Already by the late 1990s, the storefront had expanded to include music, movies, toys, and electronics, with Bezos using strategic partnerships to garner sales data, infiltrate new markets, and eventually leverage pseudo-monopoly power to force one-sided contracts on partners and take over market shares (Stone, 2013). This expansion, only slightly slowed by the dot.com crash, has continued to accelerate. Today, Amazon websites receive about 2.5 billion discrete visits each month, and Amazon's share of US e-commerce during the pandemic year of 2021 reached almost 57 percent. Even while Amazon has in some ways struggled to cope with the unexpected demands of the COVID-19 moment, its dominance in the US and European markets has remained unquestioned and mostly unchallenged as projections and expectations continue to be revised upwards by market analysts. Only the giant Chinese e-commerce leaders, Alibaba and Tencent, have anything like the power and influence of Amazon worldwide.

For more than a quarter of a century, Amazon has either been the first to imagine and implement a vast array of technological and business innovations, or has been quick to perfect its own versions of new features developed in Silicon Valley by poaching key employees from rivals, acquiring smaller companies, developing in-house versions, and throwing its weight around as the premier e-commerce platform in the United States. Yet until recently Amazon has received significantly less critical attention in the press and in academic scholarship. While scores of books and articles have been written about Apple, Google, and Facebook, there are comparatively few focused solely on Amazon. This is currently changing, as Bezos' skyrocketing to the wealthiest individual on the planet from 2017 to 2021 and ongoing labor organizing against poor conditions in warehouse and delivery operations at the company have brought Amazon into public consciousness over the past five years. It is our hope that this volume can contribute to this public reckoning and offer critical insights into some of the core issues we have seen in Amazon's business practices.

Origins of the Book

On September 7, 2017, Amazon released a request for proposals (RFP) to governments and economic development organizations in North America asking them to pitch themselves as the potential host sites of a second Amazon headquarters (HQ2). The RFP dangled the promise of over fifty thousand new full-time jobs whose average annual total compensation would exceed one hundred thousand dollars and an expected five billion dollars in capital expenditures. These entities were given a deadline of October 19, 2017, to submit reams of valuable data (real estate data, transportation data, incentive packages, education data, demographic data, etc.) to Amazon to convince it to locate its HQ2 there. While the initial RFP mentioned "incentives" twenty-one times (Stone, 2021, p. 294), perceived pressure in its hometown of Seattle shifted the company's priorities. City officials in Seattle were looking to institute a headcount tax to raise money from large corporations to combat displacement from gentrification, homelessness, and other local issues, a measure that would have increased Amazon's local tax bill by $22.5 million annually. Bezos ordered his new building near Ranier Square be leased out rather than occupied by Amazon and spent more than one hundred million dollars to avoid the tax bill, even as city officials worked to negotiate and decrease the head tax (the bill was later repealed due to pressure Amazon put on the city council). The shift in local politics in Seattle led to Amazon reevaluating its priorities and ignoring the recommendations of the HQ2 team. Bezos was now particularly focused on finding large cities with strong opportunities for recruitment in the friendliest possible political environments (Stone, 2021).

This book had its earliest origins in the announcement by Amazon in 2019 that Crystal City, in Arlington, Virginia (conveniently located just across the Potomac from Washington, DC), had been chosen as one of the sites for Amazon's HQ2. The announcement was met with conflicting and conflicted reactions. There were many reasons for the local area government and communities to welcome the inevitably huge economic impact of placing HQ2 in what was a relatively underperforming area of Northern Virginia. But equally there were many reasons to object. The transport, housing, and education infrastructures in the area were arguably already inadequate for a growing population, and the influx of thousands of new Amazon employees was also unlikely to solve existing problems of gentrification and inequality, while the incentives and bribes offered to Amazon seemed excessive. In this conflicted context, it was disappointing that Amazon's plans were greeted by our university, George Mason, with somewhat unambiguous enthusiasm in welcoming its new neighbor. As a response, the Cultural Studies doctoral program decided to arrange a conference on our campus which would be perhaps less uncritical, and we started working with local activists and grassroots organizations generally skeptical of the benefits so as to represent the case against Amazon HQ2. In the end, the conference had to be canceled because its date coincided almost exactly with the beginning of the COVID-19 pandemic. During the course of the pandemic, it seemed all the more important to not allow the issue of HQ2 to be forgotten, so we converted the planned conference into this edited volume where we have gathered a mixture of established and junior scholars, all of whose work can help us to understand the phenomenon that is Amazon. Meanwhile, our comrades in organizations like Our Revolution Arlington, Tenants and Workers, ALIGN, La ColectiVA, and DC Tech Worker Coalition continue their everyday efforts for social justice in the communities that Amazon is already affecting.

Amazon, Platform Capitalism, and Monopoly Capitalism

Amazon is the paradigmatic instance of what, after Nick Srnicek, we often now call platform capitalism. For Srnicek our current phase of capitalist accumulation is marked by the emergence of platform enterprises based on the use of data as a resource for extraction. Platform enterprises in their most basic definition facilitate interaction among different groups of economic actors (e.g., investors, producers, advertisers, consumers, etc.), often supplying these groups with the requisite tools to communicate with each other. Platforms rely upon the effects of networking interactions among the groups and normally control and regulate what Srnicek rightly calls the politics of these interactions. Those broad definitional outlines enable a variety of different kinds of platform activities, and Srnicek emphasized five different types: advertising platforms (e.g., Facebook), cloud platforms (e.g., Amazon's Amazon Web Services [AWS]), industry platforms (e.g., GE), producer platforms (e.g., Spotify), and lean platforms (e.g., AirBnB). Most platforms tend to have characteristics of more than one of those categories, but as Srnicek points out "Amazon . . . spans nearly all of the above categories" (see especially Srnicek, 2016, p. 36–50).

So although it is perhaps partly disguised by its representation as an online retailer, Amazon is in fact one of America's oldest and most successful technology platforms. At the time of writing, Amazon's market capitalization hovers at $1.12 trillion, putting it just behind Apple and Alphabet/Google, and more than double Meta/Facebook (the other members of the supposed "Big Four" of American technology companies). During the two decades or so of its rise, Amazon has been at the forefront of the majority of Silicon Valley's technological innovations: efforts to index the world; simplify and automate e-payments (e.g., 1-Click); facilitate e-reading (e.g., Topaz, Kindle, etc.); stream digital multimedia content (e.g., Audible, Video on Demand, Prime Video, MP3 Store); personalize the internet and implement recommendation engines; incorporate machine learning (e.g., Mechanical Sensei, Amabot); develop voice command through natural language processing (e.g., Alexa); domesticate artificial intelligence devices (e.g., Echo and the suite of similar devices hosting Alexa technology); scan the world's books (e.g., Search Inside the Book); implement web analytics and ad sales (e.g., Clickriver); map the world's roadways and offer street views (e.g., Block View); facilitate the gig economy (e.g., Amazon's Mechanical Turk, Amazon Fresh); automate hiring, firing, and labor management; develop facial recognition and security software (e.g., Rekognition) for domestic, commercial, and governmental use; and, perhaps most importantly, offer server services like web hosting and virtual machines for advanced computation through AWS. AWS is currently the backbone of a large portion of the commercial internet and is used by companies like Netflix, Reddit, Pinterest, Etsy, Airbnb, and LinkedIn.

AWS is reportedly the most profitable segment of Amazon, bringing in $6.5 billion in the first quarter of 2022 alone, and in 2020 was responsible for about 16 percent of Amazon's total revenues. Sara Mitchell (2021) has suggested that Amazon actually derives greater profit from its Marketplace operations, but without disclosing exact figures, and that this is a result of its skimming of revenues from sellers that use the platform. She calculates that Amazon earned 34 percent of its revenue from its marketplace in 2020. Revenues from these vendors are likely used to offset and to deliberately offer at a loss important products and services in other sectors (e.g., Amazon Prime, Amazon Fresh, or Amazon Games) as Amazon gains market share.

So while AWS is of undoubted and ever-growing importance for Amazon's revenues, its Marketplace operations are still hugely important and yet the financial details are less clear. What is clear, however, is the way that Amazon's modus operandi and the multiple ways in which it has reshaped standard business practices has overturned some of capitalism's most entrenched habits and characteristics. For example, Lina Khan has demonstrated how Amazon has led the way for capitalist corporations to integrate across previously more or less distinct business lines. That is, Amazon is now not just a retailer (in both digital and brick and mortar realms), but is now also a marketing platform, a delivery and logistics network, a payment service, a credit lender, an auction house, a major book publisher, a producer of television and films, a fashion designer, a hardware manufacturer, and a leading host of cloud server space.

Khan essentially argues that Amazon deliberately chooses monopoly over magnitude of profits and that this strategy has entailed a relentless program of integration across all aspects of the marketplace. Part of this depends upon selected areas of below-cost pricing, and the taking of deliberate losses in order to acquire market power over other vendors who are forced to use and accommodate the unavoidable infrastructure of the Amazon platform. Khan's chapter in this volume is a groundbreaking analysis of how Amazon's radical overturning of standard business practices leads us right back to venerable questions about monopolization and anticompetitive business practices. Readers should perhaps by now be familiar with Lina Khan, whose work on Amazon's antitrust profile has seen her be installed into the role of chair of the Federal Trade Commission in the Biden administration—and already her arguments have caused enough alarm in the Amazon camp that they have asked for her to be recused from investigations into the company.

Ulysses Pascal's chapter, which follows Khan's, is an enlightening analysis of exactly the means that Amazon deploys to gain the kind of control over other players that Khan discusses, and it also explicates the process by which Amazon can essentially compel its third-party vendors to use the platform, facilitating Amazon's incessant skimming of profits. Focusing on the technology and the digital infrastructure of Amazon's platform, Pascal demonstrates how what he calls "the means of value realization" are made to operate in Amazon's favor, particularly to the disadvantage of sellers on the site.

Another aspect of the landscape of the capitalist world that has been irrevocably changed by Amazon's presence and growth is what would once have been called "distribution," a term that has been displaced by emphasis on "supply chains." In the globalized economy in which Amazon is obviously a giant player, much of the character of modern production, distribution, and consumption has been refashioned by way of new and more efficient supply chains (whose fragility, however, we have witnessed during and since the global pandemic). Amazon's business fundamentally depends not just upon the smooth functioning of supply chains but also upon the ability to predict and control the flows of commodities from production to consumption and at every step along the way. The chapter here by Nikolaus Poechhacker and Eva-Maria Nyckel gives a thorough account of how such control is achieved technologically and algorithmically, but also argues that Amazon is on the cutting edge of such practices and that these practices are available to Amazon because of its market strength and only go to expand that strength.

While Amazon can be said to be changing the face of capitalism itself and establishing the structures and infrastructures by which its platform dominates and controls competitors and other businesses, it also engages in new forms of deploying, managing, and controlling labor. If Amazon dominates other businesses with the help of its platform technology, it also dominates its workforce by finding and refining news ways in which workers' activity can be incorporated with technology and machinery, ensuring workers' cooperation with machinery by the application of algorithms. Several of the chapters in this volume address the multifarious ways in which Amazon works and reworks the fundamental capital/labor relationship, and Alessandro Delfanti's chapter directly examines the ways in which digital means are used inside Amazon's many huge warehouses to mediate the relationship between the worker and the work. Delfanti concludes that Amazon's practices repeat, with a new technological variation, the chronically authoritarian nature of capitalism's relation to labor.

Practices of Resistance

Amazon's business model is founded not only on leveraging monopolistic market shares and its platform architecture, but more fundamentally on the exploitation of a growing body of international laborers. This exploitation is borne primarily by its gig economy and contract laborers, fulfillment center employees, and Whole Foods employees. Within these various sites of production, employees assemble, sort, and fulfill Amazon's ceaseless pipeline of orders in deteriorating working conditions for the company's e-commerce business and complementary subsidiaries. The difficulties fulfillment center employees have faced in organizing for better working conditions are only more daunting when it comes to gig economy workers, ranging from contract employees responsible for delivering packages in their own vehicles to digital piecemeal laborers performing "microtasks" on the Amazon Mechanical Turk platform for a pittance. In this section, chapters by Jamie Woodcock and Callum Cant, xtine burrough, and Lilly Irani reflect on the possibilities and practices of resistance within Amazon's labor force across various levels by people who carry out the work necessary to accomplish Amazon's promises to its customers.

Woodcock and Cant analyze worker writing at Amazon in their chapter and compare various experiences of work and struggle throughout different departments at Amazon. These writings from workers across several business levels provide context and detail regarding Amazon's success and struggle with consumer compliance and demand, something the authors describe as the hidden life experiences behind the work at Amazon. Throughout the chapter, candid accounts from workers reveal a sordid and bleak working environment at Amazon with warehouse conditions described as repulsive and alienating, juxtaposed with inherited automated instincts from "Turkers" and illusions of freedom from delivery drivers. The authors conclude that while angry workers may not be enough to cause widespread resistance throughout Amazon, the more that Amazon's work is platformized and divided into more atomized labor, the greater the potential is for workers to become aware of the exploitative process by which Amazon secures labor and adds to its vast accumulation of wealth.

burrough provides a visual chapter that examines works of art created through Amazon's Mechanical Turk (Mturk) platform, a crowd-sourced online work platform that divides worker tasks into smaller, more menial human intelligence tasks (HITs), one of the many so-called improvements and digitizations of Amazon's labor process. As part of her research, burrough created a worker account within the Mturk online job board and both completed HITs and posted HITs. The HITs she posted asked workers to produce creative or artistic labor, which she then spends the rest of her chapter analyzing through a lens of resistance. She asks whether a platform like Mturk could be disrupted by the very crowd-sourced workers that are employed to complete the digital sweatshop workload delegated by Amazon. She concludes from her own experiments in the platform that there is potential for coordinated resistance and disruption of Amazon's workflow within the Mturk platform.

Irani's chapter examines the difficulties that Mturk laborers face in organizing. Because of a platform like Mturk, Amazon can position itself as a high-value employer and entrepreneurial innovator by outsourcing tedium, digitizing labor, and masking that labor as high-tech mechanization. Because of this, Irani concludes, Mturk becomes an infrastructure that divides Amazon's digital workforce between "innovators" and "menial symbolic workers." She concludes by proposing the use of specially designed software for facilitating international labor organizing through Mturk.

Amazon and Culture

The fundamental social relations of capitalism are, of course, centered around the organization of the capital/labor relation, but every change in that relation implicates all other areas of capitalist culture and ideology. The chapters here by David Arditi, Lisa Daily, and Maillim Santiago each examine a particular aspect of what we might call the cultural environment of consumption. That is, as Amazon reworks the many ways it creates value and opportunities for multi-faceted consumption by innovating its Amazon Prime membership benefits, cultural formations have arisen directly through Amazon Prime's business or because of the instant gratification and monetized space Amazon Prime encourages through its features and format.

Arditi shows how Amazon Prime, the multi-faceted subscription program, alters consumer habits and expectations, at the same time as it radically expands the means of consumption. He demonstrates how Amazon Prime's multifarious features, often at an additional cost to a subscriber's base membership, encourage what he terms "unending consumption." For Arditi, unending consumption is fundamentally modeled on subscription services and positions consumers as renters rather than owners of commodities. This new model of consumption is self-perpetuating, increasingly entangling our lives with Amazon and catalyzing corporate cultural consumption and circulation. He concludes that Amazon's alarming growth and its instigation of unending consumption must be reined in by the public itself, and could be curbed by regulation of the company's power and size.

Daily investigates something similar to Arditi in the case of Amazon's takeover of the supermarket company Whole Foods in the United States. She examines the tension between former Whole Foods Chief Executive Officer John Mackey's focus on "conscious capitalism"—a business philosophy that looks to capitalism to "elevate our existence" and "lift people out of poverty"—and Amazon's corporate greed and imperialism. For Daily, the takeover may appear as a win-win scenario, where Whole Foods gains access to Amazon's logistic infrastructure, and Amazon gains enlightenment from the philosophy of conscious capitalism, but instead represents one more step in Amazon's grand scheme of economic empire. Daily shows how Amazon's erosion of workplace standards, conditions, and benefits at Whole Foods is demonstrative of how Amazon's brutalizing regime of labor infects all of its workplace operations and acquisitions.

Santiago's chapter turns to the production side of Prime Video by scrutinizing Amazon's film studio, Amazon Studios, and its operations in the context of Amazon's racialized labor practices in general. She examines what she calls "virtuous viewing," where a consumer-spectator of Prime Video is persuaded to consume Black voices by Amazon Studios in order to gain moral virtue in the wake of recent civil rights struggles. Santiago concludes that Amazon's disingenuous marketing and production practices hollow out any "virtue" in the consumption practices of the consumer-spectator. Consumption of Amazon's creative content is intended to grow the Prime e-commerce pipeline, which further exploits and silences the marginalized voices that Amazon Studios claims to amplify through their operations.

Amazon's Environmental Impact

While Amazon radically reworks the metaphorical environment of contemporary capitalism, it should not be forgotten that at the same time its presence, growth, and power has a huge impact on the literal environment of the planet. Amazon traffics as much in data as material consumer goods and thus it likely has the largest carbon footprint of all the big tech companies in the United States. Amazon's environmental impact has been repeatedly demonstrated by Amazon Employees for Climate Justice, the strongest worker organization in the company, including members high in the corporate hierarchy. In September 2020, Amazon Employees for Climate Justice staged a walkout and got major concessions from the company, including a commitment to carbon neutrality by 2040, a multi-billion dollar investment fund for companies working on decarbonization, and a series of consumer choices and guides to help green customers shop for environmentally friendly products. While the organizers did not find these commitments to go far enough, they do demonstrate that environmentalism is a key pressure point within the company that can galvanize broad coalitions both internal and external to Amazon's corporate hierarchy.

This section of the anthology is dedicated to that pressure point and looks to examine Amazon's environmental impact from a number of perspectives. In these chapters by Brett Hutchins, Libby Lester, Richard Maxwell, Toby Miller, and Whitney Monaghan, by Emily West, and by Patrick Brodie, and Paul O'Neill, Amazon's eco-violent methods of capitalist accumulation are scrutinized through a variety of Amazon's operations. From the company's climate pledges to its invasive expansion of services through physical and digital realms, Amazon's various subsidiaries pose continual threats to the environment and exacerbate the global climate crisis.

In their in-depth study, Hutchins, Lester, Maxwell, Miller, and Monaghan examine both the quick and slow violence Amazon visits upon its workforce and the environment through its business practices. They argue that quick violence affects its labor force through unsafe working conditions and an injurious work environment, while slow violence names the company's longer-term Earth-destroying production operations. The authors conclude that the organizing efforts of Amazon workers in the face of the company's eco-destructive production policies should inspire the public and limit the capitalist consumption instigated through Amazon's business model.

West scrutinizes Amazon's climate pledge, which stems from a corporate carbon accountability organization Amazon co-founded with the nonprofit Global Optimism in 2019. She analyzes this pledge through the lens of what is known about the company's environmental record and how Amazon weaponizes its own record to portray a public image of responsible green corporate policy. West concludes that while Amazon's environmental self-regulation is ostensibly more restrictive than required by the US government, Amazon is first and foremost concerned with accumulation and cannot be trusted by consumers or environmentalists to prioritize eco-regulations over its profit-seeking ventures.

Brodie and O'Neill analyze the territorial politics of AWS, the subsidiary of the company that offers cloud computing services, virtual intelligence services, and online storage space to a variety of clients, including several government branches and other private businesses. They term these politics a "regionalism" of Amazon's global infrastructures that transcends virtual and physical borders. Through their analysis, the authors show how Amazon shrouds its practices of data acquisition underneath legalities, patented technologies, and algorithms. All of these practices are difficult to trace and yet have extreme environmental impacts because of the infrastructural resources necessary to maintain the kind of immense computational power that AWS requires. They conclude that AWS' regionalism is dangerous for the environment, complicating how governments and the public can regulate Amazon's impact. The authors insist on a re-imagining of regionalisms, policies, and the virtual-physical reach of companies complicit in capitalist death cycles that are obscured due to the global, difficult-to-regulate nature of their production.

Appendix

Our volume closes with an appendix that Hiba Ali and Nina Sarnelle have titled "Art and Action," which documents a wide range of works by artists, cultural producers, and activist organizations that critically engage with Amazon. While Ali and Sarnelle note that this is by no means a comprehensive list, it does provide a window into their own works and research that helps supplement the critical scholarship in this volume. The appendix contains write ups of key artworks and creative projects organized by key themes—Gig Economy and Automation, Precarious Labor and Resistance, Sleep and Rest, Dataveillance, and Amazonification. Each of these sections contains links wherever possible to additional information, photographs, and videos online so that readers can get a sense of these works for themselves.

References

Alimahomed-Wilson, J., & Reese, E. (eds.) (2020). *The Cost of Free Shipping: Amazon in the Global Economy*. London, UK: Pluto Press.

Bayers, C. (1999, Mar. 1). The inner Jeff Bezos. *Wired*. https://www.wired.com/1999/03/bezos-3/

Delfanti, A. (2021). *The Warehouse: Workers and Robots at Amazon*. London, UK: Pluto Press

Khan, L. (2019). The Separation of Platforms and Commerce. *Columbia Law Review* 119: 4.

Lebow, S. (2022, Mar. 23). Amazon will capture nearly 40% of the US ecommerce market. *Insider Intelligence /eMarketer*. https://www.emarketer.com/content/amazon-us-ecommerce-market

Mitchell, S. (2021, Dec.) Amazon's toll road: How the tech giant funds its monopoly empire by exploiting small businesses. *Institute for Local Self-Reliance*. https://ilsr.org/amazons-toll-road/

Press, A. N. (2021, Nov. 23). Amazon is reshaping contemporary literature: An interview with Mark McGurl. *Jacobin*. https://jacobin.com/2021/11/amazon-literature-everything-less-novel-books/

Recode. (2016, Jun. 2). *Peter Thiel vs. Gawker | Jeff Bezos, CEO Amazon | Code Conference 2016* [Video]. YouTube. https://www.youtube.com/watch?v=Mf0e8M5Fxfo

Rosoff, M. (2016, Oct. 20). Jeff Bezos told what may be the best startup investment story ever. *Insider*. https://www.businessinsider.com/jeff-bezos-on-early-amazon-investors-2016-10

Srnicek, N. (2016). *Platform Capitalism*. Cambridge: Polity.

Stone, B. (2021). *Amazon Unbound: Jeff Bezos and the Invention of a Global Empire*. New York, NY: Simon & Schuster.

Stone, B. (2013). *The Everything Store: Jeff Bezons and the Age of Amazon*. New York, NY: Little, Brown and Company.

The Richest People in America. (1998, Oct. 12). *Forbes*. https://www.forbes.com/forbes/1998/1012/6208165a.html?sh=185466e81510

Turner, F. (2006). *From Counterculture to Cyberculture: Stewart Brand, the Whole Earth Network, and the Rise of Digital Utopianism*. Chicago, IL: The University of Chicago Press.

West, E. (2022). *Buy Now: How Amazon Branded Convenience and Normalized Monopoly*. Cambridge, MA: MIT Press.

PART I

~

THE POLITICAL ECONOMY OF AMAZON

CHAPTER ONE

Amazon's Antitrust Paradox

Lina Khan

"Even as Amazon became one of the largest retailers in the country, it never seemed interested in charging enough to make a profit. Customers celebrated and the competition languished."

—*The New York Times*[1]

"[O]ne of Mr. Rockefeller's most impressive characteristics is patience."

—Ida Tarbell, *A History of the Standard Oil Company*[2]

Introduction

In Amazon's early years, a running joke among Wall Street analysts was that Chief Executive Officer Jeff Bezos was building a house of cards. Entering its sixth year in 2000, the company had yet to crack a profit and was mounting millions of dollars in continuous losses, each quarter's larger than the last. Nevertheless, a segment of shareholders believed that by dumping money into advertising and steep discounts, Amazon was making a sound investment that would yield returns once e-commerce took off. Each quarter the company would report losses, and its stock price would rise. One news site captured the split sentiment by asking, "Amazon: Ponzi Scheme or Wal-Mart of the Web?"[3]

Sixteen years on, nobody seriously doubts that Amazon is anything but the titan of twenty-first-century commerce. In 2015, it earned $107 billion in revenue,[4] and, as of 2013, it sold more than its next twelve online competitors combined.[5] By some estimates, Amazon now captures 46 percent of online shopping, with its share growing faster than the sector as a whole.[6] In addition to being a retailer, it is a marketing platform, a delivery and logistics network, a payment service, a credit lender, an auction house, a major book publisher, a producer of television and films, a fashion designer, a hardware manufacturer, and a leading provider of cloud server space and computing power. Although Amazon has clocked staggering growth—reporting double-digit increases in net sales yearly—it reports meager profits, choosing to invest aggressively instead. The company listed consistent losses for the first seven years it was in business, with debts of two billion dollars.[7] While it exits the red more regularly now,[8] negative returns are still common. The company reported losses in two of the last five years, for example, and its highest yearly net income was still less than 1 percent of its net sales.[9]

Despite the company's history of thin returns, investors have zealously backed it: Amazon's shares trade at over nine hundred times diluted earnings, making it the most expensive stock in the Standard & Poor's 500.[10] As one reporter marveled, "The company barely ekes out a profit, spends a fortune on expansion and free shipping and is famously opaque about its business operations. Yet investors . . . pour into the stock."[11] Another commented that Amazon is in "a class of its own when it comes to valuation."[12]

Reporters and financial analysts continue to speculate about when and how Amazon's deep investments and steep losses will pay off.[13] Customers, meanwhile, universally seem to love the company. Close to half of all online buyers go directly to Amazon first to search for products,[14] and in 2016, the Reputation Institute named the firm the "most reputable company in America" for the third year running.[15] In recent years, journalists have exposed the aggressive business tactics Amazon employs. For instance, Amazon named one campaign "The Gazelle Project," a strategy whereby Amazon would approach small publishers "the way a cheetah would a sickly gazelle."[16] This, as well as other reporting,[17] drew widespread attention,[18] perhaps because it offered a glimpse at the potential social costs of Amazon's dominance. The firm's highly public dispute with Hachette in 2014—in which Amazon delisted the publisher's books from its website during business negotiations—similarly generated extensive press scrutiny and dialogue.[19] More generally, there is growing public awareness that Amazon has established itself as an essential part of the internet economy,[20] and a gnawing sense that its dominance—its sheer scale and breadth—may pose hazards.[21] But when pressed on why, critics often fumble to explain how a company that has so clearly delivered enormous benefits to consumers—not to mention revolutionized e-commerce in general—could, at the end of the day, threaten our markets. Trying to make sense of the contradiction, one journalist noted that the critics' argument seems to be that "even though Amazon's activities tend to reduce book prices, which is considered good for consumers, they ultimately hurt consumers."[22]

In some ways, the story of Amazon's sustained and growing dominance is also the story of changes in our antitrust laws. Due to a change in legal thinking and practice in the 1970s and 1980s, antitrust law now assesses competition largely with an eye to the short-term interests of consumers, not producers or the health of the market as a whole; antitrust doctrine views low consumer prices, alone, to be evidence of sound competition. By this measure, Amazon has excelled; it has evaded government scrutiny in part through fervently devoting its business strategy and rhetoric to reducing prices for consumers. Amazon's closest encounter with antitrust authorities was when the Justice Department sued other companies for teaming up against Amazon.[23] It is as if Bezos charted the company's growth by first drawing a map of antitrust laws, and then devising routes to smoothly bypass them. With its missionary zeal for consumers, Amazon has marched toward monopoly by singing the tune of contemporary antitrust.

This chapter maps out facets of Amazon's power. In particular, it traces the sources of Amazon's growth and analyzes the potential effects of its dominance. Doing so enables us to make sense of the company's business strategy and illuminates anticompetitive aspects of its structure and conduct. This analysis reveals that the current framework in antitrust—specifically its equating competition with "consumer welfare," typically measured through short-term effects on price and output[24]—fails to capture the architecture of market power in the twenty-first-century marketplace. In other words, the potential harms to competition posed by Amazon's dominance are not cognizable if we assess competition primarily through price and output. Focusing on these metrics instead blinds us to the potential hazards.

My argument is that gauging real competition in the twenty-first-century marketplace—especially in the case of online platforms—requires analyzing the underlying structure and dynamics of markets. Rather than pegging competition to a narrow set of outcomes, this approach would examine the competitive process itself. Animating this framework is the idea that a company's power and the potential anticompetitive nature of that power cannot be fully understood without looking to the structure of a business and the structural role it plays in markets. Applying this idea involves, for example, assessing whether a company's structure creates certain anticompetitive conflicts of interest, whether it can cross-leverage market advantages across distinct lines of business, and whether the structure of the market incentivizes and permits predatory conduct.

This is the approach I adopt in this chapter. I begin by exploring—and challenging—modern antitrust law's treatment of market structure. The first section gives an overview of the shift in antitrust away from economic structuralism in favor of price theory and identifies how this departure has played out in two areas of enforcement: predatory pricing and vertical integration. The second section questions this narrow focus on consumer welfare as largely measured by prices, arguing that assessing structure is vital to protect important antitrust values. The chapter then uses the lens of market structure to reveal anticompetitive aspects of Amazon's strategy and conduct. The subsequent section documents Amazon's history of aggressive investing and loss leading, its company strategy, and its integration across many lines of business. The fourth section identifies two instances in which Amazon has built elements of its business through sustained losses, crippling its rivals, and two instances in which Amazon's activity across multiple business lines poses anticompetitive threats in ways that the current framework fails to register. The chapter then assesses how antitrust law can address the challenges raised by online platforms like Amazon. The fifth section considers what capital markets suggest about the economics of Amazon and other internet platforms. Section six offers two approaches for addressing the power of dominant platforms: (1) limiting their dominance through restoring traditional antitrust and competition policy principles and (2) regulating their dominance by applying common carrier obligations and duties.

The Chicago School Revolution: The Shift Away from Competitive Process and Market Structure

One of the most significant changes in antitrust law and interpretation over the last century has been the move away from economic structuralism. In this section, I trace this history by sketching out how a structure-based view of competition has been replaced by price theory and exploring how this shift has played out through changes in doctrine and enforcement.

Broadly, economic structuralism rests on the idea that concentrated market structures promote anticompetitive forms of conduct.[25] This view holds that a market dominated by a very small number of large companies is likely to be less competitive than a market populated with many small- and medium-sized companies. This is because (1) monopolistic and oligopolistic market structures enable dominant actors to coordinate with greater ease and subtlety, facilitating conduct like price-fixing, market division, and tacit collusion; (2) monopolistic and oligopolistic firms can use their existing dominance to block new entrants; and (3) monopolistic and oligopolistic firms have greater bargaining power against consumers, suppliers, and workers, which enables them to hike prices and degrade service and quality while maintaining profits.

This market structure-based understanding of competition was a foundation of antitrust thought and policy through the 1960s. Subscribing to this view, courts blocked mergers that they determined would lead to anticompetitive market structures. In some instances, this meant halting horizontal deals—mergers combining two direct competitors operating in the same market or product line—that would have handed the new entity a large share of the market.[26] In others, it involved rejecting vertical mergers—deals joining companies that operated in different tiers of the same supply or production chain—that would "foreclose competition."[27] Centrally, this approach involved policing not just for size but also for conflicts of interest—like whether allowing a dominant shoe manufacturer to extend into shoe retailing would create an incentive for the manufacturer to disadvantage or discriminate against competing retailers.[28]

The Chicago School approach to antitrust, which gained mainstream prominence and credibility in the 1970s and 1980s, rejected this structuralist view.[29] In the words of Richard Posner, the essence of the Chicago School position is that "the proper lens for viewing antitrust problems is price theory."[30] Foundational to this view is a faith in the efficiency of markets, propelled by profit-maximizing actors. The Chicago School approach bases its vision of industrial organization on a simple theoretical premise: "[R]ational economic actors working within the confines of the market seek to maximize profits by combining inputs in the most efficient manner. A failure to act in this fashion will be punished by the competitive forces of the market."[31]

While economic structuralists believe that industrial structure predisposes firms toward certain forms of behavior that then steer market outcomes, the Chicago School presumes that market outcomes—including firm size, industry structure, and concentration levels—reflect the interplay of standalone market forces and the technical demands of production.[32] In other words, economic structuralists take industry structure as an entryway for understanding market dynamics, while the Chicago School holds that industry structure merely reflects such dynamics. For the Chicago School, "[w]hat exists is ultimately the best guide to what should exist."[33]

Practically, the shift from structuralism to price theory had two major ramifications for antitrust analysis. First, it led to a significant narrowing of the concept of entry barriers. An entry barrier is a cost that must be borne by a firm seeking to enter an industry but is not carried by firms already in the industry.[34] According to the Chicago School, advantages that incumbents enjoy from economies of scale, capital requirements, and product differentiation do not constitute entry barriers, as these factors are considered to reflect no more than the "objective technical demands of production and distribution."[35] With so many "entry barriers . . . discounted, all firms are subject to the threat of potential competition . . . regardless of the number of firms or levels of concentration."[36] In this view, market power is always fleeting—and hence antitrust enforcement rarely needed.

The second consequence of the shift away from structuralism was that consumer prices became the dominant metric for assessing competition. In his highly influential work, *The Antitrust Paradox*, Robert Bork asserted that the sole normative objective of antitrust should be to maximize consumer welfare, best pursued through promoting economic efficiency.[37] Although Bork used "consumer welfare" to mean "allocative efficiency,"[38] courts and antitrust authorities have largely measured it through effects on consumer prices. In 1979, the Supreme Court followed Bork's work and declared that "Congress designed the Sherman Act as a 'consumer welfare prescription'"[39]—a statement that is widely viewed as erroneous.[40] Still, this philosophy wound its way into policy and doctrine. The 1982 merger guidelines issued by the Reagan administration—a radical departure from the previous guidelines, written in 1968—reflected this newfound focus. While the 1968 guidelines had established that the "primary role" of merger enforcement was "to preserve and promote market structures conducive to competition,"[41] the 1982 guidelines said mergers "should not be permitted to create or enhance 'market power,'" defined as the "ability of one or more firms profitably to maintain prices above competitive levels."[42] Today, showing antitrust injury requires showing harm to consumer welfare, generally in the form of price increases and output restrictions.[43]

It is true that antitrust authorities do not ignore nonprice effects entirely. The 2010 Horizontal Merger Guidelines, for example, acknowledge that enhanced market power can manifest as nonprice harms, including in the form of reduced product quality, reduced product variety, reduced service, or diminished innovation.[44] Notably, the Obama administration's opposition to one of the largest mergers proposed on its watch—Comcast/TimeWarner—stemmed from a concern about market access, not prices.[45] And by some measures, the Federal Trade Commission (FTC) has alleged potential harm to innovation in roughly one-third of merger enforcement actions in the last decade.[46] Still, it is fair to say that a concern for innovation or nonprice effects rarely animates or drives investigations or enforcement actions—especially outside of the merger context.[47] Economic factors that are easier to measure—such as impacts on price, output, or productive efficiency in narrowly defined markets—have become "disproportionately important."[48]

Two areas of enforcement that this reorientation has affected dramatically are predatory pricing and vertical integration. The Chicago School claims that "predatory pricing, vertical integration, and tying arrangements never or almost never reduce consumer welfare."[49] Both predatory pricing and vertical integration are highly relevant to analyzing Amazon's path to dominance and the source of its power. In the following, I offer a brief overview of how the Chicago School's influence has shaped predatory pricing doctrine and enforcers' views of vertical integration.

Predatory Pricing

Through the mid-twentieth century, Congress repeatedly enacted legislation targeting predatory pricing. Congress, as well as state legislatures, viewed predatory pricing as a tactic used by highly capitalized firms to bankrupt rivals and destroy competition—in other words, as a tool to concentrate control. Laws prohibiting predatory pricing were part of a larger arrangement of pricing laws that sought to distribute power and opportunity. However, a controversial Supreme Court decision in the 1960s created an opening for critics to attack the regime. This intellectual backlash wound its way into Supreme Court doctrine by the early 1990s in the form of the restrictive "recoupment test."

The earliest predatory pricing case in America was the government's antitrust suit against Standard Oil, which reached the Supreme Court in 1911.[50] As detailed in Ida Tarbell's exposé, *A History of the Standard Oil Company*, Standard Oil routinely slashed prices in order to drive rivals from the market.[51] Moreover, it cross-subsidized: Standard Oil charged monopoly prices[52] in markets where it faced no competitors; in markets where rivals checked the company's dominance, it drastically lowered prices in an effort to push them out. In its antitrust case against the company, the government argued that a suite of practices by Standard Oil—including predatory pricing—violated section 2 of the Sherman Act. The Supreme Court ruled for the government and ordered the break-up of the company.[53] Subsequent courts cited the decision for establishing that in the quest for monopoly power, "price cutting became perhaps the most effective weapon of the larger corporation."[54]

Recognizing the threat of predatory pricing executed by Standard Oil, Congress passed a series of laws prohibiting such conduct. In 1914 Congress enacted the Clayton Act[55] to strengthen the Sherman Act and included a provision to curb price discrimination and predatory pricing.[56] The House Report stated that section 2 of the Clayton Act was expressly designed to prohibit large corporations from slashing prices below the cost of production "with the intent to destroy and make unprofitable the business of their competitors" and with the aim of "acquiring a monopoly in the particular locality or section in which the discriminating price is made."[57]

Congress also acted to protect state "fair trade" laws that further safeguarded against predatory pricing. Fair trade legislation granted producers the right to set the final retail price of their goods, limiting the ability of chain stores to discount.[58] When the Supreme Court targeted these "resale price maintenance" efforts, Congress stepped up to defend them. After the Supreme Court in 1911 struck down the form of resale price maintenance enabled by fair trade laws,[59] Congress in 1937 carved out an exception for state fair trade laws through the Miller-Tydings Act.[60] When the Supreme Court in 1951 ruled that producers could enforce minimum prices only against those retailers that had signed contracts agreeing to do so,[61] Congress responded with a law making minimum prices enforceable against nonsigners too.[62]

Another byproduct of the "fair trade" movement was the Robinson-Patman Act of 1936. This act prohibited price discrimination by retailers among producers and by producers among retailers.[63] Its aim was to prevent conglomerates and large companies from using their buyer power to extract crippling discounts from smaller entities, and to keep large manufacturers and retailers from teaming up against rivals.[64] Like laws banning predatory pricing, the prohibition against price discrimination effectively curbed the power of size. Section 3 of the act addressed predatory pricing directly by making it a crime to sell goods at "unreasonably low prices for the purpose of destroying competition or eliminating a competitor."[65] While predatory price cutting gave rise to civil liability and remedies under the Clayton Act, the Robinson-Patman Act attached criminal penalties as well.[66]

This series of antitrust laws demonstrates that Congress saw predatory pricing as a serious threat to competitive markets. By the mid-twentieth century, the Supreme Court recognized and gave effect to this congressional intent. The Court upheld the Robinson-Patman Act numerous times, holding that the relevant factors were whether a retailer intended to destroy competition through its pricing practices and whether its conduct furthered that purpose.[67] However, not all instances of below-cost pricing were illegitimate. Liquidating excess or perishable goods, for example, was considered fair game.[68] Only "sales made below cost without legitimate commercial objective and with specific intent to destroy competition" would clearly violate section 3.[69] In other cases, the Court distinguished between competitive advantages drawn from superior skill and production, and those drawn from the brute power of size and capital.[70] The latter, the Court ruled, were illegitimate.[71]

In *Utah Pie Co. v. Continental Baking Co.*, the Court further reinforced the illegitimacy of predatory pricing.[72] Utah Pie and Continental Baking were competing manufacturers of frozen dessert pies. A locational advantage gave Utah Pie cheaper access to the Salt Lake City market, which it used to price goods below those sold by competitors. Other frozen pie manufacturers, including Continental, began selling at below-cost prices in the Salt Lake City market, while keeping prices in other regions at or above cost. Utah Pie brought a predatory pricing case against Continental. The Supreme Court ruled for Utah Pie, noting that the pricing strategies of its competitors had diverted business from Utah Pie and compelled the company to further lower its prices, leading to a "declining price structure" overall.[73] Additionally, Continental had admitted to sending an industrial spy to Utah Pie's plant to gain information to sabotage Utah's business relations with retailers, a fact the Court used to establish "intent to injure."[74]

The decision was controversial. Continental's conduct had loosened the grip of a quasi-monopolist. Prior to the alleged predation, Utah Pie had controlled 66.5 percent of the Salt Lake City market, but following Continental's practices, its share dropped to 45.3 percent.[75] Penalizing conduct that had made a market *more* competitive as predatory seemed perverse. As Justice Stewart noted in the dissent, "I cannot hold that Utah Pie's monopolistic position was protected by the federal antitrust laws from effective price competition."[76]

The case presented an opportunity for critics of predatory pricing laws to attack the doctrine as misguided. In an article labeling *Utah Pie* "the most anticompetitive antitrust decision of the decade," Ward Bowman, an economist at Yale Law School, argued that the premise of predatory pricing laws was wrong.[77] He wrote, "The Robinson-Patman Act rests upon a presumption that price discrimination can or might be used as a monopolizing technique. This, as more recent economic literature confirms, is at best a highly dubious presumption."[78] Bork, meanwhile, said of the decision, "There is no economic theory worthy of the name that could find an injury to competition on the facts of the case. Defendants were convicted not of injuring competition but, quite simply, of competing."[79] He described predatory pricing generally as "a phenomenon that probably does not exist" and the Robinson-Patman Act as "the misshapen progeny of intolerable draftsmanship coupled to wholly mistaken economic theory."[80] Other scholars, particularly those from the rising Chicago School, also weighed in to criticize *Utah Pie*.[81]

As the writings of Bowman and Bork suggest, the Chicago School critique of predatory pricing doctrine rests on the idea that below-cost pricing is irrational and hence rarely occurs.[82] For one, the critics argue, there was no guarantee that reducing prices below cost would either drive a competitor out or otherwise induce the rival to stop competing. Second, even if a competitor were to drop out, the predator would need to sustain monopoly pricing for long enough to recoup the initial losses *and* successfully thwart entry by potential competitors, who would be lured by the monopoly pricing. The uncertainty of its success, coupled with its guarantee of costs, made predatory pricing an unappealing—and therefore highly unlikely—strategy.[83]

As the influence and credibility of these scholars grew, their thinking shaped government enforcement. During the 1970s, for example, the number of Robinson-Patman Act cases that the FTC brought dropped dramatically, reflecting the belief that these cases were of little economic concern.[84] Under the Reagan administration, the FTC all but entirely abandoned Robinson-Patman Act cases.[85] Bork's appointment as Solicitor General, meanwhile, gave him a prime platform to influence the Supreme Court on antitrust issues and enabled him "to train and influence many of the attorneys who would argue before the Supreme Court for the next generation."[86]

The Chicago School critique came to shape Supreme Court doctrine on predatory pricing. The depth and degree of this influence became apparent in *Matsushita Electric Industrial Co. v. Zenith Radio Corp.*[87] Zenith, an American manufacturer of consumer electronics, brought a Sherman Act section 1 case accusing Japanese firms of conspiring to charge predatorily low prices in the US market in order to drive American companies out of business.[88] The Supreme Court granted certiorari to review whether the Third Circuit had applied the correct standard in reversing the district court's grant of summary judgment to Matsushita—an inquiry that led the Court to assess the reasonableness of assuming the alleged predation.[89]

Citing Bork's *The Antitrust Paradox*, the Court concluded that predatory pricing schemes were implausible and therefore could not justify a reasonable assumption in favor of Zenith. "As [Bork's work] shows, the success of such schemes is inherently uncertain: the short-run loss is definite, but the long-run gain depends on successfully neutralizing the competition," the Court wrote.[90] "For this reason, there is a consensus among commentators that predatory pricing schemes are rarely tried, and even more rarely successful."[91]

In addition to adopting Bork's cost-benefit framing, the Court echoed his concern that price competition could be mistaken for predation. In *The*

Antitrust Paradox, Bork wrote, "The real danger for the law is less that predation will be missed than that normal competitive behavior will be wrongly classified as predatory and suppressed."[92] Justice Powell, writing for the 5-4 majority in *Matsushita*, echoed Bork: "[C]utting prices in order to increase business often is the very essence of competition. Thus mistaken inferences in cases such as this one are especially costly, because they chill the very conduct the antitrust laws are designed to protect."[93]

Although *Matsushita* focused on a narrow issue—the summary judgment standard for claims brought under section 1 of the Sherman Act, which targets coordination among parties[94]—it has been widely influential in monopolization cases, which fall under section 2. In other words, reasoning that originated in one context has wound up in jurisprudence applying to totally distinct circumstances, even as the underlying violations differ vastly.[95] Subsequent courts applied *Matsushita*'s predatory pricing analysis to cases involving monopolization and unilateral anticompetitive conduct, shaping the jurisprudence of section 2 of the Sherman Act.[96] The lower courts seized on *Matsushita*'s central point: the idea that "predatory pricing schemes are rarely tried, and even more rarely successful."[97] The phrase became a talisman against the existence of predatory pricing, routinely invoked by courts in favor of defendants.

In *Brooke Group Ltd. v. Brown & Williamson Tobacco Corp.*,[98] the Supreme Court formalized this premise into a doctrinal test. The case involved cigarette manufacturing, an industry dominated by six firms.[99] Liggett, one of the six, introduced a line of generic cigarettes, which it sold for about 30 percent less than the price of branded cigarettes.[100] Liggett alleged that when it became clear that its generics were diverting business from branded cigarettes, Brown & Williamson, a competing manufacturer, began selling its own generics at a loss.[101] Liggett sued, claiming that Brown & Williamson's tactic was designed to pressure Liggett to raise prices on its generics, thus enabling Brown & Williamson to maintain high profits on branded cigarettes. A jury returned a verdict in favor of Liggett, but the district court judge decided that Brown & Williamson was entitled to judgment as a matter of law.[102]

Importantly, Liggett's accusation was that Brown & Williamson would recoup its losses through raising prices on *branded* cigarettes, not the generics cigarettes it was steeply discounting. Building on the analysis introduced in *Matsushita*, the Court held that Liggett had failed to show that Brown & Williamson would be able to execute the scheme successfully by recouping its losses through supracompetitive pricing. "Evidence of below-cost pricing is not alone sufficient to permit an inference of probable recoupment and injury to competition," Justice Kennedy wrote for the majority.[103] Instead, the plaintiff "must demonstrate that there is a likelihood that the predatory scheme alleged would cause a rise in prices above a competitive level that would be sufficient to compensate for the amounts expended on the predation, including the time value of the money invested in it"[104]—a requirement now known as the "recoupment test."

In placing recoupment at the center of predatory pricing analysis, the Court presumed that direct profit maximization is the singular goal of predatory pricing.[105] Furthermore, by establishing that harm occurs *only* when predatory pricing results in higher prices, the Court collapsed the rich set of concerns that had animated earlier critics of predation, including an aversion to large firms that exploit their size and a desire to preserve local control. Instead, the Court adopted the Chicago School's narrow conception of what constitutes this harm (higher prices) and how this harm comes about—namely, through the alleged predator raising prices on the previously discounted good.[106]

Today, succeeding on a predatory pricing claim requires a plaintiff to meet the *Brooke Group* recoupment test by showing that the defendant would be able to recoup its losses through sustaining supracompetitive prices. Since the Court introduced this recoupment requirement, the number of cases brought and won by plaintiffs has dropped dramatically.[107] Despite the Court's contention—that "predatory pricing schemes are rarely tried and even more rarely successful"—a host of research shows that predatory pricing can be "an attractive anticompetitive strategy" and has been used by dominant firms across sectors to squash or deter competition.[108]

Vertical Integration

Analysis of vertical integration has similarly moved away from structural concerns. Vertical integration arises when "two or more successive stages of production and/or distribution of a product are combined under the same control."[109] For most of the last century, enforcers reviewed vertical integration under the same standards as horizontal mergers, as set out in the Sherman Act, the Clayton Act, and the Federal Trade Commission Act. Vertical integration was banned whenever it threatened to "substantially lessen competition"[110] or constituted a "restraint of trade"[111] or an "unfair method of competition."[112] However, the Chicago School's view that vertical mergers are generally procompetitive has led enforcement in this area to significantly drop.

Serious concern about vertical integration took hold in the wake of the Great Depression, when both the law and economic theory became sharply critical of the phenomenon.[113] Thurman Arnold, the Assistant Attorney

General in the 1930s, targeted vertical ownership achieved through both mergers and contractual provisions, and by the 1950s courts and antitrust authorities generally viewed vertical integration as anticompetitive. Partly because it believed that the Supreme Court had failed to use existing law to block vertical integration through acquisitions, Congress in 1950 amended section 7 of the Clayton Act to make it applicable to vertical mergers.[114]

Critics of vertical integration primarily focused on two theories of potential harm: leverage and foreclosure. Leverage reflects the idea that a firm can use its dominance in one line of business to establish dominance in another. Because "horizontal power in one market or stage of production creates 'leverage' for the extension of the power to bar entry at another level," vertical integration combined with horizontal market power "can impair competition to a greater extent than could the exercise of horizontal power alone."[115] Foreclosure, meanwhile, occurs when a firm uses one line of business to disadvantage rivals in another line. A flourmill that also owned a bakery could hike prices or degrade quality when selling to rival bakers—or refuse to do business with them entirely. In this view, even if an integrated firm did not directly resort to exclusionary tactics, the arrangement would still increase barriers to entry by requiring would-be entrants to compete at two levels.

When seeking to block vertical combinations or arrangements, the government frequently built its case on one of these theories—and, through the 1960s, courts largely accepted them.[116] In *Brown Shoe v. United States*, for example, the government sought to block a merger between a leading manufacturer and a leading retailer of shoes on the grounds that the tie-up would "foreclos[e] competition" and "enhanc[e] Brown's competitive advantage over other producers, distributors and sellers of shoes."[117] The Court acknowledged that the Clayton Act did not "render unlawful *all* . . . vertical arrangements," but held that this merger would undermine competition by "foreclos[ing] . . . independent manufacturers from markets otherwise open to them."[118] In other words, the concern was that—once merged—the combined entity would forbid its retailing arm from stocking shoes made by competing independent manufacturers. Calling this form of foreclosure "the primary vice of a vertical merger,"[119] the Court noted it was also largely inevitable: "Every extended vertical arrangement by its very nature, for at least a time, denies to competitors of the supplier the opportunity to compete for part or all of the trade of the customer-party to the vertical arrangement."[120] In his partial concurrence, Justice Harlan observed that the deal would enable Brown to "turn an independent purchaser into a captive market for its shoes," thereby "diminish[ing] the available market for which shoe manufacturers compete."[121] The Court enjoined the merger.[122]

Another reason courts cited for blocking these arrangements was that vertical deals eliminated potential rivals—a recognition of how a merger would reshape industry structure. Upholding the FTC's challenge of Ford purchasing an equipment manufacturer, the Court noted that before the acquisition, Ford had helped check the power of the manufacturers and had a "soothing influence" over prices.[123] An outside firm "may someday go in and set the stage for noticeable deconcentration," the Court wrote.[124] "While it merely stays near the edge, it is a deterrent to current competitors."[125] In other words, the threat of potential entry by Ford—the fact that, premerger, it *could* have internally expanded into equipment manufacturing—had played an important disciplining role. Relatedly, the Court observed that when a company in a competitive market integrates with a firm in an oligopolistic one, the merger can have "the result of transmitting the rigidity of the oligopolistic structure" of one industry to the other, "thus reducing the chances of future deconcentration" of the market.[126] The Court required Ford to divest the manufacturer.[127]

In the 1950s—while Congress, enforcement agencies, and the courts recognized potential threats posed by vertical arrangements—Chicago School scholars began to cast doubt on the idea that vertical integration has anticompetitive effects.[128] By replacing market transactions with administrative decisions within the firm, they argued, vertical arrangements generated efficiencies that antitrust law should promote. And if integration failed to yield efficiencies, then the integrated firm would have no cost advantages over unintegrated rivals, therefore posing no risk of impeding entry. They further argued that vertical deals would not affect a firm's pricing and output policies, the primary metrics in their analysis. Under this framework, only horizontal mergers affect competition, as "[h]orizontal mergers increase market share, but vertical mergers do not."[129]

Chicago School theory holds that concerns about both leverage and foreclosure are misguided. Under the "single monopoly profit theorem," the amount of profit that a firm can extract from one market is fixed and cannot be expanded through extending into an adjacent market if the two products are used in fixed proportions.[130] Under this premise, not only does monopoly leveraging not pose any competitive concern, but—as it can only be motivated by efficiencies, not profits—it is actually procompetitive when it does occur.

The traditional worries about foreclosure, Bork claimed, were unfounded, as "[p]redation through vertical merger is extremely unlikely."[131] A manufacturer would not favor its retail subsidiary over others unless it was cheaper to do so—in which case, Bork argued, discriminating would yield efficiencies that the firm would pass on to consumers. Additionally, any manufacturer that sought to privilege its own retailer would face "entrants who would arrive in sky-darkening swarms for the profitable alternatives."[132] In other words, Bork's take was that vertical integration generally would not create forms of market power that firms could use to hike prices or constrain output. In the rare case that vertical integration *did* create this form of market power, he believed that it would be disciplined by actual or potential entry by competitors.[133] In light of this, antitrust law's aversion to vertical arrangements was, Bork argued, irrational. "The law against vertical mergers is merely a law against the creation of efficiency."[134]

With the election of President Reagan, this view of vertical integration became national policy. In 1982 and 1984, the Department of Justice (DOJ) and the FTC issued new merger guidelines outlining the framework that officials would use when reviewing horizontal deals.[135] The 1984 version included guidelines specific to vertical deals.[136] Part of a sweeping effort to overhaul antitrust enforcement, the new guidelines narrowed the circumstances in which the agencies would challenge vertical mergers.[137] Although the guidelines acknowledged that vertical mergers could sometimes give rise to competitive concerns, in practice the change constituted a de facto approval of vertical deals. The DOJ and FTC did not challenge even one vertical merger during President Reagan's tenure.[138]

Although subsequent administrations have continued reviewing vertical mergers, the Chicago School's view that these deals generally do not pose threats to competition has remained dominant.[139] Rejection of vertical tie-ups—standard through the 1960s and 1970s—is extremely rare today[140]; in instances where agencies spot potential harm, they tend to impose conduct remedies or require divestitures rather than block the deal outright.[141] The Obama administration took this approach with two of the largest vertical deals of the last decade: Comcast/NBC and Ticketmaster/LiveNation. In each case, consumer advocates opposed the deal[142] and warned that the tie-up would concentrate significant power in the hands of a single company,[143] which it could use to engage in exclusionary practices, hike prices for consumers, and dock payments to content producers, such as television screenwriters and musicians. Nonetheless, the DOJ attached certain behavioral conditions and required a minor divestiture, ultimately approving both deals.[144] The district court held the consent decrees to be in the public interest.

Why Competitive Process and Structure Matter

The current framework in antitrust fails to register certain forms of anticompetitive harm and therefore is unequipped to promote real competition—a shortcoming that is illuminated and amplified in the context of online platforms and data-driven markets. This failure stems both from assumptions embedded in the Chicago School framework and from the way this framework assesses competition.

Notably, the present approach fails even if one believes that antitrust should promote only consumer interests. Critically, consumer interests include not only cost but also product quality, variety, and innovation. Protecting these long-term interests requires a much thicker conception of "consumer welfare" than what guides the current approach. But more importantly, the undue focus on consumer welfare is misguided. It betrays legislative history, which reveals that Congress passed antitrust laws to promote a host of political economic ends—including our interests as workers, producers, entrepreneurs, and citizens. It also mistakenly supplants a concern about process and structure (i.e., whether power is sufficiently distributed to keep markets competitive) with a calculation regarding outcome (i.e., whether consumers are materially better off).

Antitrust law and competition policy should promote not welfare but competitive markets. By refocusing attention back on process and structure, this approach would be faithful to the legislative history of major antitrust laws. It would also promote actual competition—unlike the present framework, which is overseeing concentrations of power that risk precluding real competition.

Price and Output Do Not Cover the Full Range of Threats to Consumer Welfare

As discussed in the first section of this chapter, modern doctrine assumes that advancing consumer welfare is the sole purpose of antitrust. But the consumer welfare approach to antitrust is unduly narrow and betrays congressional intent, as evident from legislative history and as documented by a vast body of scholarship. I argue in this chapter that the rise of dominant internet platforms freshly reveals the shortcomings of the consumer welfare framework and that it should be abandoned.

Strikingly, the current approach fails *even if* one believes that consumer interests should remain paramount. Focusing primarily on price and output undermines effective antitrust enforcement by delaying intervention until market power is being actively exercised, and largely ignoring whether and how it is being acquired. In other words, pegging anticompetitive harm to high prices and/or lower output—while disregarding the market structure and competitive process that give rise to this market power—restricts intervention to the moment when a company has already acquired sufficient dominance to distort competition.

This approach is misguided because it is much easier to promote competition at the point when a market risks becoming less competitive than it is at the point when a market is no longer competitive. The antitrust laws reflect this recognition, requiring that enforcers arrest potential restraints to competition "in their incipiency."[145] But the Chicago School's hostility to false positives—and insistence that market power and high concentration both reflect and generate efficiency[146]—has undermined this incipiency standard and enfeebled enforcement as a whole. Indeed, enforcers have largely abandoned section 2 monopolization claims,[147] which—by virtue of assessing how a single company amasses and exercises its power—traditionally involved an inquiry into structure. By instead relying primarily on price and output effects as metrics of competition, enforcers risk overlooking the structural weakening of competition until it becomes difficult to address effectively, an approach that undermines consumer welfare.

Indeed, growing evidence shows that the consumer welfare frame has led to higher prices and few efficiencies, failing by its own metrics.[148] It arguably has further contributed to a decline in new business growth, resulting in reduced opportunities for entrepreneurs and a stagnant economy.[149] The long-term interests of consumers include product quality, variety, and innovation—factors best promoted through both a robust competitive process and open markets. By contrast, allowing a highly concentrated market structure to persist endangers these long-term interests, since firms in uncompetitive markets need not compete to improve old products or tinker to create news ones. Even if we accept consumer welfare as the touchstone of antitrust, ensuring a competitive process—by looking, in part, to how a market is structured—ought to be key. Empirical studies revealing that the consumer welfare frame has resulted in higher prices—failing even by its own terms—support the need for a different approach.

Antitrust Laws Promote Competition to Serve a Variety of Interests

Legislative history reveals that the idea that "Congress designed the Sherman Act as a 'consumer welfare prescription'"[150] is wrong.[151] Congress enacted antitrust laws to rein in the power of industrial trusts, the large business organizations that had emerged in the late nineteenth century. Responding to a fear of concentrated power, antitrust sought to distribute it. In this sense, antitrust was "guided by principles."[152] The law was "*for* diversity and access to markets; it was *against* high concentration and abuses of power."[153]

More relevant than any single goal was this general vision. When Congress passed the Sherman Act in 1890, Senator John Sherman called it "a bill of rights, a charter of liberty," and stressed its importance in political terms.[154] On the floor of the Senate he declared,

> If we will not endure a king as a political power, we should not endure a king over the production, transportation, and sale of any of the necessities of life. If we would not submit to an emperor, we should not submit to an autocrat of trade, with power to prevent competition and to fix the price of any commodity.[155]

In other words, what was at stake in keeping markets open—and keeping them free from industrial monarchs—was freedom.

Animating this vision was the understanding that concentration of economic power also consolidates political power, "breed[ing] antidemocratic political pressures."[156] This would occur through enabling a small minority to amass outsized wealth, which they could then use to influence government. But it would also occur by permitting "private discretion by a few in the economic sphere" to "control the welfare of all," undermining individual and business freedom.[157] In the lead up to the passage of the Sherman Act, Senator George Hoar warned that monopolies were "a menace to republican institutions themselves."[158]

This vision encompassed a variety of ends. For one, competition policy would prevent large firms from extracting wealth from producers and consumers in the form of monopoly profits.[159] Senator Sherman, for example, described overcharges by monopolists as "extortion which makes the people poor,"[160] while Senator Richard Coke referred to them as "robbery."[161] Representative John Heard announced that trusts had "stolen millions from the people,"[162] and Congressman Ezra Taylor noted that the beef trust "robs the farmer on the one hand and the consumer on the other."[163] In the words of Senator James George, "[t]hey aggregate to themselves great enormous wealth by extortion which makes the people poor."[164]

Notably, this focus on wealth transfers was not solely economic. Leading up to the passage of the Sherman Act, price levels in the United States were stable or slowly decreasing.[165] If the exclusive concern had been higher prices, then Congress could have focused on those industries where prices were, indeed, high or still rising. The fact that Congress chose to denounce unjust redistribution suggests that something else was at play—namely, that the public was "angered less by the reduction in their wealth than by the way in which the wealth was extracted."[166] In other words, though the harm was being registered through an economic effect—a wealth transfer—the underlying source of the grievance was also political.[167]

Another distinct goal was to preserve open markets in order to ensure that new businesses and entrepreneurs had a fair shot at entry. Several Congressmen advocated for the Federal Trade Commission Act because it would help promote small business. Senator James Reed expressly noted that Congress' aim in passing the law was to keep markets open to independent firms.[168] When discussing the Sherman Act, Senator George lamented that if large-scale industry were allowed to grow unchecked, it would "crush out all small men, all small capitalists, all small enterprises."[169]

Through the 1950s, courts and enforcers applied antitrust laws to promote this variety of aims. While the vigor and tenor of enforcement varied, there was an overarching understanding that antitrust served to protect what Justice Louis Brandeis called "industrial liberty."[170] Key to this vision was the recognition that excessive concentrations of private power posed a public threat, empowering the interests of a few to steer collective outcomes. "Power that controls the economy should be in the hands of elected representatives of the people, not in the hands of an industrial oligarchy," Justice William O. Douglas wrote.[171] Decentralizing this power would ensure that "the fortunes of the people will not be dependent on the whim or caprice, the political prejudice, the emotional stability of a few self-appointed men."[172]

As described in the first section of this chapter, Chicago School scholars upended this traditional approach, concluding that the only legitimate goal of antitrust is consumer welfare, best promoted through enhancing economic efficiency. Notably, some prominent liberals—including John Kenneth Galbraith—ratified this idea, championing centralization.[173] In the wake of high inflation in the 1970s, Ralph Nader and other consumer advocates also came to support an antitrust regime centered on lower prices, according with the Chicago School's view.[174] By orienting antitrust toward material rather than political ends, both the neoclassical school and its critics effectively embraced concentration over competition.[175]

Focusing antitrust exclusively on consumer welfare is a mistake.[176] For one, it betrays legislative intent, which makes clear that Congress passed antitrust laws to safeguard against excessive concentrations of economic power. This vision promotes a variety of aims, including the preservation of open markets, the protection of producers and consumers from monopoly abuse, and the dispersion of political[177] and economic control.[178] Secondly, focusing on consumer welfare disregards the host of other ways that excessive concentration can harm us—enabling firms to squeeze suppliers and producers, endangering system stability (e.g., by allowing companies to become too big to fail),[179] or undermining media diversity,[180] to name a few. Protecting this range of interests requires an approach to antitrust that focuses on the neutrality of the competitive process and the openness of market structures.

Promoting Competition Requires Analysis of Process and Structure

The Chicago School's embrace of consumer welfare as the sole goal of antitrust is problematic for at least two reasons. First, as described in the previous section titled "Antitrust Laws Promote Competition to Serve a Variety of Interests," this idea contravenes legislative history, which shows that Congress passed antitrust laws to safeguard against excessive concentrations of private power. It recognized, in turn, that this vision would protect a host of interests, which the sole focus on "consumer welfare" disregards. Second, by adopting this new goal, the Chicago School shifted the analytical emphasis away from *process*—the conditions necessary for competition—and toward an *outcome*—namely, consumer welfare.[181] In other words, a concern about structure (is power sufficiently distributed to keep markets competitive?) was replaced by a calculation (did prices rise?).[182] This approach is inadequate to promote real competition, a failure that is amplified in the case of dominant online platforms.

Antitrust doctrine has evolved to reflect this redefinition. The recoupment requirement in predatory pricing, for example, reflects the idea that competition is harmed only if the predator can ultimately charge consumers supracompetitive prices.[183] This logic is agnostic about process and structure; it measures the health of competition primarily through effects on price and output. The same is true in the case of vertical integration. The modern view of integration largely assumes away barriers to entry, an element of structure, presuming that any advantages enjoyed by the integrated firm trace back to efficiencies.[184]

More generally, modern doctrine assumes that market power is not inherently harmful and instead may result from and generate efficiencies. In practice, this presumes that market power is benign *unless* it leads to higher prices or reduced output—again glossing over questions about the competitive process in favor of narrow calculations.[185] In other words, this approach equates harm entirely with whether a firm *chooses* to exercise its market power through price-based levers, while disregarding whether a firm has *developed* this power, distorting the competitive process in some other way.[186] But allowing firms to amass market power makes it more difficult to meaningfully check that power when it is eventually exercised. Companies may exploit their market power in a host of competition-distorting ways that do not directly lead to short-term price and output effects.

I propose that a better way to understand competition is by focusing on competitive process and market structure.[187] By arguing for a focus on market structure, I am not advocating a strict return to the structure-conduct-performance paradigm. Instead, I claim that seeking to assess competition without acknowledging the role of structure is misguided. This is because the best guardian of competition is a competitive process, and whether a market is competitive is inextricably linked to—even if not solely determined by—how that market is structured. In other words, an analysis of the competitive process and market structure will offer better insight into the state of competition than do measures of welfare.

Moreover, this approach would better protect the range of interests that Congress sought to promote through preserving competitive markets, as described in the section titled "Antitrust Laws Promote Competition to Serve a Variety of Interests." Foundational to these interests is the distribution of ownership and control—inescapably a question of structure. Promoting a competitive process also minimizes the need for regulatory involvement. A focus on process assigns government the task of creating background conditions, rather than intervening to manufacture or interfere with outcomes.[188]

In practice, adopting this approach would involve assessing a range of factors that give insight into the neutrality of the competitive process and the openness of the market. These factors include (1) entry barriers, (2) conflicts of interest, (3) the emergence of gatekeepers or bottlenecks, (4) the use of and control over data, and (5) the dynamics of bargaining power. An approach that took these factors seriously would involve an assessment of how a market is structured and whether a single firm had acquired sufficient power to distort competitive outcomes.[189] Key questions involving these factors would be: What lines of business is a firm involved in, and how do these lines of business interact? Does the structure of the market create or reflect dependencies? Has a dominant player emerged as a gatekeeper so as to risk distorting competition?

Attention to structural concerns and the competitive process are especially important in the context of online platforms, where price-based measures of competition are inadequate to capture market dynamics, particularly given the role and use of data.[190] As internet platforms mediate a growing share of both communications and commercial activity, ensuring that our framework fits how competition actually works in these markets is vital. In the following, I document facets of Amazon's power, trace the source of its growth, and analyze the effects of its dominance. Doing so through the lens of structure and process enables us to make sense of the company's strategy and illuminates anticompetitive aspects of its business.

Amazon's Business Strategy

Amazon has established dominance as an online platform thanks to two elements of its business strategy: a willingness to sustain losses and invest aggressively at the expense of profits, and integration across multiple business lines.[191] These facets of its strategy are independently significant and closely interlinked—indeed, one way it has been able to expand into so many areas is through foregoing returns. This strategy—pursuing market share at the expense of short-term returns—defies the Chicago School's assumption of rational, profit-seeking market actors. More significantly, Amazon's choice to pursue heavy losses while also integrating across sectors suggests that in order to fully understand the company and the structural power it is amassing, we must view it as an integrated entity. Seeking to gauge the firm's market role by isolating a particular line of business and assessing prices in that segment fails to capture both (1) the true shape of the company's dominance and (2) the ways in which it is able to leverage advantages gained in one sector to boost its business in another.

Willingness to Forego Profits to Establish Dominance

Recently, Amazon has started reporting consistent profits, largely due to the success of Amazon Web Services, its cloud computing business.[192] Its North America retail business runs on much thinner margins, and its international retail business still runs at a loss.[193] But for the vast majority of its twenty years in business, losses—not profits—were the norm. Through 2013, Amazon had generated a positive net income in just over half of its financial reporting quarters. Even in quarters in which it did enter the black, its margins were razor-thin, despite astounding growth.

Amazon's Profits[194]

Just as striking as Amazon's lack of interest in generating profit has been investors' willingness to back the company.[195] With the exception of a few quarters in 2014, Amazon's shareholders have poured money in despite the company's penchant for losses. On a regular basis, Amazon would report losses, and its share price would soar.[196] As one analyst told the *New York Times*, "Amazon's stock price doesn't seem to be correlated to its actual experience in any way."[197]

Analysts and reporters have spilled substantial ink seeking to understand the phenomenon. As one commentator joked in a widely circulated post, "Amazon, as best I can tell, is a charitable organization being run by elements of the investment community for the benefit of consumers."[198]

In some ways, the puzzlement is for naught: Amazon's trajectory reflects the business philosophy that Bezos outlined from the start. In his first letter to shareholders, Bezos wrote:

> We believe that a fundamental measure of our success will be the shareholder value we create over the *long term*. This value will be a direct result of our ability to extend and solidify our current market leadership position. . . . We first measure ourselves in terms of the metrics most indicative of our market leadership: customer and revenue growth, the degree to which our customers continue to purchase from us on a repeat basis, and the strength of our brand. We have invested and will continue to invest aggressively to expand and leverage our customer base, brand, and infrastructure as we move to establish an enduring franchise.[199]

In other words, the premise of Amazon's business model was to establish scale. To achieve scale, the company prioritized growth. Under this approach, aggressive investing would be key, even if that involved slashing prices or spending billions on expanding capacity, in order to become consumers' one-stop shop. This approach meant that Amazon "may make decisions and weigh tradeoffs differently than some companies," Bezos warned.[200] "At this stage, we choose to prioritize growth because we believe that scale is central to achieving the potential of our business model."[201]

The insistent emphasis on "market leadership" (Bezos relies on the term six times in the short letter)[202] signaled that Amazon intended to dominate. And, by many measures, Amazon has succeeded. Its year-on-year revenue growth far outpaces that of other online retailers.[203] Despite efforts by big-box competitors like Walmart, Sears, and Macy's to boost their online operations, no rival has succeeded in winning back market share.[204]

One of the primary ways Amazon has built a huge edge is through Amazon Prime, the company's loyalty program, in which Amazon has invested aggressively. Initiated in 2005, Amazon Prime began by offering consumers unlimited two-day shipping for seventy-nine dollars.[205] In the years since, Amazon has bundled in other deals and perks, like renting e-books and streaming music and video, as well as one-hour or same-day delivery. The program has arguably been the retailer's single biggest driver of growth.[206] Amazon does not disclose the exact number of Prime subscribers, but analysts believe the number of users has reached sixty-three million—nineteen million more than in 2015.[207] Membership doubled between 2011 and 2013; analysts expect it to "easily double again by 2017."[208] By 2020, it is estimated that half of US households may be enrolled.[209]

As with its other ventures, Amazon lost money on Prime to gain buy-in. In 2011 it was estimated that each Prime subscriber cost Amazon at least ninety dollars a year—fifty-five dollars in shipping, thirty-five dollars in digital video—and that the company therefore took an eleven dollar loss annually for each customer.[210] One Amazon expert tallies that Amazon has been losing one billion to two billion dollars a year on Prime memberships.[211] The full cost of Amazon Prime is steeper yet, given that the company has been investing heavily in warehouses, delivery facilities, and trucks, as part of its plan to speed up delivery for Prime customers—expenditures that regularly push it into the red.[212]

Despite these losses—or perhaps because of them—Prime is considered crucial to Amazon's growth as an online retailer. According to analysts, customers increase their purchases from Amazon by about 150 percent after they become Prime members.[213] Prime members comprise 47 percent of Amazon's US shoppers.[214] Amazon Prime members also spend more on the company's website—an average of fifteen hundred dollars annually, compared to $625 spent annually by non-Prime members.[215] Business experts note that by making shipping free, Prime "successfully strips out paying for . . . the leading consumer burden of online shopping."[216] Moreover, the annual fee drives customers to increase their Amazon purchases in order to maximize the return on their investment.[217]

As a result, Amazon Prime users are both more likely to buy on its platform and less likely to shop elsewhere. "[Sixty-three percent] of Amazon Prime members carry out a paid transaction on the site in the same visit," compared to 13 percent of non-Prime members.[218] For Walmart and Target, those figures are 5 percent and 2 percent, respectively.[219] One study found that less than 1 percent of Amazon Prime members are likely to consider competitor retail sites in the same shopping session. Non-Prime members, meanwhile, are eight times more likely than Prime members to shop between both Amazon and Target in the same session.[220] In the words of one former Amazon employee who worked on the Prime team, "It was never about the $79. It was really about changing people's mentality so they wouldn't shop anywhere else."[221] In that regard, Amazon Prime seems to have proven successful.[222]

In 2014, Amazon hiked its Prime membership fee to ninety-nine dollars.[223] The move prompted some consumer ire, but 95 percent of Prime members surveyed said they would either definitely or probably renew their membership regardless,[224] suggesting that Amazon has created significant buy-in and that no competitor is currently offering a comparably valuable service at a lower price. It may, however, also reveal the general stickiness of online shopping patterns. Although competition for online services may seem to be "just one click away," research drawing on behavioral tendencies shows that the "switching cost" of changing web services can, in fact, be quite high.[225]

No doubt, Amazon's dominance stems in part from its first-mover advantage as a pioneer of large-scale online commerce. But in several key ways, Amazon has achieved its position through deeply cutting prices and investing heavily in growing its operations—both at the expense of profits. The fact that Amazon has been willing to forego profits for growth undercuts a central premise of contemporary predatory pricing doctrine, which assumes that predation is irrational precisely because firms prioritize profits over growth.[226] In this way, Amazon's strategy has enabled it to use predatory pricing tactics without triggering the scrutiny of predatory pricing laws.

Expansion into Multiple Business Lines

Another key element of Amazon's strategy—and one partly enabled by its capacity to thrive despite posting losses—has been to expand aggressively into multiple business lines.[227] In addition to being a retailer, Amazon is a marketing platform, a delivery and logistics network, a payment service, a credit lender, an auction house, a major book publisher, a producer of television and films, a fashion designer, a hardware manufacturer, and a leading provider of cloud server space and computing power.[228] For the most part, Amazon has expanded into these areas by acquiring existing firms.[229]

Involvement in multiple, related business lines means that, in many instances, Amazon's rivals are also its customers. The retailers that compete with it to sell goods may also use its delivery services, for example, and the media companies that compete with it to produce or market content may also use its platform or cloud infrastructure. At a basic level this arrangement creates conflicts of interest, given that Amazon is positioned to favor its own products over those of its competitors.

Critically, not only has Amazon integrated across select lines of business, but it has also emerged as central infrastructure for the internet economy. Reports suggest this was part of Bezos' vision from the start. According to early Amazon employees, when the chief executive officer founded the business, "his underlying goals were not to build an online bookstore or an online retailer, but rather a 'utility' that would become essential to commerce."[230] In other words, Bezos' target customer was not only end-consumers but also other businesses.

Amazon controls key critical infrastructure for the internet economy—in ways that are difficult for new entrants to replicate or compete against. This gives the company a key advantage over its rivals: Amazon's competitors have come to depend on it. Like its willingness to sustain losses, this feature of Amazon's power largely confounds contemporary antitrust analysis, which assumes that rational firms seek to drive their rivals out of business. Amazon's game is more sophisticated. By making itself indispensable to e-commerce, Amazon enjoys receiving business from its rivals, even as it competes with them. Moreover, Amazon gleans information from these competitors as a service provider that it may use to gain a further advantage over them as rivals—enabling it to further entrench its dominant position.

Establishing Structural Dominance

Amazon now controls 46 percent of all e-commerce in the United States.[231] Not only is it the fastest-growing major retailer, but it is also growing faster than e-commerce as a whole.[232] In 2010, it employed 33,700 workers; by June 2016, it had 268,900.[233] It is enjoying rapid success even in sectors that it only recently entered. For example, the company "is expected to triple its share of the U.S. apparel market over the next five years."[234] Its clothing sales recently rose by $1.1 billion—even as online sales at the six largest US department stores fell by over five hundred million dollars.[235]

These figures alone are daunting, but they do not capture the full extent of Amazon's role and power. Amazon's willingness to sustain losses and invest aggressively at the expense of profits, coupled with its integration across sectors, has enabled it to establish a dominant structural role in the market.

In the sections that follow, I describe several examples of Amazon's conduct that illustrate how the firm has established structural dominance.[236] These examples—its handling of e-books and its battle with an independent online retailer—focus on predatory pricing practices. These cases suggest ways in which Amazon may benefit from predatory pricing even if the company does not raise the price of the goods on which it lost money. The other examples, Fulfillment-by-Amazon (FBA) and Amazon Marketplace, demonstrate how Amazon has become an infrastructure company, both for physical delivery and e-commerce, and how this vertical integration implicates market competition. These cases highlight how Amazon can use its role as an infrastructure provider to benefit its other lines of business. These examples also demonstrate how high barriers to entry may make it difficult for potential competitors to enter these spheres, locking in Amazon's dominance for the foreseeable future. All four of these accounts raise concerns about contemporary antitrust's ability to register and address the anticompetitive threat posed by Amazon and other dominant online platforms.

Below-Cost Pricing of Bestseller E-Books and the Limits of Modern Recoupment Analysis

Amazon entered the e-book market by pricing bestsellers below cost. Although this strategic pricing helped Amazon to establish dominance in the e-book market, the government perceived Amazon's cost cutting as benign, focusing on the profitability of e-books in the aggregate and characterizing the company's pricing of bestsellers as "loss leading" rather than predatory pricing. This failure to recognize Amazon's conduct as anticompetitive stems from a misunderstanding of online markets generally and of Amazon's strategy specifically. Additionally, analyzing the issues raised in this case suggests that Amazon could recoup its losses through means not captured by current antitrust analysis.

In late 2007, Amazon rolled out the Kindle, its e-reading device, and launched a new e-book library.[237] Before introducing the device, Chief Executive Officer Jeff Bezos had decided to price bestseller e-books at $9.99,[238] significantly below the twelve to thirty dollars that a new hardback typically costs.[239] Critically, the wholesale price at which Amazon was buying books from publishers had not dropped; it was instead choosing to price e-books below cost.[240] Analysts estimate that Amazon sold the Kindle device below manufacturing cost too.[241] Bezos' plan was to dominate the e-book selling business in the way that Apple had become the go-to platform for digital music.[242] The strategy worked: through 2009, Amazon dominated the e-book retail market, selling around 90 percent of all e-books.[243]

Publishers, fearing that Amazon's $9.99 price point for e-books would permanently drive down the price that consumers were willing to pay for all books, sought to wrest back some control. When the opportunity came to partner with Apple to sell e-books through the iBookstore store, five of the "Big Six" publishers introduced agency pricing, whereby publishers would set the final retail price and Apple would get a 30 percent cut.[244] After securing this deal, MacMillan, one of the "Big Six," demanded that Amazon, too, adopt this pricing model.[245] Though it initially refused and delisted MacMillan's books,[246] Amazon ultimately relented, explaining to readers that "we will have to capitulate and accept Macmillan's terms because Macmillan has a monopoly over their own titles."[247] Other publishers followed suit, halting Amazon's ability to price e-books at $9.99.[248]

In 2012, the DOJ sued the publishers and Apple for colluding to raise e-book prices.[249] In response to claims that the DOJ was going after the wrong actor—given that it was Amazon's predatory tactics that drove the publishers and Apple to join forces—the DOJ investigated Amazon's pricing strategies and found "persuasive evidence lacking" to show that the company had engaged in predatory practices.[250] According to the government, "from the time of its launch, Amazon's e-book distribution business has been consistently profitable, even when substantially discounting some newly released and bestselling titles."[251]

Judge Cote, who presided over the district court trial, refrained from affirming the government's conclusion.[252] Still, the government's argument illustrates the dominant framework that courts and enforcers use to analyze predation—and how it falls short. Specifically, the government erred by analyzing the profitability of Amazon's e-book business in the aggregate and by characterizing the conduct as "loss leading" rather than potentially predatory pricing.[253] These missteps suggest a failure to appreciate two critical aspects of Amazon's practices: (1) how steep discounting by a firm on a platform-based product creates a higher risk that the firm will generate monopoly power than discounting on nonplatform goods and (2) the multiple ways Amazon could recoup losses in ways other than raising the price of the same e-books that it discounted.

On the first point, the government argued that Amazon was not engaging in predation because in the *aggregate*, Amazon's e-books business was profitable. This perspective overlooks how heavy losses on particular lines of e-books (bestsellers, for example, or new releases) may have thwarted competition, even if the e-book business as a whole was profitable. That the DOJ chose to define the relevant market as e-books—rather than as specific lines, like bestseller e-books—reflects a deeper mistake: the failure to recognize how the economics of platform-based products differ in crucial ways from nonplatform goods.[254] As a result, the DOJ analyzed the e-book market as it would the market for physical books.

One indication of this failure to appreciate the difference between physical books and e-books is that the government and Judge Cote treated Amazon's below-cost pricing as loss leading,[255] rather than as predatory pricing.[256] The difference between loss leading and predatory pricing is not spelled out in law, but the distinction turns on the nature of the below-cost pricing, specifically its intensity and the intent motivating it. Judge Cote's use of "loss leading" revealed a view that "Amazon's below-cost pricing was (a) selective rather than pervasive, and (b) not intended to generate monopoly power."[257] On this view, Amazon's aim was to trigger additional sales of other products sold by Amazon, rather than to drive out competing e-book sellers and acquire the power to increase e-book prices.[258] In other words, because Amazon's alleged short-term aim was to sell more e-readers and e-books—rather than to harm its rivals and raise prices—its conduct is considered loss leading rather than predatory pricing. What both the DOJ and the district court missed, however, is the way in which below-cost pricing in this instance entrenched and reinforced Amazon's dominance in ways that loss leading by physical retailers does not.

Unlike with online shopping, each trip to a brick-and-mortar store is discrete. If, on Monday, Walmart heavily discounts the price of socks and you are looking to buy socks, you might visit, buy socks, and—because you are already there—also buy milk. On Thursday, the fact that Walmart had discounted socks on Monday does not necessarily exert any tug; you may return to Walmart because you now know that Walmart often has good bargains, but the fact that you purchased socks from Walmart on Monday is not, in itself, a reason to return.

Internet retail is different. Say on Monday, Amazon steeply discounts the e-book version of Harper Lee's *Go Set a Watchman*, and you purchase both a Kindle and the e-book. On Thursday, you would be inclined to revisit Amazon—and not simply because you know it has good bargains. Several factors extend the tug. For one, Amazon, like other e-book sellers, has used a scheme known as "digital rights management," which limits the types of devices that can read certain e-book formats.[259] Compelling readers to purchase a Kindle through cheap e-books locks them into future e-book purchases from Amazon.[260] Moreover, buying—or even browsing—e-books on Amazon's platform hands the company information about your reading habits and preferences, data the company uses to tailor recommendations and future deals.[261] Replicated across a few more purchases, Amazon's lock-in becomes strong. It becomes unlikely that a reader will then purchase a Nook and switch to buying e-books through Barnes & Noble, even if that company is slashing prices.

Put differently, loss leading pays higher returns with platform-based e-commerce—and specifically with digital products like e-books—than it does with brick-and-mortar stores. The marginal value of the first sale and early sales in general is much higher for e-books than for print books because there are lock-in effects at play, due both to technical design and the possibilities for and value of personalization.

By treating e-commerce and digital goods the same as physical stores and goods, both the government and Judge Cote missed the anticompetitive implications of Amazon's below-cost pricing. Though the immediate effect of Amazon's pricing of bestseller e-books may have been to sell more e-books generally, that tactic has also positioned Amazon to dominate the market in a way that sets it up to raise future prices. In this context, the traditional distinction between loss leading and predatory pricing is strained.

Instead of recognizing that the economics of platforms meant that below-cost pricing on a platform-hosted good would tend to facilitate long-term dominance, the government took comfort that the industry was "dynamic and evolving" and concluded that the "presence and continued investment by technology giants, multinational book publishers, and national retailers in e-books businesses" rendered an Amazon-dominated market unlikely.[262] Yet Amazon's early lead has, in fact, translated to long-term dominance. It controls around 65 percent of the e-book market today,[263] while its share of the e-reader market hovers around 74 percent.[264] Players that appeared up-and-coming even a few years ago are now retreating from the market. Sony closed its US Reader store and is no longer introducing new e-readers to the US market.[265] Barnes & Noble, meanwhile, has slashed funding for the Nook by 74 percent.[266] The only real e-books competitor left standing is Apple.[267]

Because the government deflected predatory pricing claims by looking at aggregate profitability, neither the government nor the court reached the question of recoupment. Given that—under current doctrine—whether below-cost pricing is predatory turns on whether a firm recoups its losses, we should examine how Amazon could use its dominance to recoup its losses in ways that are more sophisticated than what courts generally consider or are able to assess.

Most obviously, Amazon could earn back the losses it generated on best-seller e-books by raising prices of either particular lines of e-books or e-books as a whole. This intraproduct market form of recoupment is what courts look for. However, it remains unclear whether Amazon has hiked e-book prices because, as the *New York Times* noted, "[i]t is difficult to comprehensively track the movement of prices on Amazon," which means that any evidence of price trends is "anecdotal and fragmentary."[268] As Amazon customers can attest, Amazon's prices fluctuate rapidly and with no explanation.[269]

This underscores a basic challenge of conducting recoupment analysis with Amazon: it may not be apparent when and by how much Amazon raises prices. Online commerce enables Amazon to obscure price hikes in at least two ways: rapid, constant price fluctuations and personalized pricing.[270] Constant price fluctuations diminish our ability to discern pricing trends. By one account, Amazon changes prices more than 2.5 million times each day.[271] Amazon is also able to tailor prices to individual consumers, known as first-degree price discrimination. There is no public evidence that Amazon is currently engaging in personalized pricing,[272] but online retailers generally are devoting significant resources to analyzing how to implement it.[273] A major topic of discussion at the 2014 National Retail Federation annual convention, for example, was how to introduce discriminatory pricing without triggering consumer backlash.[274] One mechanism discussed was highly personalized coupons sent at the point of sale, which would avoid the need to show consumers different prices but would still achieve discriminatory pricing.[275]

If retailers—including Amazon—implement discriminatory pricing on a wide scale, each individual would be subject to his or her own personal price trajectory, eliminating the notion of a single pricing trend. It is not clear how we would measure price hikes for the purpose of recoupment analysis in that scenario. There would be no obvious conclusions if some consumers faced higher prices while others enjoyed lower ones. But given the magnitude and accuracy of data that Amazon has collected on millions of users, tailored pricing is not simply a hypothetical power.[276] Discerning whether and by how much Amazon raises book prices will be more difficult than the *Matsushita* or *Brooke Group* Courts could have imagined.[277]

It is true that brick-and-mortar stores also collect data on customer purchasing habits and send personalized coupons. But the types of consumer behavior that internet firms can access—how long you hover your mouse on a particular item, how many days an item sits in your shopping basket before you purchase it, or the fashion blogs you visit before looking for those same items through a search engine—is uncharted ground. The degree to which a firm can tailor and personalize an online shopping experience is different in kind from the methods available to a brick-and-mortar store—precisely because the type of behavior that online firms can track is far more detailed and nuanced. And unlike brick-and-mortar stores—where everyone at least *sees* a common price (even if they go on to receive discounts)—internet retail enables firms to entirely personalize consumer experiences, which eliminates any collective baseline from which to gauge price increases or decreases.

The decision of which product market in which Amazon may choose to raise prices is also an open question—and one that current predatory pricing doctrine ignores. Courts generally assume that a firm will recoup by increasing prices on the same goods on which it previously lost money. But recoupment across markets is also available as a strategy, especially for firms as diversified across products and services as Amazon. Reporting suggests the company did just this in 2013, by hiking prices on scholarly and small-press books and creating the risk of a "two-tier system where some books are priced beyond an audience's reach."[278] Although Amazon may be recouping its initial losses in e-books through markups on physical books, this cross-market recoupment is not a scenario that enforcers or judges generally consider.[279] One possible reason for this neglect is that Chicago School scholarship, which assumes recoupment in single-product markets is unlikely, also holds recoupment in multiproduct scenarios to be implausible.[280]

Although current predatory pricing doctrine focuses only on recoupment through raising prices for consumers, Amazon could also recoup its losses by imposing higher fees on publishers. Large book retailer chains like Barnes & Noble have long used their market dominance to charge publishers for favorable product placement, such as displays in a storefront window or on a prominent table.[281] Amazon's dominance in the e-book market has enabled it to demand similar fees for even the most basic of services. For example, when renewing its contract with Hachette last year, Amazon demanded payments for services including the preorder button, personalized recommendations, and an Amazon employee assigned to the publisher.[282] In the words of one person close to the negotiations, Amazon "is very inventive about what we'd call standard service. . . . They're teasing out all these layers and saying, 'If you want that service, you'll have to pay for it.'"[283] By introducing fees on services that it previously offered for free, Amazon has created another source of revenue. Amazon's power to demand these fees—and recoup some of the losses it sustained in below-cost pricing—stems from dominance partly built through that same below-cost pricing. The fact that Amazon has itself vertically integrated into book publishing—and hence can promote its own content—may give it additional leverage to hike fees. Any publisher that refuses could see Amazon favor its own books over the publisher's, reflecting a conflict of interest I discuss further in the section titled "Amazon Marketplace and Exploiting Data." It is not uncommon for half of the titles on Amazon's Kindle bestseller list to be its own.[284]

While not captured by current antitrust doctrine, the pressure Amazon puts on publishers merits concern.[285] For one, consolidation among book sellers—partly spurred by Amazon's pricing tactics and demands for better terms from publishers—has also spurred consolidation among publishers. Consolidation among publishers last reached its heyday in the 1990s—as publishing houses sought to bulk up in response to the growing clout of Borders and Barnes & Noble—and by the early 2000s, the industry had settled into the "Big Six."[286] This trend has cost authors and readers alike, leaving writers with fewer paths to market and readers with a less diverse marketplace. Since Amazon's rise, the major publishers have merged further—thinning down to five, with rumors of more consolidation to come.[287]

Second, the increasing cost of doing business with Amazon is upending the publishers' business model in ways that further risk sapping diversity. Traditionally, publishing houses used a cross-subsidization model whereby they would use their best sellers to subsidize weightier and riskier books requiring greater upfront investment.[288] In the face of higher fees imposed by Amazon, publishers say they are less able to invest in a range of books. In a recent letter to DOJ, a group of authors wrote that Amazon's actions have "extract[ed] vital resources from the [book] industry in ways that lessen the diversity and quality of books."[289] The authors noted that publishers have responded to Amazon's fees by both publishing fewer titles and focusing largely on books by celebrities and bestselling authors.[290] The authors also noted, "Readers are presented with fewer books that espouse unusual, quirky, offbeat, or politically risky ideas, as well as books from new and unproven authors. This impoverishes America's marketplace of ideas."[291]

Amazon's conduct would be readily cognizable as a threat under the pre–Chicago School view that predatory pricing laws specifically and antitrust generally promoted a broad set of values. Under the predatory pricing jurisprudence of the early and mid-twentieth century, harm to the diversity and vibrancy of ideas in the book market may have been a primary basis for government intervention. The political risks associated with Amazon's market dominance also implicate some of the major concerns that animate antitrust laws. For instance, the risk that Amazon may retaliate against books that it disfavors—either to impose greater pressure on publishers or for other political reasons—raises concerns about media freedom. Given that antitrust authorities previously considered diversity of speech and ideas a factor in their analysis, Amazon's degree of control, too, should warrant concern.

Even within the narrower "consumer welfare" framework, Amazon's attempts to recoup losses through fees on publishers should be understood as harmful. A market with less choice and diversity for readers amounts to a form of consumer injury. That DOJ ignored this concern in its suit against Apple and the publishers suggests that its conception of predatory pricing fails to capture overlooks the full suite of harms that Amazon's actions may cause.[292]

Amazon's below-cost pricing in the e-book market—which enabled it to capture 65 percent of that market,[293] a sizable share by any measure—strains predatory pricing doctrine in several ways. First, Amazon is positioned to recoup its losses by raising prices on less popular or obscure e-books, or by raising prices on print books. In either case, Amazon would be recouping outside the original market where it sustained losses (bestseller e-books), so courts are unlikely to look for or consider these scenarios. Additionally, constant fluctuations in prices and the ability to price discriminate enable Amazon to raise prices with little chance of detection. Lastly, Amazon could recoup its losses by extracting more from publishers, who are dependent on its platform to market both e-books and print books. This may diminish the quality and breadth of the works that are published, but since this is most directly a supplier-side rather than buyer-side harm, it is less likely that a modern court would consider it closely. The current predatory pricing framework fails to capture the harm posed to the book market by Amazon's tactics.

Acquisition of Quidsi and Flawed Assumptions About Entry and Exit Barriers

In addition to using below-cost pricing to establish a dominant position in e-books, Amazon has also used this practice to put pressure on and ultimately acquire a chief rival. This history challenges contemporary antitrust law's assumption that predatory pricing cannot be used to establish dominance. While theory may predict that entry barriers for online retail are low, this account shows that in practice significant investment is needed to establish a successful platform that will attract traffic. Finally, Amazon's conduct suggests that psychological intimidation can discourage new entry that would challenge a dominant player's market power.

In 2008, Quidsi was one of the world's fastest growing e-commerce companies.[294] It oversaw several subsidiaries: Diapers.com (focused on baby care), Soap.com (focused on household essentials), and BeautyBar.com (focused on beauty products). Amazon expressed interest in acquiring Quidsi in 2009, but the company's founders declined Amazon's offer.[295]

Shortly after Quidsi rejected Amazon's overture, Amazon cut its prices for diapers and other baby products by up to 30 percent.[296] By reconfiguring their prices, Quidsi executives saw that Amazon's pricing bots—software "that carefully monitors other companies' prices and adjusts Amazon's to match"—were tracking Diapers.com and would immediately slash Amazon's prices in response to Quidsi's changes.[297] In September 2010, Amazon rolled out Amazon Mom, a new service that offered a year's worth of free two-day Prime shipping (which usually cost seventy-nine dollars a year).[298] Customers could also secure an additional 30 percent discount on diapers by signing up for monthly deliveries as part of a service known as "Subscribe and Save."[299] Quidsi executives "calculated that Amazon was on track to lose $100 million over three months in the diaper category alone."[300]

Eventually, Amazon's below-cost pricing started eating into Diapers.com's growth, and it "slowed under Amazon's pricing pressure."[301] Investors, meanwhile, "grew wary of pouring more money" into Quidsi, given the challenge from Amazon.[302] Struggling to keep up with Amazon's pricing war, Quidsi's owners began talks with Walmart about potentially selling the business. Amazon intervened and made an aggressive counteroffer.[303] Although Walmart offered a higher final bid, "the Quidsi executives stuck with

Amazon, largely out of fear."[304] The FTC reviewed the Amazon-Quidsi deal and decided that it did not trigger anticompetitive concerns.[305] Through its purchase of Quidsi, Amazon eliminated a leading competitor in the online sale of baby products. Amazon achieved this by slashing prices and bleeding money,[306] losses that its investors have given it a free pass to incur—and that a smaller and newer venture like Quidsi, by contrast, could not maintain.

After completing its buy-up of a key rival—and seemingly losing hundreds of millions of dollars in the process—Amazon went on to raise prices. In November 2011, a year after buying out Quidsi, Amazon shut down new memberships in its Amazon Mom program.[307] Though the company has since reopened the program, it has continued to scale back the discounts and generous shopping terms of the original offer. As of February 2012, discounts that had previously been 30 percent were reduced to 20 percent, and the one year of free Prime membership was cut to three months.[308] In November 2014, the company hiked prices further: members purchasing more than four items in a month would no longer receive the general 20 percent discount, and the 20 percent discount on baby wipes—one of the program's top-selling products—was cut to 5 percent.[309] Summarizing the series of changes, one journalist observed, "The Amazon Mom program has become much less generous than it was when it was introduced in 2010."[310] In online forums where consumers expressed frustrations with the changes, several users said they would be taking their business from Amazon and returning to Diapers.com—which, other users pointed out, was no longer possible.[311] Through its strategy, Amazon now holds a strong position in the baby product market.[312]

Amazon's conduct runs counter to contemporary predatory pricing thinking, which contends that predation is no path to buying up a competitor. In *The Antitrust Paradox*, Bork wrote, "[T]he modern law of horizontal mergers makes it all but impossible for the predator to bring the war to an end by purchasing his victim. To accomplish the predator's purpose, the merger must create a monopoly" and law "would preclude the attainment of the monopoly necessary to make predation profitable."[313] For sectors with low entry costs, Bork writes, this strategy is precluded by the constant possibility of reentry by other players. "A shoe retailer can be driven out rapidly, but reentry will be equally rapid."[314] In fields in which entry costs are high, Bork argued that exit by competitors is unlikely because management would need to believe that the predation had rendered the value of their facilities negligible. For instance, "[r]ailroading, which involves specialized facilities, is difficult to enter, but the potential victim of predation would be difficult to drive out precisely because railroad facilities are not useful in other industries."[315]

Does online retailing of baby products resemble shoe retailing or railroading? Given the absence of formal barriers, entry should be easy: unlike railroading, selling baby products online requires no heavy investment or fixed costs. However, the economics of online retailing are not quite like traditional shoe retailing. Given that attracting traffic and generating sales as an independent online retailer involves steep search costs, the vast majority of online commerce is conducted on platforms, central marketplaces that connect buyers and sellers. Thus, in practice, successful entry by a potential diaper retailer carries with it the cost of attempting to build a new online platform, or of creating a brand strong enough to draw traffic from an existing company's platform. As several commentators have observed, the practical barriers to successful and sustained entry as an online platform are very high, given the huge first-mover advantages stemming from data collection and network effects.[316] Moreover, the high exit barriers that Bork assumes for railroads—namely, that they would have to be convinced their facilities were worth more as scrap than as a railroad—do not apply to online platforms. Investment in online platforms lies not in physical infrastructure that might be repurposed, but in intangibles like brand recognition. These intangibles can be absorbed by a rival platform or retailer with greater ease than a railroad could take over a competing line.[317] In other words, online retailers like Quidsi face the high entry barriers of a railroad coupled with the relatively low exit costs typical of brick-and-mortar retailers—a combination that Bork, and the courts, failed to consider.

Courts also tend to discount that predators can use psychological intimidation to keep out the competition.[318] Amazon's history with Quidsi has sent a clear message to potential competitors—namely that unless upstarts have deep pockets that allow them to bleed money in a head-to-head fight with Amazon, it may not be worth entering the market. Even as Amazon has raised the price of the Amazon Mom program, no newcomers have recently sought to challenge it in this sector, supporting the idea that intimidation may also serve as a practical barrier.[319]

As the world's largest online retailer, Amazon serves as a default starting point for many online shoppers: one study estimates that 44 percent of US consumers "go directly to Amazon first to search for products."[320] Moreover, the swaths of data that Amazon has collected on consumers' browsing and searching histories can create the same problem that Google's would-be competitors encounter: "an insurmountable barrier to entry for new competition."[321] Though at least one venture opened shop with an eye to challenging Amazon,[322] its founders recently sold the firm to Walmart[323]—a move that suggests that the only players positioned to challenge Amazon are the existing giants. However, even this strategy has skeptics.[324] While established brick-and-mortar retailers like Target have tried to lure online consumers through discounts and low delivery costs,[325] Amazon remains the major online seller of baby products.[326] Although Amazon established its dominance in this market through aggressive price cutting and selling steeply at a loss, its actions have not triggered predatory pricing claims. In part, this is because prevailing theory assumes—per Bork's analysis—that market entry is easy enough for new rivals to emerge any time a dominant firm starts charging monopoly prices.

In this case, Amazon raised prices by cutting back discounts and (at least temporarily) refusing to expand the program. Even if a firm viewed the unmet demand as an invitation to enter, several factors would prove discouraging in ways that the existing doctrine does not consider. In theory, online retailing itself has low entry costs since anyone can set up shop online, without significant fixed costs. But in practice, successful entry in online markets is a challenge, requiring significant upfront investment. It requires either building up strong brand recognition to draw users to an independent site, or using an existing platform, such as Amazon or eBay, which can present other anticompetitive challenges.[327] Indeed, most independent retailers choose to sell through Amazon[328]—even when the business relationship risks undermining their business. The fact that no real rival has emerged, even after Amazon raised prices, undercuts the assumption embedded in current antitrust doctrine.

Amazon Delivery and Leveraging Dominance Across Sectors

As its history with Quidsi shows, Amazon's willingness to sustain losses has allowed it to engage in below-cost pricing in order to establish dominance as an online retailer. Amazon has translated its dominance as an online retailer into significant bargaining power in the delivery sector, using it to secure favorable conditions from third-party delivery companies. This in turn has enabled Amazon to extend its dominance over other retailers by creating the FBA service and establishing its own physical delivery capacity. This illustrates how a company can leverage its dominant platform to successfully integrate into other sectors, creating anticompetitive dynamics. Retail competitors are left with two undesirable choices: either try to compete with Amazon at a disadvantage or become reliant on a competitor to handle delivery and logistics.

As Amazon expanded its share of e-commerce—and enlarged the e-commerce sector as a whole—it started comprising a greater share of delivery companies' business. For example, in 2015, UPS derived one billion dollars of business from Amazon alone.[329] The fact that it accounted for a growing share of these firms' businesses gave Amazon bargaining power to negotiate for lower rates.[330] By some estimates, Amazon enjoyed a 70 percent discount over regular delivery prices.[331] Delivery companies sought to make up for the discounts they gave to Amazon by raising the prices they charged to independent sellers,[332] a phenomenon recently termed the "waterbed effect."[333] As scholars have described,

> [T]he presence of a waterbed effect can further distort competition by giving a powerful buyer now a two-fold advantage, namely, through more advantageous terms for itself and through higher purchasing costs for its rivals. What then becomes a virtuous circle for the strong buyer ends up as a vicious circle for its weaker competitors.[334]

To this twofold advantage Amazon added a third perk: harnessing the weakness of its rivals into a business opportunity. In 2006, Amazon introduced FBA, a logistics and delivery service for independent sellers.[335] Merchants who sign up for FBA store their products in Amazon's warehouses, and Amazon packs, ships, and provides customer service on any orders. Products sold through FBA are eligible for service through Amazon Prime—namely, free two-day shipping and/or free regular shipping, depending on the order.[336] Since many merchants selling on Amazon are competing with Amazon's own retail operation and its Amazon Prime service, using FBA offers sellers the opportunity to compete at less of a disadvantage.

Notably, it is partly because independent sellers faced higher rates from UPS and FedEx—a result of Amazon's dominance—that Amazon succeeded in directing sellers to its new business venture.[337] In many instances, orders routed through FBA were still being shipped and delivered by UPS and FedEx, since Amazon relied on these firms.[338] But because Amazon had secured discounts unavailable to other sellers, it was cheaper for those sellers to go through Amazon than to use UPS and FedEx directly. Amazon had used its dominance in the retail sector to create and boost a new venture in the delivery sector, inserting itself into the business of its competitors.

Amazon has followed up on this initial foray into fulfillment services by creating a logistics empire. Building out physical capacity lets Amazon further reduce its delivery times, raising the bar for entry yet higher. Moreover, it is the firm's capacity for aggressive investing that has enabled it to rapidly establish an extensive network of physical infrastructure. Since 2010, Amazon has spent $13.9 billion building warehouses,[339] and it spent $11.5 billion on shipping in 2015 alone.[340] Amazon has opened more than 180 warehouses,[341] twenty-eight sorting centers, fifty-nine delivery stations that feed packages to local couriers, and more than sixty-five Prime Now hubs.[342] Analysts estimate that the locations of Amazon's fulfillment centers bring it within twenty miles of 31 percent of the population and within twenty miles of 60 percent of its core same-day base.[343] This sprawling network of fulfillment centers—each placed in or near a major metropolitan area—equips Amazon to offer one-hour delivery in some locations and same-day in others (a service it offers free to members of Amazon Prime).[344] While several rivals initially entered the delivery market to compete with Prime shipping, some are now retreating.[345] As one analyst noted, "Prime has proven exceedingly difficult for rivals to copy."[346]

Most recently, Amazon has also expanded into trucking. Last December, it announced it plans to roll out thousands of branded semi-trucks, a move that will give it yet more control over delivery, as it seeks to speed up how quickly it can transport goods to customers.[347] Amazon now owns four thousand truck trailers and has also signed contracts for container ships, planes,[348] and drones.[349] As of October 2016, Amazon had leased at least forty jets.[350] Former employees say Amazon's long-term goal is to circumvent UPS and FedEx altogether, though the company itself has said it is looking only to supplement its reliance on these firms, not supplant them.[351]

The way that Amazon has leveraged its dominance as an online retailer to vertically integrate into delivery is instructive on several fronts. First, it is a textbook example of how the company can use its dominance in one sphere to advantage a separate line of business. To be sure, this dynamic is not intrinsically anticompetitive. What should prompt concern in Amazon's case, however, is that Amazon achieved these cross-sector advantages in part due to its bargaining power. Because Amazon was able to demand heavy discounts from FedEx and UPS, other sellers faced price hikes from these companies—which positioned Amazon to capture them as clients for its new business. By overlooking structural factors like bargaining power, modern antitrust doctrine fails to address this type of threat to competitive markets.

Second, Amazon is positioned to use its dominance across online retail and delivery in ways that involve tying, are exclusionary, and create entry barriers.[352] That is, Amazon's distortion of the delivery sector in turn creates anticompetitive challenges in the retail sector. For example, sellers who use FBA have a better chance of being listed higher in Amazon search results than those who do not, which means Amazon is tying the outcomes it generates for sellers using its retail platform to whether they also use its delivery business.[353] Amazon is also positioned to use its logistics infrastructure to deliver its own retail goods faster than those of independent sellers that use its platform and fulfillment service—a form of discrimination that exemplifies traditional concerns about vertical integration. And Amazon's capacity for losses and expansive logistics capacities mean that it could privilege its own goods while still offering independent sellers the ability to ship goods more cheaply and quickly than they could by using UPS and FedEx directly.

Relatedly, Amazon's expansion into the delivery sector also raises questions about the Chicago School's limited conception of entry barriers. The company's capacity for losses—the permission it has won from investors to show negative profits—has been key in enabling Amazon to achieve outsized growth in delivery and logistics. Matching Amazon's network would require a rival to invest heavily and—in order to viably compete—offer free or otherwise below-cost shipping. In interviews with reporters, venture capitalists say there is no appetite to fund firms looking to compete with Amazon on physical delivery.[354] In this way, Amazon's ability to sustain losses creates an entry barrier for any firm that does not enjoy the same privilege.

Third, Amazon's use of Prime and FBA exemplifies how the company has structurally placed itself at the center of e-commerce. Already 44 percent of American online shoppers begin their online shopping on Amazon's platform.[355] Given the traffic, it is becoming increasingly clear that in order to succeed in e-commerce, an independent merchant will need to use Amazon's infrastructure. The fact that Amazon competes with many of the businesses that are coming to depend on it creates a host of conflicts of interest that the company can exploit to privilege its own products.

The dominant framework in antitrust today fails to recognize the risk that Amazon's dominance poses for discrimination and barriers to new entry. In part, this is because—as with the framework's view of predatory pricing—the primary harm that registers within the "consumer welfare" frame is higher consumer prices. On the Chicago School's account, Amazon's vertical integration would only be harmful if and when it chooses to use its dominance in delivery and retail to hike fees to consumers. Amazon has already raised Prime prices.[356] But antitrust enforcers should be equally concerned about the fact that Amazon increasingly controls the infrastructure of online commerce—and the ways in which it is harnessing this dominance to expand and advantage its new business ventures. The conflicts of interest that arise from Amazon both competing with merchants and delivering their wares pose a hazard to competition, particularly in light of Amazon's entrenched position as an online platform. Amazon's conflicts of interest tarnish the neutrality of the competitive process. The thousands of retailers and independent businesses that must ride Amazon's rails to reach market are increasingly dependent on their biggest competitor.

Amazon Marketplace and Exploiting Data

As described earlier, vertical integration in retail and physical delivery may enable Amazon to leverage cross-sector advantages in ways that are potentially anticompetitive but not understood as such under current antitrust doctrine. Analogous dynamics are at play with Amazon's dominance in the provision of *online* infrastructure, in particular its Marketplace for third-party sellers. Because information about Amazon's practices in this area is limited, this section necessarily will be brief. But to capture fully the anticompetitive features of Amazon's business strategy, it is vital to analyze how vertical integration across internet businesses introduces more sophisticated—and potentially more troubling—opportunities to abuse cross-market advantages and foreclose rivals.

The clearest example of how the company leverages its power across online businesses is Amazon Marketplace, where third-party retailers sell their wares. Because Amazon commands a large share of e-commerce traffic, many smaller merchants find it necessary to use its site to draw buyers.[357] These sellers list their goods on Amazon's platform, and the company collects fees ranging from 6 percent to 50 percent of their sales from them.[358] More than two million third-party sellers used Amazon's platform as of 2015, an increase from the roughly one million that used the platform in 2006.[359] The revenue that Amazon generates through Marketplace has been a major source of its growth: third-party sellers' share of total items sold on Amazon rose from 36 percent in 2011[360] to over 50 percent in 2015.[361]

Third-party sellers using Marketplace recognize that using the platform puts them in a bind. As one merchant observed, "You can't really be a high-volume seller online without being on Amazon, but sellers are very aware of the fact that Amazon is also their primary competitor."[362] Evidence suggests that their unease is well founded. Amazon seems to use its Marketplace "as a vast laboratory to spot new products to sell, test sales of potential new goods, and exert more control over pricing."[363] Specifically, reporting suggests that "Amazon uses sales data from outside merchants to make purchasing decisions in order to undercut them on price" and give its own items "featured placement under a given search."[364] Take the example of Pillow Pets, "stuffed-animal pillows modeled after NFL mascots" that a third-party merchant sold through Amazon's site.[365] For several months, the merchant sold up to one hundred pillows per day.[366] According to one account, "just ahead of the holiday season, [the merchant] noticed Amazon had itself beg[u]n offering the same Pillow Pets for the same price while giving [its own] products featured placement on the site."[367] The merchant's own sales dropped to twenty per day.[368] Amazon has gone head-to-head with independent merchants on price, vigorously matching and even undercutting them on products that they had originally introduced. By going directly to the manufacturer, Amazon seeks to cut out the independent sellers.

In other instances, Amazon has responded to popular third-party products by producing them itself. Last year, a manufacturer that had been selling an aluminum laptop stand on Marketplace for more than a decade saw a similar stand appear at half the price. The manufacturer learned that the brand was AmazonBasics, the private line that Amazon has been developing since 2009.[369] As one news site describes it, initially, AmazonBasics focused on generic goods like batteries and blank DVDs. "Then, for several years, the house brand 'slept quietly as it retained data about other sellers' successes.'"[370] As it now rolls out more AmazonBasics products, it is clear that the company has used "insights gleaned from its vast Web store to build a private-label juggernaut that now includes more than 3,000 products."[371] One study found that in the case of women's clothing, Amazon "began selling 25 percent of the top items first sold through marketplace vendors."[372]

It is true that brick-and-mortar retailers sometimes also introduce private labels and may use other brands' sales records to decide what to produce. The difference with Amazon is the scale and sophistication of the data it collects. Whereas brick-and-mortar stores are generally only able to collect information on actual sales, Amazon tracks what shoppers are searching for but cannot find, as well as which products they repeatedly return to, what they keep in their shopping basket, and what their mouse hovers over on the screen.[373]

In using its Marketplace this way, Amazon increases sales while shedding risk. It is third-party sellers who bear the initial costs and uncertainties when introducing new products; by merely spotting them, Amazon gets to sell products only once their success has been tested. The anticompetitive implications here seem clear: Amazon is exploiting the fact that some of its customers are also its rivals. The sources of this power are (1) its dominance as a platform, which effectively necessitates that independent merchants use its site; (2) its vertical integration—namely, the fact that it both sells goods as a retailer and hosts sales by others as a marketplace; and (3) its ability to amass swaths of data, by virtue of being an internet company. Notably, it is this last factor—its control over data—that heightens the anticompetitive potential of the first two.

Evidence suggests that Amazon is keenly aware of and interested in exploiting these opportunities. For example, the company has reportedly used insights gleaned from its cloud computing service to inform its investment decisions.[374] By observing which start-ups are expanding their usage of Amazon Web Services, Amazon can make early assessments of the potential success of upcoming firms. Amazon has used this "unique window into the technology startup world" to invest in several start-ups that were also customers of its cloud business.[375]

How Amazon has cross-leveraged its advantages across distinct lines of business suggests that the law fails to appreciate when vertical integration may prove anticompetitive. This shortcoming is underscored with online platforms, which both serve as infrastructure for other companies and collect swaths of data that they can then use to build up other lines of business. In this way, the current antitrust regime has yet to reckon with the fact that firms with concentrated control over data can systematically tilt a market in their favor, dramatically reshaping the sector.[376]

How Platform Economics and Capital Markets May Facilitate Anticompetitive Conduct and Structures

As the previous section mapped out, aspects of Amazon's conduct and structure may threaten competition yet fail to trigger scrutiny under the analytical framework presently used in antitrust. In part this reflects the "consumer welfare" orientation of current antitrust laws, as critiqued in the section titled "Why Competitive Process and Structure Matter." But it also reflects a failure to update antitrust for the internet age. This section examines how online platforms defy and complicate assumptions embedded in current doctrine. Specifically, it considers how the economics and business dynamics of online platforms create incentives for companies to pursue growth at the expense of profits, and how online markets and control over data may enable new forms of anticompetitive activity.

Economists have analyzed extensively how platform markets may pose unique challenges for antitrust analysis.[377] Specifically, they stress that analysis applicable to firms in single-sided markets may break down when applied to two-sided markets, given the distinct pricing structures and network externalities.[378] These studies often focus on the challenge that two-sided platforms face in attracting both sides—the classic coordination problem of having to attract buyers without an established line of sellers, and vice versa.[379] Economists tend to conclude that—given the particular challenges of two-sided markets[380]—antitrust should be forgiving of conduct that might otherwise be characterized as anticompetitive.[381]

Legal analysis of online platforms is comparatively undertheorized. The Justice Department's case against Microsoft under section 2 of the Sherman Act, initiated in the 1990s, remains the government's most significant case involving two-sided markets—even as platforms have emerged as central arteries in our modern economy. Starting in 2011, the FTC pursued an investigation into Google, partly in response to allegations that the company uses its dominance as a search engine to cement its advantage and exclude rivals in other lines of business. While the FTC closed the investigation without bringing any charges, leaks later revealed that FTC staff had concluded that Google abused its power on three separate counts.[382] The European Union has brought charges against Google for violating antitrust laws.[383]

For the purpose of competition policy, one of the most relevant factors of online platform markets is that they are winner-take-all. This is due largely to network effects and control over data, both of which mean that early advantages become self-reinforcing. The result is that technology platform markets will yield to dominance by a small number of firms. Walmart's recent purchase of the one start-up that had sought to challenge Amazon in online retail—Jet.com—illustrates this reality.[384]

Network effects arise when a user's utility from a product increases as others use the product. As popularity compounds and is reinforcing, markets with network effects often tip toward oligopoly or monopoly.[385] Amazon's user reviews, for example, serve as a form of network effect: the more users that have purchased and reviewed items on the platform, the more useful information other users can glean from the site.[386] As the Fourth Circuit has noted, "[O]nce dominance is achieved, threats come largely from outside the dominated market, because the degree of dominance of such a market tends to become so extreme."[387] In this way, network effects act as a form of entry barrier.

A platform's control over data, meanwhile, can also entrench its position.[388] Access to consumer data enables platforms to better tailor services and gauge demand. Involvement *across* markets, meanwhile, may permit a company to use data gleaned from one market to benefit another business line.[389] Amazon's use of Marketplace data to advantage its retail sales, as described in the previous section, is an example of this dynamic. Control over data may also make it easier for dominant platforms to enter new markets with greater ease. For example, reports now suggest that Amazon may dramatically expand its footprint in the ad business, "leveraging its rich supply of shopping data culled from years of operating a massive e-commerce business."[390] In other words, control over data, too, acts as an entry barrier.

Given that online platforms operate in markets where network effects and control over data solidify early dominance, a company looking to compete in these markets must seek to capture them. The most effective way is to chase market share and drive out one's rivals—even if doing so comes at the expense of short-term profits, because the best guarantee of long-term profits is immediate growth. Due to this dynamic, striving to maximize market share at the expense of one's rivals makes predation highly rational; indeed, it would be irrational for a business *not* to frontload losses in order to capture the market. Recognizing that enduring early losses while aggressively expanding can lock up a monopoly, investors seem willing to back this strategy.

As the introduction and third section describe, Amazon has charted immense growth while investing aggressively—both by expanding provision of physical and online infrastructure and by pricing goods below cost. Amazon's stock price has soared despite a history of razor-thin—or even negative—margins. In essence, investors have given Amazon a free pass to grow without any pressure to show profits. The firm has used this edge to expand wildly and dominate online commerce.

The idea that investors are willing to fund predatory growth in winner-take-all markets also holds in the case of Uber. Although the dynamics of the online retail market are distinct from those of ridesharing, Uber's growth trajectory is worth analyzing for general insight into how investors enable platform dominance. In 2015, news reports revealed that Uber had an operating loss of $470 million on $415 million in revenue, confirming suspicions that the company has been bleeding money for the sake of achieving steep growth and acquiring market share.[391] In China, the company has lost more than one billion dollars a year.[392] The strategy of aggressive price competition and brazen leadership coupled with soaring growth prompted immediate comparisons to Amazon.[393] Like Amazon, Uber has drawn immense interest from investors. As of July 2015, its valuation hit nearly fifty-one billion dollars, equaling the record set by Facebook in 2012.[394] It recently secured an additional $3.5 billion in investment, bringing its total funds to $13.5 billion—a figure "far greater than most companies raise even during an initial public offering," which Uber has avoided.[395]

One might dismiss this phenomenon as irrational investor exuberance. But another way to read it is at face value: the reason investors value Amazon and Uber so highly is because they believe these platforms will, eventually, generate huge returns. As one venture capitalist recently remarked, if he had to "put his entire capital in a single company and hold it for the next 10 years," he would choose Amazon. "I don't see any cleaner monopoly available to buy in the public markets right now."[396] In other words, that these platform companies are undertaking consistent, steep losses and still generating strong investor backing suggests that the markets expect Amazon and Uber to recoup these losses.

While investors have unambiguously endorsed and funded online platforms' quest to bleed money in their race to draw users, antitrust doctrine fails to acknowledge this strategy. In the past, the Supreme Court's analysis has embraced the efficient market hypothesis (EMH), the idea that market prices reflect all available information.[397] The Justice Department also acknowledges that market information—for example, the financial terms of an acquisition—may "be informative regarding competitive effects."[398] Applying EMH in this instance overwhelmingly suggests that these platforms are positioned to recoup their losses. Yet bringing a predatory pricing suit against an online platform would be almost impossible to win in light of the recoupment requirement. Strikingly, the market is reflecting a reality that our current laws are unable to detect.[399]

In addition to overlooking why online platform dynamics make predation especially rational, current doctrine also fails to appreciate how a platform might recoup losses. For one, investor support allows Amazon to strategize and operate on a time horizon far longer than what the *Brooke Group* or *Matsushita* Courts confronted. Raising prices in a third year after enduring losses for two is different from engaging in a decade-long quest to become the dominant online retailer and provider of internet infrastructure. That longer timeline, meanwhile, makes available more recoupment mechanisms. Not only has Amazon inaugurated an entire generation into online shopping through its platform, but it has expanded into a suite of additional businesses and amassed significant troves of data on users. This data enables it both to extend its tug over customers through highly tailored personal shopping experiences, and, potentially, to institute forms of price discrimination, as described in the section titled "Below-Cost Pricing of Bestseller E-Books and the Limits of Modern Recoupment Analysis." Both the latitude granted by investors and control over data equip an incumbent platform to recoup losses in ways less obviously connected to the initial form of below-cost pricing.

These recoupment mechanisms may also be more sophisticated than what a judge or even rivals would be able to spot. This last point becomes even more apparent in the context of Uber, whose dynamic pricing has conditioned users not to expect a stable or regular price. While Uber claims that its algorithms set prices to reflect real-time supply and demand, initial research has found that the company manipulates the availability of both.[400] Moreover, it routinely gives away discount coupons to select users, effectively charging users different prices, even for the same service at the same time.[401]

Although platforms form the backbone of the internet economy, the way that platform economics implicates existing laws is relatively undertheorized.[402] Amazon's conduct suggests that predatory pricing and integration across related business lines are emerging as key paths to establishing dominance—aided by the control over data that dominant platforms enjoy.

But because current predatory pricing doctrine defines recoupment in overly narrow terms, competitors generally have not been able to make an effective legal case. Similarly, because current doctrine largely discounts entry barriers, the anticompetitive effects of vertical integration are difficult to cognize under the existing framework. Roadblocks to these claims persist even as Amazon's valuation and share price point to a strong market expectation of recoupment and profits.

There are signs that enforcers are becoming more attuned to the special factors that may render current antitrust analysis inadequate to promote competition in internet platform markets. For example, in 2014 the United States successfully challenged a merger between two leading providers of online ratings and reviews platforms. In its complaint, the DOJ acknowledged that data-driven industries can be characterized by network effects, which increase switching costs and entry barriers.[403] Recent comments by FTC Commissioner Terrell McSweeny—noting that data can act as a barrier to entry and that "competition enforcers can and should assess the competitive implications of data"—also suggest that top officials are assessing how to revise their tools and framework for gauging competition in platform markets.[404]

While this burgeoning recognition is heartening, the unique features of platform markets require a more thorough evaluation of how antitrust is applied. Because scale is both vital to platforms' business model and helps entrench their dominant position, antitrust should reckon with the fact that pursuing growth at the expense of returns is—contra to current doctrine—highly rational. An approach more attuned to the realities of online platform markets would also recognize the variety of mechanisms that businesses may use to recoup losses, the longer time horizon on which recoupment might occur, and the ways that vertical integration and concentrated control over data may enable new forms of anticompetitive conduct. Revising antitrust to reflect the dynamics of online platforms is vital, especially as these companies come to mediate a growing share of communications and commerce.

Two Models for Addressing Platform Power

If it is true that the economics of platform markets may encourage anticompetitive market structures, there are at least two approaches we can take. Key is deciding whether we want to govern online platform markets through competition or want to accept that they are inherently monopolistic or oligopolistic and regulate them instead. If we take the former approach, we should reform antitrust law to prevent this dominance from emerging or to limit its scope. If we take the latter approach, we should adopt regulations to take advantage of these economies of scale while neutering the firm's ability to exploit its dominance.

Governing Online Platform Markets Through Competition

Reforming antitrust to address the anticompetitive nature of platform markets could involve making the law against predatory pricing more robust and strictly policing forms of vertical integration that firms can use for anticompetitive ends. Importantly, each of these doctrinal areas should be reformulated so that it is sensitive to preserving the competitive process and limiting conflicts of interest that may incentivize anticompetitive conduct.

Predatory Pricing

While predatory pricing technically remains illegal, it is extremely difficult to win predatory pricing claims because courts now require proof that the alleged predator would be able to raise prices and recoup its losses.[405] Revising predatory pricing doctrine to reflect the economics of platform markets, where firms can sink money for years given unlimited investor backing, would require abandoning the recoupment requirement in cases of below-cost pricing by dominant platforms. And given that platforms are uniquely positioned to fund predation, a competition-based approach might also consider introducing a presumption of predation for dominant platforms found to be pricing products below cost.

Several reasons militate in favor of a presumption of predation in such cases. First, firms may raise prices years after the original predation, or raise prices on unrelated goods, in ways difficult to prove at trial. Second, firms may raise prices through personalized pricing or price discrimination, in ways not easily detectable. Third, predation can lead to a host of market harms *even if* the firm does not raise consumer prices. Within a consumer welfare framework, these harms include degradation of product quality and sapping diversity of choice.[406] Such harms may arise if Amazon uses its bargaining power to extract better terms from producers and suppliers, who, in turn, slash investments to meet its demands. Within a broader framework—which seeks to protect the full range of interests that antitrust laws were enacted to safeguard—the potential harms include lower income and wages for employees, lower rates of new business creation, lower rates of local ownership, and outsized political and economic control in the hands of a few.[407]

Introducing a presumption of predation would involve identifying when a price is below cost, a subject of much debate. The Supreme Court has not addressed the issue, but most appellate courts have said that average variable cost is the right metric.[408] This chapter does not advocate the adoption of one particular measure over others. Admittedly, "below cost" is an imperfect filter, especially because what constitutes the relevant cost may vary depending on the industry or cost structure. And the specific definition of "costs" that courts and enforcers adopt may ultimately be less significant if the test for predatory pricing also permits a business justification defense, which would help screen against false positives.[409] A business justification defense could cover compensating a buyer for taking the risk of buying a new product, expanding demand to a level that will allow the entrant to achieve scale economies, keeping prices at competitive levels while expecting costs to decline, and matching competition.[410]

Whether a platform is dominant enough to trigger the presumption could be assessed through its market share: those holding greater than, say, 40 percent of the market in any given line of service (e.g., cloud computing, ridesharing) might be designated "dominant." Rather than measuring this market share nationally, enforcers would look to levels of local control; a ridesharing platform that held only 35 percent of the national market but 75 percent of the Nashville market would still be considered dominant for the purpose of price-cutting in Nashville.

Vertical Integration

The current approach to antitrust does not sufficiently account for how vertical integration may give rise to anticompetitive conflicts of interest, nor does it adequately address the way a dominant firm may use its dominance in one sector to advance another line of business. This concern is heightened in the context of vertically integrated platforms, which can use insights generated through data acquired in one sector to undermine rivals in another. Potential ways to address this deficiency include scrutinizing mergers that would enable a firm to acquire valuable data and cross-leverage it, or introducing a prophylactic ban on mergers that would give rise to conflicts of interest.

One way to address the concern about a firm's capacity to cross-leverage data is to expressly include it in merger review.[411] Under the current approach, only mergers over a particular monetary threshold require agency review[412]—yet the monetary value of a deal may not be a good proxy for the scope and scale of data at stake. Thus it could make sense for the agencies to automatically review any deal that involves exchange of certain forms (or a certain quantity) of data. Data that gave a player deep and direct insight into a competitor's business operations, for example, might trigger review. Under this regime, Facebook's purchases of WhatsApp and Instagram,[413] for instance, would have received greater scrutiny from the antitrust agencies, in recognition of how acquiring data can deeply implicate competition. International transactions granting foreign corporations access to data on US users would also require close review. Uber's decision to sell its China operations to Didi Chuxing, China's dominant ridesharing service—a deal through which Uber will also gain partial ownership over its main US rival, Lyft[414]—is one deal that would prompt scrutiny under this regime.[415]

A stricter approach would place prophylactic limits on vertical integration by platforms that have reached a certain level of dominance. This would recognize that a platform's involvement across multiple related lines of business can give rise to conflicts of interest by creating circumstances in which a platform has an incentive to privilege its own business and disadvantage other companies.[416] Seeking to prevent the industry structures that *create* these conflicts of interest may prove more effective than policing these conflicts. Adopting this prophylactic approach would mean banning a dominant firm from entering any market that it already serves as a platform—in other words, from competing directly with the businesses that depend on it.[417] In the case of Amazon, for example, this prophylactic approach would prohibit the company from running *both* a dominant retail platform and a dominant platform for third-party sellers. These two businesses would have to be separated into different entities, in part to prevent Amazon from using insights from its role as a third-party host to benefit its retail business, as it reportedly does now.[418]

This form of prophylactic ban has a long history in banking law.[419] A core principle of banking law is the separation of banking and commerce.[420] "U.S. commercial banks generally are not permitted to conduct any activities that do not fall within . . . the statutory concept of 'the business of banking.'"[421] More specifically, the Bank Holding Company Act of 1956 forbids firms that own or control a US bank from engaging in business activities other than banking or managing banks.[422] The main exception is that a bank that qualifies as a "financial holding company" "may conduct broader activities that are 'financial in nature,' including securities dealing and insurance underwriting."[423]

The policy goals of this regime are worth reviewing because they have analogues in antitrust and competition policy. The main justifications for preserving the separation between banking and commerce have "included the needs to preserve the safety and soundness of insured depository institutions, to ensure a fair and efficient flow of credit to productive [businesses], and to prevent excessive concentration of financial and economic power in the financial sector."[424] All three concerns are linked to the fact that banks serve as critical intermediaries in our economy. The "safety and soundness" concern traces to the idea that our banking system is too vital to be subject to the risks of other business activities.[425] The concern about fairness and efficiency centers on the idea that allowing banks to be affiliated with commercial companies may encourage banks to issue credit on the basis of how those lending decisions will affect their commercial affiliates, thereby distorting competition. The practices this may trigger—"price discrimination, unfair restriction of access to credit, and other anticompetitive banking practices"—would both "hurt the individual commercial companies not affiliated with banks" and undermine national "productivity and growth."[426] Lastly, seeking "the prevention of excessive concentration of economic . . . power" among "large financial-industrial conglomerates" recognizes that this market power tends to concentrate political power[427] while also creating systemic dangers of "too-big-to-fail" conglomerates.[428]

Like bank holding companies, Amazon—along with a few other dominant platforms—now plays a crucial role in intermediating swaths of economic activity. Amazon itself effectively controls the infrastructure of the internet economy. This level of concentrated control creates hazards analogous to those recognized in banking law. In light of this control, the conflicts of interest created through Amazon's expansion into distinct lines of business are especially troubling. As in banking, enabling an essential intermediating entity to compete with the companies that depend on it creates bad incentives. Allowing a vertically integrated dominant platform to pick and choose to whom it makes its services available, and on what terms, has the potential to distort fair competition and the economy as a whole.

The other two concerns—safety and soundness, and excessive economic and political power—are also worth considering. It is true that Amazon (and other dominant platforms like Uber and Google) have extended directly into financial services.[429] But its level of involvement in these businesses, at least at the current scale, is unlikely to concentrate financial risk in ways that warrant concern. Rather, the systemic risks created by concentration among platforms are of a different kind. One involves concentration of data. That a huge share of consumer retail data may be concentrated within a single company makes hacks of or technical failures by that company all the more disruptive. The 2013 hack into Target's system—as a result of which up to 110 million consumers had personal information stolen[430]—could have been orders of magnitude more disruptive had the hacked entity been Amazon. A few instances where Amazon Web Services crashed led to disruptions for scores of other businesses, including Netflix.[431]

Lastly, there is sound reason to ask whether permitting Amazon to leverage its platform to integrate across business lines hands it undue economic and political power.[432] While this subject invites much deeper consideration than what this chapter will provide, studies interviewing the host of businesses that now depend on Amazon—retailers, manufacturers, publishers, to name a few—reveal that the power it wields is acute.[433] History suggests that allowing a single actor to set the terms of the marketplace, largely unchecked, can pose serious hazards. Limiting Amazon's reach through prophylactic bans on vertical integration—and thereby forcing it to split up its retail and Marketplace operation, for example—would help mitigate this concern.

Governing Dominant Platforms as Monopolies Through Regulation

As described previously, one option is to govern dominant platforms through promoting competition, thereby limiting the power that any one actor accrues. The other is to accept dominant online platforms as natural monopolies or oligopolies, seeking to regulate their power instead. In this section, I sketch out two models for this second approach, traditionally undertaken in the form of public utility regulations and common carrier duties. Industries that historically have been regulated as utilities include commodities (water, electric power, gas), transportation (railroads, ferries), and communications (telegraphy, telephones).[434] Critically, a public utility regime aims at eliminating competition: it accepts the benefits of monopoly and chooses instead to limit how a monopoly may use its power.[435]

Although largely out of fashion today, public utility regulations were widely adopted in the early 1900s as a way of regulating the technologies of the industrial age. Animating public utility regulations was the idea that essential network industries—such as railroads and electric power—should be made available to the public in the form of universal service provided at just and reasonable rates. The Progressive movement of the early twentieth century embraced public utility as a way to use government to steer private enterprise toward public ends. It was precisely because essential network industries often required scale that unregulated private control over these sectors often led to abuse of monopoly power. Famously, the Interstate Commerce Commission—which instituted a form of common carriage for railroads—was created partly in response to the abusive conduct of railroads, whose control over an essential facility enabled them to pick winners and losers among farmers.[436]

In the United States, the first case applying public utility regulations to a private business was *Munn v. Illinois*, in which the Supreme Court upheld state legislation establishing maximum rates that companies could charge for the storage and transportation of grain.[437] When one "devotes his property to a use in which the public has an interest, he, in effect, grants to the public an interest in that use, and must submit to be controlled by the public for the common good," Chief Justice Waite wrote.[438] "[W]hen private property is devoted to a public use, it is subject to public regulation."[439] While the decision ushered into doctrine the principle of common carriers, the question of when a business was truly "affected with the public interest" was highly contested.[440]

Most importantly, "public utility was seen as a common, collective enterprise aimed at managing a series of vital network industries that were too important to be left exclusively to market forces."[441] At the level of policy, public utility regulations also enabled "utilities to secure capital at lower cost and to channel it into very large technological systems," and thus was a way to "socialize the costs of building and operating" a centralized system while "protecting consumers from the potential abuses associated with natural monopoly."[442]

Given that Amazon increasingly serves as essential infrastructure across the internet economy, applying elements of public utility regulations to its business is worth considering.[443] The most common public utility policies are (1) requiring nondiscrimination in price and service, (2) setting limits on rate-setting, and (3) imposing capitalization and investment requirements. Of these three traditional policies, nondiscrimination would make the most sense, while rate-setting and investment requirements would be trickier to implement and, perhaps, would less obviously address an outstanding deficiency.

A nondiscrimination policy that prohibited Amazon from privileging its own goods and from discriminating among producers and consumers would be significant. Given that many of the most notable anticompetitive concerns around Amazon's business structure arise from its vertical integration and the resulting conflicts of interest, applying a nondiscrimination scheme would curb the anticompetitive risk. This approach would permit the company to maintain its involvement across multiple lines of business and permit it to enjoy the benefits of scale while mitigating the concern that Amazon could unfairly advantage its own business or unfairly discriminate among platform users to gain leverage or market power.[444] Coupling nondiscrimination with common carrier obligations—requiring platforms to ensure open and fair access to other businesses—would further limit Amazon's power to use its dominance in anticompetitive ways.

Rate setting would be trickier. This would involve setting a ceiling on the prices that Amazon can charge to both producers and consumers. Traditionally, governments used rate setting by identifying a "fair return" that a company deserved for its investment, and then calculated consumer or producer prices accordingly.[445] But calculating "fair return" may prove more challenging in the online platform context than it did with traditional public utilities. One potential source of difficulty is that Amazon has invested so widely across such a range of projects that it is not clear which the government should peg to "rate of return." Another complicating factor is that part of Amazon's investment in these platforms, so far, has involved losing money through below-cost pricing.

Lastly, it is not clear that imposing capitalization and investment requirements would be necessary. A traditional reason for these policies has been that that the economics of creating and running a utility can be unfavorable, occasionally leading private companies to scrimp on investing and upkeep. In Amazon's case, the company is choosing to expand at a speed and scale that is pushing it into the red—but it is not clear that the activity is intrinsically loss generating. That said, a public utility regime could also be justified on the basis that succeeding as an online platform requires incurring heavy losses—a model that Amazon and Uber have pursued. This approach would treat market-share chasing losses as a capital investment,[446] suggesting the public utility domain may be appropriate.

Practically, ushering in a public utility regime may prove challenging. Public utility regulations suffered an intellectual and policy attack around mid-century. For one, critics challenged the theory of natural monopoly as an ongoing rationale for regulation, arguing that rapid economic and technological change would render monopolies temporary problems. Second, critics portrayed public utility as a form of corruption, a system in which private industry executives colluded with public officials to enable rent seeking. Ultimately, these lines of criticism substantially thinned the very concept of public utility.[447] The trend was part of a broader effort to idealize competitive markets and assume that nonintervention was almost always superior to interference. Although the concept of public utility regulation remains somewhat maligned today, there are signs that a robust movement to apply utility-like regulations to services that widely register as public—such as the internet—can catch wind. The core of the net neutrality debates, for example, involved foundational discussions about how to regulate the communication infrastructure of the twenty-first century.[448] The net neutrality regime ultimately adopted falls squarely in the common carrier tradition.

Given Amazon's growing share of e-commerce as a whole, and the vast number of independent sellers and producers that now depend on it, applying some form of public utility regulation could make sense. Nondiscrimination principles seem especially apt, given that conflicts of interest are a primary hazard of Amazon's vertical power. One approach would apply public utility regulations to *all* of Amazon's businesses that serve other businesses. Another would require breaking up parts of Amazon and applying nondiscrimination principles separately (e.g., to Amazon Marketplace and Amazon Web Services as distinct entities). That said, given the political challenges of ushering in such a regime, strengthening and reinforcing traditional antitrust principles may—in the short run—prove most feasible.

A lighter version of the regulatory approach would be to apply the essential facilities doctrine. This doctrine imposes sharing requirements on a natural monopoly asset that serves as a necessary input in another market. As Sandeep Vaheesan explains:

> This doctrine rests on two basic premises: first, a natural monopolist in one market should not be permitted to deny access to the critical facility to foreclose rivals in adjacent markets; second, the more radical remedy of dividing the facility among multiple owners, while mitigating the threat of monopoly leveraging, could sacrifice important efficiencies.[449]

Unlike the prophylactic ban on integration, the essential facilities route accepts consolidated ownership. But recognizing that a vertically integrated monopolist may deny access to a rival in an adjacent market, the doctrine requires the monopolist controlling the essential facility to grant competitors easy access. This duty has traditionally been enforced through regulatory oversight.

While the essential facilities doctrine has not been precisely defined, the four-factor test enumerated by the Seventh Circuit in *MCI Communications Corp. v. American Telephone & Telegraph Co.* forms the basis of an essential facility claim today.[450] Under that test, a facility is essential and must be shared if four conditions are met: (1) a monopolist controls the essential facility, (2) a competitor is unable practically or reasonably to duplicate the essential facility, (3) the monopolist is denying use of the facility to a competitor, and (4) providing the facility is feasible.[451] The *MCI* court also held that, in order to be deemed essential, the facility must be a "necessary input in a *distinct, vertically related market*."[452]

While the Supreme Court has never recognized nor articulated a standard for "essential facility," three Supreme Court rulings "are seen as having established the functional foundation" for the doctrine.[453] In 2004, however, the Court disavowed the essential facilities doctrine in dicta,[454] leading several commentators to wonder whether it is a dead letter. This decision by the Court to effectively reject its prior case law on essential facilities followed challenges on other fronts: notably from Congress, enforcement agencies, and academic scholars, all of whom have critiqued the idea of requiring dominant firms to share their property.[455]

Treating aspects of Amazon's business as "essential facilities" seems appropriate, given that factors two, three, and four of the *MCI* test are likely to hold for at least one line of business. The first factor—whether Amazon is a "monopolist"—is subject to the risk that doctrine takes an excessively narrow view of what constitutes a "monopolist," a definition that may be especially out of touch with dominance in the internet age.

Essential facilities doctrine has traditionally been applied to infrastructure such as bridges, highways, ports, electrical power grids, and telephone networks.[456] Given that Amazon controls key infrastructure for e-commerce, imposing a duty to allow access to its infrastructure on a nondiscriminatory basis makes sense. And in light of the company's current trajectory, we can imagine at least three aspects of its business could eventually raise "essential facilities"-like concerns: (1) its fulfillment services in physical delivery, (2) its Marketplace platform, and (3) Amazon Web Services. While the essential facilities doctrine has not yet been applied to the internet economy, some proposals have started exploring what this might look like.[457] Pursuing this regime for online platforms could maintain the benefits of scale while preventing dominant players from abusing their power.

Conclusion

Internet platforms mediate a large and growing share of our commerce and communications. Yet evidence shows that competition in platform markets is flagging, with sectors coalescing around one or two giants.[458] The titan in e-commerce is Amazon—a company that has built its dominance through aggressively pursuing growth at the expense of profits and that has integrated across many related lines of business. As a result, the company has positioned itself at the center of internet commerce and serves as essential infrastructure for a host of other businesses that now depend on it. This chapter argues that Amazon's business strategies and current market dominance pose anticompetitive concerns that the consumer welfare framework in antitrust fails to recognize.

In particular, current law underappreciates the risk of predatory pricing and how integration across distinct business lines may prove anticompetitive. These concerns are heightened in the context of online platforms for two reasons. First, the economics of platform markets incentivize the pursuit of growth over profits, a strategy that investors have rewarded. Under these conditions, predatory pricing becomes highly rational—even as existing doctrine treats it as irrational. Second, because online platforms serve as critical intermediaries, integrating across business lines positions these platforms to control the essential infrastructure on which their rivals depend. This dual role also enables a platform to exploit information collected on companies using its services to undermine them as competitors.

In order to capture these anticompetitive concerns, we should replace the consumer welfare framework with an approach oriented around preserving a competitive process and market structure. Applying this idea involves, for example, assessing whether a company's structure creates anticompetitive conflicts of interest, whether it can cross-leverage market advantages across distinct lines of business, and whether the economics of online platform markets incentivizes predatory conduct and capital markets permit it. More specifically, restoring traditional antitrust principles to create a presumption of predation and to ban vertical integration by dominant platforms could help maintain competition in these markets. If, instead, we accept dominant online platforms as natural monopolies or oligopolies, then applying elements of a public utility regime or essential facilities obligations would maintain the benefits of scale while limiting the ability of dominant platforms to abuse the power that comes with it.

My argument is part of a larger recent debate about whether the current paradigm in antitrust has failed. Though relegated to technocrats for decades, antitrust and competition policy have once again become topics of public concern.[459] Last year, the *Wall Street Journal* reported that "[a] growing number of industries in the U.S. are dominated by a shrinking number of companies."[460] In March 2016, the *Economist* declared, "Profits are too high. America needs a dose of competition."[461] Policy elites, too, have weighed in, issuing policy papers and hosting conferences documenting the decline of competition across the US economy and assessing the resulting harms, including a drop in start-up growth and widening economic inequality.[462] Antitrust even made it into the 2016 presidential campaign: Democrats included competition policy in their party platform for the first time since 1988, and in October of the same year, presidential candidate Hillary Clinton released a detailed antitrust platform, highlighting not only a need for more vigorous enforcement but for an enforcement philosophy that takes into account market structure.[463]

Animating these critiques is not a concern about harms to consumer welfare,[464] but the broader set of ills and hazards that a lack of competition breeds. As Amazon continues both to deepen its existing control over key infrastructure and to reach into new lines of business, its dominance demands the same scrutiny. To revise antitrust law and competition policy for platform markets, we should be guided by two questions. First, does our legal framework capture the realities of how dominant firms acquire and exercise power in the internet economy? And second, what forms and degrees of power should the law identify as a threat to competition? Without considering these questions, we risk permitting the growth of powers that we oppose but fail to recognize.

Notes

1. David Streitfeld, As Competition Wanes, Amazon Cuts Back Discounts, *New York Times* (July 4, 2013), http://www.nytimes.com/2013/07/05/business/as-competition-wanes-amazon-cuts-back-its-discounts.html [http://perma.cc/J48L-8CPZ].

2. Ida Tarbell, John D. Rockefeller: A Character Study, *McClure's Magazine* 25 (1905): 227, 245.

3. Amazon: Ponzi Scheme or Wal-Mart of the Web?, *Slate: Moneybox* (February 8, 2000), http://www.slate.com/articles/business/moneybox/2000/02/amazon_ponzi_scheme_or_walmart_of_the_web.html [http://perma.cc/XQ22-YR9K].

4. Allison Enright, Amazon Sales Climb 22% in Q4 and 20% in 2015, *Internet Retailer* (January 28, 2016), http://www.internetretailer.com/2016/01/28/amazon-sales-climb-22-q4-and-20-2015 [http://perma.cc/N6S3-XTSB].

5. Shelly Banjo and Paul Ziobro, After Decades of Toil, Web Services Remain Small for Many Retailers, *Wall Street Journal* (August 27, 2013), http://www.wsj.com/articles/SB10001424127887324906304579039101568397122 [http://perma.cc/C8QJ-JYRN].

6. Olivia LaVecchia and Stacy Mitchell, Amazon's Stranglehold: How the Company's Tightening Grip Is Stifling Competition, Eroding Jobs, and Threatening Communities, *Institute for Local Self-Reliance* (November 2016), 10, http://ilsr.org/wp-content/uploads/2016/11/ILSR_AmazonReport_final.pdf [http://perma.cc/A4ND-2NDJ].

7. Amazon Posts a Profit, *CNN Money* (January 22, 2002), http://money.cnn.com/2002/01/22/technology/amazon [http://perma.cc/SMF3-2UCK].

8. Partly due to the success of Amazon Web Services, Amazon has recently begun reporting consistent profits. See Nick Wingfield, Amazon's Cloud Business Lifts Its Profit to a Record, *New York Times* (April 28, 2016), http://www.nytimes.com/2016/04/29/technology/amazon-q1-earnings.html [http://perma.cc/ZHL6-JEZU]. Though this trend departs from the history on which I focus, my analysis stands given that I am interested in (1) the losses Amazon formerly undertook to establish dominant positions in certain sectors, (2) the investor backing and enthusiasm that Amazon consistently maintained *despite* these losses, and (3) whether these facts challenge the assumption—embedded in current doctrine—that losing money is only desirable (and hence rational) *if* followed by recoupment. See ibid. ("Amazon often flip-flops between showing profits and losses, depending on how aggressively it

decides to plow money into big new business bets. Investors have granted the company much wider leeway to do so than other technology companies of its size often receive, because of its history of delivering outsize growth."); *see also infra* section titled "Amazon's Business Strategy."

9. Amazon.com, Inc., Annual Report (Form 10-K) 17 (January 29, 2016), http://www.sec.gov/Archives/edgar/data/1018724/000101872416000172/amzn-20151231x10k.htm [http://perma.cc/GB6A-YWZT].

10. Matt Krantz, Amazon Breaks Barrier: Now Most Costly Stock, *USA Today* (November 11, 2015), http://www.usatoday.com/story/money/markets/2015/11/11/amazon-pe-ratio-valuation-price/75519460 [http://perma.cc/P5BA-5REB].

11. Meagan Clark and Angelo Young, Amazon: Nearly 20 Years in Business and It Still Doesn't Make Money, but Investors Don't Seem To Care, *International Business Times* (December 18, 2013), http://www.ibtimes.com/amazon-nearly-20-years-business-it-still-doesnt-make-money-investors-dont-seem-care-1513368 [http://perma.cc/6NMH-HNC4].

12. Krantz, *supra* note 10 ("Amazon's [price/earnings ratio] isn't just high relative to the market—but the stock is richly valued even if the company achieves the high expectations investors have. Amazon's [price/earnings ratio] is now 14 times higher than the astounding 67% annual growth analysts expect long term from the company. That's an off-the-charts valuation using traditional rules of thumb. Investors start to think a stock is pricey when its [price/earnings ratio] is just 2 times its expected growth rate.").

13. See, for example, Farhad Manjoo, How Amazon's Long Game Yielded a Retail Juggernaut, *New York Times* (November 18, 2015), http://www.nytimes.com/2015/11/19/technology/how-amazons-long-game-yielded-a-retail-juggernaut.html [http://perma.cc/62WG-KQ67] ("For years, observers have wondered if Amazon's shopping business—you know, its main business—could ever really work. Investors gave Mr. Bezos enormous leeway to spend billions building out a distribution-center infrastructure, but it remained a semi-open question if the scale and pace of investments would ever pay off. Could this company ever make a whole lot of money selling so much for so little?").

14. Sam Moore, Amazon Commands Nearly Half of Consumers' First Product Search, *Bloomreach* (October 6, 2015), http://bloomreach.com/2015/10/amazon-commands-nearly-half-of-consumers-first-product-search [http://perma.cc/LVD9-F6W9].

15. Karsten Strauss, America's Most Reputable Companies, 2016: Amazon Tops the List, *Forbes* (March 29, 2016), http://www.forbes.com/sites/karstenstrauss/2016/03/29/americas-most-reputable-companies-2016-amazon-tops-the-list [http://perma.cc/MN74-K3NB]; see also Melissa Hoffmann, Amazon Has the Best Consumer Perception of Any Brand, *Adweek* (July 16, 2014), http://www.adweek.com/news/advertising-branding/amazon-has-best-consumer-perception-any-brand-158945 [http://perma.cc/FG7W-YD7N] (observing that Amazon continues to be the best-perceived brand despite negative news reports).

16. David Streitfeld, A New Book Portrays Amazon as Bully, *New York Times: Bits Blog* (October 22, 2013), http://bits.blogs.nytimes.com/2013/10/22/a-new-book-portrays-amazon-as-bully [http://perma.cc/E893-5EEN].

17. An article on Amazon's treatment of workers in its warehouses, see Spencer Soper, Inside Amazon's Warehouse, *Morning Call* (August 17, 2015), http://www.mcall.com/news/local/amazon/mc-allentown-amazon-complaints-20110917-story.html [http://perma.cc/6BXK-RPCX], was a finalist for the prestigious Loeb Award, see Morning Call's Watchdog Journalism Recognized, *Morning Call* (June 2, 2012), http://articles.mcall.com/2012-06-02/news/mc-morning-call-keystones-20120602_1_amazon-warehouse-gas-explosion-keystone-press-awards [http://perma.cc/9F3E-EBZS]. A *New York Times* piece on Amazon's white-collar workplace generated more than five million page views, ranking among the *Times*' most-read pieces of 2015. See Nick Wingfield and Ravi Somaiya, Amazon Spars with the Times over Investigative Article, *New York Times* (October 19, 2015), http://www.nytimes.com/2015/10/20/business/amazon-spars-with-the-times-over-investigative-article.html [http://perma.cc/VDG6-WZZQ].

18. David Streitfeld, *supra* note 16.

19. See Paul Krugman, Amazon's Monopsony Is Not O.K., *New York Times* (October 19, 2014), http://www.nytimes.com/2014/10/20/opinion/paul-krugman-amazons-monopsony-is-not-ok.html [http://perma.cc/KJ2E-8ZPX] ("Amazon.com, the giant online retailer, has too much power, and it uses that power in ways that hurt America.").

20. See Farhad Manjoo, Tech's "Frightful 5" Will Dominate Digital Life for Foreseeable Future, *New York Times* (January 20, 2016), http://www.nytimes.com/2016/01/21/technology/techs-frightful-5-will-dominate-digital-life-for-foreseeable-future.html [http://perma.cc/YH6N-KG6J] ("By just about every measure worth collecting, these five American consumer technology companies [Amazon, Apple, Facebook, Google, and Microsoft] are getting larger, more entrenched in their own sectors, more powerful in new sectors and better insulated against surprising competition from upstarts. Though competition between the five remains fierce—and each year, a few of them seem up and a few down—it's becoming harder to picture how any one of them, let alone two or three, may cede their growing clout in every aspect of American business and society"); Brooke Masters, Hooked on a Feeling that Amazon Is Too Addictive by Far, *Financial Times* (March 11, 2016), http://www.ft.com/intl/cms/s/0/d2d2e376-e768-11e5-bc31-138df2ae9ee6.html [http://perma.cc/X25D-6NTS].

21. At a recent hearing held by the Senate Judiciary Committee's Subcommittee on Antitrust, Competition Policy, and Consumer Rights, both Republican and Democratic senators interrogated Assistant Attorney General for Antitrust Bill Baer and Federal Trade Commission (FTC) Chair Edith Ramirez about their treatment of online platforms, and urged the Department of Justice (DOJ) and FTC to study closely the anticompetitive hazards these dominant firms may pose. See Oversight of the Enforcement of the Antitrust Laws: Hearing Before the Subcomm. on Antitrust,

Competition Policy & Consumer Rights of the S. Comm. on the Judiciary, 114th Cong. (2016); see also Oversight of the Antitrust Enforcement Agencies: Hearing Before the Subcomm. on Regulatory Reform, Commercial & Antitrust Law of the H. Comm. on the Judiciary, 114th Cong. (2015).

22. Vauhini Vara, Is Amazon Creating a Cultural Monopoly?, *New Yorker* (August 23, 2015), http://www.newyorker.com/business/currency/is-amazon-creating-a-cultural-monopoly [http://perma.cc/VZ84-8UX8].

23. See *United States v. Apple Inc.*, 952 F. Supp. 2d 638, 650 (S.D.N.Y. 2013).

24. See, for example, *Nat'l Collegiate Athletic Ass'n v. Bd. of Regents of Univ. of Okla.*, 468 U.S. 85, 107-08 (1984) ("'Congress designed the Sherman Act as a 'consumer welfare prescription.' . . . Restrictions on price and output are the paradigmatic examples of restraints of trade that the Sherman Act was intended to prohibit." [quoting *Reiter v. Sonotone Corp.*, 442 U.S. 330, 343 (1979)]); *see also infra* section titled "The Chicago School Revolution: The Shift Away from Competitive Process and Market Structure."

25. See, for example, Joe S. Bain, *Industrial Organization* (second edition, 1968); Donald F. Turner and Carl Kaysen, *Antitrust Policy: An Economic and Legal Analysis* (1959); Joe S. Bain, Workable Competition in Oligopoly: Theoretical Considerations and Some Empirical Evidence, *American Economic Review* 40 (1980), 35, 36–38. The institutionalists—scholars who emphasized the importance of social rules and organizations in producing economic outcomes—were also influential in this vein. See, for example, John R. Commons, *Legal Foundations of Capitalism* (1924).

26. See, for example, *United States v. Phila. Nat'l Bank*, 374 U.S. 321, 364-65 (1963).

27. See, for example, *Brown Shoe Co. v. United States*, 370 U.S. 294, 328-34 (1962).

28. See ibid.

29. I use "The Chicago School" to refer to the group of legal scholars and economists, primarily based at the University of Chicago, who developed neoclassical law and economics in the mid-twentieth century. But it is worth noting that a new group of scholars at the University of Chicago—such as Luigi Zingales and Guy Rolnik—have departed from the neoclassical approach and are studying market competition with an eye to power. See, for example, Raghuram and Luigi Zingales, *Saving Capitalism from the Capitalist* (2003). See generally *Promarket*, http://promarket.org/about-this-blog [http://perma.cc/G3CD-45K2] ("This is the goal of the 'ProMarket blog': to educate the public about the many ways special interests subvert competition in order to make the market system work better.").

30. Richard A. Posner, The Chicago School of Antitrust Analysis, *University of Pennsylvania Law Review* 127 (1979), 925, 932. The key assumptions of price theory are "that demand curves slope downward, that an increase in the price of a product will reduce the demand for its complement, [and] that resources gravitate to areas where they will earn the highest return." Ibid, 928.

31. Marc Allen Eisner, *Antitrust and the Triumph of Economics: Institutions, Expertise, and Policy Change* (1991).

32. See Robert H. Bork, *The Antitrust Paradox: A Policy at War with Itself* (1978).

33. Eisner, *supra* note 31, at 104.

34. George J. Stigler, *The Organization of Industry* (1968).

35. Eisner, *supra* note 31, at 105.

36. Ibid.

37. Bork, *supra* note 32, at 7 ("[T]he only legitimate goal of antitrust is the maximization of consumer welfare."); ibid, 405 ("The only goal that should guide interpretation of the antitrust laws is the welfare of consumers. . . . In judging consumer welfare, productive efficiency, the single most important factor contributing to that welfare, must be given due weight along with allocative efficiency"); see also Daniel A. Crane, The Tempting of Antitrust: Robert Bork and the Goals of Antitrust Policy, *Antitrust Law* Journal 79 (2014), 835, 847 ("Bork's big move [was] his rejection of alternatives to efficiency or consumer welfare-oriented theories of antitrust enforcement").

38. As has been widely noted, Bork defines consumer welfare not as consumer surplus but as total welfare. As a result, for Bork, outcomes that might otherwise be understood to harm consumers are not thought to reduce consumer welfare. For example, Bork concludes that wealth transfers from consumers to monopolist producers would not harm consumer welfare. See Bork, *supra* note 32, at 110 ("Those who continue to buy after a monopoly is formed pay more for the same output, and that shifts income from them to the monopoly and its owners, who are also consumers. This is not dead-weight loss due to restriction of output but merely a shift in income between two classes of consumers. The consumer welfare model, which views consumers as a collectivity, does not take this income effect into account"). For critiques of Bork's conflation of consumer welfare and allocative efficiency, see John J. Flynn, The Reagan Administration's Antitrust Policy, "Original Intent" and the Legislative History of the Sherman Act, *Antitrust Bulletin* 33 (1988), 259; Eleanor M. Fox, The Modernization of Antitrust: A New Equilibrium, *Cornell Law Review* 66 (1981), 1140; Herbert Hovenkamp, Antitrust's Protected Classes, *Michigan Law Review* 88 (1989), 1; Robert H. Lande, A Traditional and Textualist Analysis of the Goals of Antitrust: Efficiency, Preventing Theft from Consumers, and Consumer Choice, *Fordham Law Review* 81 (2013), 2349 (hereinafter Lande, A Traditional and Textualist Analysis); Robert H. Lande, Wealth Transfers as the Original and Primary Concern of Antitrust: The Efficiency Interpretation Challenged, *Hastings Law Journal* 34 (1982) 65 (hereinafter Lande, Wealth Transfers); and Maurice E. Stucke, Reconsidering Antitrust's Goals, *Boston College Law Review* 53 (2012), 551.

39. *Reiter v. Sonotone Corp.*, 442 U.S. 330, 343 (1979) (quoting Bork, *supra* note 32, at 66).

40. See Barak Orbach, Foreword: Antitrust's Pursuit of Purpose, *Fordham Law Review* 81 (2013), 2151, 2152.

41. 1968 Merger Guidelines, U.S. DEP'T JUST. 1 (1968), http://www.justice.gov/sites/default/files/atr/legacy/2007/07/11/11247.pdf [http://perma.cc/884H-BGUH]. The guidelines continue, "Market structure is the focus of the Department's merger policy chiefly because the conduct of the individual firms in a market tends to be controlled by the structure of that market." Ibid.

42. 1982 Merger Guidelines, U.S. DEP'T JUST. 2 (1982), http://www.justice.gov/sites/default/files/atr/legacy/2007/07/11/11248.pdf [http://perma.cc/7J32-ZQLY].

43. See, for example, *Ginzburg v. Mem'l Healthcare Sys., Inc.*, 993 F. Supp. 998, 1015 (S.D. Tex. 1997) ("[B]ecause 'the purpose of antitrust law is the promotion of consumer welfare,' the court must analyze the antitrust injury question from the perspective of the consumer. . . . Thus, in order to show that he suffered an antitrust injury, 'an antitrust plaintiff must prove that the challenged conduct affected the prices, quantity or quality of goods or services and not just his own welfare'" [quoting *Reazin v. Blue Cross & Blue Shield of Kan.*, 899 F.2d 951, 960 (10th Cir. 1990); *Angelico v. Lehigh Valley Hosp., Inc.*, 984 F. Supp. 308, 312 (E.D. Pa. 1997)]).

44. Horizontal Merger Guidelines, U.S. DEP'T JUST. & FTC (Aug. 19, 2010), http://www.ftc.gov/sites/default/files/attachments/merger-review/100819hmg.pdf [http://perma.cc/SQ8HAB7P].

45. See Emily Steel, Under Regulators' Scrutiny, Comcast and Time Warner Cable End Deal, *New York Times* (Apr. 24, 2015), http://www.nytimes.com/2015/04/25/business/media/comcast-time-warner-cable-deal.html [http://perma.cc/H4XS-9LMY].

46. Edith Ramirez, Chairwoman, FTC, Keynote Remarks at 10th Annual Global Antitrust Enforcement Symposium (September 20, 2016) (citing Richard J. Gilbert and Hillary Greene, Merging Innovation into Antitrust Agency Enforcement of the Clayton Act, *George Washington Law Review* [2015], 1919, 1933, http://www.ftc.gov/public-statements/2016/09/keynote-remarks-ftc-chairwoman-edith-ramirez [http://perma.cc/FNS8-6FL9]).

47. And even merger review has "migrated towards assessing what is measurable—namely short-term pricing effects, primarily understood under their unilateral effects theory, and short-term productive efficiencies." Maurice E. Stucke and Allen P. Grunes, *Big Data and Competition Policy* (2016). "Price has become the common denominator in merger review." Ibid at 109.

48. Ibid at 108.

49. Crane, *supra* note 37, at 852.

50. See Christopher R. Leslie, Revisiting the Revisionist History of Standard Oil, *Southern California Law Review* 85 (2012), 573, 575.

51. See Ida Tarbell, *A History of the Standard Oil Company* (1904).

52. Monopoly price refers to the price profitably above cost that a firm with monopoly power can charge.

53. *Standard Oil Co. v. United States*, 22 U.S. 1 (1911).

54. Leslie, *supra* note 50, at 576 (quoting *United States v. A. Schrader's Son*, 264 F. 175, 181 [D. Ohio 1919], rev'd, 252 U.S. 85 [1920]).

55. Chapter 323, 38 Stat. 730 (1914) (codified as amended at 15 U.S.C. §§ 12-27, 29 U.S.C. §§ 52-53 [2012]).

56. This legislative history makes plain that section 2 of the Clayton Act "was born of a desire by Congress to curb the use by financially powerful corporations of localized price-cutting tactics which had gravely impaired the competitive position of other sellers." *FTC v. Anheuser–Busch, Inc.*, 363 U.S. 536, 543 (1959).

57. H.R. REP. NO. 63-627, at 8 (1914). Section 2 of the Clayton Act made it "unlawful for a firm to charge a low price in a targeted community while selling similar goods at a higher price elsewhere." Herbert J. Hovenkamp, United States Competition Policy in Crisis: 1890-1955, *Minnesota Law Review* 94 (2009), 311, 363.

58. Lawrence Shepard, The Economic Effects of Repealing Fair Trade Laws, *Journal of Consumer Affairs* 12 (1978), 220, 221 ("Fair trade marketing or 'resale price maintenance' enabled manufacturers to require retailers to charge producer-specified prices on certain goods").

59. See *Dr. Miles Med. Co. v. John D. Park & Sons Co.*, 220 U.S. 373 (1911).

60. Pub. L. No. 75-314, 50 Stat. 693 (1937).

61. *Schwegmann Bros. v. Calvert Distillers Corp.*, 341 U.S. 384 (1951).

62. McGuire Act, Pub. L. No. 82-542, 66 Stat. 632 (1952).

63. Pub. L. No. 74-692, 49 Stat. 1526 (codified as amended at 15 U.S.C. §§ 13, 21 [2012]).

64. See *FTC v. Henry Broch & Co.*, 363 U.S. 166, 168 (1960) ("The Robinson-Patman Act was enacted in 1936 to curb and prohibit all devices by which large buyers gained discriminatory preferences over smaller ones by virtue of their greater purchasing power").

65. 15 U.S.C. § 13(a) (2012).

66. § 3, 49 Stat. at 1528.

67. See *United States v. Nat'l Dairy Prods. Corp.*, 372 U.S. 29, 35 (1963) ("[I]n prohibiting sales at unreasonably low prices for the purpose of destroying competition, [the Act] listed as elements of the illegal conduct not only the intent to achieve a result—destruction of competition—but also the act—selling at unreasonably low prices—done in furtherance of that design or purpose").

68. See ibid at 37.

69. Ibid.

70. See, for example, *Moore v. Mead's Fine Bread Co.*, 348 U.S. 115, 119 (1954).

71. Ibid. This basis for distinguishing legitimate from illegitimate price-cutting echoed other decisions. See *FTC v. Morton Salt Co.*, 334 U.S. 37, 43 (1948) ("The legislative history of the Robinson-Patman Act makes it abundantly clear that Congress considered it to be an evil that a large buyer could secure a competitive advantage over a small buyer solely because of the large buyer's quantity purchasing ability. The Robinson-Patman Act was passed to deprive a large buyer of such advantages"); *United States v. N.Y. Great Atl. & Pac. Tea Co.*, 173 F.2d 79 (7th Cir. 1949).

72. 386 U.S. 685 (1967).

73. Ibid at 703.

74. Ibid at 696–97.

75. Ibid at 689.

76. Ibid at 706 (Stewart, J., dissenting).

77. Ward S. Bowman, Restraint of Trade by the Supreme Court: The Utah Pie Case, *Yale Law Journal* 77 (1967), 70, 86.

78. Ibid at 70.

79. Bork, *supra* note 32, at 387.

80. Ibid at 154, 382.

81. See Phillip Areeda and Donald F. Turner, *Antitrust Law: An Analysis of Antitrust Principles and Their Application* (1978), 189–90; Herbert Hovenkamp, *Economics and Federal Antitrust Law* (1985), 188–89; Richard A. Posner, *Antitrust Law: An Economic Perspective* (1976), 193–94.

82. *See* Jonathan B. Baker, Predatory Pricing After Brooke Group: An Economic Perspective, *Antitrust Law Journal* 62 (1994), 585, 586 ("The Chicago School view of predatory pricing was perhaps best captured by a 1987 dispute between two FTC Commissioners over the aptness of a metaphor: the animal that best represents price predation. For one Commissioner, predatory pricing was a 'white tiger,' an extremely rare creature. For the other Commissioner, price predation more closely resembled a 'unicorn,' a complete myth. The narrow spectrum of views between a white tiger and a unicorn fairly reflects the Chicago School view that predatory pricing is almost always irrational, and so is unlikely actually to occur" [citations omitted]).

83. See Bork, *supra* note 32, at 149–55.

84. See D. Daniel Sokol, The Transformation of Vertical Restraints: Per Se Illegality, the Rule of Reason, and Per Se Legality, *Antitrust Law Journal* 79 (2014), 1003, 1014–15.

85. Ibid.

86. Ibid at 1008.

87. 475 U.S. 574 (1986). The government argued in the case as amicus curiae in support of Matsushita. Brief for the United States as Amicus Curiae Supporting Petitioners, *Matsushita Elec. Indus. Co. v. Zenith Radio Corp.*, 475 U.S. 574 (No. 83-2004), 1985 WL 669667.

88. *Matsushita*, 475 U.S. at 577–78.

89. Ibid at 580, 588–92.

90. Ibid at 589.

91. Ibid.

92. Bork, *supra* note 32, at 157.

93. *Matsushita*, 475 U.S. at 594; see also *Cargill, Inc. v. Monfort of Colo., Inc.*, 479 U.S. 104, 116 (1986) (finding that a meat-packing company's price-cutting practices constituted vigorous competition rather than an antitrust violation).

94. Christopher R. Leslie, Predatory pricing and recoupment, *Columbia Law Review* (2013), 1695, 1702.

95. Ibid.

96. See, for example, A.A. *Poultry Farms, Inc. v. Rose Acre Farms, Inc.*, 881 F.2d 1396 (7th Cir. 1989).

97. *Matsushita*, 475 U.S. at 589.

98. 509 U.S. 209 (1993).

99. Ibid at 213.

100. Ibid at 214.

101. Ibid at 216.

102. Ibid at 218.

103. Ibid at 226.

104. Ibid.

105. See ibid at 224 ("Recoupment is the ultimate object of an unlawful predatory pricing scheme; it is the means by which a predator profits from predation. Without it, predatory pricing produces lower aggregate prices in the market, and consumer welfare is enhanced").

106. As some commentators have noted, the Court's reliance on scholarship advocating a retrenchment of enforcement against predatory pricing schemes did not reflect a dearth of opposing views. See, for example, F.M. Scherer, Conservative Economics and Antitrust: A Variety of Influences, in How the Chicago School Overshot the Mark (edited by Robert Pitofsky, 2008), 30, 33 ("Already by the time of the *Matsushita* decision, there was a substantial scholarly literature documenting what should have passed for predation by any reasonable definition and showing the rationality of sharp price-cutting by a dominant firm to discourage new entrants. Since there was a diversity of scholarly views at the time key Supreme Court pronouncements were rendered on predation, the fault for ignoring one side of the scholarship must be attributed to the Court's myopia or (without the obiter dictum) compelling facts, and not to economists' contributions" [citation omitted]); ibid at 34 ("If there was favoritism, it was not in the economic literature evaluated, but in the weighing of alternative perspectives").

107. Sokol, *supra* note 84, at 1013 ("The recoupment prong eviscerated the *Utah Pie* standard and made it nearly impossible in practice for plaintiffs to win a primary line Robinson-Patman claim going forward"). The only recent case in which plaintiffs survived a motion for summary judgment is *Spirit Airlines, Inc. v. Northwest Airlines, Inc.*, 431 F.3d 917 (6th Cir. 2005), where the court denied summary judgment on the grounds that a reasonable trier of fact could find sufficient evidence of predatory pricing.

108. Sandeep Vaheesan, Reconsidering Brooke Group: Predatory Pricing in Light of the Empirical Learning, *Berkeley Business Law Journal* (2015), 81, 82; see also Richard O. Zerbe, Jr. and Michael T. Mumford, Does Predatory Pricing Exist? Economic Theory and the Courts After Brooke Group, *Antitrust Bulletin* 41 (1996), 949, 957–64 (discussing the empirical research that companies engage in predatory pricing).

109. Robert H. Cole, General Discussion of Vertical Integration, in *Vertical Integration in Marketing* (edited by Nugent Wedding, 1952), 9.

110. Clayton Act, ch. 323, § 7, 38 Stat. 730, 731 (1914) (codified as amended at 15 U.S.C. § 18 [2012]).

111. Sherman Act, ch. 647, §§ 1, 3, 26 Stat. 209, 209 (1890) (codified as amended at 15 U.S.C. § 1 [2012]).

112. Federal Trade Commission Act, ch. 311, § 5, 38 Stat. 717, 719 (1914) (codified as amended at 15 U.S.C. § 45[a][1] [2012]).

113. See Herbert Hovenkamp, Robert Bork and Vertical Integration: Leverage, Foreclosure, and Efficiency, *Antitrust Law Journal* 79 (2014), 983, 988–92.

114. Clayton Act, ch. 1184, § 7, 64 Stat. 1125, 1125-26 (1950) (codified as amended at 15 U.S.C. § 18 [2012]); see Hovenkamp, *supra* note 113, at 985.

115. Friedrich Kessler and Richard H. Stern, Competition, Contract, and Vertical Integration, *Yale Law Journal* 69 (1959), 1, 16.

116. See, for example, *FTC v. Consol. Foods Corp.*, 380 U.S. 592, 594-95 (1965); *United States v. Yellow Cab Co.*, 332 U.S. 218, 226-27 (1947); *Miss. River Corp. v. FTC*, 454 F.2d 1083, 1091 (8th Cir. 1972); see also *Anchor Serum Co. v. FTC*, 217 F.2d 867, 873 (7th Cir. 1954) ("It would require a naive mind to conclude, as petitioner would have us do, that the arrangements under consideration could result in other than an adverse effect upon competition"). But see *United States v. Columbia Steel Co.*, 334 U.S. 495, 507-08 (1948) (finding that a vertical combination did not violate antitrust law).

117. 370 U.S. 294, 297 (1962).

118. Ibid at 324, 332.

119. Ibid at 323.

120. Ibid at 324.

121. Ibid at 372 (Harlan, J., concurring in part and dissenting in part).

122. Ibid at 294 (majority opinion).

123. *Ford Motor Co. v. United States*, 405 U.S. 562, 567 (1972) (quoting *United States v. Ford Motor Co.*, 286 F. Supp. 407, 441 [E.D. Mich. 1968]).

124. Ibid (quoting *Ford Motor Co.*, 286 F. Supp. at 441).

125. Ibid (quoting *Ford Motor Co.*, 286 F. Supp. at 441).

126. Ibid at 568.

127. Ibid at 575.

128. In an influential 1954 essay that presaged his later arguments in *The Antitrust Paradox*, Bork defended vertical integration as nearly always procompetitive. Robert Bork, Vertical Integration and the Sherman Act: The Legal History of an Economic Misconception, *University of Chicago Law Review* 22 (1954), 157, 194–201; see also Ward S. Bowman, Jr., Tying Arrangements and the Leverage Problem, *Yale Law Journal* 67 (1957), 19 (arguing that tying arrangements—a form of vertical control—cannot be used to leverage monopoly power from one market to another).

129. Bork, *supra* note 32, at 231.

130. See, for example, ibid at 372–75, 380–81; Posner, *supra* note 30, at 925, 927 ("[I]t makes no sense for a monopoly producer to take over distribution in order to earn monopoly profits at the distribution as well as the manufacturing level. The

product and its distribution are complements, and an increase in the price of distribution will reduce the demand for the product. Assuming that the product and its distribution are sold in fixed proportions . . . the conclusion is reached that vertical integration must be motivated by a desire for efficiency rather than for monopoly"); ibid at 929 ("If the [service] is already being priced at the optimal monopoly level, an increase in the price of [one component] above the competitive level will raise the total price of the service to the consumer above the optimal monopoly level and will thereby reduce the monopolist's profits").

131. Bork, *supra* note 32, at 232.

132. Ibid at 234.

133. Bork later modified his position on entry barriers when he consulted for Netscape in the Antitrust Division's challenge to Microsoft's exclusionary practices, which the company had employed primarily against Netscape. Although Bork had been a fierce critic of "leverage theory," he described Microsoft's attempt to tie its operating system to its software as a way "to leverage the [Windows] asset to make people use [Internet Explorer] instead of [Netscape] Navigator." Hovenkamp, *supra* note 113, at 996–97 (citing Robert Bork, High-Stakes Antitrust: The Last Hurrah?, in *High-Stakes Antitrust: The Last Hurrah?* [edited by Robert W. Hahn, 2003], 45–50). But in an article later commissioned by Google, Bork returned to a critique of leverage theory, deriding the idea that Google could leverage its position in the general search market to gain additional profits in downstream markets. See Robert H. Bork and J. Gregory Sidak, What Does the Chicago School Teach About Internet Search and the Antitrust Treatment of Google, *Journal of Competition Law & Economics* 8 (2012), 663, 675–77.

134. Bork, *supra* note 32, at 234.

135. *1982 Merger Guidelines*, *supra* note 42; *1984 Merger Guidelines*, U.S. DEP'T JUST. (1984), http://www.justice.gov/sites/default/files/atr/legacy/2007/07/11/11249.pdf [http://perma.cc/Y5JL-5PQS].

136. *1984 Merger Guidelines*, *supra* note 135, at 24–32.

137. Ibid.

138. William E. Kovacic, Built To Last? The Antitrust Legacy of the Reagan Administration, *Federal Bureau News and Journal* 35 (1988), 244, 245 ("Since 1981, the government antitrust agencies have issued no complaints or consent agreements in Robinson-Patman matters that originated after the arrival of Reagan appointees to head the FTC and the Justice Department. Reagan FTC leadership has said the Commission has not abandoned Robinson-Patman enforcement, but the government's failure to initiate new enforcement actions during the Reagan Administration suggests that firms are virtually immune from federal prosecution for conduct the statute proscribes"); Joseph Guinto, Antitrust Targets Vertical Deals, *Investor's Business Daily*, June 17, 1999, A01.

139. For example, Democrat-appointed antitrust leaders have also adopted the Chicago School view that most vertical mergers are benign. As then-FTC Commissioner Christine Varney (who would later go on to be assistant attorney general

for antitrust in the Obama administration) observed in a speech, "[M]ost vertical arrangements raise few competitive concerns." Christine A. Varney, Comm'r, FTC, Vertical Merger Enforcement Challenges at the FTC (July 17, 1995), http://www.ftc.gov/public-statements/1995/07/vertical-merger-enforcement-challenges-ftc [http://perma.cc/JDQ8-H5KB].

140. James B. Stewart, Why a Media Merger that Should Go Through Might Not, *New York Times* (October 25, 2016), http://www.nytimes.com/2016/10/26/business/economy/why-a-media-merger-that-should-go-through-might-not.html [http://perma.cc/NTN7-LB9N] ("'Over the last 40 to 50 years, antitrust law has evolved to be almost completely indifferent to vertical mergers,' said Tim Wu, an antitrust and internet expert at Columbia Law School").

141. By imposing conduct remedies, the antitrust agencies set out behavioral conditions that the merging parties must comply with, subject to agency oversight. By requiring divestitures, the antitrust agencies ask the merging parties to sell off a part of their business to another entity.

142. Martin H. Bosworth, Consumer Groups Oppose Comcast-NBC Merger, *Consumer Affairs* (December 3, 2009), http://www.consumeraffairs.com/news04/2009/12/comcast_nbc.html [http://perma.cc/N347-MTKQ]; David Segal, Calling Almost Everyone's Tune, *New York Times* (April 24, 2010), http://www.nytimes.com/2010/04/25/business/25ticket.html [http://perma.cc/3TT3-FHYA] ("To say this new conglomerate has inspired fear in the live-concert business doesn't capture the extent of the quaking"); Ethan Smith and Thomas Catan, Concert Deal Wins Antitrust Approval, *Wall Street Journal* (January 26, 2010), http://www.wsj.com/articles/SB10001424052748704762904575025332380117008 [http://perma.cc/FWR9-WUSR].

143. As Bork pointed out, the vertical deals would not increase the market share of either company. See Bork, *supra* note 32, at 231. In Ticketmaster/LiveNation's case, the deal instead "creates one company that will have a hand in just about every corner of the music business," Smith and Catan, *supra* note 142, while in Comcast/NBC's case, the merger created "a $30 billion media behemoth that controls not just how television shows and movies are made but how they are delivered to people's homes," Yinka Adegoke and Dan Levine, Comcast Completes NBC Universal Merger, *Reuters* (January 29, 2011), http://www.reuters.com/article/us-comcast-nbc-idUSTRE70S2WZ20110129 [http://perma.cc/EXC3-4PAU].

144. Press Release, Office of Pub. Affairs, U.S. Dep't of Justice, Justice Department Allows Comcast-NBCU Joint Venture To Proceed with Conditions (Jan. 18, 2011), http://www.justice.gov/opa/pr/justice-department-allows-comcast-nbcu-joint-venture-proceed-conditions [http://perma.cc/8FHZ-AL4W]; Press Release, Office of Pub. Affairs, U.S. Dep't of Justice, Justice Department Requires Ticketmaster Entertainment Inc. To Make Significant Changes to Its Merger with Live Nation Inc. (Jan. 25, 2010), http://www.justice.gov/opa/pr/justice-department-requires-ticketmaster-entertainment-inc-make-significant-changes-its [http://perma.cc/PZ2E-X2FL]; see also Jeremy Pelofsky and Yinka Adegoke, LiveNation, Ticketmaster

Merge; Agree to U.S. Terms, *Reuters* (January 25, 2010), http://www.reuters.com/article/us-ticketmaster-livenation-idUSTRE60O4E520100126 [http://perma.cc/QT7K-LPHA] ("'The conditions seem to be relatively benign,' said Tuna Amobi, equity analyst at Standard & Poor's. 'There are no major divestitures required. I don't know that is going to create the kind of even, competitive field that was intended'"); Smith and Catan, *supra* note 142.

145. Clayton Act, chapter 323, 38 Stat. 730 (1914) (codified as amended at 15 U.S.C. §§ 12-27, 29 U.S.C. §§ 52-53 [2012]). Former Assistant Attorney General for Antitrust Bill Baer described the incipiency standard as seeking to "prevent competitive conditions from deteriorating even when competition was not clearly problematic at the time of the lawsuit." He continued, "Second, in order to arrest potential restraints 'in their incipiency,' the Act banned these practices where their effect 'may be to substantially lessen competition.' The intent was to consider likely future effect—not just palpable impact—in determining whether these practices were illegal." Bill Baer, Assistant Att'y Gen., Antitrust Div., Dep't of Justice, Remarks at the American Bar Association Clayton Act 100th Anniversary Symposium (December 4, 2014).

146. See Hovenkamp, *supra* note 57, at 359.

147. Daniel A. Crane, Has the Obama Justice Department Reinvigorated Antitrust Enforcement?, *Stanford Law Review Online* (July 18, 2012), http://www.stanfordlawreview.org/online/has-the-obama-justice-department-reinvigorated-antitrust-enforcement [http://perma.cc/56J4-NNSP] ("The final category is monopolization cases. Over the eight years of the Bush Administration, the Justice Department filed no monopolization cases. To date, the Obama Administration has filed only one case, hardly evidencing a major shift in tactics").

148. A growing body of work shows that the consumer welfare frame has failed even on its own terms—namely, by leading to higher prices without any clear efficiency gains. See John Kwoka, *Mergers, Merger Control, and Remedies: A Retrospective Analysis of U.S. Policy* (2015); Benefits of Competition and Indicators of Market Power, *Council of Economic Advisers* (April 2016), http://www.whitehouse.gov/sites/default/files/page/files/20160414_cea_competition_issue_brief.pdf [http://perma.cc/9NMS-4U9L]; Divs. of Research & Statistics & Monetary Affairs, *Evidence for the Effects of Mergers on Market Power and Efficiency*, Federal Reserve (2016), http://www.federalreserve.gov/econresdata/feds/2016/files/2016082pap.pdf [http://perma.cc/CY4Y-DGB2].

149. See Barry C. Lynn and Lina Khan, The Slow Motion Collapse of American Entrepreneurship, *Washington Monthly* (July/August 2012), http://washingtonmonthly.com/magazine/julyaugust-2012/the-slow-motion-collapse-of-american-entrepreneurship [http://perma.cc/P9VM-9FM5]; see also Ian Hathaway and Robert E. Litan, What's Driving the Decline in the Firm Formation Rate? A Partial Explanation, *Brookings Institution* (November 2014) (documenting business consolidation as a contributing factor in the declining formation of new firms), http://www.

brookings.edu/wp-content/uploads/2016/06/driving_decline_firm_formation_rate_hathaway_litan.pdf [http://perma.cc/QA9M-ZGAT].

150. *Reiter v. Sonotone Corp.*, 442 U.S. 330, 343 (1979).

151. Heaps of scholarship delve into this legislative history. See, for example, sources cited *supra* note 38.

152. Eleanor Fox, Against Goals, 81 (2013), 2158.

153. Ibid.

154. 21 CONG. REC. 2461 (1890) (statement of Sen. Sherman).

155. Ibid at 2457 (statement of Sen. Sherman).

156. Robert Pitofsky, The Political Content of Antitrust, *University of Pennsylvania Law Review* 127 (1979), 1051.

157. Ibid.

158. 21 CONG. REC. 3146 (1890) (statement of Sen. Hoar).

159. Lande, Wealth Transfers, *supra* note 38, at 96–97.

160. 21 CONG. REC. 2461 (1890) (statement of Sen. Sherman, quoting Sen. George).

161. Ibid at 2614 (statement of Sen. Coke).

162. Ibid at 4101 (statement of Rep. Heard).

163. Ibid at 4098 (statement of Rep. Taylor).

164. Ibid at 2461 (statement of Sen. Sherman, quoting Sen. George).

165. Lande, Wealth Transfers, *supra* note 38, at 96–97.

166. Ibid at 98.

167. For a seminal discussion of why antitrust laws must take political values into account, see Pitofsky, *supra* note 156, at 1051 ("It is bad history, bad policy, and bad law to exclude certain political values in interpreting the antitrust laws. By 'political values,' I mean, first, a fear that excessive concentration of economic power will breed antidemocratic political pressures, and second, a desire to enhance individual and business freedom by reducing the range within which private discretion by a few in the economic sphere controls the welfare of all. A third and overriding political concern is that if the free-market sector of the economy is allowed to develop under antitrust rules that are blind to all but economic concerns, the likely result will be an economy so dominated by a few corporate giants that it will be impossible for the state not to play a more intrusive role in economic affairs").

168. 51 CONG. REC. 13,231 (1914) (statement of Sen. Reed).

169. 21 CONG. REC. 2598 (1890) (statement of Sen. George).

170. Louis D. Brandies, *The Curse of Bigness* (edited by Osmond K. Fraenkel, 1934), 38.

171. *United States v. Columbia Steel Co.*, 334 U.S. 495, 536 (1948) (Douglas, J., dissenting).

172. Ibid.

173. In *Economics and the Public Purpose*, Galbraith concluded that centralized planning, rather than open markets, was the best way to stabilize industries and boost prosperity. John Kenneth Galbraith, *Economics and the Public Purpose* (1973), 55.

174. See Michael Sandel, *Democracy's Discontent* (1996), 246 ("Although Nader and his followers did not disparage, as did Bork, the civic tradition of antitrust, they too rested their arguments on considerations of consumer welfare. . . . According to Nader, the 'modern relevance' of traditional antitrust wisdom lay in its consequences for 'the prices people pay for their bread, gasoline, auto parts, prescription drugs, and houses'").

175. *See* Lina Khan, New Tools To Promote Competition, *Democracy* (Fall 2016), http://democracyjournal.org/magazine/42/new-tools-to-promote-competition [http://perma.cc/VZ4N-CZBN].

176. I am by no means alone in arguing this. See, for example, Barry C. Lynn, *Cornered: The New Monopoly Capitalism and the Economics of Destruction* (2010); Fox, *supra* note 38, at 1153–54; Maurice E. Stucke, Better Competition Advocacy, *St. John's Law Review* 82 (2008), 951, 993; Stucke, *supra* note 38, at 564.

177. For a more recent argument in favor of rebalancing antitrust away from technocracy and toward democracy, see Harry First and Spencer Weber Waller, Antitrust's Democracy Deficit, *Fordham Law Review* 81 (2013), 2543, 2544 ("[A]ntitrust is also public law designed to serve public ends. Today's unbalanced system puts too much control in the hands of technical experts, moving antitrust enforcement too far away from its democratic roots").

178. See Fox, *supra* note 38, at 1153–54 ("Rather than standing for efficiency, the American antitrust laws stand against private power. Distrust of power is the one central and common ground that over time has unified support for antitrust statutes. Interests of consumers have been a recurrent concern because consumers have been perceived as victims of the abuse of too much power. Interests of entrepreneurs and small business have been a recurrent concern because independent entrepreneurs have been seen as the heart and lifeblood of American free enterprise, and freedom of economic activity and opportunity has been thought central to the preservation of the American free enterprise system. One overarching idea has unified these three concerns (distrust of power, concern for consumers, and commitment to opportunity of entrepreneurs): competition as process. The competition process is the preferred governor of markets. If the impersonal forces of competition, rather than public or private power, determine market behavior and outcomes, power is by definition dispersed, opportunities and incentives for firms without market power are increased, and the results are acceptable and fair" [citations omitted]).

179. For more on this connection, see Simon Johnson and James Kwak, *13 Bankers: The Wall Street Takeover and the Next Financial Meltdown* (2011); and Lynn, *supra* note 176.

180. The Justice Department recently cited the importance of media diversity when suing to block a merger between two newspapers. See Michaela Ross, Even for Ailing Newspapers, U.S. Says a Monopoly Is a Monopoly, *Bloomberg* (March 22, 2016), http://www.bloomberg.com/news/articles/2016-03-21/tribune-loses-out-on-local-newspaper-deal-over-antitrust-issues [http://perma.cc/U2E5-ZHM9]. For why competition policy is important for promoting media diversity, see Maurice E. Stucke

and Allen P. Grunes, Toward a Better Competition Policy for the Media: The Challenge of Developing Antitrust Policies that Support the Media Sector's Unique Role in Our Democracy, *Connecticut Law Review* 42 (2009), 101.

181. See Fox, *supra* note 152.

182. For one perspective on how the Chicago School's philosophy has shaped antitrust, see generally *How the Chicago School Overshot the Mark, supra* note 106. In his essay within this collection, Richard Schmalensee states, "Competition . . . generally means now, consumer or total welfare." Richard Schmalensee, Thoughts on the Chicago Legacy in U.S. Antitrust, in *How the Chicago School Overshot the Mark, supra* note 106, at 17.

183. See *supra* the section titled "Predatory Pricing."

184. See Bork, *supra* note 32, at 278 ("Absent the power to restrict output, the decision to eliminate rivalry can only be made in order to achieve efficiency."); see *supra* section titled "Vertical Integration."

185. See Hovenkamp, *supra* note 57, at 359 ("[T]he guiding principle of the Chicago School critique of the S-C-P paradigm was that market power is not inherently a bad thing. Indeed, often market power as well as high concentration result from efficiency").

186. One line of argument holds that the concentration of private control—and the power it hands to a few over our economy—is itself problematic, and *if* and *how* those wielding this power choose to exercise it is beside the point. See, for example, *United States v. Columbia Steel Co.*, 334 U.S. 495, 536 (1948) (Douglas, J., dissenting) ("In final analysis, size in steel is the measure of the power of a handful of men over our economy. That power can be utilized with lightning speed. It can be benign or it can be dangerous. The philosophy of the Sherman Act is that it should not exist").

187. I am not the first to argue that preserving a competitive process is vital to promoting competition. See, for example, Fox, *supra* note 38, at 1152–54. Instead, my contribution here is in (1) identifying how a consumer welfare-based approach is failing to detect and deter anticompetitive harms in the context of internet platforms, thereby (2) highlighting the need for a process-based approach as applied to internet platforms, and (3) detailing that this process-based approach would pay particular attention to entry barriers, conflicts of interest, the emergence of gatekeepers and bottlenecks, the use of and control over data, and dynamics of bargaining power.

188. This is one line of argument President Franklin Roosevelt offered in favor of robust antitrust. In a 1938 speech to Congress he said, "The enforcement of free competition is the least regulation business can expect." Franklin D. Roosevelt, Message to Congress on Curbing Monopolies, *American Presidency Project*, http://www.presidency.ucsb.edu/ws/?pid=15637 [http://perma.cc/WP9P-83RF].

189. By "distorting," I mean that a single player has enough control to dictate outcomes. This is the definition offered by Milton Friedman, a figure popular with the neoclassical school. See Milton Friedman, *Capitalism and Freedom* (2002), 119–20 ("Monopoly exists when a specific individual or enterprise has sufficient control over

a particular product or service to determine significantly the terms on which other individuals shall have access to it"). The Chicago School accepts this definition with regard to price and output, but ignores other metrics of control.

190. See Stucke and Grunes, *supra* note 47, at 107–09.

191. I am using "dominance" to connote that the company controls a significant share of market activity in a sector. I do not mean to attach the legal significance that sometimes attends "dominance."

192. See Greg Bensinger, Cloud Unit Pushes Amazon To Record Profit, *Wall Street Journal* (April 28, 2016), http://www.wsj.com/articles/amazon-reports-surge-in-profit-1461874333 [http://perma.cc/L4QS-RJ26] ("The cloud division's sales rose 64% to $2.57 billion. While that is less than one-tenth of Amazon's overall revenue, [Amazon Web Services] generated 67% of the company's operating income in the quarter").

193. Ibid.

194. Amazon's Profits, *Ben-Evans* (August 2013), http://ben-evans.com/benedictevans/2013/8/8/amazons-profits [http://perma.cc/G5JC-7XBL]; Amazon.com Inc., *Marketwatch*, http://www.marketwatch.com/investing/stock/amzn/historical [http://perma.cc/JW97-A624].

195. See Streitfeld, *supra* note 1 ("In its 16 years as a public company, Amazon has received unique permission from Wall Street to concentrate on expanding its infrastructure, increasing revenue at the expense of profit. Stockholders have pushed Amazon shares up to a record level, even though the company makes only pocket change. Profits were always promised tomorrow").

196. See, for example, Justin Dini, Amazon Losses Widen but Shares Rise After-Hours, *TheStreet* (February 2, 2000), http://www.thestreet.com/story/875924/1/amazon-losses-widen-but-shares-rise-after-hours.html [http://perma.cc/P6HJ-3VDG]; Quick Pen, What's Driving the Amazon Stock Up Despite 188% Full Year Income Drop?, *Gurufocus* (February 8, 2015), http://www.gurufocus.com/news/315124/whats-driving-the-amazon-stock-up-despite-188-full-year-income-drop [http://perma.cc/K6FJ-JWNA].

197. David Streitfeld, Amazon Reports Unexpected Profit, and Stock Soars, *New York Times* (July 23, 2015), http://www.nytimes.com/2015/07/24/technology/amazon-earnings-q2.html [http://perma.cc/WJX9-CYG7]; see also Philip Elmer-DeWitt, This Is What Drives Apple Investors Nuts About Amazon, *Fortune* (July 24, 2015), http://fortune.com/2015/07/24/apple-amazon-profits [http://perma.cc/56U5-Z2E3] (noting the same).

198. Matthew Yglesias, Amazon Profits Fall 45 Percent, Still the Most Amazing Company in the World, *Slate: Moneybox* (Jan. 29, 2013, 4:23 PM), http://www.slate.com/blogs/moneybox/2013/01/29/amazon_q4_profits_fall_45 _percent.html [http://perma.cc/J8AZ-R9S6].

199. Jeffrey P. Bezos, Letter to Shareholders, *Amazon.com, Inc.* (March 30, 1998), http://media.corporate-ir.net/media_files/irol/97/97664/reports/Shareholderletter97.pdf [http://perma.cc/793G-YML7].

200. Ibid at 2.

201. Ibid.

202. Ibid at 1–2.

203. Tonya Garcia, Amazon Accounted for 60% of U.S. Online Sales Growth in 2015, *Marketwatch* (May 3, 2016), http://www.marketwatch.com/story/amazon-accounted-for-60-of-online-sales-growth-in-2015-2016-05-03 [http://perma.cc/8C5W-8NYW] ("Amazon makes up a larger percentage of e-commerce in the U.S. than any other player, and its retail growth has outpaced overall online retail"); see also The Everything Shipper: Amazon and the New Age of Delivery, *Bi Intelligence* (June 5, 2016), http://www.businessinsider.com/the-everything-shipper-amazon-and-the-new-age-of-delivery-2016-6 [http://perma.cc/2SGJ-5ADY].

204. See Phil Wahba, This Chart Shows Just How Dominant Amazon Is, *Fortune* (November 6, 2015), http://fortune.com/2015/11/06/amazon-retailers-ecommerce [http://perma.cc/9YPV-SKM5]. The fact that Amazon was exempt from sales taxes for the first fifteen years of its existence gave it an 8 percent to 10 percent price advantage over brick-and-mortar stores. Its pricing lead over both traditional and online retailers, however, has been and still continues to be far greater than 8 percent to 10 percent. A review of a new price comparison tool stated: "And, as expected, it reported that Amazon indeed had the best prices for nearly everything we searched." Zach Epstein, Amazon Isn't Always the Cheapest Option—Here's How To Find the Best Prices, *BGR* (July 17, 2014), http://bgr.com/2014/07/17/amazon-price-comparison-tool-lowest-price [http://perma.cc/J7P3-BBY5].

205. Dawn Kawamoto, Amazon Unveils Flat-Fee Shipping, *CNET* (February 2, 2005), http://www.cnet.com/news/amazon-unveils-flat-fee-shipping [http://perma.cc/Q8FS-7SQ7].

206. It has also been a key force driving up Amazon's stock price. "Analysts describe Prime as one of the main factors driving Amazon's stock price—up 296 percent in the last two years—and the main reason Amazon's sales grew 30 percent during the recession while other retailers flailed." Brad Stone, What's in Amazon's Box? Instant Gratification, *Bloomberg Businessweek* (November 24, 2010), http://www.bloomberg.com/news/articles/2010-11-24/whats-in-amazons-box-instant-gratification [http://perma.cc/Q7VL-95DQ]; see also Tom DiChristopher, Prime Will Grow Amazon Revenue Longer than You Think: Analyst, *CNBC* (September 11, 2015), http://www.cnbc.com/2015/09/11/prime-will-grow-amazon-revenue-longer-than-you-think-analyst.html [http://perma.cc/QG8H-Z4A6] ("During Amazon's second quarter conference call, management said growing Prime adoption was one factor behind acceleration in domestic and international revenue growth").

207. Devin Leonard, Will Amazon Kill FedEx?, *Bloomberg* (August 31, 2016), http://www.bloomberg.com/features/2016-amazon-delivery [http://perma.cc/GE8F-D3BE].

208. Brad Tuttle, Amazon Prime: Bigger, More Powerful, More Profitable than Anyone Imagined, *Time* (Mar. 18, 2013), http://business.time.com/2013/03/18/

amazon-prime-bigger-more-powerful-more-profitable-than-anyone-imagined [http://perma.cc/WNL5-MC29].

209. Dan Frommer, Half of US Households Could Have Amazon Prime by 2020, *Quartz* (February 26, 2015), http://qz.com/351726/half-of-us-households-could-have-amazon-prime-by-2020 [http://perma.cc/ZW4Z-47UY].

210. Stu Woo, Amazon "'Primes' Pump for Loyalty," *Wall Street Journal* (November 14, 2011), http://www.wsj.com/articles/SB10001424052970203503204577036102353359784 [http://perma.cc/87WW-TVNW].

211. Deepa Seetharaman and Nathan Layne, Free Delivery Creates Holiday Boon for U.S. Consumers at High Cost, *Reuters* (January 2, 2015), http://www.reuters.com/article/us-retail-shipping-holidays-analysis-idUSKBN0KB0P720150102 [http://perma.cc/CPH8-932W].

212. See Elizabeth Weise, Amazon Prime Is Big, but How Big?, *USA Today* (February 3, 2015), http://www.usatoday.com/story/tech/2015/02/03/amazon-prime-10-years-old-anniversary/22755509 [http://perma.cc/5K2A-M3HA]. Amazon's filings with the Securities and Exchange Commisson show that its shipping costs have grown as a percentage of sales each year since 2009. See Amazon.com, Inc., *supra* note 9, at 26; Amazon.com, Inc., Annual Report (Form 10-K) 25 (January 30, 2013), http://www.sec.gov/Archives/edgar/data/1018724/000119312513028520/d445434d10k.htm [http://perma.cc/RX85-5RJ3]; Amazon.com, Inc., Annual Report (Form 10-K) 27 (January 29, 2010), http://www.sec.gov/Archives/edgar/data/1018724/000119312510016098/d10k.htm [http://perma.cc/L27R-CHUY].

213. Stone, *supra* note 206.

214. Brad Tuttle, How Amazon Prime Is Crushing the Competition, *Time* (January 25, 2016), http://time.com/money/4192528/amazon-prime-subscribers-spending [http://perma.cc/Y9VT-VHD5].

215. Chad Rubin, The Evolution of Amazon Prime and Their Followed Success, *Skubana* (March 31, 2016), http://www.skubana.com/e-commerce-trends/evolution-of-amazon-prime [http://perma.cc/T9ET-C6V8].

216. Ben Fox Rubin, As Amazon Marks 20 Years, Prime Grows to 44 Million Members in US, *CNET* (July 15, 2015), http://www.cnet.com/news/amazon-prime-grows-to-estimated-44-million-members-in-us [http://perma.cc/CEQ8-G996].

217. See Brad Tuttle, How Amazon Gets You To Stop Shopping Anywhere Else, *Time* (December 1, 2010), http://business.time.com/2010/12/01/how-amazon-gets-you-to-stop-shopping-anywhere-else [http://perma.cc/GLQ2-65AT].

218. Clare O'Connor, Walmart and Target Being Crowded Out Online by Amazon Prime, *Forbes* (April 6, 2015), http://www.forbes.com/sites/clareoconnor/2015/04/06/walmart-and-target-being-crowded-out-online-by-amazon-prime [http://perma.cc/CM2E-GPER].

219. Ibid.

220. Ibid.

221. Stone, *supra* note 206.

222. See Tuttle, *supra* note 217 ("What this program has done is something that's normally very difficult to accomplish: It's changed consumer habits, and, perhaps even more remarkably, it's changed them in ways that solely favor Amazon. The service is better than any freebie promotion, which even if it's good at driving traffic to the website, is short-lived. Instead, the Prime membership program gets consumers in the regular habit of at least checking with Amazon before making any online purchase").

223. Greg Bensinger, Amazon Raises Prime Subscription Price to $99 a Year, *Wall Street Journal* (March 13, 2014), http://www.wsj.com/articles/SB10001424052702303546204579436903309411092 [http://perma.cc/33TK-76GS].

224. Lance Whitney, Amazon Prime Members Will Renew Despite Price Hike, Survey Finds, *CNET* (July 23, 2014), http://www.cnet.com/news/amazon-prime-members-will-almost-all-renew-despite-price-increase [http://perma.cc/Z585-YU8P].

225. See Adam Candeub, Behavioral Economics, Internet Search, and Antitrust, *I/S* 9 (2014), 407, 409 ("[O]nline market behavior may differ from the brick and mortar world. . . . In particular, behavioral tendencies related to habit and information costs may disrupt conventional economic assumptions").

226. As Justice White wrote in his dissent in *Matsushita*, "The Court, in discussing the unlikelihood of a predatory conspiracy, also consistently assumes that petitioners valued profit maximization over growth." *Matsushita Elec. Indus. Co. v. Zenith Radio Corp.*, 475 U.S. 574, 604 (1986) (White, J., dissenting).

227. Indeed, to get a sense of Amazon's breadth, it is helpful to see the range of actors Amazon lists among its "current and potential competitors":

(1) online, offline, and multichannel retailers, publishers, vendors, distributors, manufacturers, and producers of the products we offer and sell to consumers and businesses; (2) publishers, producers, and distributors of physical, digital, and interactive media of all types and all distribution channels; (3) web search engines, comparison shopping websites, social networks, web portals, and other online and app-based means of discovering, using, or acquiring goods and services, either directly or in collaboration with other retailers; (4) companies that provide e-commerce services, including website development, advertising, fulfillment, customer service, and payment processing; (5) companies that provide fulfillment and logistics services for themselves or for third parties, whether online or offline; (6) companies that provide information technology services or products, including on-premises or cloud-based infrastructure and other services; and (7) companies that design, manufacture, market, or sell consumer electronics, telecommunication, and electronic devices.

Amazon.com, Inc., Annual Report (Form 10-K) 4 (April 6, 2016), http://phx.corporate-ir.net/External.File?item=UGFyZW50SUQ9NjI4NTg0fENoaWxkSUQ9MzI5NTMwfFR5cGU9MQ==&t=1 [http://perma.cc/96HQ-TZDT].

228. See generally ibid (describing Amazon's businesses).

229. As of 2012, Amazon had acquired or invested in over seventy companies. See Sucharita Mulpuru and Brian K. Walker, *Why Amazin Matters Now More Than Ever* (2012), 5.

230. Ibid at 17.

231. See LaVecchia and Mitchell, *supra* note 6, at 1.

232. Tiernan Ray, Amazon: All Retail's SKUs Are Belong to Them, Goldman Tells CNBC, *Barrons: Tech Trader Daily* (June 16, 2016), http://blogs.barrons.com/techtraderdaily/2016/06/16/amazon-all-retails-skus-are-belong-to-them-goldman-tells-cnbc [http://perma.cc/Z95R-JYGR] (quoting a Goldman Sachs analyst as saying, "[p]rojected ecommerce growth of 22% this year is largely thanks to Amazon," and "Amazon 'is going to outgrow that,' with perhaps 'mid to high 20s growth,' . . . given 'Amazon is taking share, and seeing acceleration in their international business'"). See generally Leonard, *supra* note 207 ("Amazon's growth has been preposterous. . . . The company is the fifth-most valuable in the world: Its market capitalization is about $366 billion, which is roughly equal to the combined worth of Walmart, FedEx, and Boeing").

233. Leonard, *supra* note 207.

234. Shelly Banjo, Amazon Eats the Department Store, *Bloomberg: Gadfly* (September 20, 2016), http://www.bloomberg.com/gadfly/articles/2016-09-20/amazon-clothing-sales-could-soon-top-macy-s [http://perma.cc/63UJ-5Y67].

235. Its clothing sales are greater than the combined online sales of its five largest online apparel competitors: Macy's, Nordstrom, Kohl's, Gap, and Victoria's Secret's parent. Ibid.

236. In some contexts, "dominance" connotes a legal definition. I am not using it in this way. See *supra* note 191.

237. See Caroline McCarthy, Amazon Debuts Kindle E-Book Reader, *CNET* (November 19, 2007), http://www.cnet.com/news/amazon-debuts-kindle-e-book-reader [http://perma.cc/VF4Z-2V77].

238. See ibid.

239. See Brad Stone, *The Everything Store* (2013); George Packer, Cheap Words, *New Yorker* (February 17, 2014), http://www.newyorker.com/magazine/2014/02/17/cheap-words [http://perma.cc/42AN-Y6UT].

240. Prior to 2009, many publishers set a wholesale price for e-books at a 20 percent discount from the equivalent physical book, at which point Amazon's $9.99 price point roughly matched the wholesale price of many of its e-books. In 2009, publishers eliminated the wholesale discount, yet Amazon continued to price e-books at $9.99. This is the point at which it clearly sold e-books below cost. See *United States v. Apple, Inc.*, 952 F. Supp. 2d 638, 649-50 (S.D.N.Y. 2013); see also Packer, *supra* note 239 ("The price was below wholesale in some cases, and so low that it represented a serious threat to the market in twenty-six-dollar hardcovers"); Jeffrey A. Trachtenberg, E-Book Sales Fall After New Amazon Contracts, *Wall Street Journal* (September 3, 2015), http://www.wsj.com/article_email/e-book-sales-weaken-amid-higher-prices-1441307826-lMyQjAxMTE1MzAxNDUwMjQ2Wj [http://perma.cc/LVZ9-DK9Y] ("Amazon was willing to buy a title for $14.99 and sell it for $9.99, taking a loss to grab market share and encourage adoption of its Kindle e-reader").

241. See Eric Savitz, Amazon Selling Kindle Fire Below Cost, Analyst Contends, *Forbes* (September 30, 2011), http://www.forbes.com/sites/ericsavitz/2011/09/30/amazon-selling-kindle-fire-below-cost-analyst-contends [http://perma.cc/3AQ8-X9LZ]; Woo, *supra* note 210 ("Mr. Munster estimated that Amazon sells each Kindle model at a loss of $10 to $15").

242. See Packer, *supra* note 239 ("In the mid-aughts, Bezos, having watched Apple take over the music-selling business with iTunes and the iPod, became determined not to let the same thing happen with books. In 2004, he set up a lab in Silicon Valley that would build Amazon's first piece of consumer hardware: a device for reading digital books. According to Stone's book, Bezos told the executive running the project, 'Proceed as if your goal is to put everyone selling physical books out of a job'").

243. *Apple*, 952 F. Supp. 2d at 649.

244. Ibid at 658–61.

245. Ibid at 672.

246. Ibid at 679.

247. Announcement: Macmillan E-Books, *Amazon* (January 31, 2010), http://www.amazon.com/forum/kindle/Tx2MEGQWTNGIMHV [http://perma.cc/K64A-RF2C]; see also *Apple*, 952 F. Supp. 2d at 680–81 (describing the struggle between the publishing houses and Amazon leading up to Amazon's capitulation).

248. *Apple*, 952 F. Supp. 2d at 681.

249. Ibid at 645.

250. Response of Plaintiff United States to Public Comments on the Proposed Final Judgment at 21, *Apple*, 952 F. Supp. 2d 638 (No. 12-CV-2826-DLC).

251. Ibid at 21–22 (quoting Complaint at 9, *Apple*, 952 F. Supp. 2d 638 (No. 12-CV-2826-DLC)).

252. *Apple*, 952 F. Supp. 2d at 708 ("This trial has not been the occasion to decide whether Amazon's choice to sell NYT Bestsellers or other New Releases as loss leaders was an unfair trade practice or in any other way a violation of law").

253. See ibid at 650 (noting that Amazon "continued to sell many NYT Bestsellers as loss leaders"); Complaint, *supra* note 251, at 9 ("From the time of its launch, Amazon's e-book distribution business has been consistently profitable, even when substantially discounting some newly released and bestselling titles"); Response of Plaintiff United States to Public Comments on the Proposed Final Judgment, *supra* note 250, at 21–22.

254. See generally Jean-Charles Rochet and Jean Tirole, Platform Competition in Two-Sided Markets, *Journal of the European Economic Association* 1 (2003), 990 (explaining the dynamics of competition in two-sided markets).

255. Traditionally, a retailer loss-leads when it prices one good below cost in order to sell more of another good, assuming that discounts on one good will attract and retain consumers. Walmart choosing to price t-shirts below cost to sell more shorts would be an example of loss leading.

256. John B. Kirkwood, Collusion To Control a Powerful Customer: Amazon, E-Books, and Antitrust Policy, *University of Miami Law Review* 69 (2014), 38–39.

257. Ibid at 39.

258. See ibid.

259. See Cory Doctorow, Why the Death of DRM Would Be Good News for Readers, Writers and Publishers, *Guardian* (May 3, 2012), http://www.theguardian.com/technology/2012/may/03/death-of-drm-good-news [http://perma.cc/H77L-7KZ8] ("If Tor sells you one of my books for the Kindle locked with Amazon's DRM, neither I, nor Tor, can authorise you to remove that DRM. If Amazon demands a deeper discount (something Amazon has been doing with many publishers as their initial ebook distribution deals come up for renegotiation) and Tor wants to shift its preferred ebook retail to a competitor like Waterstone's, it will have to bank on its readers being willing to buy their books all over again").

260. See Ana Carolina Bittar, Unlocking the Gates of Alexandria: DRM, Competition and Access to E-Books 1 (July 25, 2014) (unpublished manuscript), http://ssrn.com/abstract=2620354 [http://perma.cc/6RHH-6QM4] ("[S]ince each bookseller uses a different proprietary DRM scheme on their e-books, compatible with a limited number of reading platforms, consumers face problems with interoperability. For example, a Kindle owner cannot buy books from Barnes & Noble, and a Nook owner cannot buy books from Apple. This lack of interoperability can increase barriers to entry, switching costs, and network effects. Consequently, consumers are often locked into an e-book ecosystem, which permits booksellers to act as gatekeepers of the e-book market").

261. See Alexandra Alter, Your E-Book Is Reading You, *Wall Street Journal* (July 19, 2012), http://www.wsj.com/articles/SB10001424052702304870304577490950051438304 [http://perma.cc/6LQW-BCKJ] ("The major new players in e-book publishing—Amazon, Apple and Google—can easily track how far readers are getting in books, how long they spend reading them and which search terms they use to find books. Book apps for tablets like the iPad, Kindle Fire and Nook record how many times readers open the app and how much time they spend reading. Retailers and some publishers are beginning to sift through the data, gaining unprecedented insight into how people engage with books").

262. Response of Plaintiff United States to Public Comments on the Proposed Final Judgment, *supra* note 250, at 22.

263. October 2015 —Apple, B&N, Kobo, and Google: A Look at the Rest of the Ebook Market, *Author Earnings* (October 2015), http://authorearnings.com/report/october-2015-apple-bn-kobo-and-google-a-look-at-the-rest-of-the-ebook-market [http://perma.cc/GKN4-SA43] (noting that Amazon also sells 85 percent of indie e-books).

264. Statistics and Facts About Amazon, *Statista* (2016), http://www.statista.com/topics/846/amazon [http://perma.cc/YR3Q-D7YE].

265. Sony Gives Up on Selling E-Readers, *BBC* (August 5, 2014), http://www.bbc.com/news/technology-28663878 [http://perma.cc/D29U-W7NZ].

266. Jim Milliot, B&N Cut Nook Investment by 74% in Third Quarter, *Publishers Weekly* (March 7, 2014), http://www.publishersweekly.com/pw/by-topic/industry-news/bookselling/article/61331-b-n-cut-nook-investment-by-74-in-third-quarter.html [http://perma.cc/846M-28HZ].

267. Nor is the decline of Amazon competitors unique to e-books. "Now, with Borders dead, Barnes & Noble struggling and independent booksellers greatly diminished, for many consumers there is simply no other way to get many books than through Amazon." Streitfeld, *supra* note 1.

268. Ibid.

269. See ibid.

270. Several journalists have tracked instances of price discrimination in e-commerce. See, for example, Julia Angwin et al., The Tiger Mom Tax: Asians Are Nearly Twice as Likely To Get a Higher Price from Princeton Review, *Propublica* (September 1, 2015), http://www.propublica.org/article/asians-nearly-twice-as-likely-to-get-higher-price-from-princeton-review [http://perma.cc/L96N-SZKR]; Jennifer Valentino-Devries et al., Websites Vary Prices, Deals Based on User Information, *Wall Street Journal* (December 24, 2012), http://www.wsj.com/articles/SB10001424127887323777204578189391813881534 [http://perma.cc/BF3S-ZX3C].

271. Roberto A. Ferdman, Amazon Changes Its Prices More than 2.5 Million Times a Day, *Quartz* (December 14, 2013), http://qz.com/157828/amazon-changes-its-prices-more-than-2-5-million-times-a-day [http://perma.cc/W25A-EUNP].

272. But recent reporting does suggest that Amazon manipulates how it presents pricing in order to favor its own products. See Julia Angwin and Surya Mattu, Amazon Says It Puts Customers First. But Its Pricing Algorithm Doesn't, *Propublica* (September 20, 2016), http://www.propublica.org/article/amazon-says-it-puts-customers-first-but-its-pricing-algorithm-doesnt [http://perma.cc/RR6C-FTS4] ("[T]he company appears to be using its market power and proprietary algorithm to advantage itself at the expense of sellers and many customers").

273. See Lina Khan, Why You Might Pay More than Your Neighbor for the Same Bottle of Salad Dressing, *Quartz* (January 19, 2014), http://qz.com/168314/why-you-might-pay-more-than-your-neighbor-for-the-same-bottle-of-salad-dressing [http://perma.cc/KVL3-QCBC].

274. Ibid.

275. Ibid ("'Coupons will be the doorway in to differential pricing,' said Scott Anderson, principal consultant at FICO, which provides data analytics and decision-making services. In other words, we could all end up paying significantly different amounts for the same items, even if we see the same prices while browsing").

276. As a group of authors stated in a recent letter to the Justice Department:

[T]he corporation's detailed knowledge of the buying habits of millions of readers—which it amasses through a minute-by-minute tracking of their actions online—puts it in a powerful position to use such 'personalized' pricing and marketing to influence the decisions of readers and thereby extract the most amount of cash possible from each individual.

Letter from Authors United to William J. Baer, Assistant Att'y Gen., Antitrust Div., Dep't of Justice (July 14, 2015), http://www.authorsunited.net/july/long-document.html [http://perma.cc/L9RN-YESR]; *see also* David Streitfeld, Accusing Amazon of Antitrust Violations, Authors and Booksellers Demand Inquiry, *New York Times* (July 13, 2015), http://www.nytimes.com/2015/07/14/technology/accusing-amazon-of-antitrust-violations-authors-and-booksellers-demand-us-inquiry.html [http://perma.cc/G8QF-5LYY] (reporting on the Authors United letter to the Assistant Attorney General and its claim that Amazon seems to be "engag[ing] in content control" in its decisions to sell certain books).

277. See *supra* section titled "Predatory Pricing." For accounts of how some retailers have successfully implemented discriminatory pricing online, see *supra* note 270 and accompanying text.

278. Streitfeld, *supra* note 1.

279. See Phillip Areeda and Herbery Hovenkamp, *Fundamentals of Antitrust Law* (2010), 7–72 ("There may be cases in which a predator who makes more than one product or operates in more than one region selects only one for below-cost pricing but reaps recoupment benefits in all. . . . The courts have not dealt adequately with this problem"); Leslie, *supra* note 94, at 1720 ("Courts apparently do not appreciate the prospect of recoupment in another market"); Timothy J. Trujillo, Note, Predatory Pricing Standards Under Recent Supreme Court Decisions and Their Failure To Recognize Strategic Behavior as a Barrier to Entry, *Journal of Corporate Law* 19 (1994), 809, 813, 825 ("The . . . recoupment analysis in *Matsushita*, *Cargill*, and *Brooke* refers to recoupment only in the market in which the predation actually occurs. Thus, the Court's analyses and test . . . ignore the possibility that successful predation could occur because the dominant firm can spread its gains from predation over several markets").

280. See Leslie, *supra* note 94, at 1720–21.

281. See Randy Kennedy, Cash Up Front, *New York Times* (June 5, 2005), http://www.nytimes.com/2005/06/05/books/review/cash-up-front.html [http://perma.cc/H9L2-RUPU].

282. See James B. Stewart, Booksellers Score Some Points in Amazon's Spat with Hachette, *New York Times* (June 20, 2014), http://www.nytimes.com/2014/06/21/business/booksellers-score-some-points-in-amazons-standoff-with-hachette.html [http://perma.cc/PD34-M28S].

283. Ibid.

284. See LaVecchia and Mitchell, *supra* note 6, at 2.

285. Acquisition and maintenance of monopsony power are still recognized harms under the Sherman and Clayton Acts, even though few cases are brought today. But *cf.* Complaint at 12-13, *United States v. George's Foods, LLC*, No. 5:11-cv-00043-gec (W.D. Va. May 10, 2011) (arguing that a company's acquisition of a chicken complex would "substantially lessen competition for the purchase of broiler grower [chicken farmer] services . . . in violation of Section 7 of the Clayton Act").

286. Boris Kachka, Book Publishing's Big Gamble, *New York Times* (July 9, 2013), http://www.nytimes.com/2013/07/10/opinion/book-publishings-big-gamble.html [http://perma.cc/AP5X] ("The merger, announced last October and completed on July 1 after regulatory approval, shrinks the Big Six, which publish about two-thirds of books in the United States, down to the Big Five").

287. Ibid. Publishers have also merged divisions internally. See, for example, Alex Shephard, The Vanishing Mass Market: Penguin Merges Two Mass Market Publishing Houses To Create New Mass Market Publishing House, *Melville House* (June 26, 2015), http://www.mhpbooks.com/the-vanishing-mass-market-penguin-merges-two-mass-market-publishing-houses-merge-to-create-new-mass-market-publishing-house [http://perma.cc/F4V6-GGLU].

288. Cross-subsidization schemes can have widely different effects, depending on how the two submarkets are or are not interrelated. In Amazon's case, losses do have cross-market effects: Amazon prices below cost in order to generate higher sales in another line of business; its losses in one market *actively boost* another market. By contrast, the cross-subsidization model used by publishers has no analogous crossover effects. A publisher might decide to publish an obscure book, even if it knows it will lose money, and subsidize those losses through profits made on a more popular book. However, the publisher's choice to sustain a loss on the obscure book does not *boost* sales of its popular books. The major difference in Amazon's case is that it is an online platform. The market effects across its different segments are significant in ways that do not hold for brick-and-mortar stores or other nonplatform entities.

289. Letter from Authors United to William J. Baer, *supra* note 276.

290. Ibid.

291. Ibid.

292. That said, the DOJ did consider how rising consolidation in the media sector—specifically in the context of a proposed merger between two newspapers—would risk undermining the spread of ideas. Press Release, Office of Pub. Affairs, U.S. Dep't of Justice, Justice Department Files Antitrust Lawsuit To Stop L.A. Times Publisher from Acquiring Competing Newspapers (March 17, 2016), http://www.justice.gov/opa/pr/justice-department-files-antitrust-lawsuit-stop-la-times-publisher-acquiring-competing [http://perma.cc/3MNY-8XZE] ("Newspapers continue to play an important role in the dissemination of news and information to readers" [quoting Assistant Attorney General Bill Baer of the DOJ's Antitrust Division]).

293. At the height of its market share, this figure was closer to 90 percent. After Apple entered the market, Amazon's share fell slightly and then stabilized around 65 percent. See Packer, *supra* note 239.

294. Stone, *supra* note 239, at 297 ("Quidsi [grew] from nothing to $300 million in annual sales in just a few years").

295. Ibid at 295–96.

296. Ibid at 296.

297. Ibid; Brad Stone, The Secrets of Bezos: How Amazon Became the Everything Store, *Bloomberg* (October 10, 2013), http://www.bloomberg.com/news/

articles/2013-10-10/jeff-bezos-and-the-age-of-amazon-excerpt-from-the-everything-store-by-brad-stone [http://perma.cc/TD96-G6HV].

298. Brad Tuttle, It's Target Versus Amazon in the Battle for Moms, *Time* (September 26, 2013), http://business.time.com/2013/09/26/its-target-versus-amazon-in-the-battle-for-moms [http://perma.cc/UJE6-Y3R9].

299. Stone, *supra* note 239, at 297.

300. Ibid at 298.

301. Jason Del Ray, How Jeff Bezos Crushed Diapers.com so Amazon Could Buy Diapers.com, *All Things D* (October 10, 2013), http://allthingsd.com/20131010/how-jeff-bezos-crushed-diapers-com-so-amazon-could-buy-diapers-com [http://perma.cc/K98D-VGNP].

302. Will Oremus, The Time Jeff Bezos Went Thermonuclear on Diapers.com, *Slate* (October 10, 2013), http://www.slate.com/blogs/future_tense/2013/10/10/amazon_book_how_jeff_bezos_went_thermonuclear_on_diapers_com.html [http://perma.cc/A9JE-VNWR].

303. Stone, *supra* note 297 (noting that Amazon offered $540 million, giving Quidsi a forty-eight-hour window in which to respond and "rachet[ing] up the pressure," telling Quidsi that Bezos was "such a furious competitor [that he] would drive diaper prices to zero if they went with Walmart," in which case "the Amazon Mom onslaught would continue").

304. Ibid.

305. The FTC reviewed the deal under section 7 of the Clayton Act, the provision that governs mergers, as well as section 5 of the Federal Trade Commission Act, which targets general unfair practices. See Letter from Donald S. Clark, Sec'y, FTC, to Peter C. Thomas, Simpson Thacher & Bartlett LLP (March 23, 2011), http://www.ftc.gov/sites/default/files/documents/closing_letters/amazon.com-inc./quidsi-inc./110323amazonthomas.pdf [http://perma.cc/7E5A-LYMB]; see also Stone, *supra* note 297 ("The Federal Trade Commission scrutinized the acquisition for four and a half months, going beyond the standard review to the secondrequest phase, where companies must provide more information about a transaction. The deal raised a host of red flags, such as the elimination of a major player in a competitive category, according to an FTC official familiar with the review").

306. See Stone, *supra* note 239, at 298.

307. "At this time, [Amazon Mom is] not accepting new members," a company spokesman stated, declining to explain why. Thad Rueter, Let's Hope Amazon Doesn't Make Them Wait Until Potty Training Ends, *Internet Retailer* (November 30, 2011), http://www.internetretailer.com/2011/11/30/now-amazon-closes-membership-moms-discount-program [http://perma.cc/L76R-XEHP].

308. Thad Rueter, Amazon Tweaks Its Diaper Program, Moms Vent and a Competitor Pounces, *Internet Retailer* (February 23, 2012), http://www.internetretailer.com/2012/02/23/amazon-tweaks-diaper-program-moms-vent-competitor-pounces [http://perma.cc/GBU7-KYNF].

309. Ibid.

310. Laura Owen, Amazon Cuts the Benefits Again in Amazon Mom, Its Prime Program for Parents, *Gigaom* (September 29, 2014), http://gigaom.com/2014/09/29/amazon-cuts-the-benefits-again-in-amazon-mom-its-prime-program-for-parents [http://perma.cc/993P-JPZN].

311. In response to complaints about Amazon's abrupt change, followed by customers recommending Diapers.com, one customer stated, "Diapers.com has a different shipping program, but they were recently bought out by Amazon. I would think that their shipping policies might change soon as well." Shopaholic, Comment to Amazon Mom Benefits Misleading!, *Amazon* (June 15, 2011), http://www.amazon.com/forum/baby/ref=cm_cd_pg_pg2?_encoding=UTF8&cdForum=FxSKWDWQRZ03WU&cdPage=2&cdThread=Tx1ZC5GMKB4JEQP [http://perma.cc/E5NH-JCJ7].

312. Amazon leads the online market for baby supplies, holding 43 percent. Walmart and Target follow, with 23 percent and 18 percent, respectively. Target, Walmart, Amazon Dominate the Online Baby Goods Market, *Business Insider* (April 22, 2016), http://www.businessinsider.com/target-walmart-amazon-dominate-the-online-baby-goods-market-2016-4 [http://perma.cc/85KZ-QQCR].

313. Bork, *supra* note 32, at 153.

314. Ibid.

315. Ibid.

316. See generally Tim Wu, *The Master Switch: The Rise and Fall of Information Empires* (2010) (arguing that all American information industries since the telephone have resulted in monopolies); Candeub, *supra* note 225 (suggesting that network effects may produce anticompetitive results in the online market because of the cognitive effort necessary to switch search engines); Nathan Newman, Search, Antitrust, and the Economics of the Control of User Data, *Yale Journal on Regulation* 31 (2014), 401 (proposing a new approach to antitrust investigations that would focus on the anticompetitive effects of corporations' control of personal data); Frank Pasquale, Privacy, Antitrust, and Power, *George Mason Law Review* 20 (2013), 1009 (advocating reforms to privacy and antitrust policy to take into account the connections between market share and control over data).

317. For example, Amazon acquired Zappos.com in 2009 but chose to maintain the brand as a standalone rather than absorbing it within Amazon.com. Sarah Lacy, Amazon Buys Zappos; The Price Is $928m., Not $847m., *Techcrunch* (July 22, 2009), http://techcrunch.com/2009/07/22/amazon-buys-zappos [http://perma.cc/5NGV-P2AU].

318. See, for example, Leslie, *supra* note 94, at 1728–29.

319. Jet.com, the one company that *did* try to tackle Amazon, was recently purchased by Walmart. See Steven Davidoff Solomon, Tech Giants Gobble Start-Ups in an Antitrust Blind Spot, *New York Times: Dealbook* (August 16, 2016), http://www.nytimes.com/2016/08/17/business/dealbook/expect-little-antitrust-challenge-to-walmarts-bid-for-jet-com.html [http://perma.cc/WRC9-QGKR].

320. Moore, *supra* note 14. Google has stated that its biggest rival in search is not Bing or Yahoo, but Amazon. See Jeevan Vasagar and Alex Barker, Amazon Is Our Biggest Search Rival, Says Google's Eric Schmidt, *Financial Times* (October 13, 2014), http://www.ft.com/cms/s/0/748bff70-52f2-11e4-b917-00144feab7de.html [http://perma.cc/3PHW-77EW].

321. Newman, *supra* note 316, at 409.

322. See Vauhini Vara, Can Jet.com Take On Amazon and Win?, *New Yorker* (July 21, 2015), http://www.newyorker.com/business/currency/can-jet-com-take-on-amazon-and-win [http://perma.cc/S2K2-SMHA].

323. Shannon Pettypiece and Selina Wang, Wal-Mart To Acquire Jet.com for $3.3 Billion To Fight Amazon, *Bloomberg* (August 8, 2016), http://www.bloomberg.com/news/articles/2016-08-08/wal-mart-agrees-to-buy-jet-com-for-3-billion-to-fight-amazon [http://perma.cc/FEK9-NMR9].

324. See Grace Noto, Jet.Com Acquisition Not Enough To Challenge Amazon, Experts Say, *Bank Innovation* (August 22, 2016), http://bankinnovation.net/2016/08/jet-com-acquisition-not-enough-to-challenge-amazon-experts-say [http://perma.cc/CQ3Y-6J8X] ("[T]here remains a healthy amount of skepticism in the industry about anyone's ability to topple Amazon from its throne. 'Amazon is quite dominant and will continue to be in the foreseeable future, because the resources they are putting into ecommerce and all of their other initiatives are formidable,' said vice president and principal analyst at Forester Research Sucharita Mulpuru-Kodali. 'Walmart has slowly been gaining some share in some ways, but it's often two steps forward, one step back for them'"); Pettypiece and Wang, *supra* note 323 ("Amazon is such a machine. . . . You aren't going to out-Amazon Amazon").

325. See Tuttle, *supra* note 298.

326. See ibid (noting that Amazon's market share is double Target's).

327. See infra section titled "Amazon Marketplace and Exploiting Data."

328. See LaVecchia and Mitchell, *supra* note 6, at 18.

329. Laura Stevens and Greg Bensinger, Amazon Seeks To Ease Ties with UPS, *Wall Street Journal* (December 22, 2015), http://www.wsj.com/articles/amazon-seeks-to-ease-ties-with-ups-1450835575 [http://perma.cc/8385-A7AJ].

330. In its 10-K, UPS states that while no single customer accounts for more than 10 percent of its consolidated revenue, its business remains vulnerable to the choices of some big clients. UPS, Inc., Annual Report (Form 10-K) 15 (January 29, 2016), http://www.sec.gov/Archives/edgar/data/1090727/000109072715000008/ups-12312014x10k.htm [http://perma.cc/TU7T-B4Q4] ("[S]ome of our large customers might account for a relatively significant portion of the growth in revenue in a particular quarter or year. . . . These customers could choose to divert all or a portion of their business with us to one of our competitors, demand pricing concessions for our services, require us to provide enhanced services that increase our costs, or develop their own shipping and distribution capabilities. If these factors drove some of our large customers to cancel all or a portion of their business relationships with us, it

could materially impact the growth in our business and the ability to meet our current and long-term financial forecasts").

331. See Stephanie Clifford and Claire Cain Miller, Wal-Mart Says "Try This On": Free Shipping, *New York Times* (November 11, 2010), http://www.nytimes.com/2010/11/11/business/11shipping.html [http://perma.cc/ULM8-3ASC] ("[A]ir shipping prices for big retailers are about 70 percent less than for a small company. Shipping at Amazon costs about 4 percent of sales, and Amazon loses money on it because it offers marketing benefits. . . . [S]hipping at small sites usually costs about 35 percent of sales"). Congress passed the Robinson-Patman Act precisely to prevent this sort of "waterbed effect." As I describe earlier, Chicago School hostility to Robinson-Patman has meant that both the antitrust agencies and courts have largely stopped enforcing the law. See *supra* text accompanying notes 77–108.

332. See Laura Stevens, "Free" Shipping Crowds Out Small Retailers, *Wall Street Journal* (April 27, 2016), http://www.wsj.com/articles/for-online-shoppers-free-shipping-reigns-supreme-1461789381 [http://perma.cc/R7YL-2FTS].

333. See Paul W. Dobson and Roman Inderst, The Waterbed Effect: Where Buying and Selling Power Come Together, *Wisconsin Law Review* (2008), 331, 336–37 ("If, in contrast, the discounts to one or a few buyers were to put other buyers in a worse bargaining position to the extent of them paying even-higher prices (e.g., premiums rather than discounts) then the knock-on consequence could be higher retail prices and dampened competition. This latter case is an instance of a waterbed effect—where differential buyer power means that some buyers gain at both the relative and absolute expense of other buyers"); John Kirkwood, Powerful Buyers and Merger Enforcement, *Boston University Law Review* 92 (2012), 1485, 1544 ("[Suppose a firm] demands price or other concessions from . . . suppliers . . . [and] that those concessions nevertheless cause the suppliers to increase prices to smaller buyers or otherwise worsen their terms").

334. Dobson and Inderst, *supra* note 333, at 337.

335. Press Release, Amazon, Amazon Launches New Services To Help Small and Medium-Sized Businesses Enhance Their Customer Offerings by Accessing Amazon's Order Fulfillment, Customer Service, and Website Functionality (September 19, 2006), http://phx.corporate-ir.net/phoenix.zhtml?c=97664&p=irol-newsArticle&ID=906817 [http://perma.cc/MC8G-9LRJ].

336. Ibid ("Amazon.com customers can now use offers such as Amazon Prime and Free Super Saver Shipping when buying products with the 'Fulfilled by Amazon' icon next to the offering listing").

337. See Paul Cole, Should You Use Amazon Discounted UPS Shipping?, *Sellerengine* (2012), http://sellerengine.com/should-you-use-amazon-discounted-ups-shipping [http://perma.cc/54ND-B2WH] ("Probably the most common choice is to use Amazon's discounted rate with UPS. For many sellers, this is the way to go. It's a lower rate than you're likely to receive from UPS or FedEx if you have your own account. Currently, Amazon's UPS rate is about 20% cheaper than an average FedEx account, $.38/lb. compared to $.48/lb").

338. Before building out its own delivery operations, Amazon used (among others) UPS and FedEx. See, for example, Marcus Wohlsen, Amazon Takes a Big Step Towards Finally Making Its Own Deliveries, *Wired* (September 25, 2014), http://www.wired.com/2014/09/amazon-takes-big-step-toward-competing-directly-ups [http://perma.cc/42AT-Y4JK].

339. Daniella Kucera, Why Amazon Is on a Building Spree, *Bloomberg* (August 29, 2013), http://www.bloomberg.com/bw/articles/2013-08-29/why-amazon-is-on-a-warehouse-building-spree [http://perma.cc/999P-MLSN].

340. Leonard, *supra* note 207.

341. Greg Bensinger and Laura Stevens, Amazon's Newest Ambition: Competing Directly with UPS and FedEx, *Wall Street Journal* (September 27, 2016), http://www.wsj.com/articles/amazons-newest-ambitioncompeting-directly-with-ups-and-fedex-1474994758 [http://perma.cc/BB7F-PXJP].

342. Ibid.

343. Jillian D'Onfro, Here Are All of Amazon's Warehouses in the US, *Business Insider* (March 24, 2015), http://www.businessinsider.com/how-many-fulfillment-centers-does-amazon-have-in-the-us-2015-3#ixzz3f3AX8zda [http://perma.cc/TF8G-BJ72].

344. Bensinger and Stevens, *supra* note 341.

345. See Spencer Soper, EBay Ends Same-Day Delivery in U.S. in Face of Amazon Effort, *Bloomberg* (July 27, 2015), http://www.bloomberg.com/news/articles/2015-07-27/ebay-ends-same-day-delivery-in-u-s-in-face-of-amazon-effort [http://perma.cc/5TD9-XDC5].

346. Stone, *supra* note 206; see also JP Mangalindan, Amazon's Prime and Punishment, *Fortune* (February 21, 2012), http://fortune.com/2012/02/21/amazons-prime-and-punishment [http://perma.cc/68KL-8C5Z] ("'If you're a competing retailer, it should be in your plans that Prime will someday be a next-day or same-day delivery service with 100,000 free movies—it's going in that direction,' chimes analyst [Matt] Nemer. If that day comes, Prime won't just be a nominal loyalty program or balance sheet customer acquisition cost. It'll be a monolith few can compete with").

347. Jason Del Ray, Amazon Buys Thousands of Its Own Truck Trailers as Its Transportation Ambitions Grow, *Recode* (December 4, 2015), http://recode.net/2015/12/04/amazon-buys-thousands-of-its-own-trucks-as-its-transportation-ambitions-grow [http://perma.cc/8LBF-NCYB]; Leonard, *supra* note 207.

348. Robin Lewis, Amazon's Shipping Ambitions Are Larger than It's Letting On, *Forbes* (April 1, 2016), http://www.forbes.com/sites/robinlewis/2016/04/01/planes-trains-trucks-and-ships/#260c3aa1408c [http://perma.cc/HZ4V-KCLE].

349. Farhad Manjoo, Think Amazon's Drone Idea Is a Gimmick? Think Again, *New York Times* (August 10, 2016), http://www.nytimes.com/2016/08/11/technology/think-amazons-drone-delivery-idea-is-a-gimmick-think-again.html [http://perma.cc/9A7F-VAY6].

350. Ibid.

351. See Del Ray, *supra* note 347; see also Leonard, *supra* note 207 ("Others believe that Amazon will make a business out of its delivery network, as it did with Amazon Web Services, thereby challenging the world's leading shipping companies. . . . The fear has spread to Wall Street, where analysts say investors worry about what Amazon's strategy means for the shipping industry. 'The natural inclination among any observers of the market when they see Amazon is to be scared,' says David Vernon, a Sanford C. Bernstein analyst who tracks the shipping market. 'Amazon is the epitome of a zero-sum game'").

352. A tie is created when a firm requires consumers interested in purchasing good A to purchase good A (the tying good) and good B (the tied good) from the firm. The practice forces an unwilling customer to purchase the tied good while a refusal-to-deal turns away a willing customer. See Einer Elhauge, Tying, Bundled Discounts, and the Death of the Single Monopoly Profit Theorem, *Harvard Law Review* 123 (2009), 397, 466–67.

353. See Will Mitchell, How To Rank Your Products on Amazon—The Ultimate Guide, *StartUpBros*, http://startupbros.com/rank-amazon [http://perma.cc/6X3E-KNHF].

354. "One of the biggest themes is the challenge of getting product to your consumers, and relying on [fulfillment companies], but they don't have another option, they can't make investments [if] Amazon is in fulfillment." Ray, *supra* note 232.

355. Moore, *supra* note 14.

356. See Bensinger, *supra* note 223.

357. See Angus Loten and Adam Janofsky, Sellers Need Amazon, but at What Cost?, *Wall Street Journal* (January 14, 2015), http://www.wsj.com/articles/sellers-need-amazon-but-at-what-cost-1421278220 [http://perma.cc/4MYB-PHQN] ("If you say no to Amazon, you're closing the door on tons of sales").

358. Ibid.

359. Ibid.

360. Greg Bensinger, Competing with Amazon on Amazon, *Wall Street Journal* (June 27, 2012), http://www.wsj.com/articles/SB10001424052702304441404577482902055882264 [http://perma.cc/W9AG-BDRC].

361. Nancee Halpin, Third-Party Merchants Account for More than Three-Quarters of Items Sold on Amazon, *Business Insider* (October 16, 2015), http://www.businessinsider.com/third-party-merchants-drive-amazon-grow-2015-10 [http://perma.cc/5XL9-NTCQ].

362. Loten and Janofsky, *supra* note 357.

363. Bensinger, *supra* note 360.

364. Ibid.

365. Ibid.

366. Ibid.

367. Ibid.

368. Ibid.

369. Spencer Soper, Got a Hot Seller on Amazon? Prepare for E-Tailer To Make One Too, *Bloomberg* (April 20, 2016), http://www.bloomberg.com/news/articles/2016-04-20/got-a-hot-seller-on-amazon-prepare-for-e-tailer-to-make-one-too [http://perma.cc/79GL-5A8E].

370. Ibid (quoting a report by Skubana, an e-commerce company).

371. Ibid.

372. George Anderson, Is Amazon Undercutting Third-Party Sellers Using Their Own Data?, *Forbes* (October 30, 2014), http://www.forbes.com/sites/retailwire/2014/10/30/is-amazon-undercutting-third-party-sellers-using-their-own-data [http://perma.cc/SQE3-SEU8].

373. As one analyst said of Amazon employees, "They're data scientists. They know what people want and they're going to mop it up." Nick Bravo, Amazon Private Labels Threaten Manufacturers, *TrendSource* (July 5, 2016), http://trustedinsight.trendsource.com/trusted-insight-trends/amazon-private-labels-threaten-manufacturers [http://perma.cc/W7VE-LXSS].

374. See Alistair Barr, Amazon Finds Startup Investments in the "Cloud," *Reuters* (November 9, 2011), http://www.reuters.com/article/amazon-cloud-idUSN1E7A727Q20111109 [http://perma.cc/BH4Q-JPW7].

375. Ibid.

376. European antitrust authorities do investigate how concentrated control over data may have anticompetitive effects, and—unlike US antitrust authorities—investigated the Facebook/WhatsApp merger for this reason. Complaints from companies that their rivals are acquiring an unfair competitive advantage through acquiring a firm with huge troves of data may also prompt US authorities to take the exclusionary potential of data more seriously. In September, Salesforce announced it would urge regulators in the United States and in Europe to block Microsoft's bid to acquire LinkedIn, on grounds that the deal would foreclose competition by giving Microsoft too much control over data. See Rachael King, Salesforce.com To Press Regulators To Block Microsoft-LinkedIn Deal, *Wall Street Journal* (September 29, 2016), http://www.wsj.com/articles/salesforce-com-to-press-regulators-to-block-microsoft-linkedin-deal-1475178870 [http://perma.cc/5EZE-GVBC].

377. See David S. Evans, The Antitrust Economics of Multi-Sided Platform Markets, *Yale Journal on Regulations* 20 (2003), 325; King, *supra* note 376; David S. Evans and Richard Schmalensee, The Antitrust Analysis of Multi-Sided Platform Businesses Coase-Sandor Inst. for Law & Econ., Working Paper 623, 2012.

378. See Julian Wright, One-Sided Logic in Two-Sided Markets, *Review of Network Economics* 3 (2004), 44.

379. See David S. Evans, *Platform Economics: Essays on Multi-Sided Business* (2011), 112.

380. Two-sided markets are platforms that have two distinct user groups that offer each other network benefits.

381. See Evans, *supra* note 379, at 112 ("The pricing and investment strategies that firms in twosided markets use to 'get both sides on board' and 'balance the

interests of both sides' raise novel ones. These pricing and other business strategies are needed to solve a fundamental economic problem arising from the interdependency of demand on both sides of the market. In some cases, the product could not even exist without efforts to subsidize one side of the market or the other").

382. Brody Mullins et al., Inside the U.S. Antitrust Probe of Google, *Wall Street Journal* (March 19, 2015), http://www.wsj.com/articles/inside-the-u-s-antitrust-probe-of-google-1426793274 [http://perma.cc/H4PZ-JZ9K].

383. Mark Scott and James Kanter, Google Faces New Round of Antitrust Charges in Europe, *New York Times* (July 14, 2016), http://www.nytimes.com/2016/07/15/technology/google-european-union-antitrust-charges.html [http://perma.cc/2SYP-5Z4B].

384. See *supra* note 319.

385. Stucke and Grunes, *supra* note 47, at 163.

386. This is a form of "scale of data" network effect rather than a "traditional network effect." Ibid at 170.

387. *Novell Inc. v. Microsoft Corp.*, 505 F.3d 302, 308 (4th Cir. 2007).

388. See Guy Rolnik and Asher Schechter, Is the Digital Economy Much Less Competitive than We Think It Is?, *Promarket* (September 23, 2016), http://promarket.org/digital-economy-much-less-competitive-think [http://perma.cc/K2R6-TB7Q].

389. Interestingly, agencies have required vertically merging parties to erect firewalls to prevent anticompetitive use of data. See, for example, *In re* Coca-Cola Co., 150 F.T.C. 520, 2010 WL 9549986 (2010) (ordering Coca-Cola to set up a firewall to ensure that its merger with a bottling subsidiary does not give it access to information from its competitor, Dr. Pepper Snapple Group); Press Release, FTC, FTC Puts Conditions on Coca-Cola's $12.3 Billion Acquisition of its Largest North American Bottler (September 27, 2010), http://www.ftc.gov/news-events/press-releases/2010/09/ftc-puts-conditions-coca-colas-123-billion-acquisition-its [http://perma.cc/BP7U-EY33] (discussing the Coca-Cola settlement and a similar PepsiCo settlement).

390. Mike Shields, Amazon Looms Quietly in Digital Ad Landscape, *Wall Street Journal* (October 6, 2016), http://www.wsj.com/articles/amazon-looms-quietly-in-digital-ad-landscape-1475782113 [http://perma.cc/5ACL-MJ7D].

391. See Eric Newcomer, Uber Draws Fresh Amazon Comparisons as Growth Trumps Profit, *Bloomberg* (July 1, 2015), http://www.bloomberg.com/news/articles/2015-07-01/uber-draws-fresh-comparison-with-amazon-as-growth-trumps-profit [http://perma.cc/AYF9-9RJ7]. Uber does not just lose money in the aggregate by reinvesting more than it generates, but also by pricing rides below what it pays drivers. In other words, it is pricing below its variable costs—which enforcers traditionally read as a sign of predatory pricing. "As anyone who has taken an Uber and talked to the driver knows, sometimes the fare collected from the rider is less than what Uber pays the driver." Ibid.

392. Charles Clover and Leslie Hook, Uber Losing More than $1bn a Year in China, *Financial Times* (February 18, 2016), http://www.ft.com/content/f889f812-d664-11e5-829b-8564e7528e54 [http://perma.cc/6U6P-JQ7Q].

393. "'They're wise to expand as fast as they can,' said Lou Shipley, a lecturer at the MIT Sloan School of Management. 'I would liken it to what Amazon did with books.'" Newcomer, *supra* note 391.

394. Douglas MacMillan and Telis Demos, Uber Valued at More than $50 Billion, *Wall Street Journal* (July 31, 2015), http://www.wsj.com/articles/uber-valued-at-more-than-50-billion-1438367457 [http://perma.cc/T6GW-SY2J].

395. Leslie Hook, Uber Cranks Up Ride-Hailing Battle with $3.5 bn Saudi Investment, *Financial Times* (June 2, 2016), http://www.ft.com/content/3ac7c982-2879-11e6-8b18-91555f2f4fde [http://perma.cc/RXV8-TPBP].

396. Eugene Kim, Billionaire VC Says that Most Companies Will Eventually Pay an Amazon "Tax," *Business Insider* (January 21, 2016), http://www.businessinsider.in/Billionaire-VC-says-that-most-companies-will-eventually-pay-an-Amazon-tax/articleshow/50662558.cms [http://perma.cc/4ZGS-VSL7].

397. The Supreme Court has affirmed the validity of EMH. See *Halliburton Co. v. Erica P. John Fund*, 134 S. Ct. 2398, 2409-11, 2417 (2014).

398. *Horizontal Merger Guidelines*, *supra* note 44, at 4 ("For example, a purchase price in excess of the acquired firm's stand-alone market value may indicate that the acquiring firm is paying a premium because it expects to be able to reduce competition or to achieve efficiencies").

399. Ironically, the logic that is motivating investors—the idea that it is worth encouraging platforms to bleed money to establish a dominant position and capture the market, at which point these firms will be able to recoup those losses—maps onto the logic underpinning current predatory pricing doctrine. The main issue is how narrowly the law currently conceives of recoupment, which does not account for how Amazon can leverage its multiple lines of business.

400. See Tim Hwang and Madeleine Clare Elish, The Mirage of the Marketplace: The Disingenuous Ways Uber Hides Behind Its Algorithm, *Slate* (July 27, 2015), http://www.slate.com/articles/technology/future_tense/2015/07/uber_s_algorithm_and_the_mirage_of_the_marketplace.html [http://perma.cc/B5UR-P9PN].

401. See Felix Salmon, Why the Internet Is Perfect for Price Discrimination, *Reuters* (September 3, 2013), http://blogs.reuters.com/felix-salmon/2013/09/03/why-the-internet-is-perfectfor-price-discrimination [http://perma.cc/NZ4E-SVJJ].

402. See David Singh Grewal, Before Peer Production: Infrastructure Gaps and the Architecture of Openness in Synthetic Biology, *Stanford Technology Law Review* 20 (forthcoming 2017).

403. The Justice Department wrote, "[A]s more retailers purchase Bazaarvoice's PRR platform, the Bazaarvoice network becomes more valuable for manufacturers because it will allow . . . them to syndicate content to a greater number of retail outlets. The feedback between the manufacturers and retailers creates a network effect that is a significant and durable competitive advantage for Bazaarvoice." Complaint

at 18, *United States v. Bazaarvoice, Inc.*, No. 13-0133 2014 (N.D. Cal. Jan. 10, 2013), 2014 WL 203966.

404. Terrell McSweeny, Comm'r, FTC, Remarks to the U.S. Chamber of Commerce at TecNation 2016 (September 20, 2016), http://www.ftc.gov/system/files/documents/public_statements/985773/mcsweeny_-_tecnation_2016_9-20-16.pdf [http://perma.cc/N7GA-YN5P].

405. See *supra* section titled "Predatory Pricing."

406. See Stucke, *supra* note 38; *Horizontal Merger Guidelines*, *supra* note 44, at 2.

407. See K. Sabeel Rahman and Lina Khan, Restoring Competition in the U.S. Economy, in *Untamed: How to Check Corporate, Financial, and Monopoly Power* (Nell Abernathy et al. eds., 2016), 18.

408. See Leslie, *supra* note 94, at 1753.

409. See ibid at 1759.

410. Ibid at 1758.

411. Admittedly, this approach would not reach vertical integration that arose due to internal expansion. That type of vertical integration could be covered by the prophylactic approach discussed later.

412. For a list of FTC thresholds, see Revised Jurisdictional Thresholds for Section 7A of the Clayton Act, 81 Fed. Reg. 4,299 (January 26, 2016).

413. See Stucke and Grunes, *supra* note 47, at 74.

414. For some of the potential concerns raised by this deal, see Kevin Carty, Will Uber Rouse the Trustbusters?, *Slate* (August 9, 2016), http://www.slate.com/articles/technology/future_tense/2016/08/uber_s_deal_with_didi_chuxing_could_open_it_up_to_antitrust_scrutiny.html [http://perma.cc/F4NT-AYRZ].

415. See ibid. See generally Stucke and Grunes, *supra* note 47 (analyzing how Big Data issues relate to competition laws and policy).

416. See, for example, Scott and Kanter, *supra* note 383; Benjamin Edelman and Damien Geradin, Android and Competition Law: Exploring and Assessing Google's Practices in Mobile Harvard Bus. Sch. Negotiation, Orgs. & Mkts. Unit, Working Paper No. 17-018, 2016, 1–2, http://ssrn.com/abstract=2833476 [http://perma.cc/7JA6-RXPN].

417. This is a version of the "Separations Principle" that Tim Wu recommends for information industries. Wu, *supra* note 316, at 305 ("More than anything else, the preceding chapters chronicle the corrupting effects of vertically integrated power. A strong stake in more than one layer of the industry leaves a firm in a position of inherent conflict of interest. You can not serve two masters, and the objectives of creating information are often at odds with those of disseminating it. That is the very first reason for the Separations Principle").

418. See *supra* section titled "Amazon Marketplace and Exploiting Data."

419. This prophylactic approach has also been applied in the power industry. For example, in 1996, the Federal Energy Regulatory Commission issued a mandate requiring vertically integrated utilities to "functionally separate their generation, transmission, and distribution business, and provide transmission access to all

generators on transparent, nondiscriminatory terms." Sandeep Vaheesan, Reviving an Epithet: A New Way Forward for the Essential Facilities Doctrine, *Utah Law Review* 3 (2010), 911, 927.

420. See, for example, Saule T. Omarova, The Merchants of Wall Street: Banking, Commerce, and Commodities, *Minnesota Law Review* 98 (2013), 265, 268, 274–75; Bernard Shull, Banking and Commerce in the United States, *Journal of Banking and Finance* 18 (1994), 255, 267; Bernard Shull, The Separation of Banking and Commerce in the United States: An Examination of Principal Issues, *Financial Markets, Institutions & Instruments* 8 (1999), 1.

421. Omarova, *supra* note 420, at 268.

422. Bank Holding Company Act of 1956, Pub. L. No. 84-511, § 4, 70 Stat. 133, 135-37 (codified as amended at 12 U.S.C. §§ 1841-48 [2012]).

423. Omarova, *supra* note 420, at 268 (citing 12 U.S.C. § 1843(k)(1)(A)).

424. Ibid at 275.

425. See ibid at 275–76.

426. Ibid at 276.

427. Ibid.

428. Ibid at 275–77. Notably, several banking regulations that previously sought to prevent concentration of systemic risk in our financial system were repealed by Congress in the 1990s— leading in part to the "too-big-to-fail" crisis. See Johnson and Kwak, *supra* note 179.

429. See Sara E. Needleman and Greg Bensinger, Small Businesses Are Finding an Unlikely Banker: Amazon, *Wall Street Journal* (October 4, 2012), http://www.wsj.com/articles/SB10000872396390443493304578034103049644978 [http://perma.cc/PUH8-XFKS]; Eric Newcomer and Olivia Zaleski, Inside Uber's Auto-Lease Machine, Where Almost Anyone Can Get a Car, *Bloomberg* (May 31, 2016), http://www.bloomberg.com/news/articles/2016-05-31/inside-uber-s-auto-lease-machine-where-almost-anyone-can-get-a-car [http://perma.cc/A7AM-VZRJ]; Richard Waters and Barney Jopson, Google Makes First Foray into Credit Business, *Financial Times* (October 7, 2012), http://www.ft.com/content/55be35f2-1093-11e2-a5f7-00144feabdc0 [http://perma.cc/NC6P-2EEG].

430. Chris Isidore, Target: Hacking Hit up to 110 Million Customers, *CNN Money* (January 11, 2014), http://money.cnn.com/2014/01/10/news/companies/target-hacking [http://perma.cc/D6W3-TM75].

431. There have been some policy debates about whether Google should be considered "critical infrastructure." See, for example, Eric Engleman, Google Exception in Obama's Cyber Order Questioned as Unwise Gap, *Bloomberg* (March 5, 2013), http://www.bloomberg.com/news/articles/2013-03-05/google-exception-in-obama-s-cyber-order-questioned-as-unwise-gap [http://perma.cc/5Z2M-HVU3]. That debate has not yet extended to Amazon, but—given the growth of Amazon Web Services—it may be appropriate.

432. That platforms' concentration of economic power also concentrates political power is becoming increasingly evident. Amazon, Google, and Uber have all

shifted regulatory debates and—in some cases—directly shaped outcomes. See Liam Dillon, Uber and Lyft Are Winning at the State Capitol—Here's Why, *L.A. Times* (May 7, 2016), http:// www.latimes.com/politics/la-pol-sac-why-uber-is-winning-in-california-20160507-snap-htmlstory.html [http://perma.cc/7BRX-F39U]; Peter Elkind and Doris Burke, Amazon's (Not So Secret) War on Taxes, *Fortune* (May 23, 2013), http://fortune.com/2013 /05/23/amazons-not-so-secret-war-on-taxes [http://perma.cc/LN8G-GTNN]; Simon Marks and Harry Davies, Revealed: How Google Enlisted Members of US Congress It Bankrolled To Fight $6bn EU Antitrust Case, *Guardian* (December 17, 2015), http:// www.theguardian.com/world/2015/dec/17/google-lobbyists-congress-antitrust-brussels-eu [http://perma.cc/NLA7-KNVC]; Anna Palmer and Scott Wong, Lobbying Drives Uber's Expansion, *Politico* (September 18, 2013), http:// www.politico.com/story/2013/09/uber-taxi-lobbying-expansion-097028 [http://perma.cc/B3LA-7WUD]; Sam Jewler and Taylor Lincoln, Mission Creep-y: Google Is Quietly Becoming One of the Nation's Most Powerful Political Forces While Expanding Its Information-Collection Empire, *Public Citizen* (November 2014), http://www.citizen.org/documents/Google-Political-Spending-Mission-Creepy.pdf [http://perma.cc/83QR-X3PA]; Martin Moore, Tech Giants and Civil Power, *Centre for the Study of Media, Communication and Power* (April 2016), http:// www.kcl.ac.uk/sspp/policy-institute/CMCP/Tech-Giants-and-Civic-Power.pdf [http:// perma .cc/D76X-NALM].

433. See LaVecchia and Mitchell, *supra* note 6; Barry C. Lynn, Killing the Competition: How New Monopolies Are Destroying Open Markets, *Harper's Magazine* (February 2012), 27.

434. William Boyd, Public Utility and the Low-Carbon Future, *UCLA Law Review* 61 (2014), 1614, 1616.

435. Ibid at 1643.

436. See Christopher Leslie, Antitrust Law as Public Interest Law, *U.C. Irvine Law Review* 2 (2012), 885, 887.

437. 94 U.S. 113 (1877).

438. Ibid at 126.

439. Ibid at 130.

440. Ibid.

441. Boyd, *supra* note 434, at 1635.

442. Ibid at 1643.

443. See K. Sabeel Rahman, From Railroad to Uber: Curbing the New Corporate Power, *Boston Review* (May 4, 2015), http://bostonreview.net/forum/k-sabeel-rahman-curbing-new-corporate-power [http://perma.cc/Y6TU-E449]; K. Sabeel Rahman, Private Power and Public Purpose: The Public Utility Concept and the Future of Corporate Law in the New Gilded Age, Address at the Association of American Law Schools' 110th Annual Meeting (January 8, 2016) (transcript on file with author).

444. Net neutrality is a form of common carrier regime. For an exposition of why net neutrality and search neutrality should apply to major platforms, see Frank

Pasquale, Internet Nondiscrimination Principles: Commercial Ethics for Carriers and Search Engines, *University of Chicago Legal Forum* (2008), 263.

445. A "fair return" has been variously defined. For an overview of public utility regulatory regimes, see William A. Prendergast, *Public Utilities and the People* (1933), 2 ("What is a utility? . . . It is commonly used to denote a business the product or use of which serves the public generally. . . . [It is] a business which cannot choose its clients or customers").

446. I am indebted to David Kim for making this connection at the *Yale Law Journal* Author Seminar Workshop on October 12, 2016.

447. Boyd, *supra* note 434, at 1656.

448. *Open Internet*, Federal Communications Commission, http://www.fcc.gov/general/open-internet [http://perma.cc/ZL6S-6Q38].

449. Vaheesan, *supra* note 419, at 911.

450. 708 F.2d 1081, 1132-33 (7th Cir. 1982).

451. Ibid. This last factor allows for efficiency defenses.

452. Vaheesan, *supra* note 419, at 921.

453. Ibid at 918 (citing Marianna Lao, Networks, Access, and "Essential Facilities," *SMU Law Review* 62 [2009], 557). The three cases that Vaheesan identifies are *United States v. Terminal Railroad Ass'n*, 224 U.S. 383 (1912); *United States v. Associated Press*, 326 U.S. 1 (1945); and *Otter Tail Power Co. v. United States*, 410 U.S. 366 (1973).

454. See *Verizon Commc'ns Inc. v. Law Offices of Curtis V. Trinko, LLP*, 540 U.S. 398, 410 (2004).

455. See Brett Frischmann and Spencer Weber Waller, Revitalizing Essential Facilities, *Antitrust Law Journal* 75 (2008), 1, 3.

456. Ibid at 4.

457. For more pieces grappling with the possibility of applying the "essential facilities" doctrine to internet platforms, see Frank Pasquale, Dominant Search Engines: An Essential Cultural & Political Facility, in *The Next Digital Decade* (Berin Szoka et al. eds., 2011), 401; and Zachary Abrahamson, Comment, Essential Data, *Yale Law Journal* 124 (2014), 576.

458. See a Giant Problem, *Economist* (September 17, 2016), http://www.economist.com/news/leaders/21707210-rise-corporate-colossus-threatens-both-competition-and-legitimacy-business [http://perma.cc/DNN2-YKL3] ("[T]he most striking feature of business today is . . . the entrenchment of a group of superstar companies at the heart of the global economy. . . . But they have two big faults. They are squashing competition, and they are using the darker arts of management to stay ahead"); Davidoff Solomon, *supra* note 319.

459. In a striking speech welcoming the public and political attention toward antitrust, Assistant Attorney General for Antitrust Renata Hesse stated, "Antitrust is too important to be left solely in the hands of antitrust experts." Renata Hesse, Assistant Att'y Gen., Antitrust Div., Dep't of Justice, Remarks at the 2016 Global Antitrust Enforcement Symposium: And Never the Twain Shall Meet? Connecting

Popular and Professional Visions for Antitrust Enforcement (September 20, 2016), http://www.justice.gov/opa/speech/acting-assistant-attorney-general-renata-hesse-antitrust-division-delivers-opening [http://perma.cc/84E6-H4JB].

460. Theo Francis and Ryan Knutson, Wave of Megadeals Tests Antitrust Limits in U.S., *Wall Street Journal* (October 18, 2015), http://www.wsj.com/articles/wave-of-megadeals-tests-antitrust-limits-in-u-s-1445213306 [http://perma.cc/WA8J-ATZT].

461. Too Much of a Good Thing, *Economist* (March 26, 2016), http://www.economist.com/news/briefing/21695385-profits-are-too-high-america-needs-giant-dose-competition-too-much-good-thing [http://perma.cc/4YPA-G3HB].

462. See Eduardo Porter, With Competition in Tatters, the Rip of Inequality Widens, *New York Times* (July 12, 2016), http://www.nytimes.com/2016/07/13/business/economy/antitrust-competition-inequality.html [http://perma.cc/8Z8A-KCFJ]; America's Monopoly Problem, *New America*, http://www.newamerica.org/open-markets/events/americas-monopoly-problem [http://perma.cc/64YF-6KZV]; Marc Jarsulic et al., Reviving Antitrust, *Center for American Progress* (June 29, 2016), http://www.americanprogress.org/issues/economy/report/2016/06/29/140613/reviving-antitrust [http://perma.cc/QCV8-52TV]; Making Antitrust Work for the 21st Century, *Center for Equitable Growth*, http://equitablegrowth.org/event/making-antitrust-work-for-the-21st-century [http://perma.cc/HAX7-BRK2]; Untamed: How To Check Corporate, Financial, and Monopoly Power, *Roosevelt Institute* (2016), http://rooseveltinstitute.org/wp-content/uploads/2016/06/Untamed-Final-Single-Pages.pdf [http://perma.cc/FM9R-DXJJ].

463. See Neil Irwin, Liberal Economists Think Big Companies Are Too Powerful. Hillary Clinton Agrees, *New York Times* (October 4, 2016), http://www.nytimes.com/2016/10/05/upshot/liberal-economists-think-big-companies-are-too-powerful-hillary-clinton-agrees.html [http://perma.cc/WXA9-RX2J]; Hillary Clinton's Vision for an Economy Where Our Businesses, Our Workers, and Our Consumers Grow and Prosper Together, *Hillary Clinton*, http://www.hillaryclinton.com/briefing/factsheets/2016/10/03/hillary-clintons-vision-for-an-economy-where-our-businesses-our-workers-and-our-consumers-grow-and-prosper-together [http://perma.cc/2EHG-PT9Z] ("Promote Free and Fair Competition and Stopping Big Businesses from Hurting Small Businesses").

464. One of the most striking aspects of Hesse's speech is that she distances herself from a strict consumer-welfare-based approach—departing from current orthodoxy:

But, although we believe competition maximizes consumer welfare, the ultimate standard by which we judge practices is their effect on competition, not on consumer welfare. It is certainly relevant when a merger will lead to higher prices and reduced output because these results are hallmarks of reduced competition. But the law instructs us to examine whether a merger may substantially lessen competition and that means we must sometimes look to other evidence of harm to competition. Hesse, *supra* note 459.

CHAPTER TWO

~

Amazon 1-Click and the Value of Broken Infrastructure

Ulysses Pascal

What hides behind the modern aphorism that infrastructure is invisible until it breaks, is that infrastructure broken for some is infrastructure working for others. Susan Leigh Star popularized the idea that "the normally invisible quality of a working infrastructure becomes visible when it breaks" the same year that Amazon obtained a patent for the "Buy Now with 1-Click" button (Star, 1999; Hartmann, 1999). Though Star did not intend to describe Amazon, her proposition is operationalized in Amazon's obsession with seamless user experience design. Few of Amazon's three hundred million customers concern themselves with the processes put into action when the 1-Click button is pressed. As a patented technology that mediates 82 percent of sales on Amazon, the 1-Click button is emblematic of the invisibilized infrastructures that support Amazon's monopoly on value realization. The invisibility of the infrastructure is not testament to its working. Among Star's less cited passages is the idea that "one person's infrastructure" may be another's "difficulty" (Star 1999). In the case of Amazon, brokenness is not merely a technical inconvenience or occasional failure. Brokenness is a perpetual condition of the platform's power and profitability. Under platform capitalism, Amazon's control over the infrastructures that mediate the realization of value enable Amazon to profit from infrastructural breakdown.

Value realization is the stage in the circuit of capital accumulation where the value latent in commodities is transformed into money (Marx [1885], 1978). The valorization of commodities is not automatic—it requires infrastructures. It requires means of value realization. The 1-Click button is an emblematic component of Amazon's ownership of the means of value realization insofar as it structures the conditions of sales and purchases on the platform. The patent for the 1-Click button describes the feature as "A method and system for placing an order to purchase an item via the Internet" (Hartmann, 1999). The system collates information pertaining to user identity, billing information, shipment address, and the purchase order, enabling a remote server to process the transaction with a minimal number of clicks. In addition to data entered by the user, the server collects behavioral data regarding user preferences to train its algorithmic recommendation system. The possibility of using the 1-Click button is conditioned by a network of interlocking infrastructures for managing third-party sellers, products, and users. Though the promise of "one click" suggests an immediacy between product and user, invisiblized infrastructures mediate the production and distribution of goods.

When the 1-Click button is pressed, the order is received, processed, and packed at warehouses called Fulfillment Centers. When I took a tour of Amazon's Fulfillment Center, the first thing that surprised me was not the enormous size, densely packed aisles, nor the terse "Leadership Principles" such as "Customer Obsession," "Bias for Action," and "Frugality" posted on the walls. I was struck by how deafeningly loud it is inside. Amazon warehouses are so loud that without wearing earmuffs, radio receivers, and a microphone, we could not have discerned each other's voices. In the context of this noise, our guide gestured to the sign indicating how many days it has been since the last accident. Such accidents have become an unavoidable outcome of Amazon's business practices. The Strategic Organizing Center (2021) reports that the rate of accidents at Amazon Fulfillment Centers is 80 percent higher than at competing warehouses.

If infrastructure is that which becomes visible when it breaks, how can we make sense of infrastructures, platforms, and supply chains that "work"—at least for shareholders—because they are broken for everyone else? To begin to answer this question it is important to return to the source of Star's argument. The notion that infrastructure becomes visible when it breaks makes subtle reference to Heidegger's argument that a tool is invisible when it works. By calling infrastructure "ready-to-hand," Star alludes to Heidegger (Star, 1999, 380). For Heidegger, when a hammer is ready-to-hand, "its everyday presence has been so obvious that we have never taken notice of it" (Heidegger, [1927] 2001, 105). To understand the relation between invisibility and breakdown, we should question whether Heidegger's philosophy of the hammer scales to the infrastructures of platform capitalism.

To study the relationship between breakdown and infrastructure under platform capitalism, I trace how commoditized hammers are produced and distributed by third-party sellers on Amazon Marketplace. As hammers move through the logistical chains hidden by Amazon's seamless user interface, hammers produce what Zuboff terms behavioral surplus data (Zuboff, 2019, 17). Such data comes to inform third-party sellers, Amazon's algorithms, and the shapes that hammers now take. By addressing how a hammer is shaped and reshaped under the pressures of a hammer's movement through production, distribution, and marketing, I show how the heuristic of infrastructural invisibility fails to reveal how platforms profit from the broken infrastructures that they obscure. Amazon's Marketplace platform profits from the control of the sited conduits, linkages, and channels that data must pass through for value to be realized, and this control enables Amazon to use breakdowns in infrastructure to its advantage.

From "Ready-to-Hand" to "Just-in-Time"

Heidegger's concept of being "ready-to-hand" is only concerned with the hand of the hammer's wielder, not the hands of numerous workers the hammer passes through before it is wielded. Hammers are not only tools for hammering. Hammers are commodities produced for profit and are thereby subject to the logistics of production and distribution. During the Industrial Revolution, Marx observed that "500 varieties of hammers are produced . . . in Birmingham alone" (Marx, [1867] 1976, 460). According to Marx, hammers took on so many unique affordances because "labour can only be drained off if capital assumes the shape of the means of production required for the particular labour process in question" (Marx, [1867] 1976, 1007). Now, a search for "hammer" will produce over twenty thousand product listings (Amazon, 2021a).

Unlike the claw hammers, sledgehammers, and ball-peen hammers produced as commodities during the Industrial Revolution, the hammers on Amazon are not all designed for hammering. On Amazon Marketplace you can find hammers designed as a Father's Day gift, hammers for cosplaying as comic book heroes, and numerous low-quality, stubby, eight-ounce hammers ill-suited for hammering. If, under the Industrial Revolution, the efficiency of exploitation is contingent on the shape of industrial tools, then what shape should a tool take under platform capitalism?

Like other platforms whose power is grounded in the control of data flows, Amazon's relationship to production is what Wark terms "vectorialist" (Wark, 2019). For Wark, vectoralists are the titans of the information age, whose power renders information scarce through the control over the networks, infrastructures, and platforms of media communication. But the term "vector" suggests something broader: the class with the rights and powers over all the sited conduits, paths, and linkages that enable the transformation of surplus-value into profit. A vector is a means of value realization. The ownership of the means of value realization does not imply the end of the ownership of capital, but rather its intensification, its fracturing, and its reorganization along vectors that constrain the flow of products and services. If Wark's thesis is right, Marx's observation that the efficiency of exploitation is contingent on the shape of the means of production should be updated. We should not expect that hammers will be designed for productive efficiency. Under the pressures of platform capitalism, hammers will be molded to the particularities of value realization.

Within Amazon's platform, a hammer only works if it produces a profit, regardless of whether it affords hammering. From the perspective of a platform, the possibility that a hammer could be used to hammer is incidental to the accumulation of capital. Under platform capitalism, a hammer must conform to the requirements of global logistics chains and the rules defined by the platform itself. Before a hammer can be wieldable, it must be brandable, sampleable, reproducible, shippable, trackable, storable, packageable, reviewable, and itemizable. A hammer must be made "just-in-time" before it can be made "ready-to-hand." It is more likely for a product to be taken down because the background of the product photo fails to adhere to Amazon image guidelines of "pure white (RGB 255, 255, 255)" than because the product is defective (Amazon, 2021e). Whereas hammers produced in Birmingham were designed to increase the efficiency of labor, the hammers now listed on Amazon are designed to be bought with 1-Click.

In the search for product niches well suited for Amazon Marketplace, third-party sellers rely on research tools specifically designed to aid in the discovery of potentially profitable products. Data generated by pressing the 1-Click button on Amazon are aggregated by auxiliary platforms such as Jungle Scout. The product research tool is built around the mythos of "Jungle Sticks"—a product that repackages generic bamboo sticks as bespoke marshmallow roasters for Amazon Marketplace. The concept that a generic product can gain value from being resold as a branded innovation forms the basis of an industry that scrapes data from Amazon's product pages, often enlisting user-installed browser extensions or the Amazon Selling Partner API to collect data on the brand, weight, size, revenues, and reviews of products. Amazon's documentation describes the Selling Partner API as a system that allows merchants to "programmatically access their data on listings, orders, payments, reports, and more" (Amazon, 2021h). One research platform discloses that: "Our database is populated by users searching our site and by users of our browser extensions. Even so, we monitor the prices of about 6 million Amazon products across 9 different locales" (CamelCamelCamel, 2021b). Amazon encourages this activity. In fact, research platforms like Jungle Scout are named "Technology Partners" in Amazon's partner network. With data collected on millions of products, these tools are designed to make third-party sellers see opportunity in Amazon's Marketplace.

Research platforms use data scraped from Amazon to compute metrics of potential profitability. For example, an "Opportunity Score" compresses data on the demand, competition, and profit margins into a single number. Jungle Scout describes the "Opportunity Score" as an "algorithm graded on a scale of 1-10 where 10 is the highes [*sic*] opportunity and 1 is the lowest" (Jungle Scout, 2020b). The sales category of "hammers" received an opportunity score of three, indicating that the market is likely too crowded for new entrants to find profits. By experimenting with different search queries, product researchers are led to believe that they can discover categories with more "opportunity." With data produced from Amazon transaction history, research tools supply Amazon with aspirational entrepreneurs called third-party sellers.

Supply Chain Arbitrage

Third-party sellers are rarely manufacturers. Often, third-party sellers are supply-chain arbitrageurs who seek to capture the difference in prices between two markets by reselling generic goods as if they are unique branded products. In the community of YouTubers, Discord servers, and unaccredited online academies devoted to gaming the operating logic of Amazon Marketplace, this practice is called "private labeling." The goal is to find low weight and easily reproducible products that can be cheaply shipped from overseas manufacturers and resold at markup prices.

Materially, private labeling entails purchasing generic products from manufacturers on Alibaba and reselling the same item as a unique branded product on Amazon. In addition to established name-brand hammers, Amazon search results for "hammer" contain a preponderance of generic, small, stubby, eight-ounce hammers listed under unknown trademarks. The price of a generic hammer on Amazon is $9.72. The same "Spifflyer 8 Ounce Small Claw Hammer" is as low as $0.70 a unit on Alibaba. The difference, $9.02—a 1,288.57 percent markup—is split between freight forwarders, third-party sellers, and Amazon. Amazon profits from the sales of third-party merchants, either directly through a $0.99 charge on each item sold, or indirectly through a $39.99 monthly subscription plus additional fees, such as fulfillment fees, inventory storage fees, and a 15 to 20 percent referral fee on every product sold (Amazon, 2021c). These *faux frais* are accounted for as expenses for third-party sellers but they "constitute sources of enrichment" for Amazon (see Marx, [1885] 1978, 214). Fifty-four percent of Amazon's $386 billion revenue was fueled by its third-party sellers in 2020 (Jungle Scout, 2021).

"No Alternative Sellers"

To make third-party products trackable, scannable, indexable, and retrievable on Amazon's platform, Amazon mandates that resellers purchase universal product codes (UPCs). UPCs are algorithmically generated codes used to uniquely identify products. Every unique product is given a UPC. For example, the UPC of the "Spifflyer 8 Ounce Small Claw Hammer" is 605826466346. Though there are multiple listings of the same generic eight-ounce hammer on Amazon, each product page is associated with a different UPC. By assigning unique product codes to otherwise generic products, Amazon's algorithm concludes that there are "no alternative sellers" for the product. Even products with the exact same design and provenance can be registered as different products simply by assigning different UPCs to them.

If Amazon's algorithm treated generic hammers as if they were multiple instances of the same product, then the sellers would all be listed on the same product page. For third-party sellers, such an outcome is undesirable because only one of the seller's products can be associated with the 1-Click button. If multiple sellers are associated with one product page, an algorithm determines which seller will be compensated when a user presses the 1-Click button. The algorithm that determines the winner considers several variables, such as price, fulfillment by Amazon, and seller reputation. Using these variables, sellers compete to be the account associated with the 1-Click button because customers rarely buy from alternate sellers.

By manipulating the product metadata to make generic products nominally distinct, sellers avoid competing over the 1-Click button. When generic products are listed on Amazon with unique product identifiers, these products receive their own product pages. Sellers with their own product pages are associated with the 1-Click button by default. Using data scraped from Amazon, I calculated the number of alternative sellers on every product page from the first five pages of results for hammers. As seen in the figure, most hammers are listed as having no alternative sellers, despite being variations of the same generic, stubby, eight-ounce hammer from Alibaba.

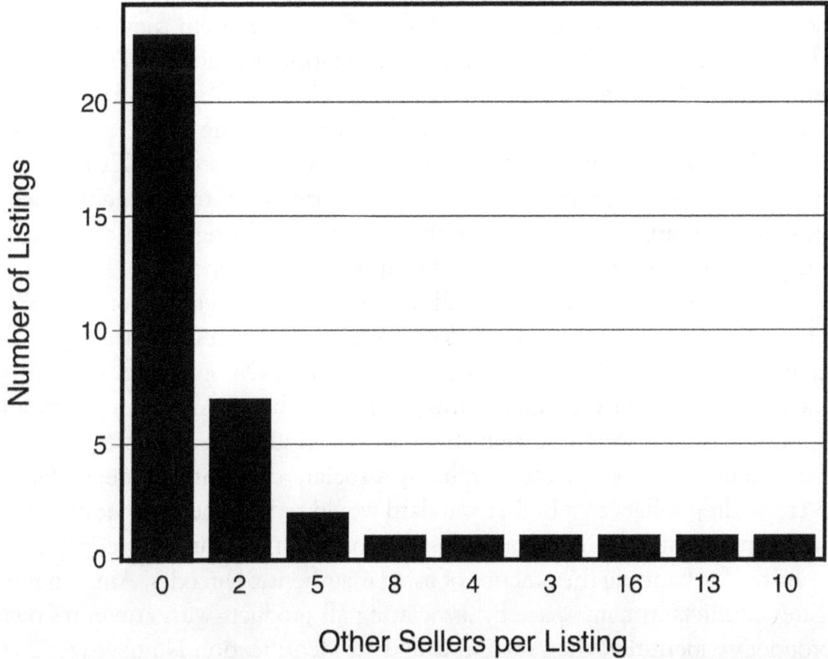

Figure 2.1. Number of "Other Sellers" for products listed in the five pages of Amazon search results for the keyword "hammer."

Instead of competing on price within a single product page, sellers compete for reviews, ratings, and reputation in Amazon search rankings. In a search for "hammer," as for any other product on Amazon, the first results are not the cheapest, but those with the highest ratings from the most customers. Under this system, the use-value of a hammer is subordinated to a brand's need to maintain positive reviews. Such a mechanism is easily gamed by paid reviewers or schemes that combine multiple different products under one heading. Though this system is broken for users who expect the same generic products to share the same price, it is convenient for Amazon, whose revenue is a percentage of the sales price.

An Algorithmic State of Exception

When searching for a hammer on Amazon, a customer is confronted by an overwhelming number of generic products and knockoffs that resemble higher quality name brand hammers. The proliferation of products is allowed because Amazon is capricious when it comes to the enforcement of its product identification guidelines. Amazon's third-party seller guidelines state that "sellers must use the correct product identifier for the item they are listing. The use of false product identification information, including UPC codes, is prohibited" (Amazon, 2021e). Authentic UPCs from GS1 cost $250 (GS1, 2021). For third-party sellers, one of the largest startup costs, other than establishing inventory, can be purchasing barcodes (James, 2020). If 341 million third-party products are sold on Amazon, the requirement placed on sellers amounts to externalizing the cost of legitimizing inventory by outsourcing over eighty-five billion dollars in UPC fees alone.

In practice, sellers have been allowed to offset the burden of the UPC requirement by purchasing the codes from gray market resellers that specialize in recycling the identifiers of obsolete products. On one hand, the proliferation of inauthentic UPCs has the potential to break Amazon's databases. If multiple sellers were to assign the same resold UPC to multiple products, the system would be unable to reliably associate data with products. However, holding sellers to a higher standard would reduce the number of sellers on the platform, costing Amazon lost revenue from fees and subscriptions.

Instead of banning the practice of using inauthentic barcodes, Amazon mitigates conflicts in namespace by associating all products with Amazon's own proprietary identifier, the Amazon Standard Identification Number (ASIN). On product pages for hammers, it is the ASIN that is listed, not the UPC. The strategy of balancing the requirement for UPCs with the use of ASINs increases the supply of third-party merchandise because sellers are *de facto* allowed to use inauthentic UPCs irrespective of what the guidelines stipulate.

The uncertainty around UPC enforcement generates a state of algorithmic exception. Amazon is known to suspend accounts without warning: "76% of sellers are concerned about Amazon shutting down their account without reason" (Jungle Scout, 2020b). However, violation of Amazon's policies does not necessarily lead to suspension. The backlog of illegitimate product listings functions like a reserve Amazon can draw upon when it is expedient. Amazon has the authority to suspend the accounts that rely on gray market UPCs, but Amazon has little incentive to do so. Not only do illegitimate sellers generate revenue for Amazon through fees, but the promise of policing knockoff sellers can also be used to entice name brands to route their commerce through Amazon's servers. Using knockoff products as leverage, Amazon gains power over the owners of brands, trademarks, and other intellectual property, enabling the extraction of valuable customer data on popular products and the monetization of large-scale orders with merchant fees (Barnett, 2020). For Amazon, the breakdown in product authentication infrastructure becomes a source of revenue, data, and control.

Means of Value Realization

By outsourcing production and product procurement to overseas manufacturers and third-party merchants, Amazon owns neither the means of production nor the bulk of the commodities sold on the platform. Amazon owns the means of value realization. Amazon owns what Srnicek (2017) calls the "bare extractive minimum." In the case of Amazon, the 1-Click button epitomizes the bare extractive minimum as a simple component of the market that over 80 percent of orders must pass through to be valorized.

Owning the means of value realization grants Amazon the power to compel third-party sellers to pay merchant fees and to subscribe to services offered by Amazon. Sellers that fail to align their business with Amazon's algorithmic policies can be denied access to the means of value realization. One service that sellers are incentivized to purchase is "Fulfillment by Amazon" (FBA). Amazon marketing material describes FBA as a solution to problems of logistics and scale. With FBA, "you store your products in Amazon's fulfillment centers, and we pick, pack, ship, and provide customer service for these products. FBA can help you scale your business and reach more customers" (Amazon, 2021c). Though FBA is not obligatory, the algorithm that computes which sellers are associated with the 1-Click button prioritizes sellers who subscribe to FBA.

Taken at its word, FBA functions as the "machine" Marx envisioned when he wrote "One merchant . . . may, by way of his operations, shorten the buying and selling time for many producers. He should then be considered as a machine that reduces the expenditure of useless energy, or helps to set free production time" (Marx, [1885] 1978, 209). This machine is a cost taken out of the value of production. In exchange for monthly membership fees, Amazon grants third-party merchants access to its logistical platform—a "machine" for product listing, warehousing, and delivery. According to Amazon's online cost calculator, a hammer sold for $9.72 can be charged $4.09 in fees, that is 42 percent of the sales price (Amazon, 2021d; see Chen et al., 2016). The substantial fee to access means of value realization prompts the question of whether the machine is in service of the merchants, or if the merchant's activity is in service of the machine.

If Amazon's infrastructure is to be regarded as a machine, it cannot be reduced to a machine for scaling the efficiency of merchant trade or reducing the expenditure of useless energy. Unlike a machine taken out of the cost of production, Amazon competes directly against the merchants it claims to support. During the congressional hearings on Big Tech and antitrust, senators pressed Jeff Bezos about Amazon's practices (House Judiciary Subcommittee on Antitrust Law, 2020). Senators were concerned that Amazon plays a "dual role" as both "marketplace operator and marketplace merchant" (Khan, 2019). Unlike the ideal-typical "multi-sided markets" described in economics textbooks where the role of broker and seller is played by different actors, Amazon plays the role of both. This is true in the market for hammers as well as in numerous other product categories. In the search results for "hammer," Amazon gives a section of the first page search results to "Amazon Basics" brand hammers—Amazon's own private label.

Amazon's private label business is supported by data collected through third-party sales on the platform (Amazon, 2021b). When the 1-Click button is pressed, Amazon keeps track of the fastest-growing product categories and users' purchasing behavior. After Jeff Bezos claimed, "we have a policy against using seller specific data to aid our private label business," he added that he "can't guarantee you that that policy has never been violated" (House Judiciary Subcommittee on Antitrust Law, 2020). Investigators have been able to confirm that the policy was indeed violated (Mattioli, 2020; Mattioli and Lombardo, 2020). Furthermore, 53 percent of sellers say, "Amazon sells its own products that directly compete with the seller's" (Jungle Scout, 2020a).

By maintaining control over the data generated from clicking the 1-Click button, Amazon can collect behavioral data about which products users will buy and which products they will avoid, while denying the same level of information to the third-party sellers on the platform. Not only can Amazon use this data to generate their own version of merchandise to compete against third-party sellers, but Amazon's control over the platform enables Amazon to systematically rank their products higher in search results. For example, in the product category of hammer, an Amazon Basics brand hammer is always in the first page of results.

The structural advantage accrued to Amazon is exacerbated by the terms and conditions of the platform. As a condition of participation, sellers relinquish access to data needed to communicate with their customers, such as email address and phone number. When a third-party seller signs up for a merchant account, the terms of agreement stipulate that "all Confidential Information will remain Amazon's exclusive property" (Amazon, 2021b). Here, "Confidential Information" is defined as information relating to Amazon customers "that is not known to the general public including, but not limited to, any information identifying or unique to specific customers, reports, insights, and other information about the services." Failure to comply with Amazon's communication policy may result in "a suspension of selling privileges in Amazon stores" (Amazon, 2022).

The asymmetry in data access allows Amazon to function as what Pistor (2020) termed a "data controller." Amazon uses sellers to collect data; it does not share data on equal terms. Amazon denies sellers the power to assetize user engagement by maintaining control over the vectors that link users to the platform (see Birch et al., 2021). Without access to the data needed to reach customers outside of the platform, sellers are locked into Amazon's Marketplace (Matsakis, 2019). These barriers to growth are reminiscent of Star's observation that stairs may seem like suitable infrastructures for climbing, but "for the person in a wheelchair, the stairs and doorjamb in front of a building are not seamless subtenders of use, but barriers" (Star, 1999). Just as Star argues that what works as infrastructure to some functions as barriers to others, the algorithmic processes behind the 1-Click button work for Amazon at the expense of third-party sellers.

Conclusion

Amazon profits from broken infrastructures. Amazon Marketplace is mediated by interlocking infrastructures for user data collection, payment processing, and product listing. Though these infrastructures are invisibilized to the consumer by the seamless user interface of the 1-Click button, the invisibility of these infrastructures should not be mistaken for the infrastructure's working.

The power to profit from broken infrastructure is built on Amazon's control over the means of value realization: the infrastructural vectors underpinning the sale and purchase of products on the platform. Owing to Amazon's control over the means of value realization, Amazon extracts fees from third-party sellers. These fees can be accounted for as *faux frais* taken out of the cost of production—as if Amazon were a machine designed to help scale businesses. Yet Amazon is more than a machine for putting third-party sellers in touch with customers. Amazon manages the relationship between sellers and customers through algorithmic incentives and platform policies. The 1-Click button is at the center of the power relationship between sellers and the platform. The button functions similarly to what Callon calls an "obligatory point of passage" (Callon, 1986). Over 80 percent of all Amazon sales are subject to the button's terms and conditions.

As a condition of access to the orders received through the 1-Click button, sellers give up rights and powers. Sellers give up the right to contact customers outside of Amazon's platform. Sellers sign away the right to own the data that their products generate. Sellers are subject to Amazon's power to suspend their accounts without reason. In addition to these asymmetries, Amazon competes directly against sellers it claims to serve.

When observed from the view of a hammer, the platform's infrastructures depart from the Heideggerian premise that infrastructure becomes visible when it breaks. The infrastructures are broken, but they remain invisibilized. Listings are saturated with low-quality products designed not for their affordances in the hands of users, but for their capacity to satisfy Amazon's algorithms. Under platform capitalism, hammers become sources for data about users, trends, and profitable niches. It would be a mistake to reduce hammers to the productivities they afford when they are ready-to-hand. On Amazon Marketplace, hammers are among millions of other tools for reproducing power asymmetries between third-party sellers and the owners of the means of value realization. The seamlessness of Amazon's 1-Click button occludes the ways in which Amazon uses its control over the means of value realization to extract profits from breakdowns in infrastructure.

References

Amazon. (2021a). Pages 1–48 of over 2,000 results for hammer. Accessed February 27, 2021. https://www.amazon.com/s?k=hammer.

Amazon. (2021b). Amazon Services Business Solutions Agreement. Accessed February 27, 2021. https://sellercentral.amazon.com/gp/help/help.html?itemID=G1791&language=en_US&ref=xx_G1791_cont_521.

Amazon. (2021c). Fulfillment by Amazon. Accessed February 27, 2021. https://sell.amazon.com/fulfillment-by-amazon.html.

Amazon. (2021d). Pricing: Let's talk numbers. Accessed February 27, 2021. https://sell.amazon.com/pricing.html?ref_=sdus_soa_priov_n#selling-plans.

Amazon. (2021e). Product Listing Guidelines. Accessed February 27, 2021. https://sellercentral.amazon.com/gp/help/external/202073140?language=en-US&ref=mpbc_200463270_cont_202073140.

Amazon. (2021f). Q4 2020 Earnings Release. Accessed February 27, 2021. https://ir.aboutamazon.com/quarterly-results/default.aspx.

Amazon. (2021g). Customer Success Stories—Amazon AWS. Amazon.com. Accessed September 30, 2021. https://aws.amazon.com/solutions/case-studies/.

Amazon. (2021h). Selling Partner API Developer Guide. Accessed February 27, 2021. https://github.com/amzn/selling-partner-api-docs/blob/main/guides/developer-guide/SellingPartnerApiDeveloperGuide.md.

Amazon. (2022). Communication Guidelines. Accessed January 4, 2022. https://m.media-amazon.com/images/G/01/SellerCentral/CommunicationGuidelines/en_GB_Communication_Guidelines.pdf.

Barnett, David. (2020). Online Platforms and Market Power, Part 5: Competitors in the Digital Economy. Accessed February 27, 2021. https://docs.house.gov/meetings/JU/JU05/20200117/110386/HHRG-116-JU05-Wstate-BarnettD-20200117.pdf.

Birch, K., Cochrane, D. T., and Ward, C. (2021). Data as Asset? The Measurement, Governance, and Valuation of Digital Personal Data by Big Tech." *Big Data & Society* 8, no. 1 (January): 1–15. doi:10.1177/20539517211017308.

CamelCamelCamel. (2021a). Best Choice 8-oz. Stubby Claw Hammer with Magnetic Nail Starter (B074D4TDVM). Accessed February 27, 2021. https://camelcamelcamel.com/product/B074D4TDVM.

CamelCamelCamel. (2021b). How Our Price Checking System Works. Accessed February 27, 2021. https://camelcamelcamel.com/blog/how-our-price-checking-system-works.

Callon, Michel. (1984). Some Elements of a Sociology of Translation: Domestication of the Scallops and the Fishermen of St. Brieuc Bay. *The Sociological Review* 32, no. 1 (May): 196–233.

Chen, Le, Mislove, Alan, and Wilson, Christo. (2016). An Empirical Analysis of Algorithmic Pricing on Amazon Marketplace. *WWW '16: Proceedings of the 25th International Conference on World Wide Web.* Montreal, April 11–15, 1339–49. New York: ACM Press. https://doi.org/10.1145/2872427.2883089.

GS1. (2021). Get Your U. P. C. Barcodes from GS1 US. Accessed February 27, 2021. https://www.gs1us.org/upcs-barcodes-prefixes/get-a-barcode.

Hartman, Peri, Bezos, Jeffrey, Kaphan, Shel, and Spiegel, Joel. (1999). Method and System for Placing a Purchase Order via a Communications Network. US Patent 20070106570A1, filed September 12, 1997, and issued September 28, 1999.

Heidegger, Martin. ([1927] 2001). *Being and Time*. Oxford: Blackwell.

House Judiciary Subcommittee on Antitrust Law. (2020). Heads of Facebook, Amazon, Apple & Google Testify on Antitrust Law. Accessed February 27, 2021. https://www.c-span.org/video/?474236-1/heads-facebook-amazon-apple-google-testify-antitrust-law.

James, Tatiana. (2020). What it ACTUALLY Costs to Start Amazon FBA (2020 UPDATE). Accessed February 27, 2021. https://www.youtube.com/watch?v=kLa4N66-viE.

Jungle Scout. (2020a). The State of the Amazon Seller 2020. Accessed February 27, 2021. https://www.junglescout.com/wp-content/uploads/2020/02/State-of-the-Seller-Survey.pdf

Jungle Scout. (2020b). What is the Opportunity Score in the Extension? Accessed February 27, 2021. https://support.junglescout.com/hc/en-us/articles/360015964774-What-is-the-Opportunity-Score-in-the-extension.

Jungle Scout. (2021). The State of the Amazon Seller in 2021. Accessed February 27, 2021. https://www.junglescout.com/amazon-seller-report/.

Khan, Lina M. (2019). The Separation of Platforms and Commerce. *Columbia Law Review* 119, no. 4: 973–1097.

Marx, Karl. ([1867] 1976). *Capital, Volume I.* Harmondsworth, England: Penguin Books.

Marx, Karl. ([1885] 1978). *Capital, Volume II.* London: Pinguin Books.

Matsakis, Louise. (2019). Amazon Cracks Down on Third-Party Apps Over Privacy Violations. *Wired Magazine*, September 18. Accessed February 27, 2021. https://www.wired.com/story/amazon-marketplace-apps-privacy/.

Mattioli, Dana. (2020). Amazon Scooped Up Data from Its Own Sellers to Launch Competing Products. *Wall Street Journal*, April 23. Accessed February 27, 2021. https://www.wsj.com/articles/amazon-scooped-up-data-from-its-own-sellers-to-launch-competing-products-11587650015.

Mattioli, Dana, and Lombardo, Cara. (2020). Amazon Met with Startups About Investing, Then Launched Competing Products. *Wall Street Journal*, July 23. Accessed February 27, 2021. https://www.wsj.com/articles/amazon-tech-startup-echo-bezos-alexa-investment-fund-11595520249.

Pistor, Katharina. (2020). Rule by Data: The End of Markets? *Law and Contemporary Problems* 83, no. 2: 101–24.

Srnicek, Nick. (2017). *Platform Capitalism*. Cambridge: Polity.

Star, Susan Leigh. (1999). The Ethnography of Infrastructure. *American Behavioral Scientist* 43, no. 3 (November): 377–91.

Strategic Organizing Center. (2021). Primed for Pain: Amazon's Epidemic of Workplace Injuries." https://thesoc.org/wp-content/uploads/2021/02/PrimedForPain.pdf

Wark, McKenzie. (2019). *Capital Is Dead.* New York: Verso.

Zuboff, Shoshana. (2019). *The Age of Surveillance Capitalism: The Fight for a Human Future at the New Frontier of Power*. New York: PublicAffairs.

CHAPTER THREE

~

Logistics of Probability

Anticipatory Shipping and the Production of Markets

Nikolaus Poechhacker and Eva-Maria Nyckel

"Prediction and explanation are exactly symmetrical. Explanations are, in effect, predictions about what has happened; predictions are explanations about what's going to happen."

—John Searle

Introduction[1]

Logistics is at the core of the global market's metabolism. Goods offered by small corner stores, supermarkets, department stores, and online retailers often traveled the world from production facilities to the consumers. Since the end of World War II, the management of the flow of goods, information, and people (i.e., logistics) has become a major driving force of global capitalism. This global movement of things is to a large extent empowered by the accumulation and circulation of information and knowledge. Knowing existing and emerging markets for one's goods poses a competitive advantage in orchestrating logistical operations (Danyluk, 2017). Logistics thereby has always been a matter of mathematics, particularly in operations research methods. However, with the emergence of digital marketplaces in the mid-1990s (Lehdonvirta, 2012), the process of market anticipation is increasingly based on data science applications and the algorithmic recognition of patterns in customer transaction data. An important element of this transformation—particularly in light of global just-in-time markets and the detachment of production and consumption—is not just the ability to transport commodities all over the globe, but also the ability to compress time and space—"especially in facilitating the movement of goods and materials" (Danyluk, 2017, 6). Data science's answer to this request is the utilization of predictive analytics for logistical systems.

On December 24, 2013, Amazon was granted the US patent *Method and System for Anticipatory Package Shipping* (Spiegel et al., 2013). The patent describes methods for shipping commodities based on the calculated probability of (potential) customers ordering goods from Amazon: with anticipatory shipping, packages are sent "in anticipation of a customer ordering items in that package, but before such an order has actually occurred" (Spiegel et al., 2013, 5). The prediction of a (potential) purchase is thereby calculated by prior patterns in tracked interactions of customers with the e-commerce platform, including purchases and click-rates. As a result, the patent suggests that the process of shipping a package will no longer be initiated by a customer pressing the buy button, but by an algorithm that predicts future demands of customers in different regions. Through this utilization of predictive analytics for shipping goods, delivery time can further be reduced, which grants an important competitive advantage. However, this compression of time based on technological foresight creates new uncertainties. Predictive analytics, based on probabilities, can and will produce incorrect deliveries—in data science identified as false positives. A system of probabilistic logistical media must therefore integrate mechanisms of dealing with these uncertainties: the logic of commodity flows has to change in a profound way to deal with the *logistics of probability*. We argue in this chapter that logistical prediction is based on two central elements. First, an infrastructural system that allows for the flexible re-routing of commodities, integrating false positives into the existing stream of goods. Second, a coupling of predictions of consumption events and the construction of markets. *Logistics of probability* pre-assumes structures of desire and demand in the targeted community, while at the same time providing methods to realize these presumptions via the entanglement of anticipatory shipping with Amazon's e-commerce portal and a second logic of prediction: Amazon's recommender system.

While logistics has always been invested in predicting markets and demand to some extent, anticipatory shipping operates on a different level. The prediction does not target the demand of a whole region for a certain type of product—the aggregation is scaled down much more. Subject to prediction are singular product purchases, resulting in packages of only some items to be distributed within the logistical infrastructure of Amazon. Instead of shipping larger amounts of goods to meet anticipated demand, singular connections between shipping and (probable) purchase are constructed and afforded through technological advances, making it necessary to integrate different strategies of distribution that show greater flexibility. The production of prediction (Mackenzie, 2015) is relying on the "total media link on a digital base" (Kittler, 1999, 2)—the digital, allowing the connection of everyone and everything with everything and everyone else. Through this, a control of commodity flows and the entanglement of digitally constructed demand and supply are enabled via algorithmic logistical media.

Algorithmic Logistical Media

The term *logistical media* was coined by John D. Peters, who particularly stresses the infrastructural role of media. The job of logistical media is—in Peters' words—"to organize and orient, to arrange people and property, often into grids" (Peters, 2015, 37). For Peters, the work of media itself can be understood as fundamentally logistical.[2] In connection to this understanding of logistical media, and taking into account that logistical infrastructures are increasingly managed through computational systems of code, media theorist Ned Rossiter (2016) defines logistical media as a coupling of infrastructure and software, having an inherent governing power: "If infrastructure makes worlds, then software coordinates them" (Rossiter, 2016, xv). While Kittler stated that "media determine our situation" (Kittler, 1999, XXXIX), Rossiter further specifies this as logistical media, specifically "software coupled with infrastructure[,] determines our situation" (Rossiter, 2016, 121). In other words, he describes logistical media as infrastructures that make the flow of materials possible on the one hand, and the operational logic that controls the flow of goods on the other:

> Logistical media—as technologies, infrastructure, and software—coordinate, capture, and control the movement of people, finance, and things. Infrastructure makes worlds. Logistics governs them. (Rossiter, 2016, 4–5)

Algorithms and software are therefore substantial elements in organizing and arranging the capacities of infrastructures to order and influence the ways in which they interact with the world. However, logistical infrastructure is a larger system that is full of frictions, which are intentional parts of this system (Gregson, Crang, and Antonopoulos, 2017). The seemingly seamless flow of goods is the result of many interruptions, where distributed spaces are used for storing, repackaging, and relocating cargo. Distribution centers are spaces of intended friction, as "logistics works through this known friction. There is purposeful pausing, or interruption, of flow that is most visible in the spatialities of storage that are critical to the achievement of coordination" (Gregson, Crang, and Antonopoulos, 2017, 390). These distribution centers are stations where the flow and relocation of cargo in the network of connected spaces are coordinated by code, creating a code/space conflation (Kitchin and Dodge, 2011). Big retailers and the logistics industry are building large "network[s] of fulfillment centers capable of dispatching goods almost anywhere in the world" (Danyluk, 2017, 9). Walmart, for example, created a huge network of distribution centers, where 90 percent of the stock is turned over every day (LeCavalier, 2016). As a result, networks of dispatch and fulfillment centers enabled logistical networks to operate as just-in-time systems, reducing extensive stock-hold inventories. With just-in-time systems, cargo containers function as storage on the road and in steady motion (Hirsch, 2013).

Amazon, as one example for these developments, also relies heavily on this specific setup of logistical infrastructures. Amazon's Marketplace is not limited to an e-commerce website but also includes fulfillment centers (i.e., Amazon's distribution centers), the identifiable packages, the stored goods, and the workers carrying, packaging, and labeling these goods. Software logic and a material infrastructure are managing all of these activities at the same time. The calculation of markets needs logistical infrastructures. In the case of anticipatory shipping, however, the logic that guides and organizes the flow of goods through the material infrastructure takes a specific form. As the patent formulates it:

> That is, at a given time, numerous speculatively shipped packages . . . may be propagating through a shipping network. When an order is placed, a closest-proximity package . . . may already be at or close to a hub . . . closest to the delivery address of the order, and thus may be available within, e.g., a day of the order placement. (Spiegel et al., 2013, 15)

Anticipatory shipping does not just need to predict consumption but also to control, track, and redirect flows of commodities. Thus, a system of constant flow of commodity with fine-grained tracking is necessary. It is not the flow of commodities that must be seamless, but the flow of data streams, RFID codes, and location trackers. Logistical media does not only include the flow of goods: it also entails the very organization of immutable mobiles, combinable in multiple ways to make it possible to apply the logic of logistics.

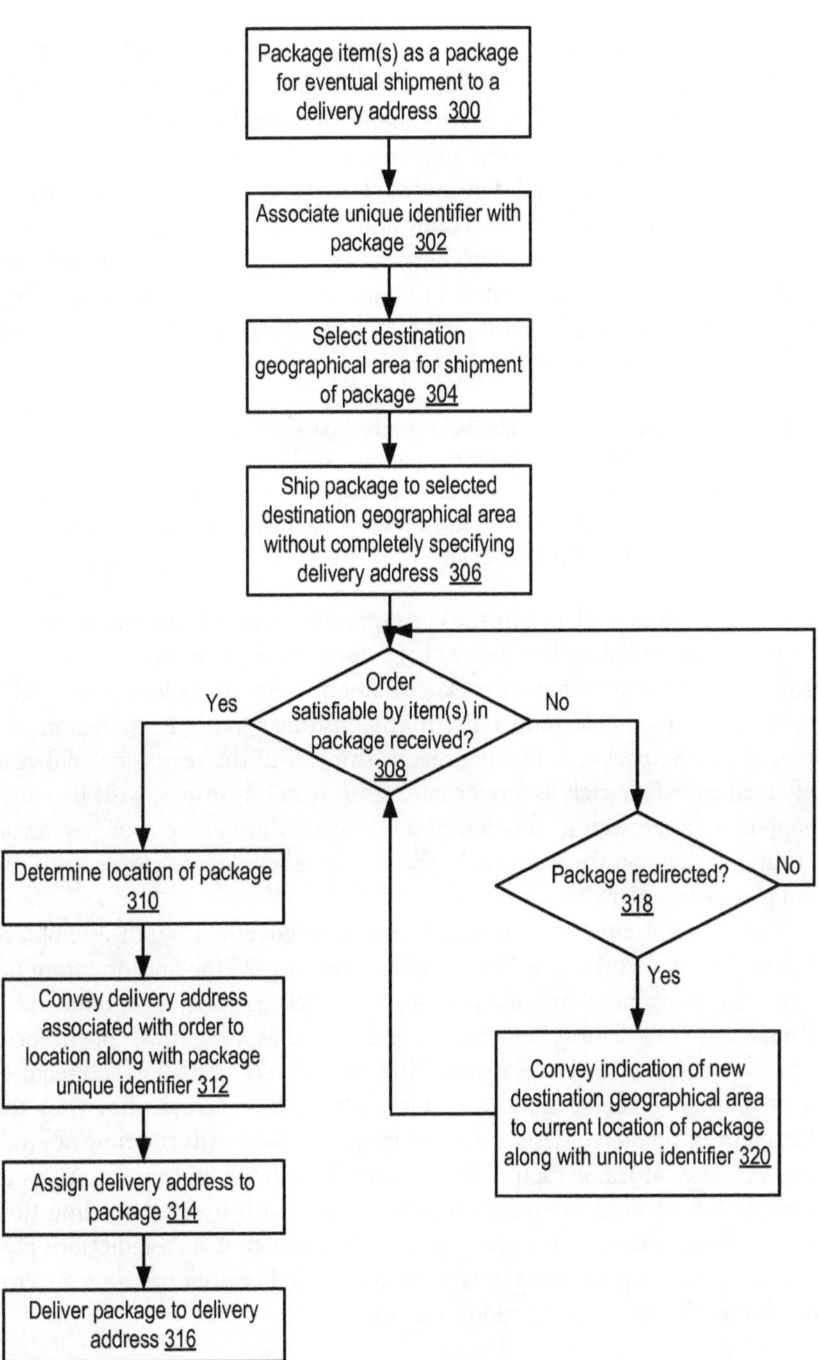

Figure 3.1. Flow Diagram of Anticipatory Shipping
(Source: Spiegel et al., 2013, p. 1.)

As Latour argues, "the logistics of immutable mobiles is what we have to admire and study" (Latour, 1987, 237). The algorithmic logic is thereby dependent on a structured environment that enables such predictions. This logic, based on predictive analytics, comes with uncertainties in the form of probabilities and false positives. The logic of Amazon's algorithmic logistics has to take that into account and develop risk management procedures. Anticipatory shipping can therefore be seen as part of this code/space production with its constant flow of commodities. As the patent describes, methods of accounting for false predictions are an integral part of the vision called anticipatory shipping.

> In one embodiment, a speculatively shipped package . . . may reach its destination geographical area before any corresponding customer order occurs. Depending on the common carrier, such a package . . . may be redirected to a different geographical area in response to actual or forecasted customer demand in that area. (Spiegel et al., 2013, 16)

When an order is placed in the corresponding area, different mechanisms of re-labeling and shipping the package come into place. As it is outlined in the patent for anticipatory package shipping, Amazon's logistics is influenced by the predicted probability that a customer in a specific region will order a specific package. The package is shipped to the region by analyzing collected user data such as former purchases, search histories, wish lists, and shopping carts as well as the duration of the user's mouse cursor resting on certain products on the website. In the best-case scenario, a customer in the area places an order.

Amazon's anticipatory shipping is a system governed by an assemblage of digital media working as "logistical devices of tracking and orientation," organizing movement in time and space as well as registering data traces (Peters, 2015, 7). The system can be understood as a logistical, operational logic as it was described by Rossiter (2016) and Peters (2015), which requires its own massive logistics infrastructure. This infrastructure allows for the alignment of predicted desires derived from user data with the flow of products. A material infrastructure with planned frictions and interruptions as moments of possible intervention is combined with a corresponding flow of data in order to enable a constant flow of goods to make predictions possible (i.e., reducing the costs of false predictions). Logistics not only governs worlds but also makes predictions less risky.

Recommendations and the Production of Markets

A central issue with capitalist modes of production in the logistical revolution is "the disjuncture between production and distribution, or supply and demand" (Bonacich and Wilson, 2008, 4). Production and consumption are detached from each other, making the issue of connecting these two aspects of each market a major problem that contemporary capitalism is facing. This issue becomes even more pressing if anticipatory shipping enacts a reality that has not yet been realized—logistic action has to be connected with emerging demand. Here the detachment is not just between production and consumption but also between delivery and locally confined consumption. The market is the mediating instance, and identifying potential customers is part of this mediation function. However, there are manifold studies arguing that we should understand markets by looking into socio-material market practices on the one hand and theories and models about those markets on the other, which are rather performative than descriptive to the exchange of values; they are "an engine, not a camera" (MacKenzie, 2006).

Along the lines of MacKenzie's argument, we can understand recommender systems as market devices that have the distinct aim of segmenting the market by identifying "smaller homogenous markets in response to differing product preferences" (Smith, 1956, 6). Following Callon's (1998) conception of markets as practical achievements of heterogeneous actors, Amazon's recommender algorithm is one important actor in the constitution of the market. Algorithmic configurations that couple demand and supply are not independent of markets, but they are actively shaping them (Callon and Muniesa, 2005). Recommender systems can be conceptualized as algorithmic configurations calculating relations between users and items, but also between users and other users as well between items—each with its different inscribed ideas about social configurations (Pöchhacker et al., 2017). As such, the algorithms are identifying and classifying items to be sold as well as different kinds of users. Based on these identifications, the supply is shaped accordingly. The e-commerce platform is using recommender algorithms to preconfigure its online market.

> Algorithmic configurations calculate encounters differently, depending on the way in which they perform these operations; each concrete market corresponds to a particular mode of organization (and calculation) of the connection between singular supplies and demands. (Callon and Muniesa, 2005, 1242)

As Callon and Muniesa argue, algorithmic configurations are technical instruments within an assemblage of marketing techniques, including cookies, click-through rates, etc., that relate people to things and, as a result, construct an economic space (Cluley and Brown, 2015). Nevertheless, in this digital marketing mode, segmentation is no longer driven by theories about identity-related demand. The construction of the user through clustering and segmentation based on data tracks is a form of what Zwick and Dholakia (2004) call "narrating consumers." As a result, "the market, in a sense, does not exist outside of traces consumers leave within databases" (Cluley and Brown, 2015, 115). Market segmentation then becomes rather an exercise of modulating consumer *dividuals* (Deleuze, 1992) with existing supply than matching existing demands with variable supply (Zwick and Denegri Knott, 2009). Calculative marketing becomes a matter of fluid reorganization and reconstruction of the individual based on changing patterns and variables (Danna and Gandy, 2002; Gandy, 2001).

Recommender systems as intermediaries (see also Morris, 2015) are reorganizing a complex and massive amount of goods. Instead of creating ads, recommendations are creating visibility by assembling personalized forms of offers. This is, ultimately, a data-driven structuring of consumer choices. Recommendation algorithms are thereby reducing complexity, which helps consumers navigate the enormous number of offered goods. Selective visibility reduces the number of goods taken into consideration and enables exploration of prior unknown items at the same time. However, this reduction in complexity does not come without side effects. By doing so, these intermediaries are also predicting the user's taste, as well as performing it (see also Beer and Burrows, 2013). MacKenzie (2006) defines the strongest form of performativity as a process in which reality is adapted to the applied model. In the case of machine learning techniques used in recommender systems, however, one can argue that the model and reality are co-shaping each other dialectically. One does not exist without the other, but the model and the observation are interdependent, where the recommender system creates a projection of past behavior in the future (Kaiser, 2015), preforming market interactions as the basis for further recommendations as well as speculative shipping. As Nigel Thrift (2004) argues, with the introduction of information technologies, the flexibility of configurations increases and becomes an object of experimentation and constant change itself. Following Thrift, this kind of prediction is a flexible and ever-adapting form of matching supply and demand—and therefore continually changing the basis for performing markets.

Performing Predictability

Anticipatory shipping, as described in Amazon's US Patent No. 8,615,473 B2 (Spiegel et al., 2013), is not independent of the market construction process. What anticipatory shipping is predicting is a preconfigured market, co-shaped and highly influenced by Amazon's e-commerce platform and recommender system. It is widely acknowledged that the recommender system of Amazon is a central part of its business model (Smith and Linden, 2017). Nevertheless, how are anticipatory shipping and recommender systems related to each other? Connecting these two forms of prediction via common centers of calculation (Latour, 1987), these media logics become entangled by predicting as well as producing their customers' demand at the same time and actively preparing the grounds for the logistics of probability.

Centers of calculation, as Latour (1987) argues, are places where references or translations of the real world, such as questionnaires and maps, are collected and made combinable. This collection of the world's traces makes the actors inside these centers of calculation able to act at a distance, recombine different parts of the world, and therefore create new possibilities for interventions. However, being able to do so involves some effort. The projection used to describe the world becomes a single point of passage for all data collected. Distributed elements in the network of goods, dispatching, and user interactions must be brought together in a common information ecology, developing standards and classifications (Bowker and Star, 2000) and integrating the captured information in databases, making it comparable (Burkhardt, 2015). In the case of Amazon's anticipatory shipping, the two forms of prediction—recommender algorithm and anticipatory shipping algorithm—do not exist independently from each other. Recommendations are based on customer data. The prediction of future purchases in a specific region, on the other hand, is based on this very database co-produced by the recommendation algorithms. Anticipatory shipping is, as the patent describes it, based on historical customer data.

> Specifically, in one embodiment, forecasting model . . . may be configured to forecast or predict customer demand for a given item. Forecasting model . . . may be configured to predict aggregate demand for items as well as demand within particular geographical areas. (Spiegel et al., 2013, 17)

Moreover:

> Demand may be predicted in various ways. For example, if a given customer has purchased a given item, other customers with similar historical shopping

> patterns (e.g., having purchased or browsed items similar to those of the given customer) may be more likely to purchase the given item, and in some embodiments forecasting model . . . may be configured to detect such possible correlations. (Spiegel et al., 2013, 18)

Following these descriptions, anticipatory shipping is not just based on purchases but also on browsing history, patterns in user ratings, and many more factors. Recommendations are placed on the e-commerce platform based on exactly these parameters. For their recommendation system, Amazon utilizes a method that allows the identification of not only the personal purchase history but also personalization based on group behavior identification. If you browse a certain item, the recommendation is based on the browsing history of other "dividuals": users who viewed this item also viewed that one. This, however, influences how actants are connected in a particular market. The recommender system becomes a calculative mode of market organization, including certain market participants and excluding others by default. Of course, this segmentation mechanism can be overcome by individual searches, but still, the interactions are highly prestructured. The recommender algorithm, while not absolutely deterministic, shapes the market; it becomes a market device (Muniesa, Millo, and Callon, 2007). Based on this market device, the anticipatory shipping is not based on an external phenomenon to be predicted but reproduces to some degree what the recommender system performed in the first place. Prediction of user choices in the form of a recommender prestructures and co-produces the data sets that are used for predictions of purchases in anticipatory shipping. The anticipation of purchases is therefore not so much the analysis of an independent and objectively given world but rests on complex interactions between algorithmic selection, logistical media, and market choices of consumers.

While recommender algorithms are performing markets that are subsequently predicted in anticipatory shipping, the models of anticipatory shipping are also being stabilized by adjusting the reality of purchased goods to match the representation of the world created in the database of Amazon. False positives, or, more simply, incorrect predictions, are attempted to be "saved" via the e-commerce platform, by offering goods to customers close to the actual location of the shipped package.

> Using a shipping model . . . may allow for increased predictability and flexibility of control of speculatively shipped packages already in transit, for example by selectively offering packages in transit to a customer depending on the proximity of those packages to the customer, or based on a customer's potential interest in items included in those packages. (Spiegel et al., 2013, 17)

Combining logistical media with digital marketplaces creates even stronger performed markets, making predictions more accurate without changing the model behind the anticipatory shipping method. Demand is not predicted but produced.

Prediction of Demand, Demands of Prediction

The technology of anticipatory shipping has not been adopted by many companies yet but promises its wide application in the future. While Amazon is often considered a key player of a technological avant-garde, others have started to adopt and adapt these methods as well.[3] However, anticipatory shipping comes with specific requirements and demands that have to be met. Predictive analytics is not a detached technology that can be applied at any time and place, but it must be embedded in a whole algorithmic ecology (Beer, 2017). Although it has often been described as such, "the algorithm" is not a mystical and powerful actor by itself (Ziewitz, 2016). The power of algorithmic systems is neither inherent to the term digital, nor is it exclusively a question of culture. In the case of Amazon's anticipatory shipping, effective prediction is based on and enabled by two crucial elements.

First, we have to account for the entanglement of digital and material infrastructures. Prediction in its probabilistic nature requires methods and procedures to account for false positives. In the case of Amazon, a dense network of sensors, RFID chips, and digital communication channels for fine-grained surveillance of shipped commodities is combined with a material infrastructure with planned frictions, interruptions, and pauses that enable the re-routing of goods accordingly. Without such an infrastructural network, false predictions would become costly—and prediction a bit less likely. Material infrastructure is a defining element enabling the revolution of logistics (Vahrenkamp, 2012) but also for organizing social life as such (Graham and Marvin, 2001). However, what increasingly holds these infrastructures together is a network of digital communication channels, coordinating flows of goods and integrating heterogeneous sites in a logistical network. Prediction relies on the coupling of digital and material infrastructures controlled from a common center of calculation.

Second, predictions of social systems are hardly ever based on observations that are unaffected by the process of prediction. In the case of Amazon's anticipatory shipping, predicting demand is based on the same data sets that are used to produce recommendations, and thereby creating demands. Thus, recommendations become a powerful tool to construct markets and connect demand and supply—recommendations are affirmatively creating what they are predicting in the first place. This has profound effects on the production of prediction as well as the production of knowledge in digitized societies. Inquiries into these interdependencies of digital culture are therefore necessary to understand epistemic and technologic practices of applied predictive analytics. Yet this entails technical questions of computability of actions as well as cultural ideas of similarity and group behavior of consumers.

In order to account for the social power of machine learning in societies that increasingly rely on algorithms as *knowledge machines*, the affordances and necessities formulated by these applications need to be understood. Interactions with algorithmic systems are stabilized by a wider network of actors, databases, data workers, protocol interfaces, and so on. The complex matter of implementing predictive analytics in logistical media can produce profound economic and political impacts. Anticipatory shipping promises to reduce delivery times tremendously, which results in competitive advantage. However, this advantage is not open to everyone. Amazon is able to stabilize and enable predictions because of its power to shape markets and control supply chains in a wide network of dispatch and fulfillment centers, and to integrate false predictions into a constant flow of goods. Yet this utilization of machine learning in logistical business is not necessarily available for all competitors, only to the ones with comparable capabilities to combine big marketplaces with highly controlled logistic infrastructures. In a more recent development, Amazon even started to establish its own package delivery service (Soper, 2017) and the controversial partner program "Amazon Flex" (Matsakis, 2019) to strengthen its independence from companies such as UPS and FedEx and to make this assemblage even stronger. As such, predictive analytics as a market device is available for the big players and stabilizes their position within increasingly consolidated markets—a development that could lead to a monopolization of (online) trade, putting pressure on competitors and consumers alike. These developments call for an ongoing investigation of technology-driven shifts in (online) markets. To do so, however, we have to accept that "we have never been modern" (Latour, 1993). Instead of approaching these questions only from a technological or economic perspective, a broad disciplinary portfolio of approaches is needed to understand the techno-political hybrids that shape contemporary markets. This includes at least dialogue and collaboration with computer scientists for a deep understanding of algorithmic phenomena in contemporary societies. Without an interdisciplinary approach, our explorations into digital cultures might come to a certain end, providing us with neither predictions nor explanations.

Notes

1. This is a reprint of: Poechhacker, Nikolaus and Eva-Maria Nyckel (2020). Logistics of Probability: Anticipatory Shipping and the Production of Markets in Marcus Burkhardt, Mary Shnayien, Katja Grashöfer (Eds.): Explorations of Digital Cultures. Lüneburg: meson press.

2. It is important to note here that Peters argues against an understanding of media that just structure and coordinate logistical operations. Instead, he considers media operations as inherently logistical.

3. In Germany, Blue Yonder is an important player in artificial intelligence solutions for retail, implementing predictive analytics to forecast demand for several companies (see, e.g., www.blue-yonder.com/en/customers/otto-price-replenishment-optimization, accessed June 21, 2019).

References

Beer, David. (2017). The Social Power of Algorithms. *Information, Communication & Society* 20, no. 1: 1–13.

Beer, David, and Burrows, Roger. (2013). Popular Culture, Digital Archives and the New Social Life of Data. *Theory, Culture & Society* 30, no. 4: 47–71.

Bonacich, Edna, and Wilson, Jake B. (2008). *Getting the Goods: Ports, Labor, and the Logistics Revolution*. Ithaca: Cornell University Press.

Bowker, Geoffrey C., and Star, Susan Leigh. (2000). *Sorting Things Out: Classification and Its Consequences*. Cambridge, MA: MIT Press.

Burkhardt, Marcus. (2015). *Digitale Datenbanken: Eine Medientheorie im Zeitalter von Big Data*. Bielefeld: transcript.

Callon, Michel. (1998). Introduction: The Embeddedness of Economic Markets in Economics. *The Sociological Review* 46, no. S1: 1–57.

Callon, Michel, and Muniesa, Fabian. (2005). Peripheral Vision: Economic Markets as Calculative Collective Devices. *Organization Studies* 26, no. 8: 1229–50.

Cluley, Robert, and Brown, Stephen D. (2015). The Dividualised Consumer: Sketching the New Mask of the Consumer. *Journal of Marketing Management* 31, no. 1–2: 107–22.

Danna, Anthony, and Gandy, Oscar H. (2002). All That Glitters Is Not Gold: Digging Beneath the Surface of Data Mining. *Journal of Business Ethics* 40, no. 4: 373–86.

Danyluk, Martin. (2017). Capital's Logistical Fix: Accumulation, Globalization, and the Survival of Capitalism. *Environment and Planning D: Society and Space* 36, no. 4: 630–47.

Deleuze, Gille. (1992). Postscript on the Societies of Control. *October* 59: 3–7.

Gandy, Oscar H. (2001). Dividing Practices: Segmentation and Targeting in the Emerging Public Sphere." In *Mediated Politics: Communication in the Future of*

Democracy, edited by W. Lance Bennett and Robert M. Entman, 141–59. New York: Cambridge University Press.

Graham, Stephen, and Marvin, Simon. (2001). *Splintering Urbanism: Networked Infrastructures, Technological Mobilities and the Urban Condition*. London/New York: Routledge Chapman & Hall.

Gregson, Nicky, Crang, Mike, and Antonopoulos, Constantinos N. (2017). Holding Together Logistical Worlds: Friction, Seams and Circulation in the Emerging "Global Warehouse." *Environment and Planning D: Society and Space* 35, no. 3: 381–98.

Hirsch, Sarah. (2013). Inhabiting the Icon: Shipping Containers and the New Imagination of Western Space. *Western American Literature* 48, no. 1: 17–40.

Kaiser, Mario. (2015). Reactions to the Future: The Chronopolitics of Prevention and Preemption. *NanoEthics* 9, no. 2: 165–77.

Kitchin, Rob, and Dodge, Martin. (2011). *Code/Space: Software and Everyday Life*. Cambridge, MA: MIT Press.

Kittler, Friedrich A. (1999). *Gramophone, Film, Typewriter*. Translated by Geoffrey Winthrop-Young and Michael Wutz. Stanford, CA: Stanford University Press.

Latour, Bruno. (1987). *Science in Action: How to Follow Scientists and Engineers through Society*. Cambridge, MA: Harvard University Press.

Latour, Bruno. (1993). *We Have Never Been Modern*. Cambridge, MA: Prentice Hall/ Harvester Wheatsheaf.

LeCavalier, Jesse. (2016). *The Rule of Logistics: Walmart and the Architecture of Fulfillment*. Minneapolis/London: University of Minnesota Press.

Lehdonvirta, Vili. (2012). A History of the Digitalization of Consumer Culture. In *Digital Virtual Consumption*, edited by Mike Molesworth and Janice Denegri-Knott, 11–28. New York: Routledge

Mackenzie, Adrian. (2015). The Production of Prediction: What Does Machine Learning Want? *European Journal of Cultural Studies* 18, no. 4–5: 429–45.

MacKenzie, Donald. (2006). *An Engine, Not a Camera: How Financial Models Shape Markets*. Cambridge, MA: MIT Press.

Matsakis, Louise. (2019, May 14). Why Amazon Is Giving Employees $10,000 to Quit. *Wired*. www.wired.com/story/amazon-delivery-paying-employees-to-quit/.

Morris, Jeremy Wade. (2015). Curation by Code: Infomediaries and the Data Mining of Taste. *European Journal of Cultural Studies* 18, no. 4–5: 446–63.

Muniesa, Fabian, Millo, Yuval, and Callon, Michel. (2007). An Introduction to Market Devices. *The Sociological Review* 55, no. October: 1–12.

Peters, John Durham. (2015). *The Marvelous Clouds: Toward a Philosophy of Elemental Media*. Chicago/London: University of Chicago Press.

Pöchhacker, Nikolaus, Burkhardt, Marcus, Geipel, Andrea, and Passoth, Jan-Hendrik. (2017). Interventionen in die Produktion algorithmischer Öffentlichkeiten: Recommender Systeme als Herausforderung für öffentlich-rechtliche Sendeanstalten. *kommunikation @ gesellschaft* 18: 25.

Rossiter, Ned. (2016). *Software, Infrastructure, Labor: A Media Theory of Logistical Nightmares*. New York: Routledge.

Smith, B., and Linden, G. (2017). Two Decades of Recommender Systems at Amazon .com. *IEEE Internet Computing* 21, no. 3: 12–18.

Smith, Wendell R. (1956). Product Differentiation and Market Segmentation as Alternative Marketing Strategies. *Journal of Marketing* 21, no. 1: 3–8.

Soper, Spencer. (2017, October 5). Amazon Is Testing Its Own Delivery Service to Rival FedEx and UPS. *Bloomberg.com*. www.bloomberg.com/news/articles/2017-10-05/amazon-is-said-to-test-own-delivery-service-to-rival-fedex-ups.

Spiegel, Joel R., McKenna, Michael T., Lakshman, Girish S., and Nordstrom, Paul G. (2013). Method and System for Anticipatory Package Shipping. United States US8615473B2, filed August 24, 2012, and issued December 24, 2013.

Thrift, Nigel. (2004). Remembering the Technological Unconscious by Foregrounding Knowledges of Position. *Environment and Planning D: Society and Space* 22, no. 1: 175–90.

Vahrenkamp, Richard. (2012). *The Logistic Revolution: The Rise of Logistics in the Mass Consumption Society*. Frankfurt am Main: Campus.

Ziewitz, Malte. (2016). Governing Algorithms: Myth, Mess, and Methods. *Science, Technology & Human Values* 41, no. 1: 3–16.

Zwick, Detlev, and Knott, Janice Denegri. (2009). Manufacturing Customers: The Database as New Means of Production. *Journal of Consumer Culture* 9, no. 2: 221–47.

Zwick, Detlev, and Dholakia, Nikhilesh. (2004). Consumer Subjectivity in the Age of Internet: The Radical Concept of Marketing Control through Customer Relationship Management. *Information and Organization* 14, no. 3: 211–36.

CHAPTER FOUR

~

Amazon Warehouse Work

Machinic Dispossession and Augmented Despotism

Alessandro Delfanti

"We are not robots!" The slogan, written on signs and shouted across picket lines, has come to be one of the most visible messages of striking Amazon workers across the world. Mobilizations at the corporation's fulfillment centers (FCs) have demanded benefits, respect of contracts, and greater worker control over schedule flexibility. They have also protested the grueling work rhythms imposed by the machines that prop up FC's logistic operations. At Amazon, technology dictates the pace of work. Machines are used to increase workers' productivity, standardize tasks, facilitate worker turnover, and ultimately gain control over the workforce. Workers are acutely aware of the uneven nature of their relation with machinery, and at the same time, they know the warehouse needs their living labor. As I was told by a manager, "technology codifies, understands and manages. But the real machine is the human: everything is done manually."[1]

To understand the relation between workers and machinery at Amazon, I rely upon early Italian *operaismo* (workerism) thinkers Mario Tronti, Romano Alquati, and Raniero Panzieri, whose studies of factory work in the 1960s conceptualized labor in innovative ways. I also combine studies of digital forms of surveillance and data capture to theorize the role of technology in structuring labor at Amazon. While scholars such as Shoshana Zuboff conceptualize surveillance capitalism as based on the "expropriation" or "extraction" of data from passive users, they tend to overlook the active role of the women and men who perform the processes that are datafied and incorporated into machinery, as well as the forces that push them to collaborate with data collection (Zuboff, 2019). *Operaismo* flips the picture to analyze capital's dependence on labor. For Tronti, "a history of the industry cannot be conceived as anything other than a history of the capital organization of productive labour" since "it is productive labour which produces capital," and from this follows that "the capitalist class is, from its birth, subordinate to the working class. Hence the necessity of exploitation" (Tronti, 1980, 29–32). In sum, capital depends on labor and needs to secure collaboration in production processes in the face of workers' unruliness. This nature of exploitation is captured by Panzieri's urge for a "dialectical awareness of the unity of the 'technical' and 'despotic' moments in the present organization of production" (Panzieri, 1961, 63). Taken on its own, technological change does not explain the labor process. It is, Panzieri suggests, simply impossible to disentangle the role of technology on the shop floor from that of capitalist domination over workers. Amazon does, in fact, need to find ways to force workers to become robots that seamlessly and efficiently abide by the rhythms automation imposes. To understand this, we need to rethink the role of men and women in the automation of both the labor process and of managerial functions. This calls for a renewed attention to the ways all-too-human power relations are entwined with the deployment of technology to organize work and control workers.

Workers themselves have written about the harsh realities of work in Amazon FCs, describing a new form of degradation of labor (Anonymous, 2018). Many perceive their job not only as physically demanding and repetitive, but also as unskilled and alienating. Their daily routine is characterized by the discipline imposed by management, and, ultimately, it is a consequence of Amazon's promise of fast and efficient product delivery to customers. As noted by a worker,

> the picker does not need much knowledge, that is not your added value. All right, picking items correctly, putting them in the tote correctly so they are not damaged, but . . . clearly if you promise to deliver quickly then you need to run to fulfill those promises.

While I analyze such degradation, I also argue that workers provide a key resource which does "add value" for Amazon's bottom line. Knowledge of FC inventory is so important that it is immediately taken away from workers and delegated to the machines. Instead, Amazon can capture and incorporate FC inventory data in the software systems that organize its fulfillment processes. In turn, the automated processes of data generation and analytics that underpin warehouse work model the relation between labor and management at

Amazon. Digital technology is used to dispossess workers of their knowledge about warehouse inventory, which is captured in the form of digital data. The information thus generated is used to automate management and use software systems to strictly control the labor process. Finally, data about all worker activities are readily made available to supervisors, augmenting management's power on the warehouse floor.

This chapter is based on research I conducted in 2017 to 2019 in a major Amazon FC located in Italy. The FC serves some of the main markets in the country. It employs up to three thousand workers during seasonal peaks and can ship tens of thousands of parcels per day. My research encompasses in-depth interviews with twenty-five warehouse workers or ex-workers at different levels of the hierarchy—from temp worker to manager—and in roles covering most major processes and departments.

Theorizing Amazon Labor

Amazon's e-commerce operations rely on over two hundred warehouses globally. Each spans hundreds of thousands of square feet and employs several thousand workers or, in Amazon corporate lingo, "associates." Work is organized around four core processes: receive, stow, pick, and pack. The first two are a part of "inbound" work. Workers at "receive" workstations unpack incoming pallets of commodities, each identified by a unique barcode. Items travel to the "stow" area, where they are grouped in bins workers carry into the "pick tower," a gigantic multi-floor area dense with thousands of shelves, numbered and divided into the cells, or bins, where the commodities are stored. The following two processes are part of "outbound" work. Workers assigned to "pick" tasks walk into the warehouse to retrieve the items ordered by Amazon customers and carry them to sorting workstations. In the "pack" area, workers receive, package, and label orders, which are then sent to shipping. The basic unit of all such processes is the omnipresent yellow tote used to move commodities around the warehouse. While many features of Amazon labor tend to be standardized across the globe, there exist different warehouses with different levels of automation. In a minority of FCs equipped with robotic shelves, workers do not walk around the aisles, but stand in workstations that are served by robots. Still, even in such partially automated workplaces the labor of storing and retrieving items remains manual and repetitive and abides by the same logics I witnessed in my fieldwork.

At the core of such logics is the fact that product barcodes allow commodities to be construed not only as inventory, but also as information to be managed (LeCavalier, 2016). In turn, this permits Amazon to rely on forms of labor that generate, manage, and trade in such digital information. The main instrument of work is the barcode scanner, which workers commonly refer to as a "gun." Workers pick one up at the beginning of their shift and use it to scan the barcode on their badge, thus logging into the system. From that moment on, the scanner mediates between workers and management, assigning tasks, communicating orders, and monitoring work. Studies of "algorithmic management" have analyzed how data-driven decision-making is automated and outsourced to digital technologies (Lee et al., 2015). This chapter is grounded in such research, but aims at theorizing digital capitalism's attempts to discipline and control labor beyond the automation of management. Specific forms of control are enacted by human managers whose work is augmented by technical and cultural rationalities rather than fully outsourced to algorithms. Other studies of algorithmic management have focused on "soft" and remote forms of control that incentivize and constrain workers' choices; for example, Uber has done so by strategically increasing pricing to convince its drivers to converge on a certain neighborhood, while data work platforms may do it by monitoring keyboard typing to discourage their workers from taking breaks (Rosenblat and Stark, 2016; Wood et al., 2019). As the balance between autonomy and control in the FC is heavily skewed toward the latter, Amazon workers are subject to quite a different regime of power.

As noted by Ursula Huws, inherent in all capitalist relations of production is the tendency to expropriate the knowledge of workers and incorporate it in machinery, like computer programs (2014). This phenomenon, described in the next two sections and which I call *machinic dispossession*, is at the center of Amazon's ability to control and subdue its workforce while ensuring it continues to amass new workers in its warehouses. Drawing inspiration from Marx, *operaismo* highlighted that capital "soaks up" living labor-power, which then confronts workers as dead labor. At Amazon, labor knowledge and cooperation are incorporated into software which is then used to strictly control the labor process downstream. The analysis of such incorporation processes is a classic focus of studies on Taylorist production. For example, in his 1970s study of factory work, Harry Braverman described management's ability to gather knowledge and use the monopoly over such knowledge to "control each step of the labor process and its mode of execution" (1974, 82). To describe how Amazon establishes such a monopoly over knowledge in its FCs to control workers, I draw upon Gilles Deleuze and Félix Guattari's concept of "machinic enslavement." Under machinic enslavement, "human beings themselves are constituent pieces of a machine . . . under the control and direction of a higher unity" (1987, 456–57). In the warehouse, the apparatus of capture that feeds machinic dispossession is based on the analysis and datafication of worker activity by central software systems. Through the incorporation of the results of their labor, machinery becomes an alien power that rules over workers, making them mere "living appendages," as Marx would say, of a labor process whose organization is dominated by algorithmic management.

In the last section, I move to an analysis of a specific form of domination that I have termed *augmented despotism*. With this concept, I turn to human managers to theorize the extent to which their role is enhanced by both the affordances provided by algorithmic dispossession and control, and a specific cultural infrastructure at play in digital capitalism. Following Panzieri, I suggest that it is futile to analyze the technical organization of labor without studying the authoritarian nature of work under capitalist relations. Panzieri described the convergence of two complementary strategies deployed by capital to subdue the workforce: "capitalist 'despotism' itself takes the shape of technological rationality. In capitalist use, not only machines, but also 'methods,' organizational forms, etc. are incorporated in capital, and confront workers as capital: as an alien 'rationality'" (1961, 61). The concept of augmented despotism is indebted to theorizations of the ways digital media extend social and communicative processes (McLuhan, 1964). For example, the metaphor of augmentation, imported from technology design, has been used to describe mediated communication processes which incorporate both the affordances of digital technologies and the established features of face-to-face social interaction (Gordon and Manosevitch, 2010).

Stow, or Machinic Dispossession

When commodities enter the warehouse, they are unboxed in the "receive" area and need to be stowed on the pick tower's shelves. The process of stowing is captured by algorithms that expropriate the results of worker activities and use this information to rationalize and increase the efficiency of the warehouse. In fact, the inventory of Amazon warehouses follows a principle of "organized disorder" or "chaotic storage," which allows for a more efficient use of storage space, as well as for the optimization of a complex form of cooperative work. By referring to this undertaking as *machinic dispossession*, I aim to stress Amazon's ability to take knowledge away from workers by incorporating it in its distant algorithmic systems. In his study of Walmart's fulfillment logistics, LeCavalier notes that the environments inhabited by workers have an "inscrutability" as they are "knowable only to the software that orchestrates the interactions and . . . determines the paths of workers"

(2016, 153). Chaotic storage is made possible by human labor, and yet it makes Amazon's warehouses even more complex to navigate for a human being than Walmart's. Faced with the impossibility of knowing the inventory in its entirety, humans "need to outsource all of this understanding to the machine," which in turn entirely determines the organization of the labor process (Danaher, 2016, 253). Workers in sum end up experiencing what Marx called "helpless dependence upon the factory as a whole" (1976, 547).

Dozens of warehouse stowers are assigned totes containing certain items, which they must place on the shelves as they walk in the pick tower, recording their position with their scanner. Stowing commodities is left at least partially to workers' autonomous decisions. With a few exceptions, such as costly electronics, there is not necessarily a specific shelf or area of the pick tower where certain classes of items are concentrated—for example, there is no designated area a worker needs to walk to so as they stow toys. Instead, these objects are distributed all over the pick tower. As they carry out this process, stowers need to abide by two main principles. First, they must distribute copies of a certain item in a number of different bins in various areas of the pick tower. This will increase the possibility that a copy of a specific commodity will be close to any given picker, thus reducing the time spent walking around the pick tower. It will also prevent bottlenecks in the case of an order surge, as several pickers simultaneously looking for the same item will not converge toward the same bin or corridor, thus avoiding slowdowns. Second, they can place items in any bin with enough room to contain them, as long as it does not contain similar types of commodities. The same item cannot be present in a bin that is horizontally or vertically adjacent. Thus, a teddy bear should not be stowed in a bin containing other stuffed animals but can be placed in a bin containing a cellphone case, several copies of a textbook, and a t-shirt. This will speed up the future labor of pickers, who will be guided to a bin that contains two identical copies of the teddy bear, but not other similar items, thus reducing mistakes.

In a pick tower of several thousand square feet, containing hundreds of shelves, distributed over a number of floors, and tens of thousands of bins, this process generates an inventory that no individual human being can navigate without the aid of Amazon's system algorithm. Stowing is a simple process, but it relies heavily on workers' dexterity. As noted by a manager, "you receive mixed totes which can contain one copy of an item and one copy of another. In a single tote you can find anything, from a CD to a soccer ball or a book. And then there are smaller and bigger bins, and if an item has been catalogued as being smaller than its actual size, that can slow you down." Stowers need to be efficient while creatively making use of available space for storing the commodities they carry. While the system algorithm can help workers avoid incorrect choices, human labor alone possesses the flexibility and speed to efficiently store in a "chaotic" manner a range of items that are different in shape, weight, volume, color, etc. What workers do not possess, or rather quickly surrender to the machine, is their knowledge of the position of the commodities they have stored. In the words of a stower worker,

> as a stower you cannot control and see where you have put a certain object. . . . You really need to pay attention to remember. There is so much different stuff in the warehouse and you just have to keep unloading carts.

To manage such complexity, the stowing process is captured through the barcode "guns" and datafied by the system algorithm. Each commodity and each bin are uniquely identified by a barcode readable through the scanner. Once the stower with the teddy bear has selected a bin, they "shoot" (scan) the commodity and bin's barcodes. Upon receiving a green light confirming that the system has recorded the item's position, only then will the worker place the item in the bin. Now the system algorithm managing the inventory knows the position of the teddy bear and can send a picker to retrieve it when an order is placed.

It is worth stressing that the data generated by the datafication and capture of stowers' work is stored and analyzed in computers that are part of Amazon's global system, meaning this system might not be situated in Europe, let alone Italy. Nonetheless, it is certainly not in the warehouse and thus workers cannot access or influence it. The machine rules from afar. The system's control is imperceptible, and yet it is omnipresent. Machinic dispossession captures and separates inventory knowledge from the subjects who have performed the activity generating the position of commodities. Individual workers are thus immediately deprived of a crucial characteristic of traditional warehouse labor. Amazon workers with previous experience in traditional warehousing stress how a crucial part of their labor was to develop tacit organizational knowledge about inventory and the processes that underpin it (Gertler, 2003). In Amazon's digital warehouses, however, a chaotic form of inventory exists in which hundreds of stowers work asynchronously in a complex form of cooperation to generate a system that that no human being could ever attempt to know in its entirety. These processes feed into Amazon's ability to algorithmically reorganize and modulate other warehouse processes. And thus the monopoly over knowledge in the warehouse resides in machinery, rather than with its human managers.

Pick, or Algorithmic Management and Control

When a customer places an order on Amazon's website, a cascade of effects begin and then reach their end on the screen of a picker's barcode scanner. The scanner tasks an associate with first retrieving the commodity and then sending it to packing and shipping. Since the process of stowing has been captured, Amazon's system software knows the position of copies of the commodity in the pick tower, calculates which copy should be assigned to each picker for efficiency, and then tasks a specific worker with retrieving it. This form of algorithmic management is based upon the standardization and taskification of the labor process made possible by this incorporation of knowledge in the machine (Lee et al., 2015; Wood et al., 2019). In turn, this allows Amazon to strictly control masses of workers who can quickly be put to work in the warehouse.

Picker is the most common entry-level job for Amazon warehouse associates and accounts for the relative majority of positions in the FC. Hundreds of pickers walk among the shelves pulling a cart that carries the tote they need to fill up with their "batch." A picker's batch is the series of tasks they are assigned; that is, a set of items to pick. The barcode scanner communicates to the picker the next commodity they are to pick, for example, showing the text "teddy bear" and an image of the item they are to retrieve. It also communicates the position on the shelves and the time in which the picker must complete the task—often a minute or so. Once again, the barcode gun is used to scan the item's barcode as well as that of the tote it is placed in after being picked. The system responds by recording and approving the process. As they move through the shelves, pickers are guided step by step by their barcode scanner, which assigns a series of tasks and guides workers through a specific route. This form of algorithmic management speeds up work and thus relegates pickers to the "Amazon pace," which means one must walk as fast as possible without running. A picker noted how this rhythm is dictated by the scanner:

> As you are loading an object onto the cart, the next one appears on the scanner. So as you are loading your cart you start moving, and as you are arriving you already take a look at what you are to pick next, you don't stop, and then you look at the shelf, is it a book or something else? In which area of the shelf is it?

The hustle that characterizes daily work at Amazon is identified by most pickers as one of the most emblematic features of warehouse work. Pickers commonly use words such as "pulling," "pushing," or "running" to describe the extremely physical nature of their daily routine. Furthermore, little craft or knowledge of the inventory is required to work as a picker. In fact, because of the rigid form of task allocation it generates, many workers perceive algorithmic management as an agent of alienation:

> You acquire those two conditioned reflexes to understand how to do this thing, and then just repeat them, anyone could do it. . . . You just need to follow the scanner, which tells you go here, go there, pick this and pick that. You don't need to do anything else, don't need to think. Eight hours can last 24 hours because you are in a limbo.

The scanner communicates to pickers, but at the same time it registers all activities performed by a worker. Again, this is not dissimilar to previously described processes of worker surveillance in gig economy companies. Warehouse labor is quantified—that is, subject to forms of calculation of workers' output, such as items picked per hour. This is immediately made visible to management, which has access to several types of information about each worker's performance. As described by a former team leader, "You log into the scanner and then they see how many pieces one does per hour. . . . It's very simple, you see a line for stowing or picking, if the line interrupts you can see if the worker has gone to the bathroom, if he stopped, you can see in which hours he was faster." The case of picking illustrates how the incorporation of knowledge in machinery makes selecting and replacing workers easier. Indeed, the automation of managerial functions based on machinic dispossession boosts Amazon's ability to sustain high turnover rates and provide the flexible workforce needed by a market characterized by sudden spikes in sales. It only takes hours to train new associates to work as pickers. Amazon training is organized around "schools," which are really crash courses for workers to learn a specific process, such as pick or receive. In turn, this permits the FC to rely on masses of workers who can quickly be put to work in the warehouse and endure work rhythms, thus fostering fast turnover of the workforce but maintaining high productivity levels. But turnover is not enough: management needs to ensure a smooth and productive relation between workers and machinery.

Management, or Augmented Despotism

"Work hard. Have fun. Make history." As workers walk into the warehouse for their shift, this slogan painted on the wall reminds them of the regime that underpins work at the FC. Technology alone does not dictate the speed of work; rather, it must be imposed through a mix of workplace discipline and worker self-discipline—isn't it fun to staff the warehouse? In sum, workers need to be persuaded that they can be controlled by machines (Grint and Woolgar, 1997). This is a common issue in capitalist relations of production. At Amazon, the typical role of the bureaucratic apparatus in Taylorist settings—to suck from living labor the information that allows managers to control flows and intensify the production process—is automated. Managers themselves must rely on system algorithms to retrieve items, assign a series of tasks, or calculate worker productivity. In fact, many leads (team leaders) or floor managers are hired straight out of school and do not have experience of warehouse work. They are tasked with political rather than organizational roles: a form of *augmented despotism* that produces new forms of domination mediated and enhanced by the use of technology to surveil and discipline workers.

At the same time, warehouse despotism is boosted by the import of elements from Silicon Valley corporations as a "cultural infrastructure" for the organization of labor on the warehouse floor.[2] In fact, the FC mimics corporate campuses such as Google's or Facebook's. This includes informal and colorful environments, foosball tables, loud music, and free goodies. Workers can (outside of their shift) relax and socialize in the canteen and other common spaces, although many describe a work experience in which "human interactions are discouraged and disincentivized if not explicitly punished . . . in the end even in the canteen there is always a lead or a manager," as I was told by a temp worker. In fact, adherence to Amazon's culture is enforced by leads and managers rather than emergent from social interactions. At the beginning of each shift, as well as before restarting work after lunch break, all workers in a certain area, say pick, are required to attend a "briefing," or "stand-up," led by management. These five-minute meetings are used by management to impose worker participation in Amazon's workplace culture. For example, workers are asked to raise their hand and suggest a "success story" in front of the rest of the team, a practice that clashes with Italian work culture and is often met with irony. During briefings, managers may also say something about the team's performance, which workers are implicitly required to celebrate. As reported by a worker, managers at times say things like "yesterday we had an insane productivity rate!" followed by applause. Another time, "a manager had come back from an experience in a different warehouse, and we applauded too."

Many workers consider the briefing a hypocritical exercise and seem to describe what Marx called capital's need to involve workers in a "caricature" of the social regulation of production while simultaneously taking away from them the very power to decide over productive processes. As described by an associate: "They try to foment you: 'guys, we have 200,000 pieces today, are we going to make it?' All bullshit that is only there to make you run more, to exalt you." Other workers describe their reaction to briefings in harsher terms: "management may round you up and tell you things like 'think about it folks, thanks to you today many children will smile, you have brought joy in the homes of thousands of families.' That's when I want to punch them." In fact, briefings seem to be geared toward ensuring the adhesion of workers to the pace dictated by algorithmic management. The pace can also be gamified through techniques derived from the service economy, such as in call center work (Woodcock, 2017). For example, Amazon managers often launch a "power hour," an hour-long period in which all workers on a team are required to "pull," or work as fast as they can. Power hours squeeze high productivity levels from associates, who in exchange may receive petty prizes, such as a company t-shirt, as well as public recognition in front of the team.

Predictably, such a workplace culture contributes to pressuring workers to accept the hustle and flexibility required by fulfillment processes. An example of such comes from a worker who said no to a request for overtime: "That time that we said no [to overtime] we had to log out in front of all the others who kept on working. It looked like the walk of shame [from *Game of Thrones*]. And I was sick that day and they would go like: 'c'mon, aren't you staying?'"

It is clear that this pressure is furthered by the casualized nature of Amazon labor. During peaks, the FC doubles its staff by including hundreds of workers hired through staffing agencies. These workers very quickly face the need to avoid expulsion from Amazon at the end of their contracts, which can last for a few weeks only. Workers describe temp workers with expressions such as "cannon fodder," who manage to work "absurd hours" under "psychological pressure" only because they are young and in good shape or do not have to worry about cooking or cleaning home after their shift. Still, a sense of insecurity dominates temp workers.

> Nobody told us we didn't have a future there, but that was the environment, the atmosphere: whatever you do we know where you are, how long you are taking, and there is lots of people who can do it better. If you don't do it, someone else will.

Managers collaborate with staffing agencies such as Adecco or Manpower, who have offices at the entrance of the FC. This is an incredible source of stress for workers as they have to deal with the uncertainty of the renewal of their contract, only being told at the end of their last if their livelihood can be sustained. As expressed by a full-time worker who had witnessed many waves of seasonal temp workers come and go: "at the beginning you quickly need to find a way to get your contract confirmed. You can be a pander, or you can run. Most people run. You have to run." Even full-time workers, who under Italian law cannot be fired, hope that keeping up with managerial requests will allow them to go up the ladder and take up more desirable roles, such as lead or problem solver. Yet the nature of work prevents many from moving vertically in the organization:

> They tell you "this is a complete meritocracy, if you are worth more than the next guy, quickly you will build a career for yourself." . . . But it's exactly the opposite: If you are faster, never call in sick with a backache, after a while your back is gone, you have carpal tunnel, psoriasis caused by stress . . . and those are the first they set aside.

This pressure is enhanced by the disciplinary role of managers, who have access to the data generated and crunched from associates' performance. This data augments supervisors' power to rank and discipline workers. The barcode gun thus becomes a tool of surveillance and communication in the service of managers, whose networked computers can access the backend of inventory software and track each associate's activity. For example, the scanner can be used to recall a picker or stower from the pick tower for a "feedback session" in which she is told that she is not meeting the team's "targets." In turn, this can put her job at risk. The despotic nature of targets is based on asymmetrical access to information, as only managers have access to the aggregated data used to calculate a worker's performance. A lead recalls how this is used to push associates to their limits: "Sometimes the manager would ask me to go tell this or that worker to push a little bit because they were slow. I checked and then said, 'but they are so fast!' How the fuck am I supposed to tell them to accelerate? But being critical doesn't lead anywhere in there."

Associates know that the opaque nature of targets is used to discipline the workforce. Some count the number of items they stow or pick per hour, for example assigning an arbitrary estimated quantity of items to a tote and then counting the totes they have emptied or loaded during a shift. This can be frustrated by the fact that managers refer to percentages, for example 80 percent of target, without disclosing the nature of the target. Some associates identify this as a factor furthering the pressure they experience: "Some days you can tell they have to give feedback, you see them all lurking with their little computers. That day I saw they were keeping an eye on me and tried to be fast but . . . they called me aside and told me . . . it is my fault if we have to work overtime."

In sum, the manager's role is to enforce worker surveillance and discipline while perpetuating a cultural construction of Amazon as a special workplace. This regime operates in parallel with machinic dispossession to secure worker collaboration in corporate goals. The construction of a cultural infrastructure based on flexibility and coolness and responding to the need to control and foster worker productivity has been identified, although in different forms, in digital capitalism corporations such as Google and Uber.[3] At Amazon, this is coupled with what Alquati identified at FIAT in the early 1960s as "parasitic management," that is, the fundamentally political nature of hierarchies and division of labor within the workplace (1961).

Conclusion

A massive infrastructure sustains the digital economy but, as noted by Ursula Huws, one should not overlook the role of "real people and real bodies" (2014). Indeed, the incorporation of worker knowledge in software systems does not eliminate the need for the control of living labor. In fact, the latter need grows with the increased technological nature of the labor process. As put by Panzieri, capital has "an absolute necessity to obtain an absolute integration of variable capital in fixed capital" (1967, 51). At Amazon, such integration is fostered through the interplay between machinic dispossession and augmented despotism, which subordinate workers to both algorithmic systems and organizational techniques.

Amazon's financial, cultural, and political power, as well as its ability to drive technological evolution, make it a perfect candidate to understand changes in the relation between labor and machinery that may reverberate beyond the walls of its FCs. Marx said that machines break the resistance which workers continue to oppose to the despotism of capital and create "new incentives which whet its insatiable appetite for the labour of others" (1976, 526). This is true in Amazon warehouses too, as they mobilize masses of workers who perform repetitive physical tasks, quickly enter production cycles, and can be expelled just as quickly. Moreover, algorithmic systems foster capital's more recent but equally insatiable appetite *for the data of others*. They are responsible for the datafication and capture of worker knowledge that is used downstream to strictly control the labor process. To optimize its ability to satiate its appetite, digital capitalism relies on forms of despotism reminiscent of the tumultuous days of early industrial capitalism while being augmented by emerging technical and cultural rationalities.

Notes

1. This chapter is an abridged version of an article published in *New Media and Society* (Delfanti, 2019). Interviews with Italian Amazon workers have been translated by the author. Participants and their personal information have been anonymized.

2. I borrow the concept of "cultural infrastructure" from Fred Turner's research on Google's corporate culture. See Turner, 2009.

3. For a broader understanding of Google and Uber's strategic use of "flexibility" and "coolness" in their cultural infrastructure to retain employees and justify employee overwork, see Turner, 2009, and Rosenblat and Stark, 2016, respectively.

References

Alquati, Romano. (1961). Tradizione e Rinnovamento Alla FIAT-Ferriere. *Democrazia Diretta.*

Anonymous. (2018, November 21). Our New Column from inside Amazon: "They Treat Us as Disposable." *The Guardian.*

Braverman, Henry. (1974). *Labour and Monopoly Capital: The Degradation of Work in the Twentieth Century*. Monthly Review Press.

Danaher, John. (2016). The Threat of Algocracy: Reality, Resistance and Accommodation. *Philosophy of Technology* 29, no. 3: 245–68.

Deleuze, Gilles, and Guattari, Félix. (1987). A *Thousand Plateaus: Capitalism and Schizophrenia.* University of Minnesota Press.

Delfanti, Alessandro. (2019). Machinic Dispossession and Augmented Despotism: Digital Work in an Amazon Warehouse. *New Media and Society* 23, no. 1: 39–55.

Gertler, Meric S. (2003). Tacit Knowledge and the Economic Geography of Context, or the Undefinable Tacitness of Being (There). *Journal of Economic Geography* 3, no. 1: 75–99.

Gordon, Eric, and Manosevitch, Edith. (2010). Augmented Deliberation: Merging Physical and Virtual Interaction to Engage Communities in Urban Planning. *New Media and Society* 13, no. 1: 75–95.

Grint, Keith, and Woolgar, Steve. (1997). *The Machine at Work: Technology, Work and Organization.* Wiley.

Huws, Ursula. (2014). *Labor in the Global Digital Economy: The Cybertariat Comes of Age*. NYU Press.

LeCavalier, Jesse. (2016). *The Rule of Logistics: Walmart and the Architecture of Fulfillment.* University of Minnesota Press.

Lee, Min Kyung, Kusbit, Daniel, Metsky, Evan, and Dabbish, Laura. (2015). Working with Machines: The Impact of Algorithmic and Data-Driven Management on Human Workers. *Proceedings of the 33rd Annual ACM Conference on Human Factors in Computing Systems*, 1603–12.

Marx, Karl. (1976). *Capital: A Critique of Political Economy*. Volume I. Penguin.

McLuhan, Marshall. (1964). *Understanding Media: The Extensions of Man*. McGraw-Hill.

Panzieri, Raniero. (1967). Lotte Operaie Nello Sviluppo Capitalistico. *Quaderni piacentini* 6, no. 29: 41–63.

Panzieri, Raniero. (1961). Sull'Uso Capitalistico Delle Macchine Nel Neocapitalismo. *Quaderni Rossi* 1: 53–72.

Rosenblat, Alex, and Stark, Luke. (2016). Algorithmic labor and information asymmetries: A case study of Uber's drivers. *International Journal of Communication* 10: 3758–84.

Tronti, Mario. (1980). The Strategy of Refusal. *Semiotext(e)* 3, no. 3: 28–34.

Turner, Fred. (2009). Burning Man at Google: A Cultural Infrastructure for New Media Production. *New Media and Society* 11, no. 1–2: 73–94.

Wood, Alex J., Graham, Mark, Lehdonvirta, Vili, and Hjorth, Isis. (2018). Good Gig, Bad Gig: Autonomy and Algorithmic Control in the Global Gig Economy. *Work, Employment and Society* 33, no. 1: 56–75.

Woodcock, Jamie. (2017). *Working the Phones: Control and Resistance in Call Centres*. Pluto Press.

Zuboff, Shoshana. (2019). *The Age of Surveillance Capitalism: The Fight for a Human Future at the New Frontier of Power*. PublicAffairs.

PART II

~

PRACTICES OF RESISTANCE

CHAPTER FIVE

~

Platforms, Resistance, Organizing

Jamie Woodcock and Callum Cant

Amazon has grown to shape increasing parts of the contemporary world. The warehouse is the backbone of Amazon's logistical operation, with an astonishing number of 'fulfilment centres' across the world: 175 covering over 150 million square feet of space (Amazon, 2019). This huge physical infrastructure has drawn in over a million workers. The impact of Amazon's growth has been the subject of much writing. Analysis has often focused on new technology, forms of control, or management techniques. For example, there has been much discussion about the working conditions in the warehouses (Briken and Taylor, 2018; Alimahomed-Wilson and Reese, 2020), as well as the use of automation and robots in the work process (Delfanti, 2021). Some writing on Amazon draws on undercover reporting (Bloodworth, 2018) or the writing of Amazon Workers and Supporters (2018). Through Amazon's expansion into digital services, like Amazon Web Services (AWS) and Mechanical Turk, the processes of the warehouse are increasingly being applied to workers beyond the company.

Given the wide range of approaches to Amazon, in this chapter we want to focus on worker writing. These draw attention to the experiences of work at different points of Amazon, highlighting the connections and similarities. There has been a proliferation of workers writing about their experiences of the work, both in the warehouses and other parts of Amazon's business. These provide glimpses of conflict and struggle across all parts of Amazon's platform of work. They bring to life experiences that are hidden from the consumer, whether behind the screen or the walls of the warehouse. More importantly, they can also provide insights, from warehouses, Mechanical Turk, and food delivery, of the ways in which workers push back against Amazon. If we want to understand resistance and organising in the wider context of Amazon, this is an important starting point.

Insights from Worker Writing

Examples of worker writing on Amazon can be found in Notes from Below, as well as through organising campaigns and elsewhere. As editors of Notes from Below, we have supported worker writers to develop their own accounts of working at Amazon. These provide an important reminder to researchers on the topic that there already many experts in the inner workings of Amazon, developing this through their day-to-day experiences. The accounts draw attention to the experiences of the work, as well as the ways that workers respond to this. For example, as Enzo (2021a) explained about his experience of working in a warehouse in Scotland:

> What I witnessed and experienced there was repulsive. Managers bullied and intimidated agency workers; COVID-19 health and safety policies were used and abused to discipline labour; precarious staff were frequently turned away from scheduled shifts, and bottles of exploited workers' urine abounded across the workplace.

In the second part, Enzo (2021b) focused on finding moments of struggle in the warehouse:

> It is not just the hum of conveyor belts and the screams of despotic managers that echo inside Amazon centres: beneath the surface, these places pulse with working class hatred and subtle acts of resistance.

This is an important part of inquiry: not just investigating work to explain how terrible it is or how bad the conditions are, but searching for moments of conflict. Throughout the pieces, Enzo reflects on the challenges for organising, trying to understand how these acts of resistance can build into something more. Similarly, John Holland (2020), a warehouse worker in the United Kingdom, explained,

> it's very difficult to establish bonds with other workers here. . . . If you were to set up a work regime primarily with the goal of hindering union organising, this is exactly how you'd do it. On top of all that, there is a big turnover in staff.

Amazon has clearly invested much time, money, and energy into preventing workers from organising in warehouses. There are large structural challenges in even bringing workers together to collectively discuss organising. However, as John Holland (2020) goes on to explain:

> It doesn't take much imagination to realise how very poorly paid we are for the amount of value we're generating for Amazon. At the time of writing Jeff Bezos has a net worth of $189 billion. If this place stopped functioning it'd probably hit the whole economy of the West Midlands with how dependent people and businesses are on online deliveries in these times. How many other workplaces can say that?

As Holland notes, Amazon workers have immense potential disruptive power, something that has only grown through the COVID-19 pandemic and the shifts in consumption during the lockdowns. However, there remain important challenges to developing sustained organising in the warehouses. Martin Harvey (2018), writing from the experiences of working at a warehouse in the United States, argued:

> Building a union at Amazon can't be done on the shop alone. A union at Amazon will be the product of organizing the class, down to the neighborhood level, and engaging the full person in their political, social, and cultural life. Our fights must be fueled by the will to be in common—to ultimately work less to be together more—and to fully augment our capacities as living, collective beings.

What these pieces highlight (and we would highly recommend going and reading them for the firsthand experience presented in them) is that the labour process and work are being reorganised in the global Amazon warehouses.

Notes from Below (2018) provide an updated framework of class composition that can help to make sense of these changes. Clearly, the technical composition—that is the way the work is organised, managed, and the use of technology—is important for understanding the political composition of how workers struggle. Large numbers of workers subjected to the discipline of the warehouse can find forms of struggle that could build on the disruptive power that Holland identified. The addition that Notes from Below adds to this is the idea of 'social composition', that is, the way that workers are organised into class society. Harvey's argument of a broader understanding of how a union at Amazon can be formed shows the importance of the communities and connections outside of the workplace, but we could also add to that the role of migration, oppression, the state and other factors beyond the walls of the warehouse.

Amazon Mechanical Turk

The growth of warehouses is only one part of Amazon. The warehouses support the e-commerce platform, providing the infrastructure to support online shopping. Behind the digital interface of the website, we know from the inquiries discussed before that there are bleak working conditions and new forms of technology being used to exploit workers. However, this was not the only kind of "new" work being created. One of the problems with running a large website is that it requires constant maintenance to ensure that the listings of commodities are up to date and that there are no duplicates. The buying process should be as smooth as it can be, both before the consumer buys something, as well as how it gets dispatched to them. In 2001, Amazon filed a patent for a 'hybrid machine/human computing arrangement' (Harinarayan, Rajaraman, and Ranganathan, 2007) to try and solve this issue. The solution that was developed became known as Amazon Mechanical Turk, a work platform that divides tasks into small human intelligence tasks. The name comes from the fake chess automaton (Levitt, 2000) that relied on a hidden person operating it. Amazon (2016) describes the service as 'artificial artificial intelligence', the human labour hidden behind the software interface. Instead of using computation to complete these small tasks, they are distributed out to workers to complete on their own.

This process is known as 'crowdsourcing' (Howe, 2006). As Lanier (2014, 178) explains, the process has 'a sense of magic, as if you can just pluck results out of the cloud at an incredibly low cost.' The workers do not need to be employed, but instead can just be engaged on a task-by-task basis. It was not long before Amazon offered this service externally, becoming popular with academic researchers and other clients, offering a low-cost way to complete surveys, image recognition, or other tasks that can be broken down. There has been a wide range of literature produced on Amazon Mechanical Turk (Irani and Silberman, 2013; Gupta et al., 2014; Hara et al., 2018; Gray and Suri, 2019).

There is also worker writing on Mechanical Turk, explaining what the work process is like in practice. As Sherry (2020), a 'Turker', explains:

> I can't remember the last day that I didn't log onto Turk on my laptop. It is not something that I have thought about, but it is a strange feeling looking back at how often I log on. I can say that I have had the convenience of working

> when I wanted to, but sometimes I would have to work double time to make it worthwhile. . . . Speaking honestly, I love Turk and it has opened so many avenues for my family.

There are some in the literature talk about the work as a kind of 'digital sweatshop' (Scholz, 2012; Pittman and Sheehan, 2016). However, what comes across in the worker writing is that it provides access to work that may not have been possible otherwise. There are examples of tips and strategies shared by workers to develop effective ways to make a living while Turking. The sweatshop analogy is one that often sees these workers as isolated and disconnected, without any possibility of fighting or bargaining for improvements in the working conditions. However, as Sherry continues, there was a moment in which she decided enough was enough:

> This meant finding a way to get a voice to Amazon, telling them that we wouldn't take this sitting down. It was time to make the Turker's voice heard: a time for change and to stand up. I believe that requesters can't be allowed to continue rejecting good and honest work just because they want to—or they want to scam the system and not pay. In turn, Amazon can't stay silent forever while their whole force of Turkers continue to be treated unfairly.

The main grievance here is that requesters—those who put work on the Turk platform—can refuse to pay without providing a reason. The platform monitors workers in great detail but leaves the requesters free to engage in activities like wage theft. Lilly Irani and Six Silberman (2013), two academic researchers, developed a software intervention to try and address this imbalance. They created a tool called Turkopticon, which seeks to reverse the panopticon-like relationship, providing a way for workers to rate requesters. Low ratings from other workers could provide a way to avoid the worst requesters, seeking to improve conditions on the platform. Turkers now run the platform, building a community of workers that can turn the frustrations of the work into action.

Amazon and Other Platforms

While Amazon offers the Turk platform to other clients, there is also another important service that Amazon sells. AWS is an on-demand cloud computer platform. It sells the computational infrastructure of Amazon as a service. In a way, this is related to the way that the retail interface has grown to sell more than products Amazon has chosen to stock, growing into a sales platform that many other smaller capitalists rely on to distribute their products.

AWS is used by many other platform companies, for example Airbnb, Apple, Baidu, Coursera, Deliveroo, Expedia, Facebook, LinkedIn, Lyft, Netflix, Slack, SoundCloud, Spotify, Twitch, Uber, and Uber Eats. These companies use the cloud services to host their offerings or use it to scale up during periods of higher demand.

This is an example of what has become known as a Pick-and-Shovel play. During the Australian gold rush, 'Walter Powell had the good sense to stop at his store and sell shovels and pickaxes at a premium, and so he suddenly became rich.' (Clifford, 1876, 172). Instead of fighting to get more of the gold during a rush, Powell's wealth came from cashing in on the desire of those who thought they could get rich. AWS is providing the digital picks and shovels for the platform gold rush. AWS accounts for 54.4 percent of Amazon's operating income. Within the remaining share, Amazon makes vast profits through advertising, as well as its original offering of the online shopfront. In 2021, third-party sellers, who use Amazon's warehouse operation to fulfil their sales, accounted for 56 percent of unit sales overall. More products were sold by third parties (with Amazon taking a commission, of course) than directly by Amazon (Davis, 2021). There are physical picks and shovels as well as the digital version.

Amazon itself tried to enter the gold rush of food delivery platforms—although they seemed to be content with just providing servers for passenger transport platforms. There is a logic to this, as Amazon has already created a complex and global logistics network to move commodities from one place to another. In the United Kingdom, for example, Amazon offers one-day delivery, same-day delivery, same-day grocery delivery (with Amazon Fresh and the fourth largest British supermarket Morrisons), and the recently defunct Amazon Now which would deliver a selection of products in London in under one hour. Amazon also attempted a fast food delivery service: Amazon Restaurants. Launched in 2016 in London, it attempted to compete with rivals Deliveroo and Uber Eats. However, two years later, the service was closed. As one industry observer noted at the time: 'it is a highly competitive market and perhaps they needed to be more than a logistics company trying to be a food company. There's an emotional component with food that maybe they didn't understand' (quoted in Prynn, 2018). There was a similar failure to enter the market in the United States. As Joshua Fruhlinger (2019) reported, Amazon 'came to the game too late.' In Los Angeles, for example, Amazon provided deliveries for 126 restaurants. The other platforms—DoorDash, Uber Eats, Grubhub, and Postmates—delivered for 15,733. In New York, that figure was 485 to 22,062. Across the whole of the United States, there were 6,235 restaurants for Amazon and 842,746 for the competitors with a ratio of 135:1 (Prynn, 2018). It is therefore no surprise that Amazon Restaurants ended in failure.

The failure led to a change of strategy for Amazon. They invested in Deliveroo, a UK-based food delivery platform that now operates across Europe, Australia, Hong Kong, Kuwait, Singapore, and the United Arab Emirates. Amazon explored buying a major stake or taking over Deliveroo. Further investment was blocked by the UK Competition and Markets Authority, which blocked the investment for almost a year (Bernal, 2021). Despite this, they continued to collaborate, particularly through AWS. Amazon (2020) claimed that 'Deliveroo relies on Amazon Web Services (AWS) in every part of its core business: accepting orders, transmitting them to restaurants, and delivering meals to customers.' As they continue: 'Deliveroo has gone all in on AWS, using it for compute and database, creating and testing ML functionality, personalizing features, customer contact centers, and intelligently dispatching drivers. It now plans to migrate services currently with other providers.' The continued growth of Deliveroo has relied on Amazon's picks and shovels. This shows how closely Deliveroo relies on Amazon to supply the many digital picks and shovels for their food delivery business.

When thinking about workers' experience of Amazon, Deliveroo workers therefore need to be considered too. They are impacted by the technologies developed by Amazon, underpinning Deliveroo's organisation of the work. Deliveroo has over fifty thousand workers in the United Kingdom. There has been a wide range of worker writing on Deliveroo. For example, as one Deliveroo rider (Waters and Woodcock, 2017) explained:

> Working for Deliveroo on a bike presents a comforting illusion of freedom. You are on a bike, you can pick your route, and to a certain degree you go at your own pace. However, this comforting illusion is regularly unravelled. Sometimes a whole shift can be unremittingly shit. In the winter you have entire weeks in the snow, wind, or rain when the weather is –3 to 3 degrees Celsius and all your shifts are in the dark. Your hands, feet, and face are numbingly cold and your body is sweating from your clothing and the exercise, but you still have to be aware of ice and wet leaves on the road and the bad judgements of other road users who are also inhibited by the conditions.

Similarly, in Notes from Below, Alice Barker (2020) explained the draw of working on the platform: 'The decent wage and promise of flexible working drew me in, both, because those sound good, but also because it wasn't another minimum wage bar job. This is an important element of the gig economy which I think is often overlooked.' In her account, she explains the conditions under which riders work:

> Some are really struggling, with long empty days hanging around waiting for an order to come in. Much has changed during my time as a courier, but it is now clear that the idea we are "all in this together" was a myth. The platforms still refuse to communicate or support workers through COVID-19.

The COVID-19 pandemic deeply impacted Deliveroo. As the pandemic spread, some of the major restaurants that Deliveroo relied upon—KFC, Burger King, and Wagamama—shut down. The rival platforms, Uber Eats and Just Eat, were outcompeting Deliveroo. Deliveroo returned to the Competition and Markets Authority to admit the platform was failing. If the investment from Amazon was not approved, they claimed the platform would close. The investment allowed Deliveroo to solidify its position, expanding the 'dark kitchens' (Garlick, 2017) or 'cloud kitchens.' These are sites away from the customer-facing restaurant that churn out food at a lower cost specifically for food delivery platforms. They have spread across the United Kingdom, increasing particularly during the COVID-19 pandemic. It is creating a new form of catering work, specifically organised to produce food quickly and efficiently for the delivery market.

Deliveroo was therefore able to go from 'fast-growing start-up, to failing firm, to on track for an [initial public offering (IPO)]' (Bernal, 2021), evading concerns from regulators in the United Kingdom to forge an increasingly closer relationship with Amazon. For example, Amazon has recently launched a Prime food delivery bundle for free delivery on Deliveroo. It has drawn a larger layer of workers into contact with Amazon, attempting to reshape their work in ways that are similar to warehouse and Mechanical Turk workers.

Conflict on Platforms

The expansion of Amazon into the food delivery operations of Deliveroo has not been without new challenges, however. There is a more complicated history of Deliveroo than the ups and downs of its share price. The first strikes at Deliveroo took place in August of 2016 (Woodcock, 2016). Workers involved in the dispute unionised with the Independent Workers Union of Great Britain, a small 'indie' union (Però, 2019). From that first incident of open struggle at Deliveroo, there have been waves of strikes that have spread across other countries that Deliveroo operates in, including the Netherlands, Germany, Spain, Belgium, France, and Italy. These strike waves involved increasing numbers of incidents, with more workers, and became increasingly synchronised (Cant, 2018).

These conflicts emerge from the organisation of the labour process at Deliveroo. There are tensions over app-based management, deactivations, issues with lack of communication, as well as the ever-present grievances over pay rates (Waters and Woodcock, 2017; Cant, 2019; Woodcock, 2020). However, despite the obstacles posed by how the work is organised, 'it is possible for workers to counterbalance the power disparities that characterise the gig economy by articulating active solidarity, which gives collective expression to the underlying antagonism of the labour process' (Tassinari and Maccarrone, 2020, 51). New worker organisations have sprung up in different countries, communicating with each other, as well as meeting in conferences of the Transnational Couriers Federation (Cant and Mogno, 2020). In a surprisingly short space of time, Deliveroo has gone from a platform that many observed would be a difficult context for workers to organise within, to the most protested platform—accounting for over a quarter of all incidents of worker protests from January 2017 to May 2020 (Joyce et al., 2020).

Platforms like Deliveroo have refigured the organisation of work in new ways that bring large numbers of workers into contact with each other. There are three important dynamics that this has involved. First, while there is no physical location or office to gather, the streets of the city become a dispersed workplace. As with all cities, there is an uneven geography, with preferred meeting points and busy restaurants where riders meet. Rather than isolating these workers, platforms have facilitated the increased connection between workers. Smartphones used in the work process have forged new links between workers on WhatsApp groups across the city. However, this leads to a second important factor: a lack of communication from platforms. Often owing to the use of bogus self-employment contacts, as well as the limited management by Deliveroo itself, it is difficult for workers to effectively communicate with the company. This prevents the mediation of disputes, leading to escalating worker action, seen with the continuing widespread use of the wildcat strike as a tactic. Third, the growth of platforms like Deliveroo has led to an internationalisation of these campaigns and the sharing of tactics and strategies by workers in different countries (Woodcock, 2021).

These different dynamics came to a culmination with Deliveroo launching an IPO in London in April 2021. As noted before, Deliveroo had almost failed before receiving investment from Amazon. The IPO gathered significant attention, but also became the focus of a worker campaign. In the run-up to the IPO, the Independent Workers Union of Great Britain organised a campaign to target the company from multiple angles. A strike was organised for the day, an investigation of pay that found riders earning as little as two British pounds per hour (Mellino, Boutaud, and Davies,

2021), and institutional investors were targeted—many withdrawing due to concerns about workers' rights (Topham, 2021). This combination led to *The Financial Times* reporting that it was the 'worst IPO in London's history' (Bradshaw and Mooney, 2021). It has also seen the emergence of a model of union organising that is beginning to push back against platforms (Woodcock and Cant, 2021).

The Logistics of Platform Struggle

Whether through directly reorganising supply chains and logistics, or through providing the digital picks and shovels to other companies, Amazon has become a key part of the contemporary world. Platforms like Deliveroo have provided an important laboratory for capital to experiment with new ways of organising work (Cant, 2019). They tend to involve the use of self-employment statuses, evading regulation, and often at the sharper end of technological change. However, while capital may have had the initiative in the first phase of platform capitalism, that period is now over. As we have argued elsewhere (Cant and Woodcock, 2019):

> Resistance is clearly already happening, from Deliveroo riders in London, Uber drivers in Bangalore, to Meituan workers in Guangzhou. A working class recomposition is rapidly under way. The key question now is understanding what forms of struggle can be successful beyond the short term and how these can be generalised more widely by the working class, both logging off platforms and breaking away from capitalism more broadly.

Platforms are increasingly forming connections between workers that were once thought of as technologically isolated or dominated by algorithmic management. The international spread of these platforms is forging new connections between worker struggles, like with the Transnational Couriers Federation.

Our argument here is that the scale and growth of Amazon may well have resulted in astronomical profits for the company. Jeff Bezos, Amazon's founder, has a personal net worth of £140 billion. It would take a UK warehouse worker at Amazon eight million years to earn that much. When Bezos uses that money to fly into space, we can also see an illustration of how remote his experiences have become from the workers who created the wealth that he has stolen—whether on the warehouse floor, Amazon Mechanical Turk, or riding for Deliveroo. This is a level of wealth so remote from the day-to-day experiences of workers that it can be hard to comprehend. For example, when Jeff Bezos heard of the cancellation of the science fiction series *The Expanse*, he promptly arranged for Amazon to buy it: 'I like watching the show, so let's make it work' (quoted in Beale, 2019). Like a feudal lord of the past, Bezos' wealth is not trickling down to anyone, but the new vassals and peasants can at least benefit from watching a space drama—although, of course, not afford to actually go into space like he will.

Anger against the accumulation of vast personal wealth is not likely to prove enough to spark widespread resistance to Amazon. However, the increasing platformisation of work at Amazon exposes the company to more potential worker anger through the exploitation of the labour process, both in person and online. In this chapter we have highlighted how the different 'hidden abodes' (Marx, 1867) of production are also points of conflict between labour and capital. In the warehouses there have been sparks of resistance, strikes, and increasing attempts to build new trade unions. In the remote work of Amazon Mechanical Turk, workers are finding ways to come together collectively, despite the significant obstacles to doing so. As Amazon supplies the infrastructure—and sometimes funding—for other parts of the platform economy, it has become part of the new workers' struggles that are unfolding.

This is why workers' experiences of these different points of Amazon is important. Instead of seeing Amazon as an organisation that is shaping increasingly more of our lives and work, it is also becoming a place where new seeds of worker power are being sown. By focusing on the experiences of different kinds of work, it is possible to see an alternative. It will be on the warehouse floor, the laptops and smartphones, the roads and waiting points that the struggle against Amazon begins. The potential of these struggles points to another direction for "Amazonisation." The different examples of worker organising, whether in warehouses, Mechnical Turk, or at Deliveroo, are each experiments from workers about how to take back control. Amazon can become a focus for these struggles, connecting workers across different kinds of work. Historically, the docks brought workers together across the world, circulating information about struggles, as well as spreading struggles themselves (Cole, 2018). Contemporary logistics has the potential to play a similar role. They can also act as 'choke points' in the global economy (Alimahomed-Wilson and Ness, 2018), something that can clearly be seen with Amazon too. If we want to find solutions to the problems of contemporary work, the use of technology, and platformisation of the economy, it begins with examining these struggles.

References

Alimahomed-Wilson, Jake, and Ness, Immanuel, eds. (2018). *Choke Points: Logistics Workers Disrupting the Global Supply Chain.* London: Pluto Press.

Alimahomed-Wilson, Jake, and Reese, Ellen, eds. (2020). *The Cost of Free Shipping: Amazon in the Global Economy*. London: Pluto Press.

Amazon. (2016). Amazon Mechanical Turk. https://www.mturk.com/mturk/welcome.

———. (2019, January 14). Why Amazon Warehouses Are Called Fulfilment Centres. *UK About Amazon*. https://www.aboutamazon.co.uk/amazon-fulfilment/our-fulfilment-centres/why-amazon-warehouses-are-called-fulfilment-centers.

———. (2020). AWS Case Study—Deliveroo. *Amazon Web Services, Inc.* https://aws.amazon.com/solutions/case-studies/deliveroo-case-study1/.

Amazon Workers and Supporters. (2018). Stop treating us like dogs! Workers organizing resistance at Amazon in Poland. In *Choke Points: Logistics Workers Disrupting the Global Supply Chain*, edited by J. Alimahomed-Wilson and I. Ness, 96–109. London: Pluto Press.

Barker, Alice. (2020). Cycling in the city. *Notes from Below*. https://notesfrombelow.org/article/cycling-city.

Beale, Lewis. (2019, December 10). Jeff Bezos' 'Favourite TV Show' Is Coming to Amazon. The Creators Say It's a Perfect Fit. *Los Angeles Times*. https://www.latimes.com/entertainment-arts/tv/story/2019-12-10/the-expanse-syfy-amazon-jeff-bezos.

Bernal, Natasha. (2021). Amazon Took a Chunk of Deliveroo. Then Things Got Interesting. *Wired UK*. https://www.wired.co.uk/article/deliveroo-pandemic-amazon.

Bloodworth, James. (2018). *Hired: Six Months Undercover in Low-Wage Britain*. London: Atlantic Books.

Bradshaw, Tim, and Mooney, Attracta. (2021, March 31). Disaster Strikes as Deliveroo Becomes 'Worst IPO in London's History' *Financial Times*. https://www.ft.com/content/bdf6ac6b-46b5-4f7a-90db-291d7fd2898d.

Briken, Kendra, and Taylor, Phil. (2018). Fulfilling the 'British Way': Beyond constrained choice—Amazon workers' lived experiences of workfare. *Industrial Relations Journal* 49, no. 5–6: 428–58.

Cant, Callum. (2018). The Wave of Worker Resistance in European Food Platforms 2016-17. *Notes from Below*. https://notesfrombelow.org/article/european-food-platform-strike-wave.

———. (2019). *Riding for Deliveroo: Resistance in the New Economy*. Cambridge: Polity.

Cant, Callum, and Clara Mogno. (2020). Platform Workers of the World, Unite! The Emergence of the Transnational Federation of Couriers. *The South Atlantic Quarterly* 119, no. 2: 401–11.

Cant, Callum, and Jamie Woodcock. (2019). The End of the Beginning. *Notes from Below*. https://notesfrombelow.org/article/end-beginning.

Clifford, John. (1876). *General Baptist Magazine*. Volume 78. London: E. Malborough & Co.

Cole, Peter. (2018). *Dockworker Power: Race and Activism in Durban and the San Francisco Bay Area*. Urbana: University of Illinois Press.

Davis, Don. (2021). Amazon Sales, Amazon Revenue and Amazon Annual Profits. *Digital Commerce 360*. https://www.digitalcommerce360.com/article/amazon-sales/.

Delfanti, Alessandro. (2018). Amazon Is the New FIAT: Political Recomposition in the Italian Digital Economy. *Notes From Below*. https://notesfrombelow.org/article/amazon-is-the-new-fiat.

———. (2021). *Warehouse: Workers and Robots at Amazon*. London: Pluto Press.

Enzo. (2021a). A Season in "Hell": Working at Amazon at the Height of the Pandemic, Part 1. *Notes From Below*. https://notesfrombelow.org/article/working-amazon-height-pandemic-part-1.

———. (2021b). Social-Distancing and Alienation: Working at Amazon at the Height of the Pandemic, Part 2. *Notes From Below*. https://notesfrombelow.org/article/social-distancing-and-alienation.

Fruhlinger, Joshua. (2019, June 24). Amazon Outnumbered: Data Shows Why Amazon Restaurants Is Shutting down Today. *B2 The Business of Business*. https://www.businessofbusiness.com/articles/amazon-restaurants-failed-because-it-got-crowded/.

Garlick, H. (2017). Dark Kitchens: Is This the Future of Takeaway?. *The Financial Times*. https://www.ft.com/content/d23c44fe-4b0b-11e7-919a-1e14ce4af89b.

Gray, Mary L., and Suri, Siddarth. (2019). *Ghost Work: How to Stop Silicon Valley from Building a New Global Underclass*. New York: Houghton Mifflin Harcourt.

Gupta, Neha, Martin, David, Hanrahan, Benjamin V., and O'Neill, Jacki. (2014). Turk-life in India. *Proceedings of the ACM International Conference on Supporting Group Work (GROUP'14)*. Sanibel Island.

Hara, Kotaro, Adams, Abi, Kristy, Milland, Saiph, Savage, Callison-Burch, Chris, and Bigham, Jeffrey. (2018). A Data-Driven Analysis of Workers' Earnings on Amazon Mechanical Turk. *CHI'18: Proceedings of the 2018 CHI Conference on Human Factors in Computing Systems Paper*, no. 449.

Harinarayan, Venky, Rajaraman, Anand, and Ranganathan, Anand. (2007). United States Patent: 7197459 - Hybrid machine/human computing arrangement. 7197459, issued 27 March 2007. https://patft.uspto.gov/netacgi/nph-Parser?Sect1=PTO1&Sect2=HITOFF&d=PALL&p=1&u=%2Fnetahtml%2FPTO%2Fsrchnum.htm&r=1&f=G&l=50&s1=7,197,459.PN.&OS=PN/7,197,459&RS=PN/7,197,459.

Harvey, Martin. (2018). A Union at Amazon? Organize the Class, Not the Shop. *Notes From Below*. https://notesfrombelow.org/article/a-union-at-amazon.

Holland, John. (2020). Amazon Inquiry: An Inquiry at a Distribution Warehouse. *Notes From Below*. https://notesfrombelow.org/article/amazon-inquiry.

Howe, Jeff. (2006). The Rise of Crowdsourcing. *Wired*. http://www.wired.com/2006/06/crowds/.

Irani, Lilly C., and Silberman, M. Six. (2013). Turkopticon: Interrupting Worker Invisibility in Amazon Mechanical Turk. *Proceedings of CHI 2013*, 611–20. New York: ACM Press.

Joyce, Simon, Neumann, Denis, Trappmann, Vera, and Umney, Charles. (2020). A Global Struggle: Worker Protest in the Platform Economy. *ETUI Policy Brief* 2. https://www.etui.org/publications/policy-briefs/european-economic-employment-and-social-policy/a-global-struggle-worker-protest-in-the-platform-economy.

Lanier, Jaron. (2014). *Who Owns the Future?* New York: Simon and Schuster.

Levitt, Gerald M. (2000). *The Turk, Chess Automaton*. Jefferson, NC: McFarland.

Marx, Karl. (1867). *Capital: A Critique of Political Economy*. Volume 1. London: Penguin Books.

———. (1880). A Workers' Inquiry. *La Revue Socialiste*. https://www.marxists.org/archive/marx/works/1880/04/20.htm.

Mellino, Emiliano, Boutaud, Charles, and Davies, Gareth. (2021). Deliveroo Riders Can Earn as Little as £2 an Hour during Shifts, as Boss Stands to Make £500m. *The Bureau of Investigative Journalism*. https://www.thebureauinvestigates.com/stories/2021-03-25/deliveroo-riders-earning-as-little-as-2-pounds.

Notes from Below. (2018). The Workers' Inquiry and Social Composition: A New Framework for Class Composition Analysis. *Notes from Below*, no. 1. https://notesfrombelow.org/article/workers-inquiry-and-social-composition.

Però, Davide. (2019). Indie Unions, Organizing and Labour Renewal: Learning from Precarious Migrant Workers. *Work, Employment and Society*. https://journals.sagepub.com/doi/abs/10.1177/0950017019885075.

Pittman, Matthew, and Sheehan, Kim. (2016). Amazon's Mechanical Turk a Digital Sweatshop? Transparency and Accountability in Crowdsourced Online Research. *Journal of Media Ethics* 31, no. 4: 260–62. https://doi.org/10.1080/23736992.2016.1228811.

Prynn, Jonathan. (2018, November 22). Amazon Takeaways Axed after Two Years Following Fierce Competition from Deliveroo. *The Evening Standard*, sec. Business. https://www.standard.co.uk/business/business-news/amazon-takeaways-axed-after-two-years-following-fierce-competition-from-deliveroo-a3996896.html.

Scholz, T. (2012). *Digital Labor: The Internet as Playground and Factory*. New York: Routledge.

Sherry. (2020). Living as a Turker: An Inquiry at Amazon Mechanical Turk. *Notes From Below*. https://notesfrombelow.org/article/living-turker.

Tassinari, Arianna, and Maccarrone, Vincenzo. (2020). Riders on the Storm: Workplace Solidarity among Gig Economy Couriers in Italy and the UK. *Work, Employment and Society* 34, no. 1: 35–54.

Topham, Gwyn. (2021). Deliveroo Dampens IPO Expectations as Investors Raise Workers' Rights Concerns. *The Guardian*, sec. Business. https://www.theguardian.com/business/2021/mar/29/deliveroo-ipo-investors-workers-rights.

Waters, Facility, and Woodcock, Jamie. (2017). Far From Seamless: A Workers' Inquiry at Deliveroo. *Viewpoint Magazine*. https://www.viewpointmag.com/2017/09/20/far-seamless-workers-inquiry-deliveroo.

Woodcock, Jamie. (2016). #Slaveroo: Deliveroo Drivers Organising in the 'Gig Economy.' *Novara*. https://novaramedia.com/2016/08/12/slaveroo-deliveroo-drivers-organising-in-the-gig-economy.

———. (2020). The Algorithmic Panopticon at Deliveroo: Measurement, Precarity, and the Illusion of Control. *Ephemera* 20, no. 3: 67–95.

Woodcock, Jamie. (2021). *The Fight Against Platform Capitalism: An Inquiry into the Global Struggles of the Gig Economy*. London: University of Westminster Press.

Woodcock, Jamie, and Cant, Callum. (2021). Platform worker organising at Deliveroo in the UK: from wildcat strikes to building power. *Journal of Labor and Society*. https://brill.com/view/journals/jlso/aop/article-10.1163-24714607-bja10050.

CHAPTER SIX

~

Disrupting Work with Play on Mturk.com

A Visual Essay

xtine burrough

In this visual essay I narrate works of art that intervene in Amazon's Mechanical Turk platform. My works reveal the humanity, expressed corporeally, if not spiritually, of a workforce invisible to the common public, and also to Chief Executive Officer Jeff Bezos. While Bezos has a flight of fancy in space, his corporation operates by the hands of its workers: "roughly 1.2 million workers" were reportedly hired by Amazon as of September 2020 (Cain and Peterson, 2020). However, this chapter is not about Amazon warehouses or any of its 1.2 million on-the-ground factory employees. While Amazon Fulfilment Centers are the visible factories where workers create the affordance for Bezos in his civilian space missions, the company hosts an invisible factory, too. Amazon's Mechanical Turk is the global labor force of crowd-sourced workers who earn pennies per minute while completing virtual piecework.

Workers on Amazon.com's Mechanical Turk website (Mturk.com) complete simple assignments, called human intelligence tasks (HITs), that are too complex for a computer but only require minimal human intelligence. Requestors (or job managers) post HITs on the Mturk virtual job board. Then workers complete the HIT in tasks such as sorting, labeling, responding to surveys, creating keywords, or translating small phrases.

When I learned of this emergent form of crowdsourcing (which seemed to me like a digital sweatshop made newly possible by distributed technologies), I was both horrified and curious. I created a worker account to experience Mturk, and worked for an hour. I earned fifty-seven cents after completing twenty-seven HITs.[1]

With my suspicions confirmed, I set out to disrupt the system. Unlike the traditional "clog in the wheel" sabotage, a physical disruption bringing factories to a halt that influence rhetorical understandings of culture jamming,[2] my first effort created HITs that felt more like play than like work, while offering a fairer compensation than the penny "awards" I saw for jobs listed on the platform.

The compensation is the tricky part of this process. It positions me, as an artist interested in hacking the system, in the seat of the requestor. There's no way around feeling unsettled in this position, but these heavy emotions are part of the process. As a creative risk-taker, I often lift the heavy concepts and truths by countering them with lightness and play. After all, it is the unfair transactional nature of the system that horrified me in the first place—so it would have to be the location, if I was going to make a disruption, of the creative action to take place. For some of the jobs, especially in my earlier works, I simply offered significantly greater "reward" values than what I saw on the Mturk.com job board. Where most jobs were offered for one cent, five cents, or ten cents (in US currency), I offered two or three dollars per job. For other jobs, I offered a monetary value that created a symbolic or conceptual connection with the work of art. In later works, I ran a pilot version of the job in which I surveyed the workers to tell me if the pay was fair, then settled on what felt more like a negotiated (or at least a considered) wage for the bulk of the workers who would respond to the next iteration of the job post.

My alternatives to the usual job tasks asked workers to perform Olympic events, submit recipes, send happy birthday messages, light candles for loved ones, trace their hands, send messages they'd like to relay to Jeff Bezos, and reflect on working during the COVID-19 pandemic. These works span from 2008 to 2022. The following visual essay showcases creative projects that have resulted from a selection of these projects.

Mechanical Olympics

The *Mechanical Olympics* are a crowdsourced version of the Olympic Games (burrough, 2008). During the Games, I pay workers on Mturk to record a performance of an Olympic event and share their video on YouTube. Throughout the Games, anyone can vote for gold medal winners on the YouTube playlist (burrough, 2021). Winners are paid a bonus payment on Mturk.com. This project began in the summer of 2008 and has been performed every two years, corresponding to the timeline of the international Olympic Games (Figure 6.1).

Figure 6.1. xtine burrough, *Mechanical Olympics,* online project with Mechanical Turk workers, 2008–2021. xtine burrough

The first time I requested workers to submit media, I thought the request would seem unfamiliar, playful, and less scripted than the usual jobs. I wondered if anyone would take the job; then I wondered if they would enact their performance seriously, humorously, poetically, or indifferently. Workers did not fail to surprise me with their responses, and at once I realized that my art of instruction (my job request) had destabilized—even if only for the time it takes a worker to perform and upload a recording of themselves skating or swimming—the purpose Amazon had intended for its platform. When seen together, the worker performances create what Brian Holmes terms the "hieroglyphs of the future" as a "multiplicity of individual expression and [sic] unity of a collective will" (Holmes, 2007, 350–51). This intervention on Mturk went unnoticed by Amazon because I followed the rules of the platform. But, for myself and the workers who accepted my HIT, the rules were folded into an artful game that subversively replaced work with play.

In August 2016, I assembled a collection of videos for this project to accompany a talk at the Dallas Museum of Art for the museum's ten-channel video wall. I watched all of the videos I had collected with fresh eyes. It was not until then that I realized I have been watching one family from India grow throughout this time. The worker's name was familiar each year, but seeing the videos he made from 2010, 2012, 2014, and 2016 all together made me realize how members of this family have been consistent players in this project. As I have written before (burrough, 2020a), if there is but one ghost in the machine that I wish I could reach out and hug, it would be the Ghosh family in Bengal, India (Figure 6.2).

Figure 6.2. Soham Ghosh performs the *Mechanical Olympics* at seven (top left) and thirteen (top right) years old. Shamik Ghosh (bottom right) and his wife (bottom left) each perform "Curling" for the Mechanical Olympics in games separated by eight years, 2018 and 2010. xtine burrough

Mediations on Digital Labor

After the *Mechanical Olympics* became a somewhat mechanical intervention to reproduce, I thought about creating a new work that would focus on the workers' bodies as passive and restful, rather than active. For this second project, my intention was, again, to use the Mturk platform against itself. In my request for workers who participated in *Mediations on Digital Labor*, I asked fifty workers to do nothing—to "not work"—for one to five minutes.

I assumed workers might meditate or take a nap, or they might collect the money and not take a break at all (burrough, 2020–2022). I left a response field as a space for creative potential and asked the workers to describe their experience. These sentiments became a central visual component in an exhibition for the project room at Grand Central Art Center in Santa Ana, California, as I rendered the workers' reflections, a text in its own right, in chalk. When viewers walked into the room, they would obscure the words on the floor. This activity seemed appropriate, as the primary visual reference to the invisible workers would also fade away as the general public entered the space (Figure 6.3).

Viewers become participants as they travel the floor of the exhibition to a video kiosk in the center of the room (Figure 6.4). Here they could see and

Figure 6.3. Film still of the floor as it becomes covered in chalked text. See this clip, which includes a pan out for a full view of the floor on Vimeo, https://vimeo.com/210541664. xtine burrough

Figure 6.4. xtine burrough, *Mediations on Digital Labor*, Grand Central Art Center Project Room, Santa Ana, California, 2015. xtine burrough

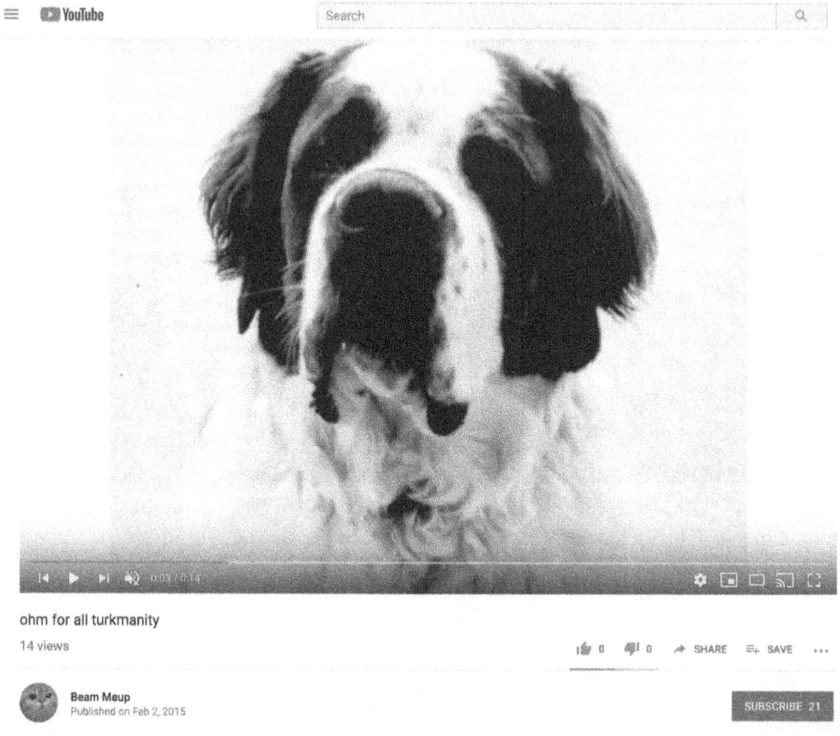

Figure 6.5. "Om [sic] for all turkmanity," a Mechanical Turk worker's response to a human intelligence task that requested the workers to chant "Om." xtine burrough

hear another set of Mechanical Turk workers, whom I paid to chant "Om." One worker sent me a video of a dog who appears to be chanting (Figure 6.5).

For gallery participants, I offered one of the USB drives hanging from the wall to anyone who volunteered to re-chalk the floor for thirty minutes. Each drive contained a single worker's chant. Counter to the invisible workers on Mturk, our bodies in the gallery would be put to work in order to make their sentiments visible. This inversion of visibility on the laboring body, from the digital workers in the cloud to our physical bodies in the gallery, was fundamental to the conceptual premise of the work of art.

A Vigil for Some Bodies

Following this exploration of workers resting or meditating, and also chanting, I hired workers to light a candle or take a moment to remember, reflect on, or say a prayer for someone whom they had loved and lost. *A Vigil for*

Some Bodies began in 2015 and continues to this writing. It consists of a single job post, annually, on the evening of October 31, a time in the year that coordinates with All Hallows' Eve/All Saints' Day and Día de los Muertos.

Workers were paid, initially, twenty-five cents for this job, the value of the iconic coin I remembered paying to light a votive in a cathedral. Upon further research I offered one dollar per job starting in 2018 as I realized the price for participation in candle lighting in the real world had increased since my childhood experiences.

I asked workers to share with me anything they wanted about their experience and collected worker's prayers, intentions, memories, and photographs. In turn, I created a series of battery-operated candles, purchased from Amazon.com, with the names of the people the workers remembered, worker IDs, and sentiments collected about these loved ones (Figure 6.6).

I tried to bring this work into an Amazon Fulfillment Center, but it was only mildly successful as the degree of surveillance in the warehouses prevented me from further intervention (Figures 6.7 and 6.8) (burrough, 2020b).

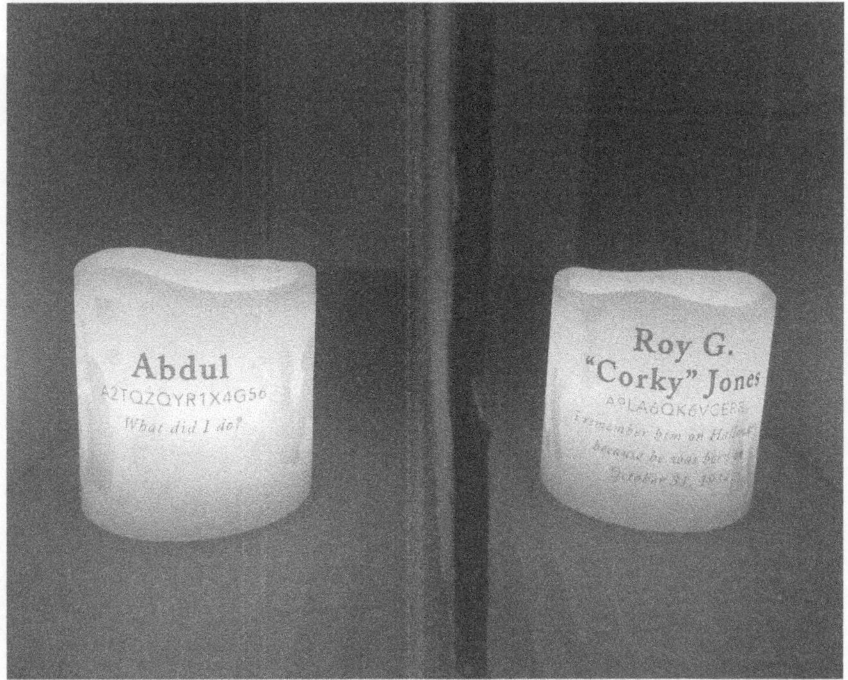

Figure 6.6. xtine burrough, *A Vigil for Some Bodies*, close-up installation view, 2016.
xtine burrough

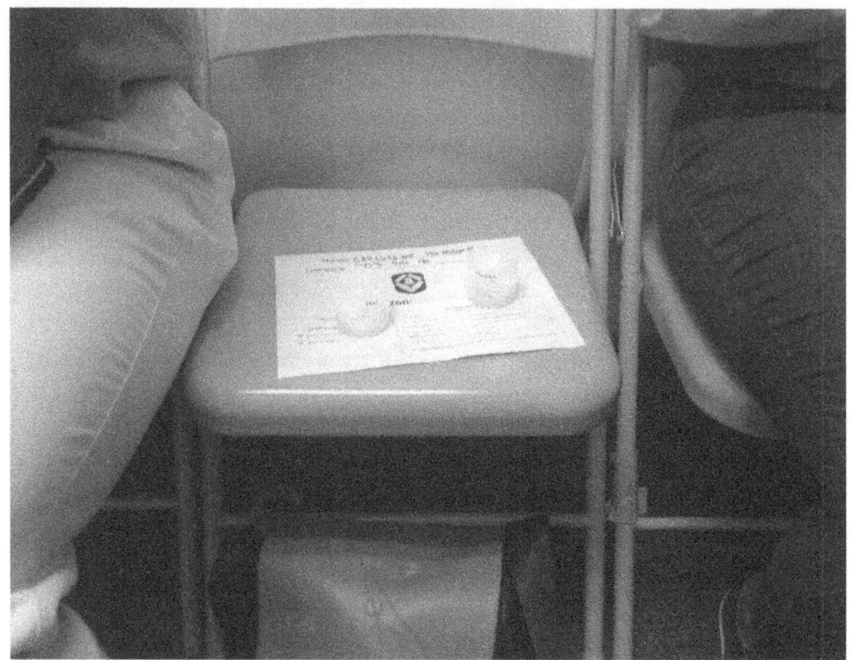

Figure 6.7. xtine burrough, *A Vigil for Some Bodies*, series. A temporary vigil while waiting for my turn to take a drug test during an Amazon Fulfillment Center seasonal job interview, November 2015, Coppell, Texas. xtine burrough

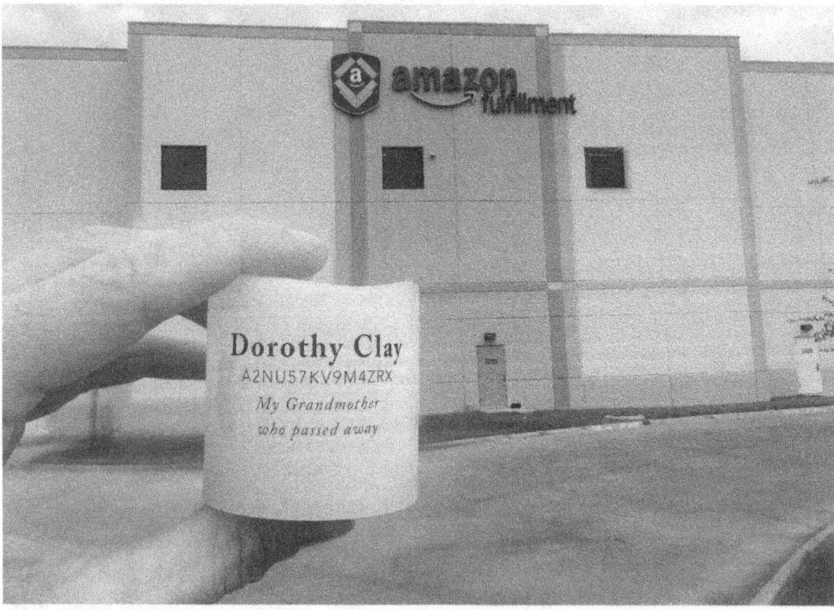

Figure 6.8. xtine burrough, *A Vigil for Some Bodies*, series. Dorothy Clay at an Amazon Fulfillment Center, Coppell, Texas, 2015. xtine burrough

Figure 6.9. ***A Vigil for Some Bodies,* Installation view, International Digital Media and Arts Association IDEAS exhibition, 2016.** xtine burrough

In 2016, I brought this project to an exhibition organized by the International Digital Media and Arts Association as an installation showcasing a vigil for workers' memories, separated by cubicles created out of cardboard boxes, or the material we most often associate with Amazon deliveries (Figure 6.9). The installation of the project enabled me to give a material form to the work and sparked conversation about my experiences in the warehouse. However, the moments of intervention captured in the photographs at the Coppell, Texas, Fulfillment Center are the closest media forms to the intention of my creative exchange with workers.

The Laboring Self: Hired Hands

In 2017, I collaborated with literary studies scholar Sabrina Starnaman for a project that explored parallels between the conditions and experiences of digital laborers and those of workers during the industrial revolution. In the exhibition *The Laboring Self*, we brought texts from the workers to the public alongside texts from writers like Emma Goldman and Morris Rosenfeld, and

Figure 6.10. "Hired Hands" from *The Laboring Self*. Installation view at the Dallas Museum of Art Center for Creative Connections, October (left) and December 2017 (right). xtine burrough

texts on weaving and sweatshops from late 1800s publications like *Life*, *The Saturday Evening Post* and *Godey's Lady's Book and Magazine*.

"Hired Hands" (Figure 6.10) calls for the public to add their sentiments to the collection of hands I created for the wall, embroidered with words workers wrote in response to the question, "How does your work affect your body?" In addition to our survey, we asked workers to trace their hands and send us an image of the tracing. I used this to laser cut replica hands from flattened and taped-together Amazon boxes. The participating public also wrote a response to our question on cardboard hands that were added to the

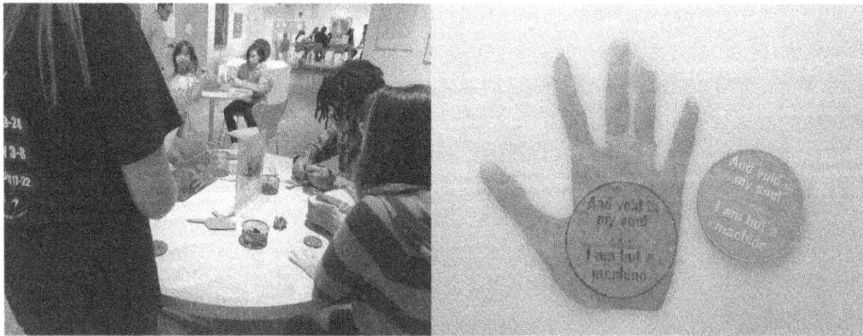

Figure 6.11. At the Center for Creative Connections in the Dallas Museum of Art, we encouraged participants to trace their hands, cut them from craft paper, and create a crayon rubbing in their palm using a round, etched disk we glued to the table. Disks held various literary quotes about labor, written during the Industrial Revolution. burrough and Starnaman, *The Laboring Self*, 2017–2018. xtine burrough

installation. In this generative installation, everyone—workers on Mturk, visitors to the museum, docents, tour groups, school-aged children—became part of the fabric of the "Hired Hands" display (Figure 6.11). In lieu of disrupting or inverting notions of labor on Mturk, this project called attention to the ways in which all bodies experience labor.

Illuminated Voices

An interactive lightbox I created for *The Laboring Self* exhibition, titled "Illuminated Voices," is charged by the power of human touch. Inside the box, sentiments from workers responding to questions about how work affects their bodies are stenciled, cut, and almost, but not quite, torn from the page (Figure 6.12). This tension of nearly being cut from the page, yielding white on white text, renders the text difficult to read. Next to the shadow box is a worker's hand cut from wood and coated in conductive ink. When a viewer places their hand on the worker's hand, LED lights are turned on inside the shadow box. Human interaction completes the circuit and renders the text inside legible. A wire from the hand connects to an Arduino Trinket, which is mounted to the back of the frame. While the "Hired Hands" installation

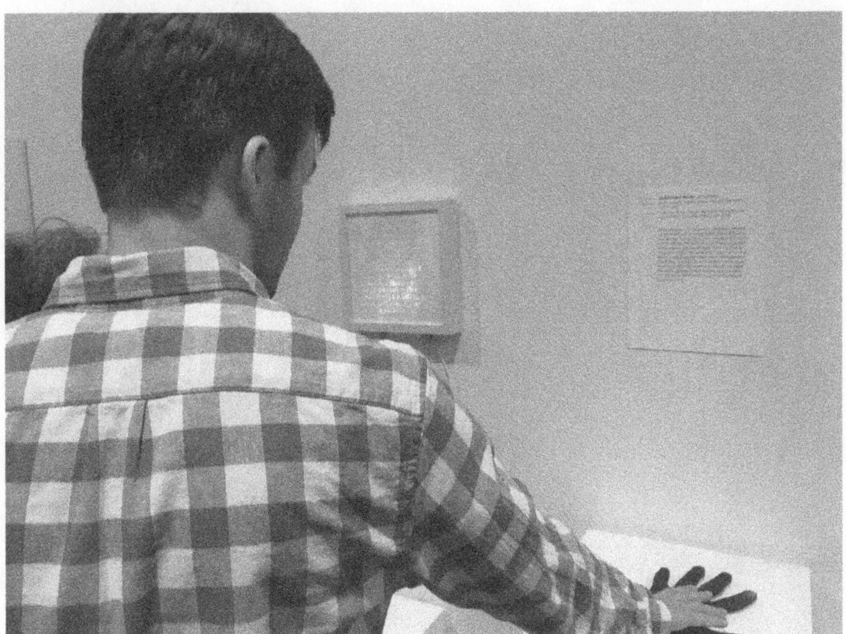

Figure 6.12. "Illuminated Voices" for *The Laboring Self*, 2017. See this work on Vimeo, https://vimeo.com/xtineburrough/illuminated-voices. xtine burrough

called for all visitors to add their voices to the work of art, "Illuminated Voices" enabled visitors to use their bodies in order to shine a light on the voice and sentiments of invisible workers.

Return to Sender

The Laboring Self also had a touring workshop, "Return to Sender," that Starnaman and I brought to campuses from the east to west coasts of the United States. After an artist talk about *The Laboring Self*, we placed workshop attendees in the precarious role of Mechanical Turk requestor. Working in groups, attendees wrote and deployed jobs for the workers with an end goal of asking the workers to share sentiments or images that they would like to have delivered to the desk of Jeff Bezos. After participants wrote jobs, and determined their wages, we posted the HITs and watched as the finished work was delivered to us in minutes. Attendees then created action-artifacts (see burrough and Starnaman, 2017) comprised of precut worker's hands on which participants transcribed worker sentiments to put their work to action by sending them along to Bezos (Figures 6.13, 6.14, and 6.15). This workshop

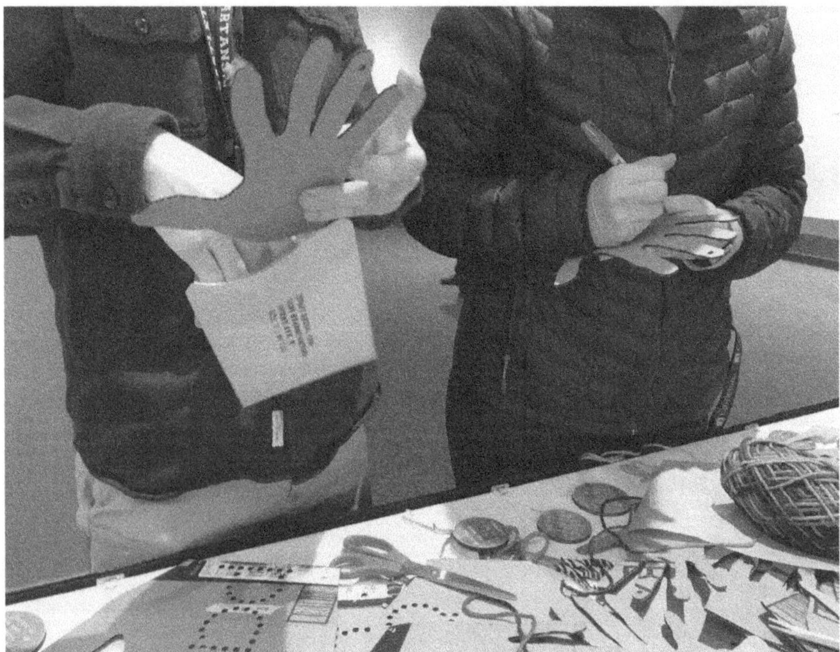

Figure 6.13. *Return to Sender* Workshop, Castleton University, Vermont, 2018.
xtine burrough

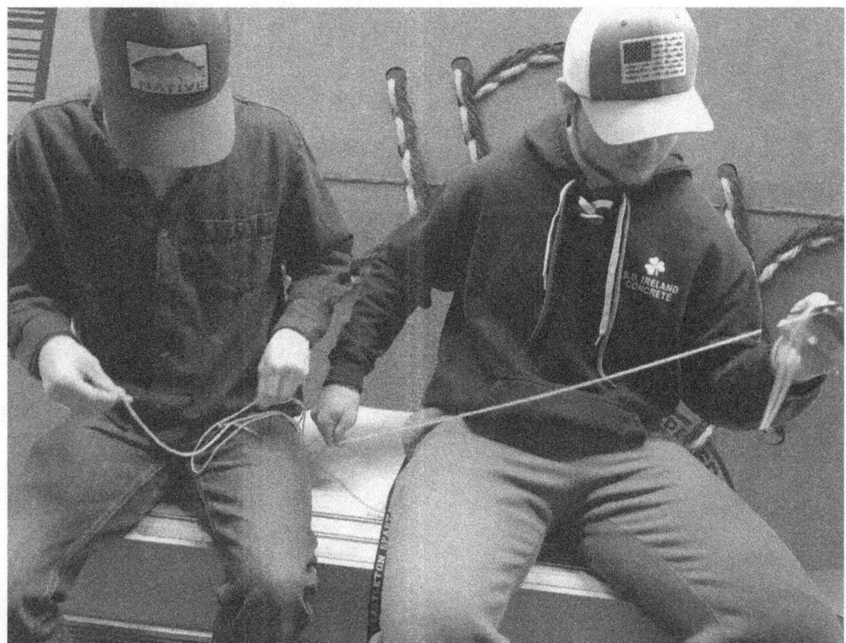

Figure 6.14. Students embroider workers' hands cut from Amazon boxes as they wait for workers to complete the job they wrote. xtine burrough

has the most in common with direct action tactics, in which the creative task is to bridge the divide between the workers and management.

Women's Work is (Screen) Saved

In 2021, I turned my attention to women workers' attitudes and sentiments about life during the COVID-19 pandemic. The Mturk platform has made many updates and changes from 2008 to 2021. In more recent years, it enables a requestor to post jobs for workers who satisfy specific demographics. I created a job that targeted women who are caregivers, putting me in conversation with working women on Mturk. As a caregiver, I, too, felt the hardships of pandemic life as the world as I once knew collapsed into the domestic sphere. *Women's Work is (Screen) Saved* is a MacOS screensaver (and set of images for Windows users) that displays reflections written by women who work on Mturk about their lives, livelihood, and relationship to work during the pandemic (Figure 6.16). While many women wrote that their lives were profoundly changed, the details shared by women workers highlights the variety of effects the pandemic has had on women around the

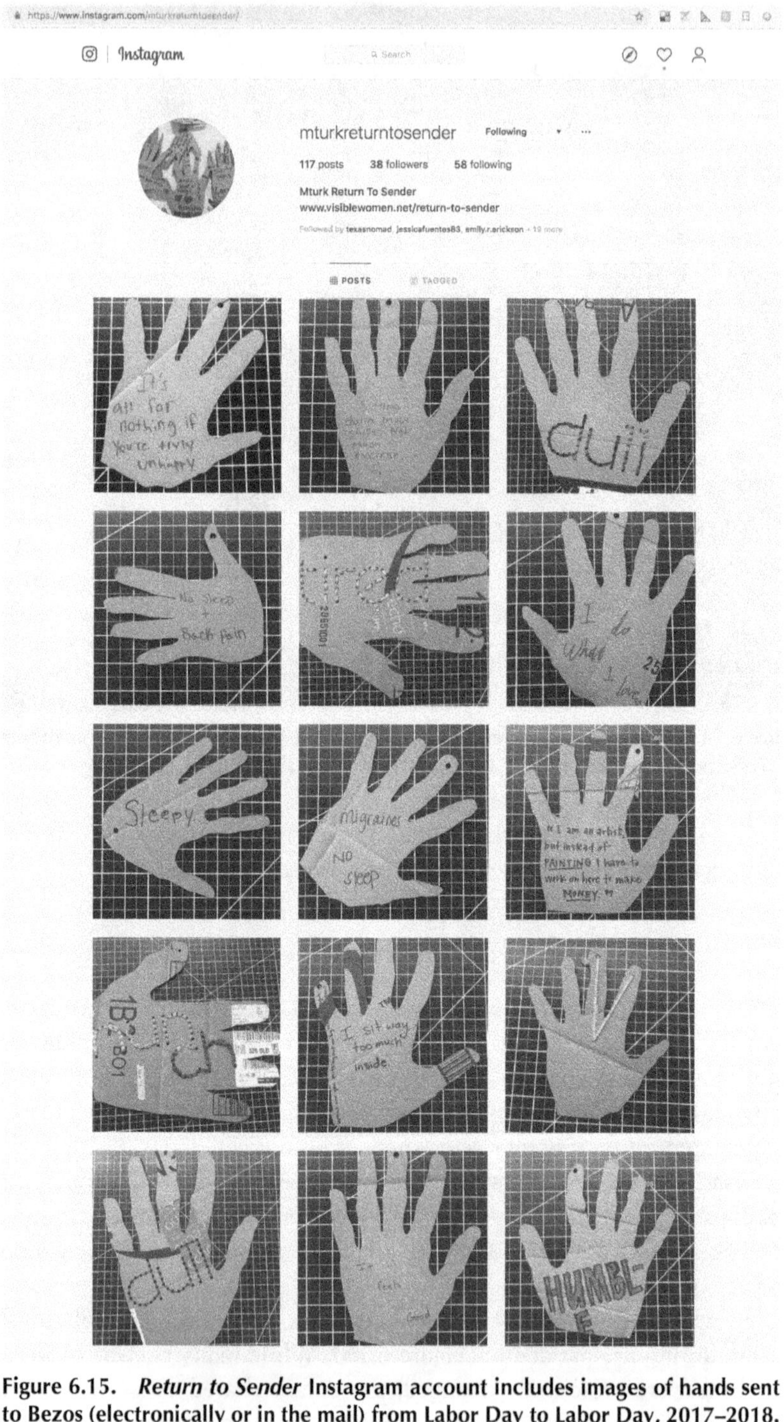

Figure 6.15. ***Return to Sender*** **Instagram account includes images of hands sent to Bezos (electronically or in the mail) from Labor Day to Labor Day, 2017–2018.**
xtine burrough

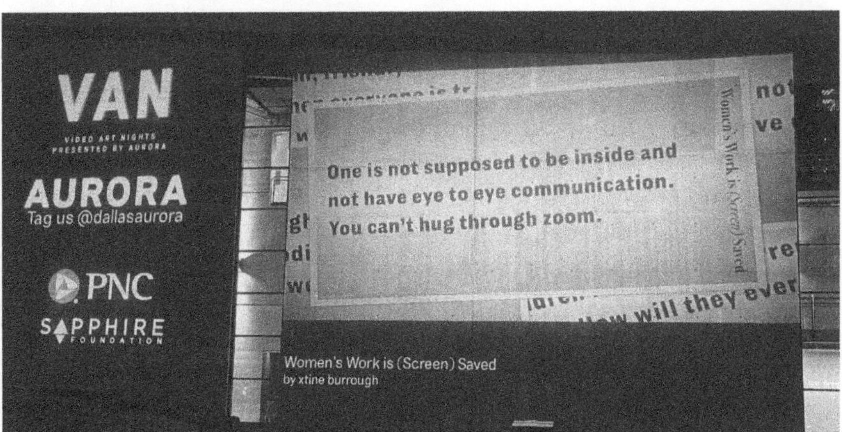

Figure 6.16. xtine burrough, *Women's Work is (Screen) Saved.* Exhibition still frame from Aurora, public art in Dallas, April 29, 2022. The project is a MacOS screensaver displaying sentiments of women who work on Mturk.com during the COVID-19 pandemic. xtine burrough

globe. Some share physical changes, citing leg pains, spinal pains, weight loss (a result of "forgetting to eat throughout the day while working from home" [burrough, 2020–2022] writes one worker), weight gain, and more. While reflecting on her relationship with her grandchildren, one woman wrote, "You can't hug through Zoom" (burrough, 2020–2022). This digital artwork was made for the screens that we were not hugging through, and the virtual worksite in home offices, kitchen tables, or upon laps on beds and couches.

Conclusion

From my first intervention on Mturk, using the platform to create a shadow, online version of the Olympic Games, to my more recent screensaver showcasing the sentiments of women workers during the global health crisis, my iterative practice disrupts, inverts, intervenes, shines a light on, and organizes the voices of the workers for a variety of public exhibition settings. Initially, my interest in Mturk was sparked by its novelty, but as the platform continued to operate with little regulatory guidelines my motivation for subverting its tools deepened. The projects showcased in this visual essay illustrate the workers' humanity and liveliness using the digital tools that exploit and abuse them. Over time, practitioners of creative resistance and culture jamming must also account for the self-doubt that creeps in during the production of a project, or more often, after it has come to a conclusion: the heavy time of reflection between projects.

Jacques Ranciere challenges the capacity of art and aesthetics for social transformation as he begins an essay with, "critical art intends to raise consciousness of the mechanisms of domination in order to turn the spectator into a conscious agent in the transformation of the world" (Renciére, 2006, 83). He goes on to underscore how unlikely it is that the act of understanding will result in social change. I find myself coming back to this quote and to arguments for and against culture jamming—questioning the value of creative resistance. It is impossible to know how transformative a work of art may be, and I am not sure that large-scale transformation is one of my long-term goals. I have garnered just enough positive feedback to sustain, on an emotional level, my creative practice, and to continue to believe it is a worthwhile endeavor. Personally, I have received messages from workers through the Mturk platform who shared their excitement, joy, good humor, and gratitude. Publicly, when Miranda Katz interviewed Mechanical Turk workers who participated in the *Mechanical Olympics* for a 2018 article she penned for *Wired* they shared that my requests were "something different," that they "paid more," and that the *Mechanical Olympics* are used "as an opportunity for family bonding" and "extra cash" (Katz, 2008). Knowing that my creative disruptions on a digital platform created an opportunity for the Ghosh family to enjoy working together and put extra cash in workers' pockets helps to alleviate doubts or second thoughts I may have as an artist working in the domain of culture jamming.

This work, having at least created short-term, local transformations that take place between me and several workers, yielded enough social impact for me to believe it is worthwhile to subvert, intervene, and flip the machine on its head. Each of these approaches may result in different concepts, and these different concepts lead to projects that reach different working publics. For instance, there are workers who repeatedly show up for *A Vigil for Some Bodies*, and they are different from the workers who consistently perform for the *Mechanical Olympics*. These two projects were expressed in different media forms for a variety of in-person and online public audiences. While I may not change the world, I will continue to use my practice to disrupt the virtual job board hosted by Amazon. While doing so, I may ever so slightly but with great intention help to push the proverbial needle away from the mega machine and toward a humanity that values generosity, contemplation, and play.

Notes

1. See my work log in Table 6.1.

2. See Mark Dery's influential essay, Culture Jamming: Hacking, Slashing, and Sniping in the Empire of Signs, https://www.markdery.com/books/culture-jamming-hacking-slashing-and-sniping-in-the-empire-of-signs-2/. Also see Christine Harold, Pranking Rhetoric: "'Culture Jamming' as Media Activism" in *Culture Jamming: Activism and the Art of Cultural Resistance*, edited by Marilyn DeLaure and Moritz Fink, 62–90. New York: NYU Press, 2017.

Table 6.1. Work Log on Amazon.com's Mechanical Turk

LOG:
4:02: logged on to mturk, accepted a human intelligence task (HIT)
4:03–4:08: read directions and waited for minutes for the site to load
4:08–4:16: completed my first HIT for five cents (label images)
4:16–4:26: completed my second HIT for nice cents (categorize a website)
4:26–4:32: completed my third HIT for one cent (actually, make that 4:34 because I made a mistake) (write an "interesting" question after reading a short article, using keywords)
4:32–4:37: completed my fourth HIT for two cents (find substitutable words); decided I liked this HIT so took a few more4:37–4:52: submitted twenty HITs (two cents each) from "Find Substitutable Words" by Powerset Knowledge
4:52–4:58: went trolling for the highest paid HITs and realized that the top dollar HITs were things I wouldn't be willing to do with my own name attached to it (sign up on websites and leave blog comments about products I've never used)
4:59–5:02: accepted new HIT for "Decide if these two products are the same or not" and made one cent per HIT on three HITs
5:02: accepted my last HIT for "Rewrite this sentence in your own words" and rewrote one sentence for four cents

References

burrough, xtine. (2008, ongoing). *Mechanical Olympics*. http://mechanicalolympics.org/.

———. (2015, ongoing). *A Vigil for Some Bodies*. http://missconceptions.net/vigil/.

———. (2015). *Mediations on Digital Labor*. Grand Central Arts Center, Santa Ana, California. http://missconceptions.net/mediations/.

———. (2020a). A Decade of Working with the Working Crowd. In *Humans Are Underrated: Art & Labor in the Amazon Economy*, edited by Johanna Gosse. *Media-N: Journal of the New Media Caucus* 16, no. 1: 116–40.

———. (2020b). Art Reel: A Vigil for Some Bodies. In *Metaphors of Internet: Ways of Being in the Age of Ubiquity*, edited by Annette Markham and Katrin Tiidenberg, 177–84. London: Peter Lang.

———. (2020–2022). *Women's Work is (Screen) Saved*. http://missconceptions.net/womensWorkScreenSaved.

———. (2021). Mechanical Olympics Channel. *YouTube*. https://www.youtube.com/user/MechanicalOlympics.

burrough, xtine, and Starnaman, Sabrina. (2017). A *Digital Korl Woman:* Students and Workers Recover the Spirit of *Life in the Iron Mills* from the Digital Factory to the Classroom. *Transformations: The Journal of Inclusive Scholarship and Pedagogy* 27, no. 2 : 121–41.

Cain, Aine, and Peterson, Hayley. (2020, September 15). Two charts show Amazon's explosive growth as the tech giant prepares to add 133,000 workers amid record online sales. *Business Insider*. https://www.businessinsider.com/amazon-number-of-employees-workforce-workers-2020-9.

DeLaure, Marilyn, and Fink, Moritz. (2017). *Culture Jamming: Activism and the Art of Cultural Resistance*. New York: NYU Press.

Holmes, Brian. (2007). The Revenge of the Concept: Artistic Exchanges, Networked Resistance. In *Art and Social Change: A Critical Reader*, edited by Will Bradley and Charles Esche, 350–68. London: Tate Publishing.

Katz, Miranda. (2018, February 18). The Quest to Recreate the Olympics with Mechanical Turk: Why one Texas professor pays Turkers to post themselves doing Olympic events on YouTube. *Wired*. https://www.wired.com/story/mechanical-turk-olympics/.

Ranciére, Jacques. (2006). Problems and Transformations in Critical Art, 2004. In *Participation*, edited by Claire Bishop, 83–95. Cambridge, MA: MIT Press.

CHAPTER SEVEN

Difference and Dependence Among Digital Workers

The Case of Amazon Mechanical Turk

Lilly Irani

In 2006, Jeff Bezos announced a new labor service masquerading as computer technology. The Amazon.com, Inc., chief executive officer explained the technology as a form of "artificial intelligence"—human workers that could be integrated directly into computer code. These human workers were marketed as part of Amazon Web Services, alongside S3 and EC21[1]—just-in-time server space and computational cycles available to programmers through routine acts of coding. Like these "software-as-a-service" systems, Bezos explained the new technology as "humans-as-a-service." That service was Amazon Mechanical Turk (AMT).

The secret of AMT was not a feat of computer engineering, statistics, or algorithms. In fact, AMT was born out of the failures of artificial intelligence to meet the needs of internet companies seeking to expand the domain of the data they could store, classify, and serve up online. Artificial intelligence, it turned out, failed to classify the cultural nuances of the images, sounds, and texts that filled web 2.0. Rather, AMT offered a virtual marketplace where programmers could ask people, rather than algorithms, to fill the gap. Workers with computers and internet connections all over the world could flexibly complete data-processing tasks around the clock. Employers seeking quick-turnaround data processing no longer had to hire more employees or even contract with an outsourcing firm; they would not even have to meet their employees, either online or face-to-face. They could simply place their data-processing tasks online, set a price for each task, and design algorithms to receive, validate, and integrate workers' processed data into computer systems. The system allowed for a kind of massively mediated microlabor—large volumes of small, independent tasks distributed to large groups of workers.

Despite Bezos' declaration of this technology's novelty, large-scale microlabor is not itself new. For a long time, homeworkers have, for instance, translated documents through correspondence; a company called *DialAmerica* paid homeworkers for each phone number they verified (Felstiner 2011). Poorly compensated data work has been the foundation of this information economy, from telegraph messenger boys to online chatroom moderators (Downey, 2014; Scholz, 2012; Schmidt, 2011; Terranova, 2000).

Compared to these prior modes of data work, however, information technology microwork platforms allow for the distribution, collection, and processing of data work at high speeds and large scales. Instead of hiring hundreds of homeworkers for a few weeks, a single person can hire sixty thousand workers for two days. This shift in speed and scale produces a qualitative change in which human workers come to be understood as computation. Employers delegate the management of these workers to algorithms, pushing labor relations into the server and out of the manager's workday. AMT is part of a larger class of microlabor platforms (e.g., CloudFactory, MobileWorks, and Crowd-Flower); these platforms provide algorithms, payments transfer, and websites where employers can place tasks, set prices or collect bids, and then electronically receive the results of the work. These systems are sometimes glossed as "crowdsourcing." A whole subfield of computer science has sprung up around these forms of data microwork and emerging strategies of technologically mediated management. The field, human computation, integrates the capacities of human workers located all over the world under the rubric of computational resources and digitized labor relations.

This chapter takes up the computational labor relations of AMT as a symptom of emerging forms and stakes of digital work. In these systems, some people are employers, entrepreneurs, and programmers (Castells, 2000, 233–36), and others simulate computation for them. Following Donna Haraway's exchange with Lisa Nakamura, I investigate "which kinds of humanness and machineness are produced out of these sorts of material-semiotic relationships" (Nakamura and Haraway, 2003). I will show the technical means by which diverse workers are rendered into computational resources, directly feeding the algorithms of entrepreneurs and Fortune 500 companies alike. The transformation of workers into a computational service, in turn, serves not only employers' labor needs and financial interests but also their desire to maintain preferred identities; that is, rather than understanding themselves as managers of information factories, employers can continue to see themselves as much-celebrated programmers, entrepreneurs, and innovators. Amazon's platform untethers these employers from the working "crowd," keeping workers behind computer screens and lines of code. Employers imagine that Turkers (as they are called colloquially) work by uncoerced choice; ignorance is not only bliss, but has consequences for what microwork-employing enterprises are financially worth.

Transforming People into "Human Computation"

Amazon operates AMT as an online marketplace infrastructure. Employers can post tasks at a set price; workers can browse and select tasks; Amazon also provides programming infrastructures and payment transfer to automate the transfer of money and bits between employers and workers. The employer-defined tasks, called human intelligence tasks, are web-based forms that specify an information task and allow workers to input responses. Tasks include structuring unstructured data (e.g., entering the information from a given webpage into an employer's structured form fields), transcribing snippets of audio, and labeling an image (e.g., as pornography or violating given terms of service). Employers specify the range of data for processing, define the structure of the form into which the data must be input, create a set of instructions for workers, and assign the task a price. Workers find and perform tasks on the AMT website. Amazon sends workers' output directly to employers' information technology systems without human intermediation.

The employer defines criteria that candidate workers must meet to access the task. These criteria include the worker's approval rating (the percentage of tasks the worker has performed that employers have approved and, by consequence, paid for), the worker's self-reported country, and whether the worker has completed certain skill-specific qualification exams offered on the platform. This filter approach to choosing workers, as compared to more individualized evaluation and selection, allows employers to request work from thousands of temporary workers in a matter of hours.

Once a worker submits completed work, the employer can choose whether to pay for it. This discretion allows employers to reject work that does not meet their needs, but also enables wage theft. Because AMT's participation agreement grants employers full intellectual property rights over submissions regardless of rejection, workers have no legal recourse against employers who reject work and then use it anyway.[2]

Today, it appears that Turkers hail largely from the United States, though Indian workers also appear in online forums from time to time. In the early days of the system, Turkers were a global workforce, though employers have always been restricted to the United States. Amazon paid in dollars, rupees, and Amazon.com gift certificates. In recent years, however, Amazon appears to have cut off international workers, instead focusing on US workers, who are understood to generate less "spam" work. Though Amazon has not publicly announced this as policy, international worker forums appear to have been abandoned, stories of new international workers joining are rare (though not unheard of), and some US workers substantiate this observation. US workers offer several advantages: they are likelier to be culturally fluent in the kinds of linguistic and categorization tasks employers delegate to AMT, and they have also developed online forums where they regulate, train, and sanction one another to produce high-quality work. Though the crowd seems unstructured, AMT employers rely on invisible social work and cultural bonds to smooth and simplify their operations.

Hiring a thousand workers for a few hours of work is no small task. Employers develop algorithmic approaches to sorting "good" work and workers from "bad." The work of management itself is semiautomated; labor relations play out in large part through routine acts of programming. As a result, Turk employers are far more likely to identify as entrepreneurs, coders, and scientists rather than owners or managers.

There are a number of approaches to deciding algorithmically which workers are doing "good" work. A common approach to vetting workers is to include tests to which employers know the answer but that look like any other data processing task. Workers that answer correctly can be authorized for future work; employers often assume those who get the wrong answer are either inadequately skilled or "spammers" trying to generate income through bad-faith work. Another approach is to hire several workers to do the same information task: employers then count the workers who offer the most common result as correct, while workers with outlier results might be denied pay or even blocked from future work. This technique is called "majority rule" (Martin et al., 2014, 6).

Within this large-scale, fast-paced, and highly mediated workforce, dispute resolution between workers and employers becomes intractable. Workers dissatisfied with a requester's work rejection can contact the requester through AMT's web interface. Amazon does not require requesters to respond, and many do not; several requesters have noted that a thousand-to-one worker-to-requester ratio makes responding cost prohibitive. In the logic of massive crowd collaborations, dispute resolution does not scale. Dahn Tamir, a large-scale requester, explained a logic I heard from several Turk employers: "You cannot spend time exchanging e-mail. The time you spent looking at the e-mail costs more than what you paid them. This has to function on autopilot as an algorithmic system . . . and integrated with your business processes" (personal communication, October 6, 2011). Instead of eliciting a response, workers' dispute messages become signals to the employer. Rick, a pseudonymous chief executive officer of a crowdsourcing start-up, explained to me that messages from workers signal the algorithm's performance in managing workers and tasks. If a particular way of determining "correctness" for a task results in a large number of disputing messages, Rick's team will look into revising the algorithm but will rarely retroactively revise decisions. Algorithmic management, here, precludes individually accountable relations (personal communication, October 5, 2011).

Purifying Innovation Work

The promise of the new media industries is expressive, creative work. Promises can never quite be fulfilled, but how people pursue them makes a difference. AMT employers cite the system as enabling them to innovate in new ways, first by outsourcing tedium, second by speeding up their experiments in production, and third by enabling labor employers to perform as software companies.

Technology has captured the imaginations of robotics engineers and critical theorists alike as a potential liberator from tedious labor. AMT's existence testifies, I argue, to the limits of automation and the persistence of tedium as a condition of human life. Within the internet industries, those who can outsource tedium and lower-value work can instead enjoy highly valued work and the promise of the creative, collaborative new-media workplace (Turner, 2009).

Jeff Howe, author of the otherwise celebratory book *Crowdsourcing*, characterizes AMT clickwork as "any number of dull, brainless, low-paid tasks that keep the Internet economy, for better or for worse, firing on all pistons. . . . Mechanical Turk allows clients to farm out the kinds of menial clickwork that we all wish computers could do, but can't" (2008). Howe explains how he used AMT to get rid of his tedious work quickly and cheaply, obtaining transcriptions of book research interviews at 10 percent of what professional transcriptionists would cost. Another engineer, Stig Hammond, explained the value of AMT through a story of a creative class workplace gone awry. Hammond (2005) tells the tale of an e-mail auto-responder program ceasing to work and the guilt he felt assigning a fast-rising support staff member to perform the work of that algorithm: "It wasn't worth it to recode the system, as we were about to migrate to a new e-mail platform. So we assigned Wamique to manually review the incoming mail, look at the request, and place the file in the appropriate directory. Mindless work, really, and I felt bad about giving it to him, but he did a great job with it. We started calling him the 'Human API.'" APIs, in software engineering parlance, are "application program interfaces"—standardized protocols for invoking a bundle of code written and stored elsewhere, and ready for reuse. APIs, and AMT more broadly, fit a broader discipline by which computer scientists working on large-scale systems bracket off complexity by studiously ignoring how the functions they depend on are implemented (Blanchette, 2011). By calling Wamique the "Human API," the manager marks both his appreciation and regret. Like a computer, Wamique performed the task tirelessly, quickly, and without the need for constant supervision or management. Like Howe, Hammond appreciates that such work must sometimes be done but it is beneath *his* coworkers. He assigns it to lower-ranking "support" staff, but he writes that AMT allows for this tedious work to be outsourced beyond the walls of the firm.

Through the redistribution of tedium, AMT requesters can reshape their roles to more closely align with the image of creative work. AMT, then, is more than a means of collaborating, sharing burdens, pooling cognitive surplus (see Benkler, 2006), and expropriating value. AMT also offers a means for new-media producers to do boundary work (see Gieryn, 1983), producing the difference between innovators and non-innovators in high tech. The boundary work is both organizational and rhetorical, manifested in both the actual division of labor that AMT enables and the symbolic consequences of those organizational acts of purification.

AMT not only enables employers to experiment quickly and identify as "innovators" rather than managers, but it also allows microwork companies to hide their labor force so they can attract capital as high-tech companies. AMT renders digital labor flexible and low-cost, but it does so to such an extent that it allows for more than the extraction of surplus value. It allows employers to experiment with the uses of human labor, exploring new business areas with little accountability or obligation to those employed in the experiments.

One large-scale requester I spoke with worked in a technology company; he used AMT both to test prototypes of products under development and to explore new business areas. He argued that AMT allowed him to work in a new way. He tinkered with microlabor the way he might have otherwise tinkered in code: "You can work in a different way, you can work much faster, you can try things. To me, the try things thing is a wonderful thing about crowdsourcing on Mechanical Turk. You don't have to get your questions perfect. . . . When I was wrong, it really didn't matter. I spent a few bucks. The loss was minimal. It inspires the willingness to try a lot of things" (personal communication). Microwork, then, enabled this engineer to tinker with human workers. The figure of the masculine tinkerer is central to American innovation myths, from Thomas Edison to Steve Jobs and his partner Steve Wozniak. AMT expands the capacity to tinker from the domain of things to the domain of people, with little expansion of consequence.

By hiding the labor and rendering it manageable through computing code, human computation platforms have generated an industry of start-ups claiming to be the future of data. Hiding the labor is key to how these start-ups are valued by investors, and thus key to the speculative but real winnings of entrepreneurs. Microwork companies attract more generous investment terms when investors perceive them as *technology companies* rather than labor companies. At one industry workshop I witnessed, a crowdsourcing start-up chief executive officer discussed the question, "Am I a labor business or an SaaS [software-as-a-service] business?" In response, a venture capital (VC) investor responded, "SaaS has a higher multiplier in the market. I was hoping it was a technology company and not a labor company when I invested!" Multipliers are rule-of-thumb quantities that appraisers of various sorts—VCs, banks, buyers—use to estimate the value of companies. Multipliers represent an attempt to guess at the relation between a company's current capital and future market value. To act as technology companies, microlabor companies must convince investors, first, that their labor force is of little risk and of little cost and, second, that their technology confers an advantage over other companies. Microlabor companies do this in part by foregrounding algorithmic techniques for managing Turkers and demonstrating a reliable flow of replaceable workers. As companies promise the ability to expand their operations quickly, so do they fuel scaling valuations.

The characterization of Turk work as menial and mindless serves the project of attributing innovation and agency to the software engineers and entrepreneurs that employ Turkers. For decades, feminist researchers of work have demonstrated that "rote" and "menial" work actually demand creativity and improvisation (Suchman and Bishop, 2000, 331; Suchman, 1995, 59). Turk work is no different. Workers I have met online include laid off teachers, mobility-impaired professionals, military retirees, agoraphobic writers, undersupported college students, stay-at-home parents, and even Malaysian programmers-in-training. This variety of backgrounds, skills, and languages benefits employers running surveys, commissioning web articles, virtualizing focus groups, getting translations, and sorting permissible web 2.0 content from policy violations.[3] Beyond Amazon's website and networks, workers participate in an ecology of forums, employer review sites, and job-sharing platforms. Tens of thousands of workers congregate on two major worker-run web forums in which workers share advice with one another, negotiate the norms of work (Martin et al., 2014), and struggle to establish more interactive and participatory relationships with employers. These collectives are sites where workers manage one another, help employers improve their tasks, and, sometimes, coordinate work refusals.

The agency of workers—both as organizers and as workers—threatens the valuation of microwork-based "software" companies in two primary ways. First, the more visible the workers in human computation become, the less the "software" companies look like software—there go the valuations. Second, a skilled labor force is not an infinite labor force; the more skilled Turkers appear, the more a microwork company may seem dependent on a limited labor pool rather than on an infinitely replaceable pool of cheap labor. Again, there goes the VC valuation.

Conclusion

I have shown three ways that AMT, like other human-computation and microlabor platforms, allows employers to sustain their identities as creative, highly valued entrepreneurs. By outsourcing tedium, tinkering with labor, and casting their work as high tech, entrepreneurs focus their own labors on that which has higher exchange and speculative value. AMT, then, becomes an infrastructure not only for data processing but also for producing the difference between "innovators" and "menial" symbolic workers.[4] Programmers who manage thousands remain flexible tinkerers with few accountabilities. AMT organizes workers for the pleasure of programmers, fitting workers into forms of late-industrial experimental production and innovation. Workers' invisibility also fuels the status of the companies that employ them. AMT, then, innovates more than cheap labor. It enables high-tech workers to manage accountabilities and maintain their high-tech image—they sustain their identities and enhance their valuations. Programmers, innovators, lean start-ups, and information technology managers reinforce their claim as the celebrated actors of knowledge-economy projects—the brains that drain, circulate, and congregate in centers of capital (Saxenian, 2005; Castells, 2000, 233–36).

What kinds of solidarities will strengthen futures of labor in the shadow of a knowledge economy? Knowledge workers of the world are divided not only by the differences among them, but also by much more difficult dependencies between them. The subjectivity of the entrepreneur is dependent on the Turker as mediated through AMT's interfaces. Ethnic studies scholar Evelyn Nakano Glenn has shown how Black and immigrant servants made possible "the woman belle ideal for white middle class women" who employed them (1985, 104). Similarly, in American late capitalism, the entrepreneurial information and communications technology ideal rests on the distanced work of Turkers who are kept variously close or at a distance, in rough accordance with the identity practices of their creative-class employers. The co-work space, the hacker space, and the start-up office offer high-status knowledge workers forms of work-based community predicated on the appropriation and distancing of other kinds of labor. This segmentation and differentiation poses a challenge for theories of immaterial labor that point us toward the immanence of the communicative, collective revolutionary subject. Some immaterial laborers are programmers, and some are Turkers. Turkers need programmers to survive; programmers need Turkers to sustain the magic of their technologies and the fun of their work. Within these relations of exploitation, where among the multitudes is liberation to be found?

Notes

1. S3 stands for Simple Storage Service, and EC2 stands for Elastic Cloud 2. These are examples of cloud computing services—data storage and processing services maintained by Amazon in data centers across the world and available to programmers on an as-needed basis. Like AMT, these services allow programmers to use computational resources without committing to the upkeep or maintenance of those resources.

2. Turker forums (e.g., mTurkGrind) and activist projects (e.g., Turkopticon) have sprung up in part to help workers share information about bad employers. Amazon, however, does not intervene in cases of wage theft or include infrastructures in AMT to prevent it.

3. AMT allows employers to disaggregate the work of the focus group participant, the translator, the journalist, and the web "community manager" according to the Babbage principle—high-cost work is subdivided so that some parts can be performed by lower-cost labor (Braverman, 1998). Yet the tasks are not so much deskilled as they are performed by members of an enlarged and, hence, more competitive labor pool.

4. I expand elsewhere on the gendered dimensions of sinking labor into infrastructure (Irani, 2013).

References

Benkler, Yochai. (2006). *The Wealth of Networks*. New Haven, CT: Yale University Press.

Blanchette, Jean François. (2011). A Material History of Bits. *Journal of the American Society for Information Science and Technology* 62, no. 6: 1042–57.

Braverman, John. (1998). *Labor and Monopoly Capital: The Degradation of Work in the Twentieth Century*. New York: Monthly Review.

Castells, Manuel. (2000). *The Rise of the Network Society*. Sussex: Wiley-Blackwell.

Downey, Greg. (2014). Making Media Work: Time, Space, Identity, and Labor in Analysis of Information and Communication Infrastructures. In *Media Technologies: Essays on Communication, Materiality, and Society*, edited by Tarleton Gillespie, Pablo Boczkowski, and Kristen Foot, 141–66. Cambridge, MA: MIT Press.

Felstiner, Alek. (2011). Working the crowd: employment and labor law in the crowdsourcing industry. *Berkeley Journal of Employment & Labor Law 32*, no 1:143-203.

Gieryn, Thomas. (1983). Boundary-Work and the Demarcation of Science from Non-Science: Strains and Interests in Professional Ideologies of Scientists." *American Sociological Review* 48: 781–95.

Hammond, Stig. (2005, November 5). Amazon's Mechanical Turk Is the Human API. *Watson, come here, I need you* (blog). www.stighammond.com/watson/webtech/.

Howe, Jeff. (2008, August 1). Mechanical Turk Targets Small Business. *Crowdsourcing.com*. www.crowdsourcing.com/cs/2008/08/index.html.

Irani, Lilly. (2013). The Cultural Work of Microwork. *New Media and Society*. nms.sagepub.com/content/early/2013/11/19/1461444813511926.abstract.

Martin, David, et al. (2014). Being a Turker. In CSCW '14: *Proceedings of the 17th ACM Conference on Computer Supported Cooperative Work and Social Computing, Baltimore, February 15–19*. New York: ACM.

Nakamura, Lisa, and Haraway, Donna. (2003). Prospects for a Materialist Informatics: An Interview with Donna Haraway." *Electronic Book Review*. www.electronicbookreview.com/thread/technocapitalism/interview.

Nakano Glenn, Evelyn. (1985). Racial Ethnic Women's Labor: The Intersection of Race, Gender, and Class Oppression. *Review of Radical Political Economics* 17, no. 3: 86–108.

Saxenian, AnnaLee. (2005). From Brain Drain to Brain Circulation: Transnational Communities and Regional Upgrading in India and China. *Studies in Comparative International Development* 40, no. 2: 35–61.

Schmidt, Kjeld. (2011). *Cooperative Work and Coordinative Practices*. London: Springer.

Scholz, Trebor. (2012). *Digital Labor: The Internet as Playground and Factory*. New York: Routledge.

Suchman, Lucy. (1995). Making Work Visible. *Communications of the* ACM 38, no. 9: 56–64.

Suchman, Lucy, and Bishop, Libby. (2000). Problematizing Innovation as a Critical Project. *Technology Analysis and Strategic Management* 12, no. 3: 327–33.

Terranova, Tiziana. (2000). Free Labor: Producing Culture for the Digital Economy. *Social Text* 18, no. 2: 33–58.

Turner, Fred. (2009). Burning Man at Google: A Cultural Infrastructure for New Media. *New Media and Society* 11, no. 1–2: 73–94.

PART III

~

AMAZON AND CULTURE

CHAPTER EIGHT

Unending Consumption

A Prime Example

David Arditi

On a typical movie night at home, my wife and I begin our search for a movie on one of our streaming services. Streaming video replaced our former trip to the local Blockbuster. While we enjoyed our trips to Blockbuster, streaming services from Netflix to HBO Max provide the promise of an unlimited catalog, much of which we pay for through our growing number of subscriptions. However, these subscriptions present an illusion of universal access limited by the licenses copyright holders agree to with streaming services. In actuality, our movie night pursuits usually bring us back to the same place so many of our shopping trips take us: Amazon.

Amazon Prime Video promises us "free" streaming of movies through our Amazon Prime subscription. If we do not find anything on Netflix, HBO Max, Disney+, etc., we turn to Amazon. After unsuccessfully scrolling through movies available through our Amazon Prime subscription, we settle on renting a movie through the service. Since our credit card information is stored on Amazon Prime, renting a movie through Amazon is far easier for us than renting through Fandango or Redbox. Whether we rent or stream free through Prime, the business model is illustrative of our relationship to cultural commodities, which has shifted from owning physical objects to renting access to content.

Amazon Prime expands the means of consumption by deploying what I call unending consumption. Unending consumption is the expansion of consumption based on a subscription model where an individual's consumption becomes constant and consistent. At the same time, their relationship to these cultural commodities shifts from one of an owner to one of a renter. Amazon's expansion of the means of consumption exemplifies a strategy to increase consumption of both material and immaterial goods by combining subscriptions with the simplicity of buying commodities. This changes our relationship to commodities and the way we consume them. How does Amazon Prime affect culture through the deployment of unending consumption? To address this question, I turn first to unending consumption to lay the groundwork for Amazon's political economic strategy to drive profits. Then I present a case study on Amazon, paying special attention to the impact Amazon Prime membership has on increasing consumption through convenience and a seemingly endless catalog of content. While Amazon feels to many technology commentators to be disruptive, I argue these changes are grease on capitalism's wheels. As Amazon changes the way we consume cultural goods, we become entrenched in ever-expanding webs of corporate cultural consumption and circulation.

Unending Consumption

Over the past twenty years, digital networks and information communication technologies have changed the way we consume goods. This is the latest shift to consumption in a long line of transformations to capitalist consumptive practices. As capitalists have wrestled with issues of supply and demand through cycles of overproduction, they have adopted what I call unending consumption. Unending consumption is a mechanism that makes consumption constant and consistent using subscription services. These subscriptions reverberate through the consumption of both material and immaterial goods. However, unending consumption does not stop with subscriptions, but rather facilitates increased consumption through customer loyalty, convenience, impulsive purchasing behavior, and incomplete access to content. In previous work (Arditi, 2021, 2018), I emphasized how subscription services produce rent-seeking consumption practices by trapping subscribers in perpetual payments for immaterial cultural goods. But we also see the proliferation of the consumption of material goods through digital retailers. As I show in the following section, Amazon is at the forefront of this approach to consumption.

While capitalism has always relied on the production of goods for sale made by underpaid workers, the emphasis of capitalism shifted from the means of production to the means of consumption (Aglietta, 2001). Capitalism used to rely on selling the same product to more people, but over the twentieth century, capitalism shifted to target the same consumers with more goods. The logic of the expansion of the means of consumption is visible with the development of recorded music, for instance. When manufacturers first began selling gramophone and phonograph players, most could not envision the market for recorded music. The novelty of the machine that could play recorded sounds was the first market. Simon Frith identifies a process whereby "people begin buying records, any records (train noises, the first compact disc releases), just to have something to play," then they buy records to have records, and finally "people begin to buy new, improved players in order to listen to specific sounds" (Frith, 2006, 233). As the novelty of the sound players wore off, gramophone manufacturers realized that many people enjoyed listening to music on them. Consequently, manufacturers began producing and selling music to play on the machines. These gramophone manufacturers would print their logos on the labels of records—hence the name record labels. This process accelerated across media following World War II. Paul Smith contends the increase in "activity-commodities (such as travel, tourism, and sports) and the massive expansion in the catchment of the electronic and print media . . . constitute just one component in capital's response to the crises of the postwar period" (Smith, 1997, 48). As the postwar crises resolved themselves, capital continued to expand the means of consumption across material and immaterial goods. By selling more consumer goods to people with disposable income, capitalists ensured the growth of capital in a way that protected against periods of diminished demand.

In *Fast Capitalism*, Ben Agger developed "fast capitalism" as a way to address the expansion of media texts under this phase of capitalism (Agger, 1988). The speed of production characterizes fast capitalism as cultural producers produce on a larger and faster scale than previous production processes permitted. However, this accelerated production created a ubiquity of cultural texts that no longer allowed people to read, watch, or listen to most texts, much less think about them. At the time of publication, *Fast Capitalism*'s emphasis was material cultural goods (analog books, CDs, VHS tapes, etc.). The material collection of these cultural artifacts stood as a visual representation of a culture of too much consumption without contemplation. Alongside Frankfurt School theorists, Agger views critical thinking as a key element to overcoming domination, but for Agger the problem extends beyond the commodity logic of the good to how the rate of production of cultural goods does not permit the careful reading and contemplation of these texts. Similarly, cultural content exists primarily in commodity form, which does not allow people to satisfy "needs outside the market/property nexus" (Andrews, 2019, 201). This accelerated phase of capitalism keeps people preoccupied and further dominated much like Theodor Adorno and Max Horkheimer argued the culture industry acted to deceive and subdue the masses (Horkheimer and Adorno, 1972). This new phase of capitalism expanded the means of consumption beyond the point where consumers could read, watch, or consume the texts they purchased. People would buy books they would never read or buy VHS tapes of movies they would never watch. When they would read or watch these books or movies, Agger claims they would move on to the next without much thought and certainly without discussing the texts with others.

With the development of digital networks, accelerated production merges with accelerated distribution. The internet deploys an open framework that allows more people to contribute to the production of texts, but we become so inundated with information that it is hard to keep up. In *Blog Theory*, Jodi Dean furthers Agger's point about time to contemplate texts by positing "the temporal take-over of theory displaces sustained critical thought, replacing it with the sense that there isn't time for thinking, that there are only emergencies to which one must react, that one can't keep up and might as well not try" (Dean, 2013, 2). Here the pace at which we cannot comprehend what is happening not only kills critical thought, but also drives revenue among a distracted mass of web-surfers who inattentively click their way through content. For Dean, "communicative capitalism" is the idea that "contemporary communications media capture their users in intensive and extensive networks of enjoyment, production, and surveillance" (Dean, 2013, 3–4). Communicative capitalism benefits from distraction by promising enjoyment while watching our every move. Furthermore, it operates (in what Vincent Mosco calls the "pay-per society") with information as a "commodity and as a means of social control" (Mosco, 1989, 28). The control happens in the current moment through the surveillance of our web activities, which changes production while it keeps us hooked. Although we feel pleasure in our consumption of online content, it functions to dominate our tastes and thoughts. By not giving us time to think, cultural commodities become tools of oppression.

The current phase of capitalism is one of unending consumption. We rarely buy our media and cultural texts, but rather license and rent them. As Aaron Perzanowski and Jason Schultz put it, we have moved from an economy based on ownership of cultural commodities to one characterized largely by rental. "Compared to sales-based models that wax and wane depending on a host of factors, subscriptions generate relatively predictable and reliable revenue streams" (Perzanowski and Schultz, 2016, 50). Content producers and distributors reduce risk by assuring revenue through subscriptions. Additionally, digital subscriptions changed consumers from owners to renters and altered the fundamental logic of many commodities, especially where it comes to streaming (Arditi, 2021). The changing form of capitalism in turn solidifies the power of a handful of large corporations. "Even as some media forms eclipse others, global conglomerates profit from the innovations while pernicious arrangements of state power benefit from a diverted populace" (Dean, 2013, 39). Our diverted attention from, not to mention willing acceptance of, cultural commodities blinds us to the actions of media conglomerates. We often do not recognize that the basic concepts of property ownership are changing alongside these shifts. Perzanowski and Schultz underscore that the problem is not only for subscription rentals, but rather a fundamental characteristic of immaterial digital goods. They summarize a case where Amazon deleted *1984* from users' devices because of a licensing conflict. While users thought they "owned" their Kindle editions of *1984*, they really licensed access. This was a capitalism so fast that many people lost the good they purchased before they could read it. This change is indicative of broader changes to the economy. Corporate conglomerates institute changes to the economy that increase profits, while these shifts change the basic structures of property and ownership in society. Again, these changes may agitate consumers, but they do not disrupt the system.

When corporations institute a streaming subscription service, it has the effect of increasing consumption beyond the subscription. For instance, the average person in America spent roughly forty-five dollars per year on recorded music for decades (Arditi, 2020). However, with the launch of Spotify and Apple Music (originally Beats Music), the recording industry increases the average consumer's spending on recorded music to $120 per year on subscriptions alone (Arditi, 2018). Some music fans may subscribe to Spotify to hear corporate music and SoundCloud to hear independent music (each ten dollars per month). The same music fan may also purchase vinyl records, which is experiencing its own resurgence (Palm, 2017, 2019). Spotify will also alert subscribers when musicians they listen to come through their town. These sales combined have a way of greatly expanding how much any individual spends on music.

Most importantly, unending consumption doesn't stop. Because most of our media consumption comes through subscriptions, we no longer own physical media artifacts. "Instead, the digital subscription model allows you to pay a flat monthly rate—or patiently endure advertisements—in exchange for access to large libraries of streaming content" (Perzanowski and Schultz, 2016, 48). We pay for access, and when we stop paying for access, we lose what we paid for. With physical media, we own the music and can use it until it breaks, we gift it, or we resell it. But with digital media, we cannot do any of these things. For example, I have owned the Red Hot Chili Peppers' *Blood Sugar Sex Magic* for thirty years, and I have listened to the album countless times for about ten dollars. However, if I listened to no other album on Spotify for a year, I would pay $120 for access to this album, and as soon as I canceled my Spotify subscription, I would no longer have access to the album. Of course, I can cancel my subscription at any time, but then I have no music. Subscriptions are unending because users want to continue to receive access; this produces constant and consistent revenue for corporations as subscribers continue to pay.

Amazon

In 1994, Jeff Bezos founded Amazon (then Cadabra) as an online bookstore. At the time, the banal launch of an online storefront when most Americans were not online did not appear to be a big deal. In hindsight, Amazon's launch would create the largest retail store in history, altering other retail arrangements around the world. However, instead of acting as a disruptive force, the launch marked another part of the process of retail realignment visible for decades. In the 1990s, big corporate book chains put small independent bookstores out of business. The big corporate bookstores of Barnes and Noble, Books-A-Million, and Borders provided large retail outlets for books, calendars, and stationary with an emphasis on a very specific market: best-selling books. They place the best-sellers in center aisles and the other rows of books are known in the book-selling industry as "wallpaper" because they create an ambiance, not sales (Grazian, 2017). The result was lower-priced books with less diversity. In contrast to big chains, most independent bookstores provided a curated assortment of books and still sold best-sellers. The big corporate bookstores put these small shops out of business. Amazon offered an essentially unlimited catalog of books available at the click of a button and delivered to your front door. In the world of academic books, this meant cheaper books available to broke students and underpaid faculty with dwindling book budgets. Amazon began selling the Kindle in 2007 followed by Barnes and Noble's Nook in 2009—electronic readers that allow users to read digital books. These electronic devices eliminated the need for physical copies of books. However, book retail is only a small part of Amazon's strategy to build customer loyalty and induce impulse shopping.

In many ways, the Kindle created the logic of unending consumption on Amazon. In this sped-up fast capitalism aided by digital networks (Agger,

2004), users could buy access to new books at a discounted rate on an impulse and never read them. However, as the case of *1984* demonstrates, a digital purchase is not the same as ownership (Perzanowski and Schultz, 2016). The lower price of eBooks is partly a function of disintermediation. As media content shifted online, the costs associated with manufacturing and distributing physical media were eliminated. This began with the realignment of the recording industry as record labels reacted to file-sharing services by moving most distribution online with Apple's iTunes Store (Arditi, 2020). The elimination of intermediaries (hence disintermediation) creates savings for these large corporations at the same time that they lower prices. With lower prices for media content, consumers are more likely to impulse buy music, books, and videos. As people purchase more media content, they run into the problem Agger described because they don't have the time to read, listen, or watch the content they purchase. The corporate temptation for eBooks stems from their ready availability and their low prices, even if people still prefer physical books. While eBooks are available cheaper than physical books, Amazon Prime Reading provides a seemingly limitless catalog of books available free to Prime subscribers (more on Prime in the next section). Books were the beginning of Amazon's expanding monopoly, but the online store caused change to far more than bookstores.

A constant refrain about Amazon is that it is disruptive (Handley, 2018). But the word disrupt is problematic in relation to Amazon. When people comment on the disruptive force of technology, they rarely define what it means for a technology to "disrupt." This is especially acute among business researchers and journalists; for instance, one academic article about Amazon entitled "Disruptions versus more disruptions: How the Amazon Dash Button is altering consumer buying patterns" (Farah and Ramadan, 2017) never articulates what disruption means nor do the authors make any attempt to show that Amazon is in fact disruptive. Disruption cannot be appropriated to mean increased business efficiency that eliminates intermediaries. To disrupt means to drastically change, alter, or destroy something. A strike can disrupt production by blocking a factory from operating. An earthquake can disrupt traffic by creating a deep fissure in a road and making the road impassable. A severe thunderstorm can disrupt a baseball game by forcing the game to be postponed or canceled. However, Amazon doesn't disrupt capitalism, but rather makes the distribution of goods more efficient. Competition is a central tenet of capitalist ideology, so competition cannot be viewed as disruptive. Because capitalism thrives on cutting out intermediaries, replacing labor with machines, reducing the general skill of labor, and competition between businesses, Amazon is more like the grease to help capitalism function than a wrench in the machine. Amazon's goal is frictionless capitalism, not disruption of capitalism.

From its beginnings in book retail, Amazon has gone on to put companies in multiple industries out of business, especially of the cultural variety. But Amazon has created more problems for the retail industry than any other industry. Big box retailers from Best Buy to Walmart have the most to lose from Amazon's economic takeover. The book-selling giant turned ubiquitous retail deliverer upended the economy of scale of other predatory retailers. However, the story of changing retail business models is not new. In the music industry, for instance, big box retailers like Best Buy and Walmart helped shutter corporate record stores such as Sam Goody and Tower Records. Earlier, Sam Goody and Tower Records contributed to the closure of mom-and-pop record stores. This is the process through which larger businesses operating on economies of scale force smaller businesses to close. Amazon has been able to put smaller retailers out of business partly because of its size and partly from predatory pricing (Sussman, 2019). Because Amazon is so large and dominant, it can sell goods close to or at a loss. This is not dissimilar to the practice by box retailers to use recorded music as loss leaders—this basically means that a store like Best Buy sells music at a loss to get customers in the store to tempt them to purchase other items. Amazon works on such a large scale that they can set prices long term, which forces other retailers out of business and further reduces its own costs by operating at a still larger scale. But the key to the strategy lies in a Prime subscription to get customers on the hook.

Prime

When Amazon launched Amazon Prime in 2005, it seemed like a way for consumers to reduce spending on shipping fees through a subscription. This subscription resembled other predigital subscriptions in which someone makes regular payments to participate in a program. For people who order frequently from Amazon, Prime offered a considerable discount. Fourteen years later, Prime appears as the free hit of heroin dealers give to people to make them addicted to the product. Today, in addition to free shipping for physical purchases, Amazon Prime opens a world of streamable entertainment all for the simple fee of $119 per year. Amazon Prime expands the means of consumption by deploying unending consumption. By offering subscribers a seemingly good deal on the delivery of commodities, Amazon entices subscribers with a long list of other goods, which ultimately fail to satisfy their needs.

Amazon Prime has a way of pulling customers into its sphere of consumption. The original purpose of Amazon Prime from a consumer perspective saved money on shipping costs. A convenient feature of an Amazon search allows the user to select only Prime products that shipped free of charge. These shipping options changed over time from free five-day shipping to the now common free two-day shipping to same-day delivery for some items in specific geographic regions. An Amazon Prime subscription not only encourages subscribers to shop from Amazon, but also makes other forms of shopping less desirable. In 2018, I bought my dad an eight-track player at the Texas Vintage Radio and Phonograph Society's auction. I was proud of myself for purchasing the device for sixteen dollars, below the minimum twenty-five-dollar bid. However, when I went to a shipping center, the cheapest service cost sixty dollars to ship it from Texas to Virginia. My excellent auctioning skills were matched by my terrible shipping skills. The problem was that my frequent use of Amazon Prime lulled me into thinking shipping was cheap. I live over twenty hours away from family, and for every birthday or holiday, I have a dozen gifts to send across the country to parents, nieces, and nephews. Amazon Prime's free shipping saves me around five to twenty dollars per person, but it also limits what I purchase. Instead of buying something at a street festival or local store, I purchase their gifts from Amazon. Not only do I purchase them through Amazon's website, I search for items that use Amazon Prime, which means I rarely use independent dealers. As Amazon has grown larger, they've also increased the number of Amazon branded products available, further limiting variety. Of course, my relatives simplify the whole process by making Amazon wish lists, which ensures that I use Amazon for the purchase.

Amazon Prime developers attempted to create a system where impulse and need drive consumption. Here again, we see the logic of big box retailers fulfilled. When you walk into a Target, you might do so to purchase a specific item like laundry detergent. When Target sells laundry detergent as a loss leader, the hope is that you go into the store to buy detergent, but also buy something from the dollar bin and grab some lightbulbs and a snack while you're there. However, if the same customer must leave their house to purchase the laundry detergent, they may put off the purchase altogether. With Amazon, the customer can think "I need laundry detergent," login to Amazon, buy the product, and have it delivered same-day free with an Amazon Prime account. Amazon then took this to the next level with the short-lived Amazon Dash Button, which consciously aimed to create impulse buying activity (Farah and Ramadan, 2017). The Amazon Dash Button was a small WiFi-networked device that corresponded to a specific product in the customer's house. Users would place a button in their laundry room, for example, and when they ran out of laundry detergent, they simply pressed the button. This would send a signal to their Amazon account and order the detergent. The instantaneity of the purchase enables no sale to be missed for Amazon. Instead of putting laundry detergent on your weekly grocery store list, Amazon receives the immediate sale. According to Vincent Mosco, the "goal is to automate consumption" (Mosco, 2017, 47). And the automation of consumption, itself, led to the downfall of the Amazon Dash Button. The button was a decidedly material object in a digital world. Instead, Amazon turned to "smart" objects such as the Samsung Washing Machine with WiFi and auto laundry dispenser. With this technology, the washing machine can send an alert to the user's phone and users can click to order more laundry detergent. Or people can use Amazon's Alexa to request new products—"Alexa, buy Tide laundry detergent." With the availability of smart devices and Alexa, Amazon streamlines purchases so consumers do not have to think about their needs.

Furthermore, as customers purchase more from Amazon they build affective relationships with the company which encourages them to purchase more items from Amazon (Ramadan, Farah, and Saada, n.d.). Because Amazon Prime subscribers are already on the hook for $119/year, they perceive every transaction with Amazon to be a sunk-cost. Purchasing laundry detergent online with a different company wouldn't make sense for the customer, not only because it would include an excessive shipping fee in comparison to Prime, but also because it would be easier to buy detergent at the grocery store than register with a new online retailer. As subscribers feel like they receive more value from their Prime subscription, they purchase more from Amazon.

It is the perception that Prime members receive something included with their subscriptions that makes media consumption on Amazon alluring. Herein lies Amazon's strategy: Amazon promotes their streaming content to encourage people to subscribe to Amazon Prime thereby enticing them to purchase more goods from Amazon. The retailer "uses SVOD [Streaming Video On-Demand] to drive customers to its Prime membership program whose members make more purchases more often than non-members" (Wayne, 2018, 726). However, Amazon's digital libraries never provide universal access and "one of the greatest challenges" according to Chuck Tryon, " has been consumers' ability to identify and locate movies and television shows they might want to see" (Tryon, 2013, 57). More often than not, subscribers need to purchase or rent content they want to watch, read, or listen to. While Amazon has by far the largest streaming video catalog included with its subscription, reports vary widely on the size of the catalog (Perry, 2021; Roettgers, 2020; Brantner, 2019); its catalog tends to be older than other services, aside from Amazon original content.

While Amazon Prime Video's library is vast, its user interface is difficult to navigate because the mix of old/new and free/paid services blur together, obscuring how a user can stream a given show or movie. Four types of streamed content are available through Amazon Prime Video. First, an Amazon Prime subscription provides access to hundreds of thousands of books, songs, shows, movies, and video games. When logged into an Amazon Prime Video app, the app limits the selections to movies and television shows. When users launch the app, Amazon Prime Video users see a range of the content available to them, curated by an algorithm that feeds videos based on a user's previous consumption. Users can filter results in a number of ways, including "free to me." The videos included with Amazon Video Prime are marked with a "Prime" logo. With this type of access, there is no confusion about ownership because Prime membership pays for access. The frustrating part for consumers stems from the changing availability of materials in the catalog. Users may think they have access to a specific film, television show, or song only to find out later they Amazon lost the license.

Second, Amazon Prime Video allows users to rent content for a limited time. Generally, renters have thirty days to begin playback and a smaller window after they begin watching it (usually one to seven days). Using the rent feature resembles using a video rental store with the added benefit of no late fees and renting from the comfort of your home. While the rental model limits when you can watch, Amazon's platform limits where you can watch it. If a renter loses their internet connection after they begin the playback, there isn't an easy way to seek a refund. Amazon's rental feature hurt video rental companies, but this is part of the longer process of changing business models—not disruption. However, the ready availability of rental content contributes to unending consumption. This is not only because it begins with a subscription, but also because people rent after they already feel like they have access. Amazon Prime subscribers end up spending more on entertainment because of the convenience of renting within Amazon's apps.

Third, users can buy content for unlimited playbacks. Despite the fact that they purchased the content, they do not "own" it. As consumption has moved away from physical goods, corporations have tested the limits of ownership. "The disappearance of hard goods, in the form of physical recordings heightens the transition from a world of cultural goods to a world of cultural services" (McCourt, 2005, 251). Because digital purchases on Amazon are licenses, the company can end a user's access at any time within the terms of agreement. The Kindle Store simply states: "Kindle Content is licensed, not sold, to you by the Content Provider" ("Kindle Store Terms of Use," 2016). The implications of licensing, not selling, books is illustrated the conflict between Amazon and George Orwell's publisher discussed earlier (Stone, 2009; Perzanowski and Schultz, 2016). Amazon had a conflict with *1984*'s publisher, so overnight, Amazon deleted copies of *1984* from users' Kindles. While less succinct than the Kindle Store's "Terms of Use," the same issue arises with Amazon Prime Video's "Terms of Use":

> **Availability of Purchased Digital Content.** Purchased Digital Content will generally continue to be available to you for download or streaming from the Service, as applicable, but may become unavailable due to potential content provider licensing restrictions or for other reasons, and Amazon will not be liable to you if Purchased Digital Content becomes unavailable for further download or streaming. ("Amazon Prime Video Terms of Use," 2021)

In other words, if you buy a season of *The Walking Dead*, you do not own it. At any time, Amazon can lose its license to the content and deny you future access to the content despite your purchase. Even when a user downloads a video to their device, digital rights management allows Amazon to strip the file from a device whenever the device is connected to the Internet. According to Ted Striphas, "the gradual and as yet incomplete emergence of a new and contradictory conjunction of the law, capitalism, culture, and technology, in which the very category of 'private property' is destabilized precisely as it is extended to encompass ever more objects and ideas" (Striphas, 2006, 253). Owning a commodity becomes obsolete as digital rights management makes cultural content "wired shut" (Gillespie, 2007). By licensing use, Amazon practices unending consumption because there is always the chance that users will have to pay for access to content once again in the future.

Fourth, Prime members can subscribe to television networks that are otherwise unavailable through Amazon Prime Video. These on-demand videos provide access to other platforms and on-demand videos through Amazon. Subscribers can watch these videos on the day of their release, but they cannot live stream the content. Michael Wayne argues bundled content creates a relationship between Amazon and television networks that provides brand affinity as a means to grow the Amazon Prime subscriber base. As more people have cut the cord, Wayne shows how Amazon's streaming channels provide a means for Prime members to subscribe to television networks without a cable subscription. Currently known as Prime Video Channels, Prime members can subscribe to Starz, AMC, Paramount+, Showtime, and more ranging from $4.99 per month to $10.99 per month. It is easy to subscribe to these channels because Prime members use their credit card on file with Amazon; their monthly subscription automatically renews through Prime. Additionally, accessing these channels through Prime Video gives Amazon access to data about users' consumption patterns. By subscribing to another service through Prime, these channels contribute to unending consumption.

Amazon is not disruptive, but rather aims to find new ways for consumers to spend more money through Amazon. "The Amazon Prime service was created, in part to encourage users to purchase directly from Amazon rather than their third-party sellers and showed that in some cases digital delivery of movies could be used as an enticement to purchase other goods or services" (Tryon, 2013, 29). A Prime subscription leads to more consumption through Amazon. The Amazon Prime Video library is a loss leader that provides members with a sense of unlimited access. However, their access is always unfulfilling as they realize they don't want to watch any of the available free content. Then they rent, buy, or subscribe to a network channel to watch the good stuff.

Conclusion

People have become used to instant access to cultural content and a seemingly unlimited library of content through Amazon Prime Video. The streaming content available through Prime entices people to subscribe. Once subscribed, Prime members want to make the most of their membership, so they buy more goods from Amazon. This is part of a vicious cycle that leads to more and more consumption through Amazon, hence unending consumption. When subscribers get on the hook for $119 per year, they want to maximize their value from their Prime subscription, but the unfulfilling streaming video options result in video rentals and more streaming subscriptions.

As Amazon continues to grow, there is a public need to rein in its size. In 2017, Amazon bought the rights to J.R.R. Tolkien's *Lord of the Rings* for $250 million with plans to create a universe rivaling Marvel Cinematic Universe or the *Star Wars* franchise (Cain, 2017). The purchase will allow Amazon to produce content with a large ready-made fan base. In May 2021, Amazon announced the acquisition of MGM Studios (Porter, 2021). The $8.45 billion purchase would give Amazon an even deeper catalog, and access to popular media franchises such as James Bond, which will also allow Amazon to enter theaters. These are big shifts that require regulation. Mergers and acquisitions across a number of industries grow Amazon's size and encourage unending consumption to continue. Amazon Prime acts like the center of a blackhole that allows Amazon to pull more content, revenue, and businesses into its gravitational force.

References

Agger, Ben. (1988). *Fast Capitalism*. Urbana, IL: University of Illinois Press.

———. (2004). *Speeding Up Fast Capitalism: Cultures, Jobs, Families, Schools, Bodies*. Boulder, CO: Routledge.

Aglietta, Michel. (2001). *A Theory of Capitalist Regulation: The US Experience*. Translated by David Fernbach. New Edition. New York: Verso.

Amazon Prime Video Terms of Use. (2021). Amazon.com Services LLC. https://www.primevideo.com/help?nodeId=202095490&view-type=content-only.

Andrews, Sean Johnson. (2019). *The Cultural Production of Intellectual Property Rights: Law, Labor, and the Persistence of Primitive Accumulation*. Philadelphia, PA: Temple University Press.

Arditi, David. (2018). Digital Subscriptions: The Unending Consumption of Music in the Digital Era. *Popular Music and Society* 41, no. 3: 302–18. https://doi.org/10.1080/03007766.2016.1264101.

———. (2020). *ITake-Over: The Recording Industry in the Streaming Era*. Second edition. Lanham, MD: Lexington Books.

———. (2021). *Streaming Culture: Subscription Platforms and the Unending Consumption of Culture*. New Milford, CT: Emerald Publishing Limited.

Brantner, Chris. (2019, January 28). Netflix Has More Certified Fresh Movies Than Prime, Hulu, and HBO Combined. *Soda* (blog). https://www.soda.com/news/netflix-movie-library-2019/.

Cain, Rob. (2017, November 14). Amazon's $250M "Lord of the Rings" Purchase Price Is 1,000 Times What Tolkien First Got For It. *Forbes*. https://www.forbes.com/sites/robcain/2017/11/14/amazons-250m-lord-of-the-rings-purchase-price-is-1000-times-what-tolkein-first-got-for-it/.

Dean, Jodi. (2013). *Blog Theory: Feedback and Capture in the Circuits of Drive*. First edition. Polity.

Farah, Maya F., and Ramadan, Zahy B. (2017). Disruptions versus More Disruptions: How the Amazon Dash Button Is Altering Consumer Buying Patterns. *Journal of Retailing and Consumer Services* 39, no. C: 54–61.

Frith, Simon. (2006). The Industrialization of Music. In *The Popular Music Studies Reader*, edited by Andy Bennett, Barry Shank, and Jason Toynbee, xxii. New York: Routledge.

Gillespie, Tarleton. (2007). *Wired Shut: Copyright and the Shape of Digital Culture*. Cambridge, MA: MIT Press.

Grazian, David. (2017). *Mix It Up: Popular Culture, Mass Media, and Society*. Second edition. Philadelphia: W. W. Norton, Incorporated.

Handley, Lucy. (2018, June 18). Amazon Is Seen as so Disruptive Because People Think They're Getting Something for Free. *CNBC*. https://www.cnbc.

com/2018/06/18/amazon-is-disruptive-because-people-think-they-get-something-free.html.

Horkheimer, Max, and Adorno, Theodor W. (1972). *Dialectic of Enlightenment*. New York: Herder and Herder.

"Kindle Store Terms of Use." (2016). Amazon Digital Services, LLC. https://www.amazon.com/gp/help/customer/display.html?nodeId=200771440.

McCourt, Tom. (2005). Collecting Music in the Digital Realm. *Popular Music and Society* 28, no. 2: 249–52. https://doi.org/10.1080/03007760500045394.

Mosco, Vincent. (1989). *The Pay-Per Society: Computers and Communication in the Information Age*. Norwood, NJ Praeger.

———. (2017). *Becoming Digital: Toward a Post-Internet Society*. Bingley, UK: Emerald Publishing Limited.

Palm, Michael. (2017). Analog Backlog: Pressing Records during the Vinyl Revival. *Journal of Popular Music Studies* 29, no. 4). https://doi.org/10.1111/jpms.12247.

———. (2019). The New Old: Vinyl Records after the Internet. In *The Dialectic of Digital Culture*, edited by David Arditi and Jennifer Miller, 149–62. Lanham, MD: Lexington Books.

Perry, Nick. (2021, April 1). Netflix vs. Amazon Prime Video. *Digital Trends* (blog). https://www.digitaltrends.com/movies/netflix-vs-amazon-prime/.

Perzanowski, Aaron, and Schultz, Jason. (2016). *The End of Ownership: Personal Property in the Digital Economy*. Cambridge, MA: The MIT Press.

Porter, Jon. (2021, May 26). Amazon Buys MGM for $8.45 Billion. *The Verge*. https://www.theverge.com/2021/5/26/22441644/amazon-mgm-acquisition-prime-video-subscription-service-james-bond.

Ramadan, Zahy, Farah, Maya F., and Saada, Rana Bou. (n.d.). Fooled in the Relationship: How Amazon Prime Members' Sense of Self-Control Counter-Intuitively Reinforces Impulsive Buying Behavior. *Journal of Consumer Behaviour* 20, no. 6: 1497–1507. Accessed September 21, 2021. https://doi.org/10.1002/cb.1960.

Roettgers, Janko. (2020, October 26). Netflix Has 400 Times More Movies than Apple TV+. Blog. *Protocol — The People, Power and Politics of Tech* (blog). https://www.protocol.com/streaming-catalogs-by-the-numbers.

Smith, Paul. (1997). *Millennial Dreams: Contemporary Culture and Capital in the North*. London: Verso.

Stone, Brad. (2009, July 18). Amazon Erases Orwell Books From Kindle." *The New York Times*. https://www.nytimes.com/2009/07/18/technology/companies/18amazon.html.

Striphas, Ted. (2006). Disowning Commodities: EBooks, Capitalism, and Intellectual Property Law. *Television & New Media* 7, no. 3: 231–60. https://doi.org/10.1177/1527476404270551.

Sussman, Shaoul. (2019). Prime Predator: Amazon and the Rationale of Below Average Variable Cost Pricing Strategies Among Negative-Cash Flow Firms. *Journal of Antitrust Enforcement* 7, no. 2: 203–19. https://doi.org/10.1093/jaenfo/jnz002.

Tryon, Chuck. (2013). *On-Demand Culture: Digital Delivery and the Future of Movies*. New Brunswick, NJ: Rutgers University Press.

Wayne, Michael L. (2018). Netflix, Amazon, and Branded Television Content in Subscription Video on-Demand Portals. *Media, Culture & Society* 40, no. 5: 725–41. https://doi.org/10.1177/0163443717736118.

CHAPTER NINE

~

Amazon Eats Whole Foods

Empire-Building and the Acquisition of Conscious Capitalism™

Lisa Daily

"These people, they just want to sell Whole Foods Market and make hundreds of millions of dollars, and they have to know that I'm going to resist that. . . . [Whole Foods Market] is my baby. I'm going to protect my kid, and they've got to knock Daddy out if they want to take it over."

—John Mackey (in Foster, 2017)

A June 2017 *Texas Monthly* article posits: "Whole Foods' eccentric founder changed the way Americans consume food. Can he survive the Wall Street forces that now want to consume him?" (Foster, 2017). Two days later, a formal announcement shared that Amazon would purchase Whole Foods Market for $13.7 billion, leaving John Mackey, the "eccentric founder" of Whole Foods Market, intact as the chief executive officer (Whole Foods Market News Release, 2017; Foster, 2017). Mackey was not interested in selling Whole Foods and referred to the activist hedge fund, Jana Partners, which bought 9 percent of the company stock and pressured radical reform or sale, as "greedy bastards" (Foster, 2017). In the days following the acquisition announcement, tremendous discussion proliferated as to why Amazon founder, billionaire, and one of the richest people in the world—Jeff Bezos—would want to purchase the natural foods grocery chain as well as what this meant for Whole Foods Market, with its approximately five hundred stores in the United States and locations in Canada and the United Kingdom. Tremendous effects also rippled through the grocery industry, with stock prices plummeting for large grocery chains, largely due to speculation of Amazon's "habit of taking a wrecking ball to any market it gets involved with" (Stevenson, 2021).

As conventionally told in this story of acquisition, John Mackey appears as the lovable mindful leader who stands up against corporate greed and evil imperialist capitalism. Not only is he a vegan who regularly goes on months-long hikes to find his flow state, but also he co-founded the Conscious Capitalism™ movement, which articulates a roadmap for the evolution of capitalism into its "awakened" state of consciousness. Through an analysis of Amazon's acquisition of Whole Foods Market, this chapter considers the tensions between John Mackey's vision of capitalism and the imperialist capitalism of the Amazon empire—surely, the antithesis to any substantive "conscious" capitalism—and examines the ramifications of the sale. I argue that the sale of Whole Foods Market to Amazon is not only *not* surprising, but rather is congruent with the evolution of the Whole Foods business model and the libertarian free-market economics that Mackey has preached for decades. The sale of Whole Foods Market to Amazon is a "win-win" for both corporations in that it strengthens the relationship between capitalist demands for expansion and extraction, efficiency, technological development, innovation, and surveillance, while also providing a more robust (and superficial) platform for ethical concerns.

And yet things can only get worse for Whole Foods Market under the umbrella of the Amazon empire. But for who? With Amazon's relentless drive for efficiency, innovation, and customer satisfaction, Whole Foods Market customers benefit immensely in material ways (although perhaps not ethically) from the further mainstreaming of organics, lower prices, the integration of Amazon Prime membership with Whole Foods discounts, easier access to Amazon lockers and returns, and the ability to order online and have one- or two-hour delivery. As an aside, most Whole Foods customers already have an Amazon Prime membership—around 75 percent—whereas only 20 percent of Amazon Prime members shop at Whole Foods (Berg and Knights, 2019, chapter 3). For Whole Foods as a company, Amazon's ownership has centralized purchasing and supplier relationships nationally, provided financial security, consolidated power, is working on the aging and incompatible technology infrastructures within Whole Foods stores, and further standardized the company. As Emily West, among others, suggests, the ubiquity of Amazon within the United States has profound effects economically, politically, and culturally. The model of relentless customer convenience actively remakes "what it means to be a consumer," but also substantially alters what it means to be a worker (West, 2022, 4). How did we get here? What culture(s) is being created, altered, or destroyed with Amazon's purchase of Whole Foods Market, and for who? I suggest, like many other critics, that workers are the losers in the persistent drive for customer innovation and satisfaction, as perhaps is any guise of capitalism with a conscious (not that I actually ever believed such was possible).[1] More broadly, Amazon must be understood not simply as a retailer or a new-to-the-game grocer, but as "indispensable infrastructure"—a technology behemoth, which "happens to sell a lot of stuff in the process" (Berg and Knights, 2022, 27).

This chapter delves into why the acquisition of Whole Foods Market by Amazon is not surprising through an abridged examination of the ethos of John Mackey and Whole Foods Market, as well as what is gained by Amazon: primarily, a way for it to reconcile its seemingly haphazard prior experimentation with the grocery industry while massively expanding its physical locations, delivery options, and automation. Throughout, I consider the cultural changes wrought by the sale, especially with regards to technological enhancements and the continued erosion of labor, even with the recent—albeit limited—2022 win for unionization at Amazon.

Love at First Sight . . .

While the sale of Whole Foods was shocking to the public, it had been in the works for months. In fact, when John Mackey said, "I'm going to protect my kid [Whole Foods], and they've got to knock Daddy out if they want to take it over," he was not necessarily alluding to a resistance against acquisition, but rather that he needed the *right* acquisition (Foster, 2017). Shortly after Jana Partners revealed their stock, Mackey and his executives were shopping proposals, namely from direct competitors such as grocery chain Albertson's. Secretly, however, they wanted Amazon. In late April 2017 and under a nondisclosure agreement, John Mackey and Jeff Bezos met at Bezos' home (Stone, 2021, 189). Amazon officially offered to buy Whole Foods Market on May 23 for forty-two dollars a share, and the $13.7 billion deal was officially announced on June 16, 2017 (ibid). Mackey recounts that it was "like falling in love" (ibid).

Neither Jeff Bezos nor John Mackey are conventional capitalists, each reimagining success differently. For Bezos, he established Amazon (Amazon.com) with plans to "define his own metrics for success, without interference from impatient outsiders . . . vowing a focus not on immediate financial returns or on satisfying the myopic demands of Wall Street, but on increasing cash flow and growing market share," while also aggressively working to lay waste to his competitors (Stone, 2021, 3). Conversely, John Mackey might be best understood as one of the "new prophets of capital," which Nicole Aschoff argues are "a new generation of storytellers telling us what's wrong with society and how to fix it" (Aschoff, 2015, 9). The catch, however, is that "the most powerful of these storytellers aren't poor or working people, they are the super-elite" who are not envisioning the eradication of capitalism but rather "a different kind of capitalism" (Aschoff, 2015, 9). While this new capitalism goes by many names, Mackey and his collaborators deem it Conscious Capitalism™, a concept they promote through various publications and an adjoined 501(c)(3) nonprofit organization with its conferences and executive leadership retreats.[2] The fundamental notion of Conscious Capitalism is that "business is good because it creates value, it is ethical because it is based on voluntary exchange, it is noble because it can elevate our existence, and it is heroic because it lifts people out of poverty and creates prosperity" (Conscious Capitalism, Inc., n.d.). In some ways, John Mackey has workshopped his notion of Conscious Capitalism over the decades since he first opened a natural foods store, SaferWay, in 1978 in Austin, Texas.[3] Back then, Mackey considered himself to be swept up in the 1960s and 1970s counterculture, practicing yoga, living in a commune, and thinking businesses were "essentially evil" (Mackey and Sisodia, 2013, 1–2). More recently, Mackey insists: "Although it may seem counterintuitive, the best way to maximize profits over the long-term is not to make them the primary goal of business" (Conscious Capitalism, 2013). Mackey even debated the father of neoliberalism, Milton Friedman, among others, about the "social responsibility of business," although notions that ethical or politically focused goods garner better profit maximization are no longer unconventional (Friedman et al., 2005).[4]

Many critics, including employees, contend that the conscious culture of Whole Foods Market eroded after the Amazon's purchase and while this may be true to some extent, the ethos of Whole Foods Market has long enacted contradictory ethics and limited worker protections (Minkin, 2021). Despite Mackey's proclamations of personal and capitalist enlightenment, he is, I suggest, a ruthless capitalist with his own history of unethical corporate practices, from building his company on the ashes of small independent health foods stores acquired by Whole Foods Market to union-busting and more recently slashing hazard pay during the COVID-19 pandemic and cutting health care benefits. The language of transcendence within Mackeyian Conscious Capitalism™ coalesces with free market economics, and toward this end, Mackey is a staunch libertarian, is antiunion, and in 2009 argued for a market-based solution to the Affordable Care Act, which came under massive scrutiny from more leftist progressive Whole Foods Market customers. Importantly, *this is not new* since Amazon purchased Whole Foods.

While Whole Foods Market continues to do tremendous work in supporting organics and natural food, environmental stewardship such as banning single-use plastic bags at checkout and plastic straws and supporting pollinators, and is working on waste reduction initiatives, it also—in a truly neoliberal and staunchly antijustice fashion—depoliticizes and individualizes such work (Davis, 2017, 225). As Davis notes, "Customers are instructed to take responsibility for these issues as individuals outside the store, not in conjunction with Whole Foods or its staff. The company's message for environmental and social transformation is essentially a philosophy of self-reform, a prescription of individual health and wellness that avoids making any demands for systemic change" (Davis, 2017, 225). Even during the Reagan era of Whole Foods Market, Mackey "adamantly objected to efforts to redress structural inequalities," asking "Why do so many people believe it is wrong for there to be inequalities in wealth among people? Should the more talented be handicapped so that no one will feel inferior or envious of them?" (Davis, 2017, 220). These sorts of callous comments continue today, as when in a 2020 interview with *The New York Times*—during the height of the COVID-19 pandemic—Mackey professed that people are obese not because of access to healthy food, a lack of health care, or lack of financial security, but because of individual choices (Gelles, 2020). These comments echo earlier comments as seen in the infamous 2009 op-ed in the *Wall Street Journal*, "The Whole Foods Alternative to Obamacare," where Mackey essentially says that poor health is "self-inflicted" (Mackey, 2009).

This belief has carried into the Whole Foods Market employee benefits, including the controversial Team Member Healthy Discount Incentive Program, which rewards individual employees for a low body mass index, low cholesterol, and other health features. In 2019, under Amazon's directive, health care benefits were slashed for part-time employees (Peterson, 2019). As G. J. Harney notes, Mackey's comments about health care are "pretty tone deaf at a time when people need actual healthcare–and particularly when his own employees are on the frontlines making sure that healthy foods and lifestyle accessories are available for those who can afford to pay" (Harney, 2020). In early 2021—again, amid a raging global pandemic—Whole Foods cut "paid breaks from 15 minutes to 10 minutes" for some regions of its store locations, noting "we are standardizing our expectations for meal and rest periods across the company to maximize Team Member safety and productivity and to best meet our operational needs" (Gurley, 2021). Higher-purpose or consciousness are clearly not the driving forces behind these changes, but rather they are motivated by productivity measures, profit, and standardization of work.

The individualist mentality further infiltrates worker protections with unionization and worker pay. Bezos and Mackey are aligned on many of these issues, as made increasingly visible during massive strides for—and some successes in—unionization as well as each company self-imposing a fifteen dollar minimum wage for hourly workers. In late March 2022, a landmark victory for the first Amazon Labor Union occurred at the JFK8 Amazon fulfillment center in Staten Island, while a neighboring warehouse voted against the union less than a month later. The victory is significant, however, in that it not only signals meaningful employee organization and collaboration within Amazon and its subsidiaries, but also in that it joins a chorus of unionization efforts of late, such as those with Starbucks. Moreover, its success comes at a $4.3 million loss to Amazon—what it spent on union-busting efforts. Apparently in JFK8, union busters "wrote the scripts for meetings and shaped anti-union messaging that papered the warehouse's bathroom stalls and hallways," and was also "sent to workers via mailings, Instagram ads, phone calls, text messages, and videos projected on screens inside the facility" (Press, 2022). Like most antiunion rhetoric, Amazon declared that it was "disappointed with the outcome of the election . . . because we believe having a direct relationship with the company is best for our employees" (Press, 2022). At Whole Foods Market, union-busting accusations have proliferated throughout the 2000s and most recently the technological auspices of Amazon have enabled further measures for worker surveillance, such as with heatmap tracking the threat of unionization in particular Whole Foods stores and assigning a "unionization risk score" (Thalen, 2020; Leon, 2020). In 2018, a forty-five-minute leaked Amazon video made headlines as it espoused antiunion tactics on how Whole Foods managers and team leaders should handle any rumblings of unionization (Menegus, 2018).[5] But long before Amazon, Mackey infamously stated, "The union is like having herpes. It doesn't kill you, but it's unpleasant and inconvenient, and it stops a lot of people from becoming your lover" (Paumgarten, 2009). Elsewhere, Mackey says that Whole Foods is not "antiunion," it is "*beyond* unions" (Lyster, 2013).

During the COVID-19 pandemic, employee criticism of Whole Foods Market—along with its Amazon overlord—reached new heights. A December 17, 2020, internal email was sent from a Whole Foods employee in Detroit, Michigan, to the entirety of Whole Foods Market employees and was circulated widely through social media and posted on the Whole Worker organization's website (Whole Worker, 2020). In the scathing letter, the employee states that "it has become abundantly clear during this pandemic that Whole Foods is obsessed with pushing us, the workers, to keep up production at the expense of our health and our customers' health" (Whole Worker, 2020). It goes on to note Whole Foods' paltry response to COVID outbreaks in its stores, the eradication of company-sponsored benefits, especially for part-time workers, the hard-fought for and then quickly taken-away two dollar hazard pay for essential workers, and the ruthless suggestion by John Mackey that healthy employees donate their paid-time off to team members experiencing a family emergency (Whole Worker, 2020).[6] Regarding the superficiality of Whole Foods core values, the letter quips: "There is no core value at Whole Foods of greater importance than pushing sales and Amazon Prime" (Whole Worker, 2020). The letter links its employee advocacy with Amazon workers, also experiencing unjust and dangerous working conditions.

Certainly, some of these changes in Whole Foods Market employee culture are due to Amazon's takeover, but based on the history of Whole Foods and its chief executive officer, John Mackey, it may also be seen as the growing pains of the company and the inherently unethical practices of Conscious Capitalism. It remains to be seen what will happen to the discourse of conscious capitalism within Whole Foods, especially as John Mackey announced his own retirement this past September 2021, taking effect September 2022, and with the current chief operating officer, Jason Buechel, to take the position as the next chief executive officer of Whole Foods Market (Whole Foods Market News Release "Retirement," 2021). Buechel has thrived at Whole Foods in part by being more Amazonian, meaning more technologically minded, including incorporating Apple Pay at stores and a partnership with Instacart starting in 2014—a relationship that has since ended. In the final section, I delve further into Amazon's actions at Whole Foods Market as well as other actions taken by Amazon to cement its influence within the grocery industry, primarily around technological innovation.

Amazon Eats Whole Foods

Whole Foods Market is but one snippet of the Amazon empire's portfolio, ranging from its online retail marketplace to contracted delivery drivers and shoppers, from its cloud-based Amazon Web Services, Ring, and Echo to facial recognition software, investments in space and in deportation airlines within the United States, Amazon Studios and streaming services, Zappos, the *Washington Post* (personally owned by Jeff Bezos), and more. So why does it matter that Amazon bought Whole Foods Market? Why did leading grocery companies plummet in stocks on the day the acquisition was announced? As indicated in *Amazon Empire: The Rise and Reign of Jeff Bezos*, it is because entire industries fear the possibility of their colonization by Amazon—that it will do for their industry what it has done to bookstores, publishers, and retailers. The acquisition of Whole Foods Market serves as yet another bellwether for the future of Amazon: it continues to extend its reach for Prime membership and data collection, it extracts productivity and labor from its workers in the name of profits, and it fully intends to transform the grocery industry through technological innovation, efficiency, and deliveries.

For Amazon, purchasing Whole Foods Market might begin to untangle its messy experimentation with groceries since 2007, all of which have largely failed (Stone, 2021, chapter 8). More particularly, it enables the convergence of online and offline shopping—"clicks and mortar"—and provides Amazon a much-needed physical storefront presence in thousands of communities, bolstering its delivery infrastructure, extending its ubiquity, and therefore Prime membership to potentially new customers, while also accessing their data (Berg and Knights, 2022, chapter 1). Further, the sale cements the Amazon empire's reach firmly within the grocery industry, seen as a "monumental blow" to industry insiders (Stevenson, 2021). Amazon continues to experiment with its own Amazon Fresh stores, a grocery store with "consistently low prices," while also launching other storefronts such as Amazon Go, a convenience-style grab and go store (Amazon, n.d.-a). In November 2021, Amazon and Starbucks partnered for the first-ever entirely "grab-and-go" Starbucks Pickup store, which opened in midtown Manhattan and uses Amazon's cashierless technology with the goal being "effortless convenience" (Starbucks, n.d.).

Increasingly, online commerce—especially when promising quick delivery—requires more physical infrastructure. As Berg and Knights suggest, "If Amazon wants to crack the grocery and pharmacy sectors, it needs stores. If Amazon want to offset rising fulfillment and customer acquisition costs, it needs stores. And if Amazon wants to further drive Prime membership, adoption of voice technology and one-hour delivery, guess what? It needs stores" (Berg and Knights, 2022, 3). In particular, the authors see Amazon as "redefin[ing] the supermarket for the 21st-century shopper—stripping out checkouts, digitizing the experience, utilizing stores for fast delivery and, crucially, engaging with shoppers in a way that it could never do online" (Berg and Knights, 2022, 3). But Whole Foods Market will also enable more frequent purchases through essential products—food.

The COVID-19 pandemic has dramatically altered the way in which people shop with deliveries, curbside or in-store pickup, and online ordering being more prevalent, although some of these changes were happening even prior to March 2020. At Whole Foods alone, it is estimated that 10 to 11 percent is online grocery purchasing, an increase of 8 to 9 percent (Stevenson, 2021). John Mackey sought Amazon in part for its technological prowess:

> One of the reasons we wanted to do this merger is we saw Amazon as a technology leader, and Whole Foods was just a follower. Since Covid struck, our online sales have tripled. Could we have done that prior to Amazon? No way. From the very first day we merged with them, they pushed us to make the changes we needed to be more effective at online delivery. (Gelles, 2020)[7]

Separate from Whole Foods, Amazon expects to increase its "online edible grocery sales . . . to $26.7 billion worldwide in 2026 from $14.5 billion in 2021" (Redman, 2021). Delivery, however, is not the primary metric of success, but rather the speed in which a delivery may occur. And Amazon and Whole Foods are still unable to compete with rapid delivery companies such as Dashmart/DoorDash, which launched fifteen-minute delivery in New York City in late December 2021 and relies upon bike couriers (Fickenscher, 2021).

Amazon will continue to push the grocery industry to become more efficient as well as more proficient in technological (and ultimately, surveillance-based) modifications under the guise of customer satisfaction and ease, but this also signals changes to work and automation. For instance, Amazon's Just Walk Out technology continues to be implemented in physical stores within the United States and abroad. Not only is it available to other retailers to purchase and utilize, but also it actively reshapes the grocery shopping experience in Amazon Fresh, Amazon Go, and Whole Foods Market stores. This technology is "made possible by a combination of computer vision, sensor fusion, and deep learning—similar to what you'd find in self-driving cars—and adds convenience to customers' grocery shopping experience by giving them the option to come in, pick up what they want, and skip the checkout when they're done" (Whole Foods Market Release "Technology," 2021). To be clear, this isn't the self-checkout lane you might be familiar with at numerous retail establishments. Rather, the technology automatically adds items the consumer picks up to the "virtual cart" and consumers "simply scan or insert their entry method again to exit" (Whole Foods Market Release "Technology," 2021). No scanning. No getting a credit card out. The system supposedly knows if you pick up and then set down a can of high-end salmon in favor of a can of tuna. And by "the system," I mean the hundreds of small cameras—the "digital tentacles"—that hang from the ceiling of any store with Just Walk Out technology (Moran, 2022).

Although there are twenty-three Amazon Fresh stores, the first store with Just Walk Out technology opened in Bellevue, Washington, in mid-2021 (Amazon, n.d.-a). A Whole Foods Market in the Glover Park neighborhood of Washington, DC, opened in February 2022 and a second is opening in Sherman Oaks, California (Acosta, 2022). What do these technologies mean for labor? Amazon has been quite vague about the number of employees at such technologically enhanced stores, but notes that employees shift their focus to customer service or stocking rather than checkouts. Another common technology in Amazon Fresh stores is the Dash Cart, a smart shopping cart, which "uses a combination of computer vision algorithms and sensor fusion to identify items you put in the cart. When you exit through the store's Amazon Dash Cart lane, sensors automatically identify the cart, and your payment is processed using the credit card on your Amazon account" (Amazon, n.d.-b). However, according to a recent leaked Amazon document obtained by *Business Insider*, Dash Cart is underperforming, only being used by 11 to 15 percent of Amazon Fresh shoppers when it anticipated at least a 30 percent adoption rate, with customers preferring human cashiers and checkout lanes (Kim, 2022). As for Amazon Go, these are convenient-style stores with a small retail footprint that rely exclusively on Amazon's Just Walk Out technology. Customers must scan a code to enter the store, collect what they'd like to buy, and then walk out. A key feature of this automation is that it is "contactless" and convenient, one of the ways in which corporations may establish more locations in smaller retail spaces. In a 2021 poll, almost 60 percent of thirty thousand people "would like to have an Amazon Go in their area and see the concept as a threat to big food retailers such as Walmart and Kroger" (Redman, 2021). To date, there are approximately thirty Amazon Go stores in the United States and United Kingdom.

One might think: Amazon purchased Whole Foods Market for $13.7 billion; why does it need to then also start its own line of grocery or other brick and mortar stores? The Amazon Fresh stores have existed long before the Whole Foods acquisition and sell foods a customer can't get at Whole Foods, such as Coke and Doritos. It is meant to entice consumers who might be looking for a lower-cost and less bourgeois grocery experience. According to journalist Seth Stevenson, the Amazon Fresh (or Go) stores "Might just be Trojan horses for Amazon's actual goal, which is same-day delivery to everybody, everywhere. Online grocery shopping has been Amazon's white whale for some time now" (Stevenson, 2021). This is increasingly proving to be true. As of March 2022, Amazon announced that it is closing "more than 50 of its physical retail stores, including two dozen bookstores and more than 30 Amazon 4-star stores" with plans to "focus more on our Amazon Fresh, Whole Foods Market, Amazon Go and Amazon Style stores and our Just Walk Out technology" (Weise, 2022). More acutely, however, Jeff Bezos seeks the total integration between online and offline, between what we need, what we think we need, or what we may not yet realize is essential for our livelihoods. Bezos jokes about his cross-sector success with Amazon: "how every time he wins a Golden Globe 'it helps [him] sell more shoes. And it does that in a very direct way'" (PBS, 2020). The physicality of commodities—to be delivered or shipped in an hour or a day—necessitates a boundedness to material space, whether it be a warehouse, a brick and mortar store, or somewhere in-between.

Whole Foods Market is merely a dot in the grand scheme of the Amazon empire's future. And in some ways, it is difficult to think about the sale of Whole Foods Market to Amazon when Jeff Bezos wants to colonize space and seems to increasingly support the militarization of police forces and American borders. The sale of Whole Foods is another story of acquisition under a brutal regime of capitalism. It is not a particularly surprising story, and we will continue to see the erosion of worker satisfaction and protections at Whole Foods under Amazon's directive as well as other efficiency and extraction measures. Whole Foods Market and its chief executive officer, John Mackey, have long upheld visions of consciousness, while simultaneously undermining its workers, communities, and concern for healthy, natural, and accessible food for all. Whole Foods has helped mainstream natural and organic foods throughout the United States, which is an admirable feat. Everyone needs to eat, and we should be concerned about increasingly mechanized, corporatized, and chemically enhanced foods. We should care about food production, food insecurity, food deserts, and advocate for structural changes to advance food sovereignty. This will be increasingly difficult to manage with the continued domination of Amazon.

Notes

1. See Brad Stone, *Amazon Unbound: Jeff Bezos and the Invention of a Global Empire* (New York: Simon & Schuster, 2021). Also see Berg and Knights, *Amazon*, and West, *Buy Now*.

2. For more, see https://www.consciouscapitalism.org as well as numerous publications: John Mackey and Raj Sisodia, *Conscious Capitalism: Liberating the Heroic Spirit of Business* (Boston: Harvard Business Review Press, 2014); John Mackey, et

al. *Conscious Leadership: Elevating Humanity through Business* (New York: Portfolio/Penguin, 2020).

3. For more on Mackey, see G. J. Harney, Whole Foods' Hippie CEO and the Lie of Enlightened Capitalism, *Current Affairs*, March 12, 2021. Also see Isaac Chotiner, The Whole Foods C.E.O. John Mackey's "Conscious Capitalism," The New Yorker, February 22, 2021.

4. Milton Friedman, John Mackey, and T. J. Rodgers, Rethinking the Social Responsibility of Business, *Reason*, October 2005. Also see Amanda Hess, The Trump Resistance Will Be Commercialized, *The New York Times*, March 17, 2017. Also see Lisa A. Daily, "We bleed for female empowerment': Mediated ethics, commodity feminism, and the contradictions of feminist politics, *Communication and Critical/Cultural Studies*, 2019. Also see Clifford A. Young and Justin Gest, Americans are spending money according to their values. Companies need to realize that, *USA Today*, October 3, 2021.

5. Clips of the leaked video are featured in *PBS Frontline*, Episode 12, Season 2020, Amazon Empire: The Rise and Reign of Jeff Bezos, aired February 18, 2020 (min 38), https://www.pbs.org/wgbh/frontline/film/amazon-empire/.

6. Also see Lauren Kaori Gurley, Whole Foods Suggests That Workers Share Paid Time Off During Coronavirus, *Vice*, March 13, 2020. https://www.vice.com/en/article/93988v/whole-foods-suggests-that-workers-share-paid-time-off-during-coronavirus. And Lois Beckett, Whole Foods workers hold "sick-out" to demand hazard pay during pandemic, *The Guardian*, March 31, 2020, https://www.theguardian.com/business/2020/mar/31/whole-foods-coronavirus-outbreak-us-health.

7. Also see Hayley Peterson, "I ultimately am not afraid to get fired": Leaked audio captures Whole Foods CEO John Mackey describing clashes with Amazon, *Business Insider*, July 13, 2018.

References

Acosta, Gina. (2022). How Amazon Plans to Transform Grocery in 2022. *Progressive Grocer*. https://progressivegrocer.com/how-amazon-plans-transform-grocery-2022.

Amazon. (n.d.-a).Amazon Fresh. Accessed May 25, 2022. https://www.amazon.com/fmc/m/20190651?almBrandId=QW1hem9uIEZyZXNo\.

Amazon. (n.d.-b). Dash Cart. Accessed May 25, 2022. https://www.amazon.com/b?ie=UTF8&node=21289116011.

Aschoff, Nicole. (2015). *The New Prophets of Capital*. New York: Verso Books.

Banker, Steve. (2019, June 25). How Amazon Changed Whole Foods. *Forbes*. https://www.forbes.com/sites/stevebanker/2019/06/25/how-amazon-changed-whole-foods/?sh=7ca9111178dd.

Beckett, Lois. (2020, March 31). Whole Foods workers hold "sick-out" to demand hazard pay during pandemic. *The Guardian*. https://www.theguardian.com/business/2020/mar/31/whole-foods-coronavirus-outbreak-us-health.

Berg, Natalie, and Knights, Miya. (2019). *Amazon: How the world's most relentless retailer will continue to revolutionize commerce*. London: Kogan Page Limited.

Berg, Natalie, and Knights, Miya. (2022). *Amazon: How the world's most relentless retailer will continue to revolutionize commerce*. Second edition. London: Kogan Page Limited.

Chotiner, Isaac. (2021, February 22). The Whole Foods C.E.O. John Mackey's "Conscious Capitalism." *The New Yorker*. https://www.newyorker.com/news/q-and-a/whole-foods-ceo-john-mackeys-conscious-capitalism.

Conscious Capitalism, Inc. (n.d.). Our philosophy. Accessed November 10, 2021. https://www.consciouscapitalism.org/philosophy.

"Conscious Capitalism": Q&A with Whole Foods CEO John Mackey. (2013, March 1). *Forbes*. https://www.forbes.com/sites/ashoka/2013/03/01/qa-with-whole-foods-ceo-john-mackey-about-conscious-capitalism/?sh=5290cca62176.

Daily, Lisa A. (2019). "We bleed for female empowerment": Mediated ethics, commodity feminism, and the contradictions of feminist politics. *Communication and Critical/Cultural Studies* 16, no. 2: 140–58.

Davis, Joshua Clark. (2017). *From Head Shops to Whole Foods: The Rise and Fall of Activist Entrepreneurs*. New York: Columbia University Press.

———. (2017, June 19). So Much for "Conscious Capitalism." *Slate*. https://slate.com/business/2017/06/whole-foods-can-drop-the-conscious-capitalism-shtick-now.html.

Fickenscher, Lisa. (2021, December 6). DoorDash opens 15-minute delivery-only grocery store in NYC. *New York Post*. https://nypost.com/2021/12/06/doordash-opens-15-minute-delivery-only-grocery-store-in-nyc/.

Foster, Tom. (2017, June). The Shelf Life of John Mackey. *Texas Monthly*. https://features.texasmonthly.com/editorial/shelf-life-john-mackey/.

Friedman, Milton, Mackey, John, and Rodgers, T. J. (2005, October). Rethinking the Social Responsibility of Business. *Reason*. https://reason.com/2005/10/01/rethinking-the-social-responsi-2/.

Gelles, David. (2020, September 24). Whole Foods Founder: The Whole World is Getting Fat. *The New York Times*. https://www.nytimes.com/2020/09/24/business/john-mackey-corner-office-whole-foods.html.

Gurley, Lauren Kaori. (2020, March 13). Whole Foods suggests that workers share paid time off during coronavirus. *Vice*. https://www.vice.com/en/article/93988v/whole-foods-suggests-that-workers-share-paid-time-off-during-coronavirus.

———. (2021, January 12). Whole Foods Is Cutting Some Workers' Paid Break Time from 15 to 10 Minutes." *Vice*. https://www.vice.com/en/article/y3gqgx/whole-foods-is-cutting-thousands-of-workers-paid-break-time-from-15-to-10-minutes

Harney, G. J. (2021, March 12). Whole Foods' Hippie CEO and the Lie of Enlightened Capitalism. *Current Affairs*. https://www.currentaffairs.org/2021/03/whole-foods-hippie-ceo-and-the-lie-of-enlightened-capitalism.

Hess, Amanda. (2017, March 17). The Trump Resistance Will Be Commercialized. *The New York Times*. https://www.nytimes.com/2017/03/17/arts/the

-trump-resistance-will-be-commercialized.html?smprod=nytcore-iphone&smid=nytcore-iphone-share&_r=0.

Kim, Eugene. (2022, February 17). Leaked document shows Amazon's ambitious physical stores plans are falling short of expectations, with far fewer people using its cashierless grocery carts than predicted. *Business Insider*. https://www.businessinsider.com/amazons-dash-cart-fresh-grocery-cashierless-ambitions-decline-in-usage-2022-2.

Leon, Harmon. (2020, April 24). Whole Foods Secretly Upgrades Tech to Target and Squash Unionizing Efforts." *Observer*. https://observer.com/2020/04/amazon-whole-foods-anti-union-technology-heat-map/.

Lyster, Lauren. (2013, February 6). Whole Foods Isn't Anti-Union, Its Beyond Unions: Whole Foods Co-Ceo John Mackey. *Yahoo Finance*. https://finance.yahoo.com/blogs/daily-%20ticker/whole-foods-isn-t-anti-union-beyond-unions-152024101.html.

Mackey, John. (2009, August 11). The Whole Foods alternative to Obamacare. *The Wall Street Journal*. https://www.wsj.com/articles/SB10001424052970204251404574342170072865070.

Mackey, John. (2020, November 12). *Freakanomics* podcast. Interview by Stephen J. Dubner. Season 10, episode 11. https://freakonomics.com/podcast/season-10-episode-11/.

Mackey, John, and Sisodia, Raj. (2013). *Conscious Capitalism: Liberating the Heroic Spirit of Business*. Boston: Harvard Business Review Press.

Mackey, John, et al. (2020). *Conscious Leadership: Elevating Humanity through Business*. New York: Portfolio/Penguin.

Menegus, Bryan. (2018, September 26). Amazon's Aggressive Anti-Union Tactics Revealed in Leaked 45-Minute Video. *Gizmodo*. https://gizmodo.com/amazons-aggressive-anti-union-tactics-revealed-in-leake-1829305201.

Minkin, Tracey. (2021, July). What–If Anything–is Left to Love about Whole Foods? *Austin Monthly*. https://www.austinmonthly.com/what-if-anything-is-left-to-love-about-whole-foods/.

Moran, Catherine Douglas. (2022, March 8). Inside the Store: The first Whole Foods with Just Walk Out is beautiful. Just don't look up. *Grocery Dive*. https://www.grocerydive.com/news/inside-the-store-the-first-whole-foods-with-just-walk-out-is-beautiful-ju/619799/.

Paumgarten, Nick. (2009, December 27). Food Fighter. *The New Yorker*. https://www.newyorker.com/magazine/2010/01/04/food-fighter.

PBS Frontline. (2020, February 18). Amazon Empire: The Rise and Reign of Jeff Bezos. Episode 12. https://www.pbs.org/wgbh/frontline/film/amazon-empire/.

Peterson, Hayley. (2018, July 13). "I ultimately am not afraid to get fired": Leaked audio captures Whole Foods CEO John Mackey describing clashes with Amazon. *Business Insider*. https://www.businessinsider.com/whole-foods-ceo-john-mackey-clashes-with-amazon-2018-6.

———. (2019, September 12). Whole Foods is Cutting Medical Benefits for hundreds of part-time workers. *Business Insider*. https://www.businessinsider.com/whole-foods-cuts-medical-benefits-for-part-time-workers-2019-9.

Press, Alex N. (2022, April 1). A Stunning New Chapter Begins for Amazon Warehouse Workers. *Jacobin*. https://jacobinmag.com/2022/04/amazon-labor-union-victory-jfk8-staten-island-bessemer.

Redman, Russell. (2021, February 24). Amazon Go draws high interest from U.S. shoppers. *Supermarket News*. https://www.supermarketnews.com/retail-financial/amazon-go-draws-high-interest-us-shoppers.

———. (2021, July 15). Amazon to nearly double online edible grocery sales by 2026. *Supermarket News*. https://www.supermarketnews.com/online-retail/amazon-nearly-double-online-edible-grocery-sales-2026.

Starbucks. (n.d.). Starbucks Pickup. Accessed May 26, 2022. https://www.starbucks.com/ways-to-order/pickup-with-amazon-go/.

Stevenson, Seth. (2021, June 28)."It's finally clear why Amazon bought Whole Foods. *Slate*. https://slate.com/business/2021/06/why-amazon-bought-whole-foods-groceries-online.html.

———. (2021, June 25). Organic and Inorganic Growth: The Story of Whole Foods. *Thrilling Tales of Modern Capitalism*. Podcast. https://slate.com/podcasts/thrilling-tales-of-modern-capitalism/2021/06/amazon-whole-foods-why.

Stone, Brad. (2021). *Amazon Unbound: Jeff Bezos and the Invention of a Global Empire*. New York: Simon & Schuster.

Thalen, Mikael. (2020, April 20). Whole Foods using "heat map tool" to track potential unionization at stores. *Daily Dot*. https://www.dailydot.com/debug/whole-foods-heat-map-tool-unions/.

Weise, Karen. (2022, March 2). Amazon plans to shut down more than 50 brick-and-mortar stores. *The New York Times*. https://www.nytimes.com/2022/03/02/technology/amazon-closing-stores.html.

West, Emily. (2022). *Buy Now: How Amazon Branded Convenience and Normalized Monopoly*. Cambridge, MA: The MIT Press.

Whole Foods Market News Release. (2017, June 16). Amazon to Acquire Whole Foods Market. https://media.wholefoodsmarket.com/amazon-to-acquire-whole-foods-market.

———. (2021, September 8)."Whole Foods Market to Launch Just Walk Out Technology at Two Stores Next Year https://media.wholefoodsmarket.com/whole-foods-market-to-launch-just-walk-out-technology-at-two-stores-next-year.

———. (2021, September 30). Co-Founder and CEO Announces Retirement. https://media.wholefoodsmarket.com/co-founder-and-ceo-john-mackey-announces-retirement.

Whole Foods Market. (n.d.). Whole Foods Market History. Accessed December 20, 2021. https://www.wholefoodsmarket.com/company-info/whole-foods-market-history.

———. (n.d.). Our Core Values. Accessed November 15, 2021. https://www.wholefoodsmarket.com/mission-values/core-values.

Whole Worker. (2020, December 17). Whole Worker December Mass Email. https://www.wholeworker.org/press/december-mass-email.

Young, Clifford A., and Gest, Justin. (2021, October 3). Americans are spending money according to their values. Companies need to realize that. *USA Today*. https://www.usatoday.com/story/opinion/2021/10/02/american-shopping-habits-companies-politicized/5887912001/?gnt-cfr=1.

CHAPTER TEN

~

Virtuous Viewing and Amazon Studios

Maillim Santiago

With the onset of the global COVID-19 pandemic, the meanings and modes of activism and community inevitably morphed. While the first few months of the pandemic saw most people abiding by stay-at-home orders while stockpiling essentials, a string of murders of unarmed Black Americans (George Floyd, Breanna Taylor, and Ahmaud Arbery, among many others) toward the end of May 2020 inspired a fresh wave of civil rights protests across the world. For those unable to join mass-scale demonstrations in the streets, Instagram accounts would compile slideshows of resources aimed at other forms of activism: sharing bail funds, Venmos, and petitions, or explaining basic critical race theory to educate a virtual public. It took only a few days of this social media wave for digital streaming platforms to take notice of the cultural shift and to quickly adjust to the moment.

Netflix, Prime Video, Hulu, and The Criterion Channel are among the many streaming platforms that began organizing their landing pages to include "Black voices" among the genres advertised, sandwiched between Action/Adventure and Comedies. As more people were arrested, brutalized, or killed by a militarized police authority, the call to become active consumers of "Black content" spurred the phenomenon I call "virtuous viewing." Virtuous viewing is a means of content consumption—primarily on these platforms—that is construed as a method of activism; if a consumer-spectator participates in virtuous viewing, then they can be presumed to have done their part in supporting the BIPOC community and they often do not feel the need to more materially redress past discrimination and marginalization, thus reducing their "activism" to slacktivism (Christensen, 2011, 1). This mode of slacktivism was encouraged and cultivated by companies who sent out newsletters to their subscribers in June 2020, promising hiring changes and/or solidarity with the Black community. This fed these companies' profits, while at the same time peddling an implied notion that this was ethical viewing: it was certainly a subscriber's moral responsibility to consume "Black voices" as attentively as they would True Crime or Horror (Francis, Gryta, and Trentmann, 2022).

All these companies are complicit in racial exploitation in some form or another, but none more so than Amazon, Inc., particularly due to their sheer size, revenue, and variety of goods and services offered. Amazon also remains unique from most other technology, goods, and service companies by having a fully functioning film studio as part of its services and branding. In this piece, I will examine the function and purpose of Amazon Studios, especially how they brand themselves as a distributor of "radical" creative content, using evidence provided by Amazon founder and former Chief Executive Officer Jeff Bezos and current chief executive officer of Amazon Studios, Jennifer Salke. Then, I will outline the racialized labor practices of Amazon at large, foregrounding how racism and sexism structure the workforce that sustains Amazon's ballooning business, particularly in the way Amazon maintains a consistent flow of low-wage Black and brown workers within their labor force. Finally, I will emphasize how the labor practices of Amazon as a corporation, as epitomized by what goes on at its warehouses—a wrangling and suppression of a brown and Black labor workforce—is laundered by Amazon Studios, which attempts to cover up these abuses by making content "to amplify stories from fresh and bold perspectives" and to encourage "virtuous viewing" (Baysinger, 2021). One might even say that Amazon Studios functions as a propaganda arm of the corporation that increasingly receives prestige and profits in Hollywood and the global media community. Furthermore, consumer-spectators of Prime Video who engage in "virtuous viewing" are complicit in generating revenue for Amazon and thus are tacitly supporting and furthering their exploitative and racist labor practices.

Amazon Studios and Prime Video

In 2006, streaming services like Netflix were coming into their own. Renting a movie digitally was becoming common, paving the way for the first iteration of Amazon's streaming service, Prime Video. Once the streaming sphere became more sophisticated in the early 2010s, Amazon revamped its video service and acquired films through purchases. Thanks to Bezos' deep pockets,

Amazon could acquire films and organize them into two different tiers: films that were "free" for Prime users, and films that users, Prime or not, had to pay to access. As Prime Video grew its digital library, the steps to expand Amazon's streaming service into a fully functional film studio were visible on November 16, 2010, when Amazon announced "a new website that lets users upload scripts and sample movies and then use community tools to evaluate and edit each other's work" (Fritz, 2010). To get started, Amazon signed a first-look deal with Warner Bros., who would help distribute and produce the content submitted via the Amazon Studios' website. First-look deals are struck by film studios with a creative client (in this case, Amazon Studios) where that client will develop a project and take it to the studio for the project to be greenlit, securing production and distribution. The studio can decide to turn down the developed project, which then allows the client to pitch the project outside of the deal (Thrasher, 2021). First-look deals are usually secured when a studio is eager to see what a specific client can develop. This initial foray into film producing would be one of the many Trojan horses unleashed by Amazon that facilitated its disruption of the film industry, mirroring the structural disruption its parent company had already introduced to other industries.

It takes so much financial, social, and cultural capital to reach the point of film studio functionality in Hollywood that the landscape for film studios has only shrunk since the days of Hollywood's studio system in the early twentieth century. As of 2018, Amazon Studios has become its own film studio, handling its theatrical and after-market distribution as well as the preproduction and principal photography stages of each of its productions. Furthermore, the company is one of the few streaming services that doubles as a film studio. Even more, Amazon has fully outpaced the capability of film studios like Warner Bros. or Sony Pictures, demonstrating its power with the unprecedented $8.45 billion purchase in summer 2021 of the oldest film studio in American history, Metro-Goldwyn-Mayer, and sparking a backlash from Hollywood creatives and calls for the Federal Trade Commission to investigate the purchase (Goldsmith, 2021). Amazon Studios is a conglomerate tied to its parent company; as of June 2022, only The Walt Disney Company with Disney+ could be considered to operate similarly to Amazon Studios/Prime Video. Amazon Studios was founded in 2010. The Walt Disney Company, as a film studio, was founded in 1923.

Amazon's seemingly limitless budget to buy and make creative content for Amazon Studios and Prime Video has disrupted the independent film industry by out-pricing film purchases in the tens of millions of dollars since their first record-breaking purchase of *Manchester By the Sea* at Sundance

Film Festival in 2016. Now, in 2022, streamers like Amazon and Netflix are the main purchasers in independent film markets, causing a shuttering down of independent production and distribution companies similar to how Amazon facilitated the disruption of bookstores and retail markets with the company's initial success. Aside from this market disruption, Amazon Studios' unbounded budgets for television and film content they create and distribute, along with the double-tiered rental and "free" model, gives them the most comprehensive video library in the streaming era. This abundance of "everything for everyone" is the hook Amazon, and its executives invest in for Prime Video because it brings the consumer-spectator back to Prime overall where they will be reminded, even goaded by advertising, for the latest Lightning Deal on Prime.

Additionally, when Prime Video and Amazon Studios markets their content as highlighting social justice issues, such as institutionalized racism, the company sets the ground for the complicity of the consumer-spectator in virtuous viewing. In 2018, Salke said: "[Our goal is] emphasizing diversity both above and below the line . . . [bringing] their vision to a global audience who is hungry for revolutionary, authentic content" (Lee, 2019). Amazon

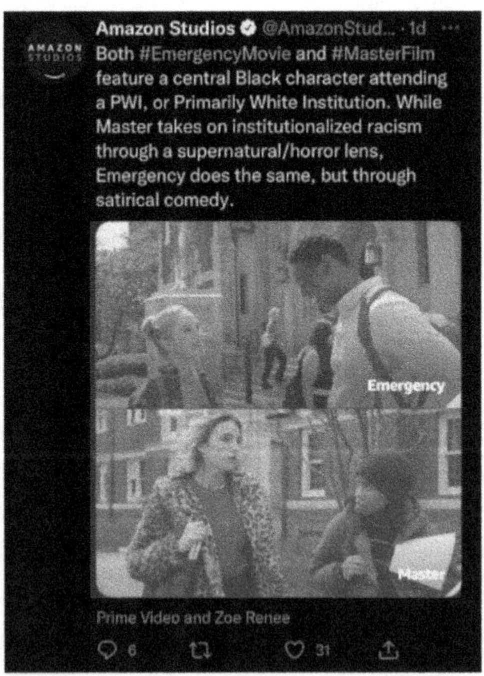

Figure 10.1. Amazon Studios' tweet from June 5, 2022, promoting *Emergency* (2022) and *Master* (2022).

Studios is implying with its marketing, material support, and press releases for "diverse" content that they are not complicit in the issues brought up in these films and television series. In fact, Amazon Studios is the loudspeaker for these visions. Furthermore, to be aware of these systemic issues that affect Black and brown people, the "hungry" consumer-spectator should go watch "revolutionary, authentic content" content on Prime Video where they also will be reminded to buy goods that creates the pipeline that will exploit the Black and brown people affected by Amazon's own institutionalized racism.

Amazon, Logistics, and Race

Amazon first broke into the market as a books-only webstore in 1994, hastening the slow decay of physical bookstores in the coming decades (Williams, 2020, Location No. 1270). Throughout the late 1990s, Jeff Bezos—Amazon's founder and chief executive officer—expanded Amazon's services, from launching affiliate programs to merging competitive internet companies into its brand until Amazon finally increased its retail offerings beyond books by 1999. Amazon also became a lot more than a retailer as it swelled in economic value where the largest portion of Amazon's profits came from Amazon Web Services (AWS). As the company built the largest online store on the web, storage space and computing power became vital. As a result, Amazon built its own web-hosting services that now boasts clients including Airbnb, British Petroleum, C-SPAN, General Electric, Monsanto, Netflix, Soundcloud, Ticketmaster, and many more. Studies estimate that AWS "controls nearly half, 47.8 percent as of 2019, of the public-cloud infrastructure, worth over $32 billion" (Williams, 2020, Location No. 1323).

This hosting service provides a virtual infrastructure to various government agencies as well, particularly the US government. The details of these numerous collaborations are not public, but their existence confirms the government's reach is as large as Amazon's, a company known to sell its users' data for a variety of purposes. For example, one AWS client is the Immigration Control and Enforcement (ICE) agency. The AWS cloud for ICE "hosts digital immigration case files . . . as well as biometric data on 230 million humans" (Williams, 2020, Location No. 1355). This aids ICE in deporting and detaining undocumented immigrants, making Amazon complicit in this process while the company makes a profit on the exchange. This partnership has made Amazon a target for protest by its workers and immigration rights' activists.

These are not the only Amazon services and products that fortify the company's role in surveillance capitalism (Zuboff, 2019). As a supplement to Amazon's Ring video doorbell, Amazon created a facial recognition platform, Rekognition, shortly after the introduction of their Echo speakers. Since its debut, Rekognition has been marketed to local US police forces as a cheap add-on function to its web services, costing six to twelve dollars a month. This technology, house by house and block by block, aids in building an authoritarian state in an increasingly militarized society which overpolices Black and brown bodies. Ring is also marketed to police forces; over four hundred law enforcement agencies are currently using it. Its usability "helps to create a wider surveillance network for police . . . with infrastructure owned by Amazon" (Williams, 2020, Location No. 1432). In other words, Amazon's technologies and services that are sold to, and used by, governmental forces actively support a police state that disproportionately targets Black and brown Americans.

Aside from creating products and services that surveil and subjugate marginalized populations, Amazon's most egregious abuse of power stems from the exploitation of its racialized workforce. Last-mile logistics workers allow Amazon to deliver on its promise to the consumer: quick, precise, and "free" shipping through Amazon Prime. These delivery workers "complete the final steps of goods delivery, ensuring Amazon Prime packages are delivered on time to a consumer's place of residence" (Alimahomed-Wilson, 2020, Location No. 2062). As Amazon expands its workforce, so too its active antagonism toward unions grows, and the exploitation and racialization of its essential and overworked labor force continues, particularly through structural moves intended to keep brown and Black workers right where they are in their menial positions and pay.

An example of this structural divide between warehouse workers and upwards mobility at the company is shown through the Amazon Technology Academy. In 2017, Amazon executives and diversity staff pushed a memo to Bezos that "propose[d] that Amazon could begin inviting warehouse employees, who are disproportionately Black and Latinx compared to corporate staff, to apply for a technical training program called the Amazon Technology Academy" (Del Rey, 2021). Although the Amazon Technology Academy was eventually founded in 2017, Bezos' response to the call for diversity at the time leaked via *The New York Times* from a staff meeting: "Mr. Bezos said that adding more diversity to the leadership team would happen slowly because of low turnover in its ranks" (Wingfield, 2017). Warehouse employees were not accepted into the academy until 2019; less than a year later, Amazon's hiring surge to cover COVID-19 demand would make an already disproportionate number of Black and brown employees face deadlier stakes amid poor working conditions and workplace abuses during a global pandemic.

In March 2020, the COVID-19 pandemic changed how the world would communicate, shop, travel, be entertained, and work for the foreseeable future. The health crisis spurred lockdowns around the globe, particularly hitting Hollywood hard due to its crowd-gathering nature across all levels of its functioning: producing, filming, exhibiting, and consuming. While theaters were shuttered and productions halted, a few select companies and services thrived in this new environment. The biggest winner of all seemed to be Amazon and Bezos, the man himself earning $34.6 billion just between mid-March and mid-May (Frank, 2020). While Amazon Studios stopped all of its productions, Prime Video saw more traffic than ever as streaming soared more than 60 percent with all the global stay-at-home orders (Keegan, 2020, 10). Meanwhile, the general public was encouraged, at times legally required, to stay home as much as possible, instigating record-high online sales for goods and commodities. Yet there was a racialized labor workforce for Amazon, primarily consisting of Black and brown people, who needed to fulfill these demands in the face of an unprecedented global health crisis.

These Black and brown employees "are producers of value; that is, they (not its consumers) are the source of the incredible wealth of this capitalist giant and its multi-billionaire boss Jeff Bezos" (Moody, 2020, Location No. 899). Yet these workers are limited in their freedoms on the clock, from timed bathroom breaks to working through injuries and sicknesses, without any job security should their bodies give out under the immense pressure necessary to maintain Amazon's promises to the consumer. For these workers' sacrifices, Amazon has maintained a culture of fear over their workers, once sending out supervisory emails with the subject line, "YOU CAN SLEEP WHEN YOU'RE DEAD" for those employees who fail to keep up with demand, eventually firing those who were not susceptible to these tactics of intimidation (Streitfeld, 2021). For the value produced by Black and brown workers, Amazon gives them two options: submit to dehumanizing work conditions or be fired and slandered for attempting to challenge the corporate hegemony exerted by Amazon supervisors and managers (Kantor and Weise, 2022).

Additionally, these producers of value are disproportionately hired from marginalized communities, especially in high-volume concentrated regions. For example, in the Los Angeles region, delivery drivers and last-mile logistics workers "are also increasingly becoming defined as racialized-gendered jobs . . . mostly men of color of Latinx descent, are overrepresented across the last-mile sector" (Alimahomed-Wilson, 2020, Location No. 2300). In 2021, *Vox* conducted an investigation of Amazon's racialized hiring practices, leading with eyewitness information from a former Amazon global manager of diversity, Chanin Kelly-Rae, who quit after less than a year at the job because "Amazon's corporate workplace has deep, systemic issues that disadvantage Black employees and workers from other underrepresented backgrounds" (Del Rey, 2021). The investigation extended into warehouse statistics, revealing racial abuses and treatment, such as in the example of Christian Smalls, while also reiterating that this is not just one company's racist workplace practices; Amazon is the second-largest private-sector employer in the United States. Swaths of brown and Black Americans rely on the company to survive, many times because Amazon might be the only reliable or available employer in both isolated or high-volume areas. Yet the company is complicit in subjugating this racialized workforce, either through its collaboration with the state or refusing benefits to logistics workers as some examples. As Kelly-Rae states, "They have access to our lives in more ways than any other company. The best thing they can do when creating opportunity is make sure that opportunity is enjoyed universally and not kept from some because of who they are" (Del Rey, 2021).

This context for how Amazon operates, as well as its virtual and physical reach, is essential to an understanding of Amazon Studios and its practices. Many of Amazon's goals and purposes are outlined by Bezos, a white American entrepreneur who trades off the title of richest man in the world biweekly with Tesla Chief Executive Officer Elon Musk. Bezos is part of a ruling class of white male executives who accumulate excessive wealth by exploiting the health and labor of last-mile and warehouse workers along racial, ethnic, and gendered lines. This underpaid workforce is composed of "non-supervisory blue-collar warehouse workers . . . disproportionately Latinx or African American workers that commonly face racial discrimination and live in areas of concentrated poverty and unemployment" (Struna and Reese, 2020, Location No. 2460). The structural racism and xenophobia these workers face are embedded in, and have become crucial for, Amazon's success. This structural racism is built into Amazon Studios as well, in its content acquisition and marketing practices.

Virtuous Viewing and Amazon

The already frayed social fabric of America was torn on May 25, 2020, when George Floyd was murdered by Minneapolis police officers (Hill et al., 2020). That night, protests broke out across the country, sparking a civil rights movement that lasted through the summer and continues to the time of writing. Within a week, Netflix, Amazon, Hulu, HBO, and other Hollywood corporations began using their social media accounts to "stand with" the

Black Lives Matter movement (Low and Yap, 2020). Amazon Studios posted on Twitter, "Together we stand with the Black community—colleagues, artists, writers, storytellers, producers, our viewers—and all allies in the fight against racism and injustice." Then on June 3, Amazon announced a ten million dollar donation to "organizations that are working to bring about social justice and improve the lives of Black and African Americans" (About Amazon, 2020). The same announcement also stated that Amazon employees themselves collectively donated $8.5 million, a figure which Amazon matched, totaling the company's respective donation to $18.5 million. But to put this donation into perspective, producing just one episode of Amazon's popular show, *The Man in the High Castle*, cost seven to eleven million dollars (Spangler, 2017). This philanthropic effort thus pales in comparison to the ever-growing multi-billion-dollar revenue Bezos has pocketed during the pandemic; even worse, with the unprecedented rise in demands for goods and services, exploitative labor conditions worsened for the very employees for which his company was supposedly advocating. For example, early in the pandemic, several brown and Black warehouse employees located in the Inland Empire—where the first Amazon warehouses were built—made their dissatisfaction and concern public through Facebook, changing their profile pictures "to include an orange circle that read: 'I CAN'T STAY HOME . . . I WORK AT AMAZON'" (Hayasaki, 2021). This move instigated a wave of workers to organize on Facebook under the group IE Amazonians Unite. In this online group, "a petition posted specifically for the employees of the Eastvale warehouse demanded that 'the facility must be shut down for a minimum of two weeks.' The petition also pushed for paid leave while the facility was sterilized, free worker testing for the virus, hazard pay, child-care pay and subsidies." In response, Amazon offered unpaid time off for anyone concerned about working in the pandemic conditions.

On September 24, 2020, Amazon Studios' building in downtown Los Angeles had a FlyBy Ad declaring their solidarity: AMPLIFY BLACK VOICES. On this ad, which could only be seen via drone or reproduced in promotional material, are the logos of Prime Video and Amazon Studios. There is simple white lettering contrasted on a black sheet: bold, stark, and demanding. But who is this advertisement speaking to? It certainly is not for Amazon Studios themselves; they are passing the buck, demanding the looker amplify Black voices by consuming Black voices as a spectator, subscriber, and consumer of Prime Video and Amazon Studios. The implication is the consumer is morally richer, more virtuous, if they engage with this content on Prime Video. The advertisement is a business expense, thus a tax write-off, and a grand metaphor for the concept of virtuous viewing. Furthermore,

Figure 10.2. Amazon Studios' FlyBy Ad from September 24, 2020, located in downtown Los Angeles.

once consumers are on Prime Video, they are on Amazon's landing page—an intention Bezos openly publicized regarding Amazon Studios in 2015: "You can have the best technology, you can have the best business model, but if the storytelling [at Amazon Studios] isn't amazing, it won't matter. Nobody will watch. And then you won't sell more shoes" (Jarvey, 2015).

The practice of viewership motivated by superficial virtue (and virtue signaling) became widely promoted by all major streaming services in the summer of 2020. "Black voices" or "Black content" became its own browsable genre. "Black voices" themselves become a commodity for Amazon Studios—one to promote with advertisements and as a genre on Prime

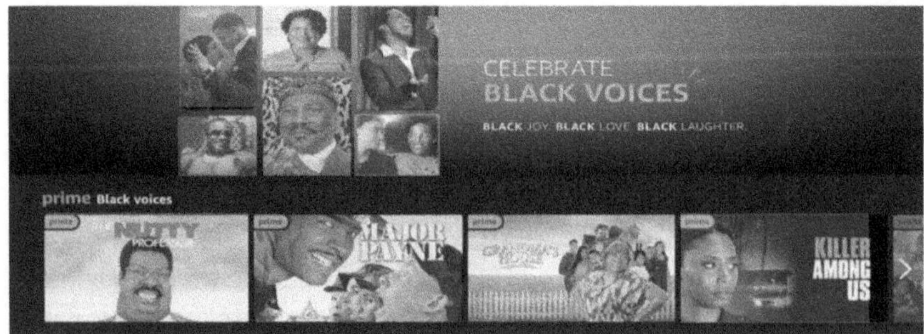

Figure 10.3. November 2021 banner for "Black voices" on Prime Video.

Figure 10.4. June 2022 banner for "Black voices" on Prime Video.

Video's platform. The category of "Black voices" shows up on Prime Video's landing page, falling right between Action & Adventure and Children & Family. Once a user selects the category, the page is organized in two tiers: free to Prime users and pay to view. Examining the "Black voices" landing page on Prime Video reveals what kind of Black voices Amazon finds value in amplifying.

A banner featuring the "Black voices" Amazon amplifies on Prime Video's landing page consists of several Black cultural icons from years past and present. The first titles to browse under this content collection are from major producers, directors, and actors within the Black community, including Eddie Murphy and *The Nutty Professor* series, a Wayans Brothers film, and Tyler Perry productions. These are already very successful Black entertainers outside of their association with Amazon Studios. One thing to note is that every month, Prime Video does change the layout of its Black voices section.

For June 2022, Prime Video focuses on the nationally ordained "Black Music Month," which was first coined by President Jimmy Carter in 1979. The landing page for "Black voices" in June 2022 looks entirely different than the ones for previous months that prioritize content titles that contain "Black voices." Instead, content featuring exclusively Black musicians take up the first few categories of the landing page.

When looking at the voices Amazon is amplifying with Prime Video selections, there is a class demarcation to who holds value for Amazon Studios versus who is actually producing the value for Amazon at large, including

Figure 10.5. June 2022 "Black voices" landing page on Prime Video.

Figure 10.6. June 2022 "Black voices" landing page on Prime Video.

their creative properties with Amazon Studios. Successful Black entertainers are the voices Amazon is amplifying while their Black employees are being fired, abused, or threatened for attempting to amplify their own struggles against the conglomerate. Meanwhile, Prime Video and Amazon Studios weaponize the language of civil rights movements to market their "revolutionary and authentic" content; all the while, Bezos' open admission that creative content drives the company's material goals exploits the very voices they are silencing in the value-generating process. This is where the contradictions and hollowness of "virtuous viewing" arise, a practice that became increasingly common since the first wave of Black Lives Matter–influenced organizing. "Amplify Black voices" becomes "amplify Black faces"; neither demand an intentional nor reflective process.

Within the free content section for "Black voices," there is a subsection dedicated just for Amazon Originals. Closer inspection of this selection reveals that the labels of "Black voices" and "Black lead" are used quite liberally. *The Marvelous Mrs. Maisel* is among the first entries in this section, a show that did not have a Black main character until its third season. And once it did, criticism of the character's relationship to the story world arose from Black and non-Black critics alike (Venable, 2019).

As of writing this chapter in June 2022, the second Amazon Original spotlighted under "Amazon Originals | Black Lead" is the film *Bingo Hell*, directed by Gigi Saul Guerrero, a non-Black Mexican Canadian filmmaker. The "Black lead" in the film is the only Black character, who has ten minutes of screentime and the most violent death in the entire film.

Figure 10.7. June 2022 "Amazon Originals | Black Lead" section on Prime Video.

Furthermore, nothing about the inclusion of Grover Coulson's character, Clarence, implies any thoughtful reflection toward the film's themes or narrative development; instead, he is treated as the stereotypical sacrificial Black character in mainstream horror cinema, his presence an afterthought, and by the director's admission, the victim of the "bloodiest scene." This character is what Amazon considers as a "lead" within "Black voices"; there is no Black voice at the center of the film, only one commodified Black face and death.

Even within the "Black led" content Amazon greenlights from Black creatives, there have been complaints from within the Black community

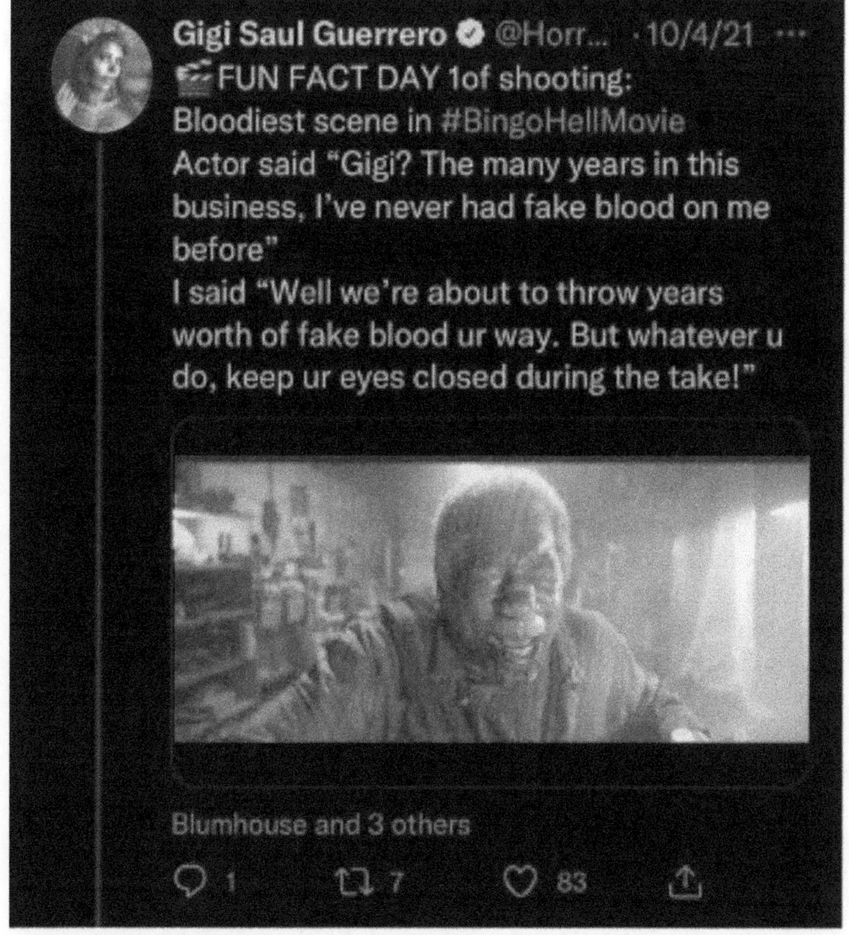

Figure 10.8. Gigi Saul Guerrero's tweet from October 4, 2021 describing the "bloodiest scene" from her film, *Bingo Hell* (2021)

itself about the commodifiable nature of Black pain that complicates any virtuosity that could be gained from "virtuous viewing." In April 2021, *Them*, an Amazon Original, was released. The series was created by Lena Waithe, an already successful Black writer, actor, director, and producer. When the series was released, it was bombarded with terrible reviews and accusations of clout-chasing Jordan Peele, known to the public now as a horror auteur (Crowley, 2021). Waithe has long faced backlash from the Black community with her other creative properties, such as *The Chi* and *Queen & Slim*, for exploiting Black trauma and stereotypes for white financiers/producers and audiences: "Even as she professes to represent the Black community that she belongs to, she perpetuates the traumatic narratives inherent in too much of Black-centric media. This is a fine line that many creators of content about painful experiences, whether it be drugs or death or brutal racism, must walk. But Waithe might walk it perhaps too much, and not well" (Frank, 2021). *Them* continued this trend in Waithe's long career in content production for white producers. In the case of *Them*, Waithe created and produced a "Blacks in horror" series for Amazon Studios that emphasizes brutal violence to Black bodies in their difference above all rather than exploring the complexity of Blackness in the face of the many anxieties Waithe brushes past in her establishment of the story world (Means Coleman, 2011). How "virtuous" can the viewing be if what is witnessed on screen is the degradation of fictional Black bodies in the name of genre and cultural trends while also contributing to, by consuming from, a company that uses Black and brown bodies as cultural and logistical capital?

Moreover, Amazon has proven they have an active interest in squashing any "revolutionary content" within their own workforce, such as union-busting Black-majority warehouses. Thus who is allowed access to this revolution they claim to curate and support and how is that revolution defined? Steve McQueen's *Small Axe* films, while about leftist West Indians in Britain, are made for an American production company that has largely no stake in revolutionary representations that come outside of America. Barry Jenkins' *Underground Railroad* series, while highly regarded within the Black cultural milieu for prestige television, is a big budget historical series about a past all too many Americans ascribe to "very long past," among them Amazon Studios' leadership themselves. Yet what these series do is feed the cultural capital of both the viewers participating in virtuous viewing and the Hollywood prestige Amazon Studios, Bezos, and his leadership team savor for making safe, nonrevolutionary content with Black creators.

Conclusion

Despite Amazon's transparent intentions behind corporate posturing and content curation with Amazon Studios, visibility for Black creators and Black actors is paramount to ensuring nonproblematized media representations. While the practice of virtuous viewing tends to fetishize Black pain for entertainment, there is room to critique and appreciate the content found in such spaces. Though some content produced by Amazon Studios and made by Black creators could be considered important to the Black cultural milieu, within the context of white supremacist capitalist patriarchy, creative content is culturally, socially, and economically compromised. Where the issue becomes particularly stark is when the machinations of the corporation are revealed. Amazon Studios and Prime Video were created with the intention of growing Amazon's customer base and Bezos' reputation in Hollywood. Every project greenlit at Amazon Studios has the goal of feeding the consumer-spectator back into the Prime pipeline. If this is the case, then Amazon Studios and Amazon's logistical practices cannot be separated. The structural racism built into Amazon's employment practices, practices that keep Amazon's hiring and turnover high, is reflected in the structural logics of Amazon Studios—from content acquisition, to marketing, and distribution. The branches work toward the same endgame through different methods and are expected to be symbiotic in their result. This means that Amazon Studios' investment in the amplification of Black voices is not for itself or for the sake of justice, but always for the sake of Amazon's bottom line regardless of other motivations. The virtue then falls on the viewer, who consumes content on Amazon, often leading to purchases that racialized bodies fulfill to comply with Amazon's marketing promises. Even if a purchase is not secured with every stream on Prime Video, the hollow act of virtuous viewing content from "Black voices" varies from supporting culturally Black creators to participating in forms of marketable blackface, such as in *Bingo Hell*. Viewers then espouse this faux cultural capital and give undue credit to Amazon and Amazon Studios for sharing content that uplifts "Black voices." Even more insidious, virtuous viewing and the values it performs works to distract from the exploitative and racist labor practices that undergird the entire Amazon corporation.

What Amazon's practices—both at large and as a fully functioning film studio—do is virtue signal from a company that actively participates in the subjugation and surveillance of racialized bodies, weaponizing their own diversity initiatives and content acquisition practices to put the onus of racial inequality onto their consumers and even their employees. Amazon

Studios' messaging is it wants to be a loudspeaker for Black voices and revolutionary and authentic content, but only if these voices and content fit a certain economic status/image and are just revolutionary enough, which is to say, nonthreatening to the white centrist capitalist class in their US home base. If Amazon Studios (and Amazon as a whole) truly cares about Black voices, where is the attention to the Black employees that are struggling as a result of Amazon's labor practices? If Amazon cares about Black voices, why did the company sink an unprecedented amount of money into union-busting their largely Black Bessemer, Alabama, warehouse; engage in tactics that "included an anti-union website, Twitch ads, mailers, care packages, text messages, compulsory meetings, fliers in bathroom stalls"; change the timer of the stoplight right outside the warehouse; or install a USPS Amazon-monitored ballot drop box at the location's entrance (Gurley, 2021)? Why would they hire an antiunion consultant at the rate of thirty-two hundred dollars a day to assist with these efforts (Fang, 2021)? The messaging is clear: Black people can be creative partners for white executives to profit off of their "revolutionary" content while simultaneously exploiting the most vulnerable of marginalized populations to reach their consumer-based goals.

Thus, the question arises: how virtuous could the viewing be on Prime Video? Amazon's pandering to the Black community is no different from what many corporations have done since 2020, including pledging donations to nebulous causes with little follow-through. Virtuous viewing is designed for white consumer-spectators to feed themselves moral capital without a second thought to how their consumption abuses the bodies and minds of racialized workers whose symbolic humanity on screen becomes the consumer-spectator's commodified virtue. What does set Amazon apart is its own inflated self-worth, figuratively and literally. Bezos wants to win the culture and prestige war for Amazon Studios, in part by growing a reputation for underrepresented content behind and on the screen. As the viewership for these properties skyrocket, Prime subscribers spend more time and money on Amazon Prime, churning a pipeline whose directives land on its racialized and exploited labor force. Bezos is only able to accomplish his goals by simultaneously exploiting Black employees and ensuring creative partnerships with Black creators of a certain prestige. Every move made by Amazon Studios to highlight its commitment to racial equity is intimately tied to its oppressive labor practices, its participation in surveillance capitalism, and subjugation of its racialized nonsupervisory workforce. If the onus is on the consumer-spectator to amplify Black and diverse voices, then the consumer-spectator should push beyond the boundaries of virtuous viewing and amplify all Black and diverse voices victimized and weaponized by Amazon's practices across its various subsidiaries.

References

Alimahomed-Wilson, Jake, and Reese, Ellen, eds. (2020). *The Cost of Free Shipping: Amazon in the Global Economy*. London: Pluto Press.

About Amazon. (2020, June 3). Amazon Donates $10 Million to Organizations Supporting Justice and Equity. https://www.aboutamazon.com/news/policy-news-views/amazon-donates-10-million-to-organizations-supporting-justice-and-equity.

Baysinger, Tim. (2021, January 19). Riz Ahmed Signs First-Look TV Deal With Amazon Studios. *The Wrap*. https://www.thewrap.com/riz-ahmed-signs-first-look-tv-deal-with-amazon-studios/.

Christensen, Henrik Serup. (2011, February). Political Activities on the Internet: Slacktivism or Political Participation by Other Means?" *First Monday*. https://doi.org/10.5210/fm.v16i2.3336.

Crowley, James. (2021, April 10). Lena Waithe Faces Backlash over Scenes of Graphic, Racist Violence in "Them." *Newsweek*. https://www.newsweek.com/lena-waithe-backlash-amazon-them-twitter-racist-violence-1582650.

Del Rey, Jason. (2021, February 26). Bias, Disrespect, and Demotions: Black Employees Say Amazon Has a Race Problem. *Vox*. https://www.vox.com/recode/2021/2/26/22297554/amazon-race-black-diversity-inclusion.

Del Rey, Jason. (2021, June 15). Amazon's Black Employees Say the Company's HR Department Is Failing Them. *Vox*. https://www.vox.com/recode/22524538/amazon-diversity-black-employees-human-resources-department.

Fang, Lee. (2021, February 10). Amazon Hired Koch-Backed Anti-Union Consultant to Fight Alabama Warehouse Organizing." *The Intercept*. https://theintercept.com/2021/02/10/amazon-alabama-union-busting-koch/.

Francis, Theo, Gryta, Thomas, and Trentmann, Nina. (2022, January 1). U.S. Companies Are Thriving Despite the Pandemic—or Because of It. *The Wall Street Journal*. https://www.wsj.com/articles/u-s-companies-are-thriving-despite-the-pandemic or-because-of-it-11641033005.

Frank, Allegra. (2021, May 23). Why the Internet Turned on Lena Waithe. *Slate*. https://slate.com/culture/2021/05/lena-waithe-controversy-master-of-none.html.

Frank, Robert. (2020, May 21). American Billionaires Got $434 Billion Richer during the Pandemic. *CNBC*. https://www.cnbc.com/2020/05/21/american-billionaires-got-434-billion-richer-during-the-pandemic.html.

Fritz, Ben. (2010). Amazon Studios; The Online Retailing Giant Wants to Turn Ideas Submitted by Users into Movies. *The Los Angeles Times*. https://search.proquest.com/docview/792980137?pq-origsite=primo.

Goldsmith, Jill. (2021, August 31). WGA, Public Interest Groups Ask FTC To Block Amazon-MGM Deal; Slam "Clear Pattern Of Monopolistic Practices.'" *Deadline*. https://deadline.com/2021/08/wga-ftc-amazon-mgm-merger-1234825214/.

Gurley, Lauren Kaori. (2021, April 9). Amazon Has Enough Votes to Bust Bessemer Union. *Vice*. https://www.vice.com/en/article/v7m5dd/amazon-has-enough-votes-to-bust-bessemer-union.

Hayasaki, Erika. (2021, February 18). Amazon's Great Labor Awakening. *The New York Times*. https://www.nytimes.com/2021/02/18/magazine/amazon-workers-employees-covid-19.html.

Hill, Evan, Tiefenthäler, Ainara, Triebert, Christiaan, Jordan, Drew, Willis, Haley, and Stein, Robin. (2020, June 1). How George Floyd Was Killed in Police Custody. *The New York Times*. https://www.nytimes.com/2020/05/31/us/george-floyd-investigation.html.

Jarvey, Natalie. (2015, July 15). Amazon's Hollywood Shopping Cart Secrets. *The Hollywood Reporter*. https://www.hollywoodreporter.com/tv/tv-features/amazon-prime-day-hollywood-shopping-808533/.

Kantor, Jodi, and Weise, Karen. (2022, April 2). How Two Best Friends Beat Amazon. *The New York Times*. https://www.nytimes.com/2022/04/02/business/amazon-union-christian-smalls.html.

Keegan, Rebecca. (2020). So Now What, Hollywood? There May Not Be a Return to "Normal." *Hollywood Reporter* 426 (March): 9–13.

Lee, Ashley. (2019, February 27). A Year after Frances McDormand's Oscars Speech, Are Inclusion Riders Making Progress? *The Los Angeles Times*. https://www.latimes.com/entertainment/la-et-mn-inclusion-riders-oscars-year-later-20190227-story.html.

Low, Elaine, and Yap, Audrey Cleo. (2020, May 31). Netflix, Hulu, Amazon, HBO and Other Hollywood Players Take a Stand in Support of Black Lives Matter Movement Amid George Floyd Protests. *Variety*. https://variety.com/2020/tv/news/netflix-hulu-amazon-hbo-black-lives-matter-george-floyd-protests-1234621292/.

Means Coleman, Robin R. (2011). *Horror Noire: Blacks in American Horror Films from the 1890s to Present*. New York: Routledge.

Spangler, Todd. (2018, March 15). Amazon Spent $107 Million on 'Man in the High Castle' Season 2. *Variety*. https://variety.com/2018/digital/news/amazon-documents-internal-spending-originals-man-in-high-castle-1202727642/.

Streitfeld, David. (2021, March 16). How Amazon Crushes Unions. *The New York Times*. https://www.nytimes.com/2021/03/16/technology/amazon-unions-virginia.html.

Thrasher, Lisa. (2021, January 27). Special Pod: Film Business w/ Lisa Thrasher. Interview by May Santiago. *Horrorspiria*. Audio, 48:04. https://www.horrorspiria.com/episodes/2021/1/27/special-pod-film-business-w-lisa-thrasher.

Venable, Malcolm. (2019, December 13). The Marvelous Mrs. Maisel Continues Its Rose-Colored Denial of Racism in Season 3. *TV Guide*. https://www.tvguide.com/news/marvelous-mrs-maisel-season-3-shy-baldwin/.

Wingfield, Nick. (2017, October 20). Inside Amazon, Diversity Concerns Flare Up After Harassment Accusations. *The New York Times*. https://www.nytimes.com/2017/10/20/technology/amazon-sexual-harassment.html.

Zuboff, Shoshana. (2019). *The Age of Surveillance Capitalism: The Fight for a Human Future at the New Frontier of Power*. First edition. PublicAffairs.

PART IV

~

ENVIRONMENTAL IMPACT

CHAPTER ELEVEN

Quick and Slow Violence[1]

The Age of Billionaire Biodiversity

Brett Hutchins, Libby Lester, Richard Maxwell, Toby Miller, and Whitney Monaghan

> "We are heartbroken & horrified by the deaths of 6 Amazon workers in IL w/ many more injured after a tornado blew thru a warehouse. Amazon has a history of knowingly putting workers in harm's way"
>
> —Amazon Employees for Climate Justice, https://twitter.com/AMZNforClimate/status/1470385760754880517

> "Amazon is destroying millions of items of unsold stock every year, products that are often new and unused. . . . Undercover filming from inside Amazon's Dunfermline warehouse reveals the sheer scale of the waste: Smart TVs, laptops, drones, hairdryers, top of the range headphones, computer drives, books galore, thousands of sealed face masks—all sorted into boxes marked 'destroy.' . . . An ex-employee . . . told us: 'From a Friday to a Friday our target was to generally destroy 130,000 items a week.'"
>
> —Richard Pallot (2021)

Violence may be defined "as an event or action that is immediate in time, explosive and spectacular in space . . . erupting into instant sensational visibility" (Nixon, 2011, 2). That dominant understanding in popular, governmental, and scholarly discourse holds that violence is dramatic and rapid (Miller, 2021). But there is a much less human and dramatic, but equally destructive, form: "slow violence." It is enacted by the dread hand of development, capital, international organizations, and states. Such violence

> occurs gradually and out of sight, a violence of delayed destruction that is dispersed across time and space, an attritional violence that is typically not viewed as violence at all. . . . neither spectacular nor instantaneous, but rather incremental and accretive, its calamitous repercussions playing out across a range of temporal scales. (Nixon, 2011, 2)

Amazon is responsible for both forms of violence—the quick kind, that its warehouse workers suffer in terms of everything from soul-destroying drudgery to constant surveillance and unsafe conditions, and the slower kind, generated by the company's Earth-destroying policies and practices. The two meet when warehouses are built in areas subject to dangerous weather, which leads to casualties from climate change, and in predominantly working-class communities of color, where diesel trucks, planes, and trains pollute the necessities of everyday life (Calma and Schiffer, 2021). That encounter of quick and slow violence takes place in an epoch of "billionaire biodiversity conservation" (Jones, 2021), today's gilded age of *faux* environmentalism.

Confronted by orders to destroy unsold products and the constant invigilation of their work targets, employees enact Amazon policies even as their sense of autonomy and social and environmental justice are violated. When they take action, per thousands who have signed up to join Amazon Employees for Climate Justice, they face derision, suspension, and loss of employment (Heubel, 2020). Meanwhile, trapped by the firm's monopoly-capital warehousing costs, companies that have inventory held by Amazon agree to the destruction of their goods rather than pay exorbitant rent. The remains head for unsustainable destinations (Pallot, 2021).

The two forms of violence are largely secreted from the population by the silky veil of consumer ideology: the ease of life as an Amazon customer is predicated on ignoring the experiences of fellow workers, citizens, and the natural environment.

Consumer electronics, of the kind that are central to Amazon's business, are profoundly linked to progress and desire. A "technological sublime" incarnates the quasi-sacred power that many societies have bestowed on modern high-tech machinery. Once beautified by seductive design and marketing, their awesome, hypnotic, even scary qualities are said to draw customers inescapably toward them (Nye, 1994).

The emergence of the technological sublime is attributed to post–Second World War Japanese and Western engineering and design triumphs, when technological power has supposedly supplanted nature's capacity to inspire alarm and astonishment. This potent blend of magic and science has a lengthy lineage. In the nineteenth century, people were supposedly governed by electrical impulses, and telegraphy was conceived of as a physical manifestation of human intellect that matched the essence of humanity to the performance of labor. In the early twentieth century, radio waves were said to move across "the ether," a mystical substance that could contact the dead and cure cancer. During the interwar period, it was claimed that the human "sensorium" had been retrained by technology. And throughout the 1950s and 1960s, machines were thought to embody and even control consciousness (Miller, 1998).

In our own time, this strange enchantment attaches to wireless communication, cellphones, tablets, high-definition televisions, IMAX cinema, mobile computing, and virtual reality: one more cliché dalliance with new technology's supposedly innate capacity to endow users with transcendence. That banality makes it no less powerful, because of the interests it dutifully serves and the cult of newness it successfully reproduces (Ogan et al., 2009).

Consumers experience the technological sublime via "the Fetishism which attaches itself to the products of labour" as if they were "independent beings" (Marx, 1987, 77). A "materiality paradox" exists: the greater the frenzy to buy goods for their immaterial cultural meaning, the greater the need for material resources (Schor, 2010, 40–41).

A typical assessment of the internet from the technological sublime fantasizes that "the emergence of the Knowledge Economy [is] ending the old linear relationship between output and energy use (*i.e.* partially de-coupling growth and energy use)" (Houghton, 2009). *Bourgeois* economists argue that the newer media have streamlined hitherto inefficient markets, enriching people in zones where banking services and commercial information are scarce, due to distance and terrain. Exaggerated claims for the magic of the internet in places that lack electricity, plumbing, fresh water, hospital care, and the like boast of "the complete elimination of waste," massive reductions in poverty and corruption, and individual *empowerment* (Jensen, 2007).

Internet production, distribution, and shopping are said to obliterate geography, sovereignty, and hierarchy, replacing them with truth and beauty. A deregulated, individuated, technologized world makes consumers into producers, frees the disabled from confinement, encourages new subjectivities, rewards intellect and competitiveness, links people across cultures, and allows billions of flowers to bloom in a postpolitical cornucopia. As if invoking Hegel, this solipsistic discourse exalts in human mastery, avowing that one can put one's "will into everything," such that an object or place "becomes *mine*." This "I" has "the right of absolute proprietorship" of everything, both natural and not (Hegel, 1954, 242–43, 248–50; 1988, 50, 61, 154).

Such cybertarianism is laden with jargon, half-truths, and nonsense, per the logic of possessive individualism that animates it (Macpherson, 1990). In reality, toxic manufacturing has moved to the Global South, pollution levels are rising worldwide, and energy consumption is accelerating in residential and institutional sectors, accompanying increased information and consumer technology usage. Recent research into the ecological impact of internet use in the Global North argues for its environmental utility per se, but not in the context of the increases in gross domestic product it facilitates (Özpolat, 2021).

For this is the most material era of history. In 1965, fewer "than 12 materials were in wide use: wood, brick, iron, copper, gold, silver, and a few plastics." Today, there is a comprehensive "materials basis to modern society": the computer chip that enabled us to compose and edit this chapter contains more than sixty of them (Graedel et al., 2015). New materials are taken as signs of progress, and it is true that developments in the alloys that bind them together and form new ones can diminish greenhouse gas emissions. But the notion of endless growth and progress fails to acknowledge that unearthing these things is a drain on natural resources, we have a finite supply of the basic ingredients of modern material life, and substitutes rarely deliver equivalent quality.

Those materials do not simply evaporate once the manufactures they enable are abandoned. On a typical day, each person in the world generates 1.2 kilograms of postconsumer waste (a bullshit average that distorts contributions from the ruling and middle class, corporations, and the state) (Hoornweg and Bhada-Tata, 2012). In 2021, electronic waste (e-waste) totaled 57.4 metric tons worldwide—heavier than the Great Wall of China, Earth's weightiest artificial object. The figure is predicted to reach 74 metric tons by 2030, thanks to the proliferation of electronics with short lifecycles and limited repair options (WEEE Forum, 2021).

Those numbers result from economic growth achieved through the division of labor, with the human and environmental costs externalized by capitalism. So much for a supposedly dematerialized age, an era of effortless postindustrial weightlessness.

The A-Word

> "A whole generation of first-in-the-family college graduates—now working as peons for Uber or delivering groceries for Amazon—are unlikely to imagine their future as solar panel installers or software technicians for an otherwise fully automated trucking company. For

every 'green power' job created, automation and depressed demand will probably dispose of five or ten traditional jobs."

—Mike Davis (2020b, 17)

We might immediately understand the syntagm "Amazon" and "environment" as denoting the effects of climate change on a great South American river. But what is the climate impact of one of our biggest companies that bears that name, reportedly chosen with dual purposes: to appear early in alphabetical lists and capture nature's riparian might? How green is Amazon?

When Amazon began in 1994, it sold printed books produced from trees, inter alia. A widely cited study says that once an owner has read 22.5 books on a Kindle, its carbon emissions have been offset; but the firm's secrecy about production practices make this more guesswork than fact (Ritch, 2009), and later evidence problematizes the claim (Roy, 2020; Naicker and Cohen, 2016).

Its electronic sales overtook paper- and hardbacks in 2010 (Malik, 2017). By that time, the company had branched out to selling most commodities imaginable, except animals, to the point where today it is almost "monopolizing the qualities of daily life" (Harvey, 2020, 49). This massive expansion forms part of a wider, wildly successful strategy of waste: to lose money initially but become dominant in markets through endless overproduction, overdistribution, overconsumption, and overdestruction (Quiggin, 2022, 179).

Amazon reportedly shipped five billion items worldwide via Prime in 2017 (Save the Post Office, 2018) and now accounts for 50 percent of US electronic commerce, followed by eBay, Apple, Walmart, and Home Depot, which together hold about 16 percent (Lunden, 2018; Mies, 2017; Rojo, 2021). Estimates from before the COVID-19 syndemic suggested one hundred million parcels would be delivered in the United States each day by 2026 (López, 2020). In 2016, transportation of consumer goods accounted for more carbon emissions than electricity plants for the first time since 1979 (Rojo, 2021), and the A-word has a vast, if largely invisible, warehouse and postal service. Its role in polluting ports across the west coast is a segment of an air-quality crushing supply chain from China that has caused tens of thousands of deaths (Robertson, 2021; Anenberg et al., 2019).

Since Amazon became a publicly traded company in 1997, the volume of corrugated cardboard production has doubled. US recycling corrugated cardboard boxes grew from that point, reaching 93 percent of recovery in 2015 because of grocery and big-box retail companies, which routinely repackaged cardboard waste for sale to paper pulpers (Weise, 2018). The industry even promised 100 percent recovery (Corrugated Packaging Alliance, 2016). But 2018 saw a decline of about three hundred thousand tons in recycled cardboard waste. That burden had shifted onto customers, who only send a quarter of cardboard for salvage. Amazon and other electronic retailers increasingly use less bulky plastic sacks for delivery to cut transportation costs (Young, 2019). These sacks are ineligible for curbside collection—and COVID-19 saw new restrictions on such services (see https://www.plasticfilmrecycling.org/recycling-bags-and-wraps/find-drop-off-location/).

The bottom line is that millions of objects have been wrapped in plastic and cardboard and delivered by thousands of newly hired drivers, as logistics expanded, waste multiplied, and purchases became simultaneously more personal and less hands-on—quasi-intimate home delivery, but no casual interactions while wandering around malls (Boudreau, 2021). Perhaps 23.5 million pounds of the company's plastic packaging waste ended up in oceans, rivers, and lakes in 2020, whose resident creatures mistake these toxic items for foodstuffs. That amounts to dumping a vanload of plastic in the ocean every hour of every day (Oceana, 2021).

Amazon Web Services

Amazon Web Services (AWS) began in 2005. It is "the world's most comprehensive and broadly adopted cloud platform, offering over 200 fully featured services from data centers globally" (Amazon, n.d.-b). AWS generates almost half of Amazon's operating income (Novet, 2021). It works with advertising, vehicular, educational, financial, gaming, governmental, and military sectors of the economy, inter alia. That seems an impressive example of innovation; but in reality, the A-word relies on a gruesome clientelism. In the United States, for instance, hundreds of former officials—creatures both great and small—have been systematically brought onto the payroll. They have duly delivered immensely profitable government contracts, from the Pentagon, Justice, Treasury, and others. Amazon explains that "we're committed to hiring builders who are dedicated to helping our customers accomplish their critical missions" (quoted in Lippman and Birnbaum, 2021). Right. Builders. Needless to say, the revolving door of "builders" works both ways; the Biden administration is replete with former executives from the A-word and its boyfrenemies (Schaffer, 2021).

Some of Amazon's "builders" are athletes. It took advantage of commercial television's loss of advertising revenue and decreased prices during the syndemic to buy the rights to broadcast and sponsor big-time association football, tennis, the National Football League, cricket, and baseball, thereby drawing subscribers to Prime to watch and buy as well as gaining goodwill to distract attention from its labor practices and environmental record (Hutchins et al., 2019; Poindexter, 2021). *The Economist* sees this as breaching television's "last redoubt" ("Brace," 2021). Regulators throw their hands in the air; sports welcome the money; consumers commit; television networks fume (Kayali et al., 2021; Robert, 2021). Nothing is said of the Carbon Trust's finding that people watching football via mobile devices multiply their footprint tenfold in comparison with television (http://www.carbontrust.com/media/360767/carbon-bootprint-infographic.pdf).

The cloud is not some beautiful, natural phenomenon as its name might suggest, delivering the water necessary for life. It's human-made and destructive. AWS has become a monumental contributor to environmental violence through its hegemony of cloud computing, whether that be your method of reading this chapter or your enjoyment of Netflix and its kind. The company has gone on to dwarf its boyfrenemies Microsoft and Google in its data-center carbon footprint: 44.4 MtCO2e in 2020 by contrast with sixteen for Microsoft and 1.5 for Google. It emits the same amount of carbon pollution each year as France (Mosco, 2014; de Laubier, 2022; Berthelot, 2022; Pitron, 2021).

The A-word boasts of its investments in wind and solar energy to power AWS, but as more and more companies rely on it, the use of electricity increases, along with the need to replace equipment. Amazon uses lots of dirty energy and doesn't like anyone publicizing the fact (Oberhaus, 2019); for example, its presence in France relies on a supply of 155 megawatts, akin to the needs of a city of millions (Pitron, 2021).

In 2021, Greenpeace estimated that data centers' electricity consumption around the world was somewhere between the amount of energy India and Japan used annually and would continue to grow at a rapid pace (Greenpeace International, 2012). But although global data traffic increased about "30 times over 2005-2015 . . . computing capacity per amount of energy for a typical one socket rack server has increased 100-fold" (Malmodin and Lundén, 2018, 11). The International Energy Agency confirms that data centers' average global electricity consumption stabilized after 2010 (2017, 105–06). The US Department of Energy found that in the United States, which has about a third of the market, electricity use by data centers ceased growing that year and remained at about 1.8 percent of total national consumption through 2014 (Shehabi et al., 2016).

Data centers' electricity consumption would have doubled over the period sans improved efficiency (International Energy Agency, 2017, 105). Hyperscale data centers are replacing smaller, less-efficient systems. One server in a hyperscale data center can cover 3.75 servers in other locations (Shehabi et al., 2016, 36; Hussain et al., 2019). The emergence of fog and edge computing, where information is closer to users than is the case with clouds, also promises greener solutions (Buyya and Srirama, 2019).

But there are barriers to a full "hyperscale shift": security, regulation (Shehabi et al., 2016, 46), and resistance from industries where instant data transmission is critical. In the financial sector, for example, milliseconds count (Lewis, 2014; Zook and Grote, 2017). Existing hyperscale data centers are located too far from flash traders to deliver real-time transmission (Cantu and Reiners, 2019; Krugman, 2014). Not all data centers perform sustainably, especially smaller ones (the vast majority) and those located in countries with a dirty electricity mix (Malmodin and Lundén, 2018, 14). As more businesses move to AWS and its competitors, data centers must restrict their carbon footprint (Pearce, 2018).

COVID-19

> "[T]he world has clearly undergone a massive shift in 2020 with the emergence of COVID-19. We are, first and foremost, focused on the safety of our employees and contractors around the world. It is important that we help our customers through this difficult time, and Amazonians are working around the clock to get necessary supplies delivered directly to the doorsteps of people and organizations who need them."
>
> —Amazon (2020)

> "Covid-19 . . . is key to new patterns of accumulation, . . . intensifying dynamics of labour exploitation. . . . Amazon Fulfilment Centres, . . . staffed often by migrant labour, have become hotspots of infection at the same time as work rhythms and conditions have worsened."
>
> —Adam Fishwick and Nicholas Kiersey (2021, 239)

Goldman Sachs gleefully proclaimed COVID-19 to be "a structural catalyst for a commodity supercycle" ("Commodity Prices," 2021). The syndemic has been "a Great Unequalizer," forcing and accelerating a middle-class convergence into inequality for Global South and North alike as multinational corporations abandon those classes, other than as consumers (Therborn, 2020, 85–86). But fear not. Amazon thoughtfully offered to assist with vaccine distribution as part of a desired expansion into digital health, pharmaceuticals—and obtaining personal and collective information about the population's health (Luthi, 2021).

The firm doubled its number of employees during the COVID bonanza, to a million (Lippman and Birnbaum, 2021). It clearly needed to do so—in the first ten months of the crisis, Amazon's stock price rose by a mere 65 percent and profits by fourteen billion dollars, while its principal bureaucrat Jeff Bezos' fortune increased by $75.6 billion (Kinder and Stateler, 2020). US electronic commerce sales in general leapt by a third in 2020; Amazon's share was US$263.5 billion (Boudreau, 2021).

During COVID's first year, the A-word's carbon emissions shot up by a fifth, the equivalent of fifteen coal plants or 140 billion burning barrels of oil, even though capital's overall carbon footprint diminished dramatically. The corporation's plastic packaging waste increased by more than a quarter, to almost six hundred million pounds—enough to circle the Earth hundreds of times (Boudreau, 2021; Heilweil, 2021; Pisani and Associated Press, 2021; Oceana, 2021).

Meanwhile, Amazon was supporting and benefiting from antiscience. In keeping with the wild popularity of the antivaccine books and snake-oil COVID "cures" it peddles, the firm donated tens of thousands of dollars to the antivaccination movement—just part of its commitment to what administrative researchers politely euphemize as misinformation (Schreiber, 2021).

Conclusion

> "When you see Amazon advertise its Climate Pledge, think about the workers who are most at risk & who Amazon leaves w/o protection from extreme weather."
>
> —Amazon Employees for Climate Justice, https://twitter.com/AMZNforClimate/status/1470385786713513989

Amazon's "Climate Pledge" of net-zero carbon emissions by 2040 attracted hundreds of corporate chorines to sign on, from Verizon to Visa (see https://www.theclimatepledge.com/). It focuses on renewable energy credits, which help maintain fossil-fuel hegemony elsewhere on the grid. The "Pledge" fails any reasonable test of transparency, excluding its supply chain from future promises and failing to counter the fact that its data centers frequently depend on dirty energy. And it carries no penalties or legal sanctions for infractions (Amazon, 2019; Jardim, 2020; Pardilla, 2021). This represented not only an exemplar of propaganda for external purposes; it was also an attempt to stave off criticisms from within, among a ginger group, Amazon Employees for Climate Justice, whose public profile and astute politicking were rare threats to profiteering in the era of the syndemic (Stone, 2021).

Amazon provides a variety of services to global petroleum firms such as Shell and BP, from the cloud to artificial intelligence (Amazon, n.d.-a). One of its strategic money-making priorities is "automating the climate crisis" (Merchant, 2019), notably via its own brand of motor oil (Ladd, 2018). Destruction of the climate via big oil is an important part of Amazon's business (Greenpeace, 2020) as it boasts a "digital oilfield of the future" (Ramos, 2020). The A-word joined Exxon, big pharma, Alphabet, Microsoft, Disney, and others beyond the Magic Kingdom in a multi-million dollar lobbying campaign contra the 2021 US infrastructure-climate bill (Milman, 2021). A-word greenwashing was signaled by its 2020 takeover of the site of the 1962 World's Fair, modestly renamed the Amazon Climate Pledge Arena (Climate Pledge Arena, n.d.). The unveiling occurred a mere two days after the company's Sustainability Report disclosed a 15 percent increase in its carbon footprint. Other numerous attempts to elude democratic regulation see such pitiful managerial euphemisms as the "Self Regulatory Initiative" and "Climate Neutral Data Centre Pact" that lay laughable claim to "lead the transition to a climate neutral economy" (Bourne, 2021).

The astounding revelations from ITV's investigative team about the firm instructing its workforce to destroy millions of unsold items a year mentioned earlier (Pallot, 2021) drew an immense international backlash. It emerged that although German legislation stopped Amazon from destroying new products, the A-word got around this by ordering workers to cut up clothing that could then be deemed used and hence liable for destruction (Abelvik-Lawson, 2021).

Amazon looked to score points as well as evading scandal and the law. It soon announced "Fulfilment by Amazon" programs, which would putatively be in the vanguard of a circular economy by allowing third-party vendors to reclaim their items in A-word warehouses (Shead, 2021). The corporation's "Day One Team" assured us this would "give returned and unsold inventory new life . . . next steps for Amazon in helping to build a circular economy" (Amazon, 2021). Orwell lives. Mendacity and illegality are not enough for these people. One must appear to be a leader in all things virtuous.

Beyond the world of euphemism, Amazon's mix of oligopolistic power and oligarchic networking finds pluralist political scientists throwing their hands in the air and saying it should be brought into the world of global governance—not as a self-interested lobbyist, but as a legitimate, formal actor within civil society which will help forge a new multilateralism (Higgott, 2022, 107). This is because

> [T]he moment you go into amazon.com, you are outside capitalism, and you are inside a platform that provides everything for you. It's equivalent of walking down the high street only to discover that every shop is owned by the same man, every product sold is distributed by the same company that owns the shops. The tarmac is owned by the same company, the air you breathe is owned by the same company, and what your eyes see is directed by the same company. This is what happens on Amazon. What you see on Amazon right now is directed by the company. (Varoufakis, 2021, 422)

Corporations like Amazon long to participate in social planning and private welfare, helping to define policy issues and manage public programs alongside the third sector. Via foundation support, corporate sponsorship, and executive largesse, multinationals have become bigger sources of global aid than states—and they remorselessly promote that fact, along with their compliance with voluntary codes of restraint. This movement into the public sector parallels their takeover of natural state monopolies through the neoliberal privatization of water, power, the military, telecommunications, incarceration, and so on. "Partnerships" between civil society and multi-nationals show they are dominated by capital's methods and interests (Rondinelli, 2002; Dagnino, 2003; Goranova and Ryan, 2014). In the words of *The Economist*, far from a reflexively critical voice when it comes to business, "The human face that CSR applies to capitalism goes on each morning, gets increasingly smeared by day and washes off at night" (Crook, 2005, 4).

It would be defeatist and self-defeating to invite the A-word and its boyfrenemies to participate in global governance. Climate justice can be achieved beyond the state, but not through their kind (Umbers and Moss, 2021). We should learn to reassess not only our daily routines but also our policy imagination to look for a collectively influenced response—via green supply chains and a public-service-oriented infrastructure of communication and consumption (Davis, 2020a).

That's not easy to do, especially when the bourgeois media fawn over so-called tech companies. Few press reports have pointed out Amazon's record: about a third of the site's top featured books on climate change promote climate denial. And Bezos' three-minute space jaunt earned him more column inches from NBC, CBS, and ABC than the networks' entire 2020 coverage of climate change (Macdonald, 2021; Cooper, 2021).

Shocked—shocked—by the fragility and beauty he had witnessed, the great executive in the skies—and beyond—descended to rejoin his people and immediately pledged a billion dollars to conservation. Make that two billion, carefully and lovingly reannounced a few weeks later, at the 26th

Conference of the Parties. Jeff proclaimed that "[t]op-down programs fail to include communities," notably indigenous people, vowing/threatening that "[w]e won't make those same mistakes" (Greenfield, 2021; Jones, 2021).

Contra the space cadet on high, who was indeed speaking "top-down" as he alighted from a chap's very own spacecraft, there are valuable intellectual/activist resources of hope in longstanding debates about the environment and our place in it.

Kant gave an impassioned account of the natural world as equally beautiful and sublime, aesthetic and awesome. That paradoxical amalgam forced him to confront a terrifying place where "the shadows of the boundless void into the abyss before me." This raised a horrifying specter: an apocalyptic vision that one day we may realize there is nothing left, nothing else, nothing beyond (2011, 17).

Edmund Burke acknowledged that all generations were "temporary possessors and life-renters" of the natural and social world. People must maintain "chain and continuity" rather than act ephemerally, as if they were "flies of a summer," thus ensuring "a partnership not only between those who are living, but between those who are living, those who are dead, and those who are to be born." This would sustain "the great primeval contract of eternal society" (1986, 192–95). Such intergenerational care has long been a centerpiece of African American environmental thought (Smith, 2007).

Engels recognized that "nature does not just exist, but *comes into being* and passes *away*" (1946, 9). He noted anthropocentrism's peculiar faith in "the *absolute immutability of nature*. In whatever way nature itself might have come into being, once present it remained as it was as long as it continued to exist . . . everything would remain as it had been since the beginning" (1946, 6). In that context, Rosa Luxemburg criticized "bankrupt politicians" who "seek refuge and repose in nature" without observing that its very existence was compromised and shortened by industrial capital (1970, 335). Marcuse realized that:

> the demands of ever more intense exploitation come into conflict with nature itself, since nature is the source and locus of the life-instincts which struggle against the instincts of aggression and destruction. And the demands of exploitation progressively reduce and exhaust resources: the more capitalist productivity increases, the more destructive it becomes. This is one sign of the internal contradictions of capitalism. . . .
>
> [Nature] is a dimension *beyond* labor, a symbol of beauty, of tranquility, of a nonrepressive order. Thanks to these values, nature was the very negation of the market society. (1972)

Human labor's transformation and marshaling of nature has immiserated as well as sustained the workers who service growth and profit. There can be no better example in the current conjuncture than the experience of many workers hired by Amazon, whose struggles for union recognition, human rights, and safe conditions are well-documented (Ross, 2021, 16). We must open our eyes to the human origins of Amazon's business. Of course, that doesn't just apply to electronics: we rarely think about the origins of our soap, clothes, or cars. They seemingly appear online fully formed, without any outward sign of their histories. It is a healthy reminder that somewhere, someone, makes and circulates the things we need and want (Merk, 2021).

The sense of a future made in our present must be borne in mind as we energize our Kindle and open our Whole Foods delivery—but not just as customers, per the "E-Shopper Barometer" (DPDgroup, 2020). Rather, we should do so as citizens and workers, such that we can appreciate the peril for employees and Earth alike engendered by our consumer ease. Otherwise, as a recent study in the delightfully named journal *Cogent Business & Management* indicates, environmental sympathies drop away from individual actions when consumption is in play (Rao et al., 2021). In the case of Amazon, while younger customers fret about its carbon footprint, this does not alter their conduct ("Amazon Shoppers," 2020).

Extinction Rebellion responded to revelations about Amazon's systematic destruction of goods in wasteful and unsustainable ways by blockading its warehouses in the United States, the Netherlands, Britain, and Germany in 2021 to protest the corporation's "exploitative and environmentally destructive business practices, disregard for workers' rights in the name of company profits, as well as the wastefulness of Black Friday" ("Extinction Rebellion," 2021). Within a few days, hundreds of thousands of the company's customers petitioned it to offer plastic-free choices (Delma, n.d.). Greenpeace reacted to ITV's revelations by criticizing Amazon for "a business model built on greed and speed." *Vox* declared "Jeff Bezos Commits $1 Billion to Conservation as Amazon Destroys the World" (Abelvik-Lawson, 2021; Heilweil, 2021).

Meanwhile, US Amazon workers could celebrate the 2021 holiday season. They gained the right to organize, contra the employer harassment they had habitually faced ("Amazon Settles," 2021). Such visions, not those of a Bezos aloft, should inspire us, connecting nature to capital and labor as constitutive variables of analysis and favoring regulation of business and work to comply with ecological principles, limiting consumption by restricting the generation of need and the exploitation of scarcity, thereby binding the twin arms of capitalism in a controlling embrace that refuses violence, quick and slow alike.

Note

1. Some of the research presented in this chapter was supported by an Australian Research Council Discovery grant (DP200103360).

References

Abelvik-Lawson, Helle. (2021, June 28). Why Amazon is Throwing Away Millions of Unused Products—And How We Can Stop Them. *Greenpeace* https://www.greenpeace.org.uk/news/stop-amazon-throwing-away-millions-unused-products/.

Amazon. (2019). Press release: Amazon co-founds The Climate Pledge, setting goal to meet the Paris Agreement 10 years early. https://press.aboutamazon.com/news-releases/news-release-details/amazon-co-founds-climate-pledge-setting-goal-meet-paris.

———. (2020). All In: Staying the Course on Our Commitment to Sustainability https://sustainability.aboutamazon.com/.

———. (2021). Amazon's new programmes give returned and unsold inventory new life. https://blog.aboutamazon.co.uk/sustainability/amazons-new-programmes-give-returned-and-unsold-inventory-new-life.

———. (n.d.-a). AWS energy. https://aws.amazon.com/energy/?energy-blog.sort-by=item.additionalFields.createdDate&energy-blog.sort-order=desc.

———. (n.d.-b). Cloud computing with AWS. https://aws.amazon.com/what-is-aws.

Amazon Settles with NLRB to Give Workers Power to Organize. (2021, December 24). *Times-Republican*. https://www.timesrepublican.com/news/money-markets/2021/12/amazon-settles-with-nlrb-to-give-workers-power-to-organize/.

Amazon Shoppers Won't Abandon Ship. (2020, March 18). *Inbound Logistics*. https://www.inboundlogistics.com/cms/article/amazon-shoppers-wont-abandon-ship/.

Anenberg, Susan, Miller, Joshua, Henze, Daven, and Minares, Ray. (2019). *A Global Snapshot of the Air Pollution-Related Health Impacts of Transportation Sector Emissions in 2010 and 2015*. International Council on Clean Transportation/Climate & Clean Air Coalition. https://theicct.org/sites/default/files/publications/Global_health_impacts_transport_emissions_2010-2015_20190226.pdf.

Berthelot, Benoît. (2022, January 7). La lourde facture environnementale des data centers. *Capital*. https://www.capital.fr/entreprises-marches/la-lourde-facture-environnementale-des-data-centers-1424800.

Boudreau, Catherine. (2021, November 18). Shopping Online Surged During Covid. Now the Environmental Costs Are Becoming Clearer. *Politico*. https://www.politico.com/news/2021/11/18/covid-retail-e-commerce-environment-522786.

Bourne, James. (2021, January 21). AWS, Google, Cloud, Equinox Among Europe Climate Neutral Data Centre Pact Founders. *TechForge Media.* https://cloudcomputing-news.net/news/2021/jan/21/aws-google-cloud-equinix-among-europe-climate-neutral-data-centre-pact-founders/.

Brace for the Amazon Effect on Live Sport. (2021, April 10). *The Economist.* https://www.economist.com/business/2021/04/10/brace-for-the-amazon-effect-on-live-sport.

Burke, Edmund. (1986). *Reflections on the Revolution in France and on the Proceedings in Certain Societies in London Relative to That Event.* Edited by Conor Cruise O'Brien. Harmondsworth: Penguin.

Buyya, Rajkumar, and Srirama, Satish Narayana, eds. (2019). *Fog and Edge Computing: Principles and Paradigms.* Hoboken: Wiley.

Calma, Justine, and Schiffer, Zoe. (2021, May 25). Amazon Workers Demand Company Quit Polluting Near Communities of Color. *The Verge.* https://www.theverge.com/2021/5/25/22453516/amazon-workers-pollution-petition-letter-demand.

Cantu, Marissa, and Reiners, Lee. (2019, April 24). High-Frequency Trading Comes to Cryptocurrency. *FinReg.* https://sites.law.duke.edu/thefinregblog/2019/04/24/high-frequency-trading-comes-to-cryptocurrency/.

Climate Pledge Arena. (n.d.). Climate Pledge Arena info. https://climatepledgearena.com/arena-info.

Commodity Prices Are Surging. (2021, January 16). *Economist.* https://www.economist.com/finance-and-economics/2021/01/12/commodity-prices-are-surging.

Cooper, Evlondo. Twitter Post. July 20, 2021, 5:51 PM. https://twitter.com/EvlondoCooper/status/1417603055822929921.

Corrugated Packaging Alliance. (2016). *Corrugated Packaging—A Recycling Success Story* http://www.corrugated.org/wp-content/uploads/PDFs/WhitePapers/CPARecyclingWhitePaperAugust2016.pdf.

Crook, Clive. (2005, January 22). The Good Company. *The Economist* 3–4.

Dagnino, Evelina. (2003). Citizenship in Latin America: An Introduction. *Latin American Perspectives* 30, no. 2: 3–17.

Davis, Mike. (2020a, April 6). How to Save the Postal Service. *The Nation.* https://www.thenation.com/article/politics/usps-profiteering-nationalize-amazon/.

———. (2020b). Trench Warfare: Notes on the 2020 Election. *New Left Review* 126: 5–32.

de Laubier, Charles. (2022, January 9). Pourquoi le numérique contribue de plus en plus au réchauffement climatique. *Le Monde.* https://www.lemonde.fr/economie/article/2022/01/09/le-numerique-dans-le-piege-climatique_6108779_3234.html.

Delma, Nicole. (n.d.). Get Amazon to offer plastic-free packaging options. Petition.

DPDgroup. (2020, February 10). DPDgroup's e-shopper barometer 2019 identifies regular e-shoppers as the driving force in European e-commerce. https://www.dpd.com/group/en/2020/02/10/dpdgroups-e-shopper-barometer-2019

Engels, Frederick. (1946). *The Dialectics of Nature.* Translated and edited by Clemens Dutt. London: Lawrence and Wishart.

Extinction Rebellion Targets Amazon Warehouses in UK in Black Friday Protests. (2021, November 26). *ITV*. https://www.itv.com/news/2021-11-26/extinction-rebellion-targets-amazon-warehouses-across-uk-on-black-friday.

Fishwick, Adam, and Kiersey, Nicholas. (2021). Afterword: Living in the Catastrophe. In *Post-Capitalist Futures: Political Economy Beyond Crisis and Hope*. Edited by Adam Fishwick and Nicholas Kiersey, 239–48. London: Pluto Press.

Goranova, Maria, and Verstegen Ryan, Lori. (2014). Shareholder Activism: A Multidisciplinary Review. *Journal of Management* 40, no. 5: 1230–68.

Graedel, Thomas E., Harper, E. M., Nassar, N. T., and Reck, Barbara K. (2015). On the Materials Basis of Modern Society. *Proceedings of the National Academy of Sciences of the United States of America* 112, no. 20: 6295–300.

Greenfield, Patrick. (2021, September 21). "'Earth Looks Fragile from Space': Jeff Bezos Pledges $1bn to Conservation." *Guardian*. https://www.theguardian.com/environment/2021/sep/21/earth-is-fragile-from-space-jeff-bezos-pledges-1bn-to-conservation-age-of-extinction.

Greenpeace. (2020). *Oil in the Cloud: How Tech Companies are Helping Big Oil Profit from Climate Destruction*. https://www.greenpeace.org/usa/reports/oil-in-the-cloud/#ref-18?link_id=1&can_id=78b5188883d26fd2bbbb8f335655c47e&source=email-take-action-today-to-fight-climate-denial-4&email_referrer=email_818960&email_subject=big-tech-3-big-oil-upcoming-action.

Greenpeace International. (2012). *How Clean is Your Cloud?* https://www.greenpeace.org/international/publication/6986/how-clean-is-your-cloud/.

Harvey, David. (2020). *The Anti-Capitalist Chronicles*. Edited by Jordan T. Camp and Chris Caruso. London: Pluto Press.

Hegel, Georg Wilhelm Friedrich. (1954). *The Philosophy of Hegel*. Edited by Carl J. Friedrich. Translated by Carl J. Friedrich, Paul W. Friedrich, W. H. Johnston, L. G. Struthers, B. Bosanquet, W. M. Bryant, and J. B. Baillie. New York: Modern Library.

———. (1988). *Lectures on the Philosophy of World History. Introduction: Reason in History*. Translated by H. B. Nisbet. Cambridge: Cambridge University Press.

Heilweil, Rebecca. (2021, September 21). Jeff Bezos Commits $1 Billion to Conservation as Amazon Destroys the World. *Vox*. https://www.vox.com/recode/2021/9/21/22686233/jeff-bezos-conservation-climate-amazon.

Heubel, Ben. (2020). Can the Winner Take it All? *E&T Magazine* 15, no. 5: 46–49.

Higgott, Richard. (2022). *States, Civilisations and the Reset of World Order*. London: Routledge.

Hoornweg, Daniel, and Bhada-Tata, Perinaz. (2012). *What a Waste: A Global Review of Solid Waste Management*. Washington: World Bank.

Houghton, John. (2009). ICT and the Environment in Developing Countries: Opportunities and Developments. Organization for Economic Co-operation and Development. https://documents.pub/document/ict-and-the-environment-in-developing-countries-opportunities-and-rev-3-31-august.html.

Hussain, Sardar Mehboob, Wahid, Abdul, Ali Shah, Munam, Akhunzada, Adnan, Khan, Faheem, ul Amin, Noor, Arshad, Saba, and Ali, Ihsan. (2019). Seven Pillars to Achieve Energy Efficiency in High-Performance Computing Data Centers. In *Recent Trends and Advances in Wireless and IoT-Enabled Networks*. Edited by Mian Ahmad Jan, Fazlullah Khan, and Muhammad Alam, 93–105. Cham: Springer.

Hutchins, Brett, Li, Bo, and Rowe, David. (2019) Over-the-Top Sport: Live Streaming Services, Changing Coverage Rights Markets, and the Growth of Media Sport Portals. *Media, Culture & Society* 41, no. 7: 975–94.

International Energy Agency. (2017). *Digitalization and Energy*. https://www.iea.org/digital/

Jardim, Elizabeth. (2020, January 27). Microsoft, Google, Amazon—Who's the Biggest Climate Hypocrite? *Greenpeace*. https://www.greenpeace.org/usa/microsoft-google-amazon-energy-oil-ai-climate-hypocrite/.

Jensen, Robert. (2007). The Digital Provide: Information Technology, Market Performance, and Welfare in the South Indian Fisheries Sector. *Quarterly Journal of Economics* 122, no. 3: 879–924.

Jones, Benji. (2021, November 2). What Happens When Billionaires Jump on the Biodiversity Bandwagon. *Vox*. https://www.vox.com/down-to-earth/22686696/jeff-bezos-amazon-billionaires-biodiversity-conservation.

Kant, Immanuel. (2011). *Observations on the Feeling of the Beautiful and Sublime and Other Writings*. Edited by Patrick Frierson and Paul Guyer. Cambridge: Cambridge University Press.

Kayali, Laura, Walker, Ali, and Leali, Giorgio. (2021, June 17). Why Amazon's Move into European Sports is Unstoppable. *Político*. https://www.politico.eu/article/amazon-europe-sport-football-tv/.

Kinder, Molly, and Stateler, Laura. (2020, December 22). Amazon and Walmart Have Raked in Billions in Additional Profits During the Pandemic, and Shared Almost None of it with Their Workers. *Brookings*. https://www.brookings.edu/blog/the-avenue/2020/12/22/amazon-and-walmart-have-raked-in-billions-in-additional-profits-during-the-pandemic-and-shared-almost-none-of-it-with-their-workers/.

Krugman, Paul. (2014, April 13). Three Expensive Milliseconds. *New York Times* A23.

Ladd, Brittain. (2018, September 14). Amazon is in the Oil Business, Proving no Industry is Amazon Proof. *Forbes*. https://www.forbes.com/sites/brittainladd/2018/09/14/amazon-is-in-the-oil-business/?sh=54712aaa48f8.

Lewis, Michael. (2014). *Flash Boys*. New York: W. W. Norton & Company.

Lippman, Daniel, and Birnbaum, Emily. (2021, June 4). The Secret Behind Amazon's Domination in Cloud Computing." *Político*. https://www.politico.com/news/2021/06/04/amazon-hiring-former-government-officials-491878.

López, Antonio. (2020). Online Shopping, Friend or Foe of the Environment? *Sacyr*. https://www.sacyr.com/en/-/la-compra-online-aliada-o-enemiga-del-medio-ambiente.

Lunden, Ingrid. (2018). Amazon's Share of the US E-commerce Market is now 49%, or 5% of All Retail Spend. *TechCrunch*. https://techcrunch.com/2018/07/13/amazons-share-of-the-us-e-commerce-market-is-now-49-or-5-of-all-retail-spend/.

Luthi, Susannah. (2021, January 23). Amazon's Offering to Help Biden's Vaccine Push. There May be a Reason Why. *Politico*. https://www.politico.com/news/2021/01/23/amazon-covid-vaccine-distribution-461525.

Luxemburg, Rosa. (1970). *Rosa Luxemburg Speaks*. Edited by Mary-Alice Waters. New York: Pathfinder Press.

Macdonald, Ted. (2021, April 13). In 2020, Broadcast TV Networks Mentioned Climate Solutions in Less Than 30% of Overall Climate Change Coverage." *Media Matters*. https://www.mediamatters.org/broadcast-networks/2020-broadcast-tv-networks-mentioned-climate-solutions-less-30-overall-climate.

Macpherson, C. B. (1990). *The Political Theory of Possessive Individualism: Hobbes to Locke*. Oxford: Oxford University Press.

Malik, Eddy. (2017, July 3). Amazon history timeline. *Office Timeline*. https://www.officetimeline.com/blog/amazon-history-timeline.

Malmodin, Jens, and Lundén, Dag. (2018). The Energy and Carbon Footprint of the Global ICT and E&M Sectors 2010-2015. *Sustainability* 10, no. 9. https://www.mdpi.com/2071-1050/10/9/3027/htm.

Marcuse, Herbert. (1972). Ecology and Revolution. *Liberation* 16: 10–12.

Marx, Karl. (1987). *Capital: Vol. 1: A Critical Analysis of Capitalist Production*. Third edition. Translated by Samuel Moore and Edward Aveling. Edited by Frederick Engels. New York: International Publishers.

Merchant, Brian. (2019, February 21). How Google, Microsoft, and Big Tech Are Automating the Climate Crisis. *Gizmodo*. https://gizmodo.com/how-google-microsoft-and-big-tech-are-automating-the-1832790799.

Merk, Jeroen. (2021). *Human Rights Risks in the ICT Supply Chain*. https://www.ed.ac.uk/files/atoms/files/human_rights_risks_in_the_ict_supply_chain_0.pdf

Mies, Will. (2017, May 26). US Box Demand "Back in Growth Mode Again" with a Major Boost from E-Commerce, Speakers Tell FBA. *RISI TechnologyChannels*. https://technology.risiinfo.com/mills/north-america/us-box-demand-back-growth-mode-again-major-boost-e-commerce-speakers-tell-fba.

Miller, Toby. (1998). *Technologies of Truth: Cultural Citizenship and the Popular Media*. Minneapolis: University of Minnesota Press.

———. (2021). *Violence*. London: Routledge.

Milman, Oliver. (2021, October 1). Apple and Disney Among Companies Backing Groups Against US Climate Bill. *Guardian*. https://www.theguardian.com/us-news/2021/oct/01/apple-amazon-microsoft-disney-lobby-groups-climate-bill-analysis.

Mims, Christopher. (2014, April 18). Amazon and Google Are in an Epic Battle to Dominate the Cloud—And Amazon May Already Have Won. *Quartz*. https://qz.com/196819/how-amazon-beat-google-attempt-to-dominate-the-cloud-before-it-even-got-started/.

Mosco, Vincent. (2014). *To the Cloud: Big Data in a Turbulent World.* Boulder: Paradigm Publishers.

Naicker, Vinesh, and Cohen, Brett. (2016). A Life Cycle Assessment of E-Books and Printed Books in South Africa. *Journal of Energy in Southern Africa* 27, no. 2: 68–77.

Nixon, Robert. (2011). *Slow Violence and the Environmentalism of the Poor.* Cambridge, MA: Harvard University Press.

Novet, Jordan. (2021, April 29). Amazon's Cloud Division Reports 32% Revenue Growth. *CNBC.* https://www.cnbc.com/2021/04/29/aws-earnings-q1-2021.html.

Nye, David E. (1994). *American Technological Sublime.* Cambridge, MA: MIT Press.

Oberhaus, Daniel. (2019, December 10). Amazon, Google, Microsoft: Here's Who Has the Greenest Cloud. *Wired.* https://www.wired.com/story/amazon-google-microsoft-green-clouds-and-hyperscale-data-centers/.

Oceana. (2021). *Exposed: Amazon's Enormous and Rapidly Growing Plastic Pollution Problem.* https://oceana.org/reports/amazon-report-2021/.

Ogan, Christine L., Bashir, Manaf, Camaj, Lindita, Luo, Yunjuan, Gaddie, Brian, Pennington, Rosemary, Rana, Sonia, and Salih, Mohammed. (2009). Development Communication: The State of Research in an Era of ICTs and Globalization. *Gazette* 71, no. 8: 655–70.

Özpolat, Aslı. (2021). How Does Internet Use Affect Ecological Footprint?: An Empirical Analysis for G7 Countries. *Environment, Development and Sustainability.* https://doi.org/10.1007/s10668-021-01967-z.

Pallot, Richard. (2021, June 22). Amazon Destroying Millions of Items of Unsold Stock in One of its UK Warehouses Every Year, ITV News Investigation Finds." *ITV*https://www.itv.com/news/2021-06-21/amazon-destroying-millions-of-items-of-unsold-stock-in-one-of-its-uk-warehouses-every-year-itv-news-investigation finds.

Pardilla, Ambar. (2021, June 17). What Amazon's Climate Pledge Means, According to Experts. *NBC.* https://www.nbcnews.com/select/shopping/amazon-climate-pledge-ncna1271192.

Pearce, Fred. (2018, April 3). Energy Hogs: Can World's Huge Data Centers Be Made More Efficient? *Yale Environment 360.* https://e360.yale.edu/features/energy-hogs-can-huge-data-centers-be-made-more-efficient.

Pisani, Joseph, and Associated Press. (2021, June 30). Amazon's Carbon Footprint Grew by This Much Last Year. *Fortune.* https://fortune.com/2021/06/30/amazon-carbon-footprint-pollution-grew/.

Pitron, Guillaume. (2021, November). No Such Place as the Cloud. Translated by Charles Goulden. *Le monde diplomatique.* https://mondediplo.com/2021/11/09digital-waste.

Poindexter, Owen. (2021, June 21). Amazon's Aggressive Expansion into Sports Continues. *Front Office Sports.* https://frontofficesports.com/amazon-wants-all-the-live-sports/.

Quiggin, John. (2022). *Economics in Two Lessons: Why Markets Work So Well, and Why They Can Fail So Badly*. Princeton: Princeton University Press.

Ramos, Juan Pablo. (2020, June 23). Amazon, Microsoft y la hipocresía con el medio ambiente. *Cletofilia*. https://cletofilia.com/amazon-microsoft-y-la-hipocresia-con-el-medio-ambiente/.

Rao, Prakash, Balasubramanian, Sreejith, Vihari, Nitin, Jabeen, Shazi, Shukla, Vinaya, and Chanchaichujit, Janya. (2021). The E-Commerce Supply Chain and Environmental Sustainability: An Empirical Investigation on the Online Retail Sector. *Cogent Business & Management* 8, no. 1. https://doi.org/10.1080/23311975.2021.1938377.

Ritch, Emma. (2009). *The Environmental Impact of Amazon's Kindle*. https://gato-docs.its.txstate.edu/jcr:4646e321-9a29-41e5-880d-4c5ffe69e03e/thoughtsereaders.pdf.

Robert, Aurélien. (2021, December 20). Amazon Prime Video Ligue 1: Comment s'abonner pour voir le foot français? *CNET*. https://www.cnetfrance.fr/news/amazon-prime-video-ligue-1-comment-s-abonner-pour-voir-le-foot-francais-39927383.htm.

Robertson, Angeline. (2021). *Shady Routes: How Big Retail and Their Carriers Pollute Along Key Ocean Shipping Corridors*. https://shipitzero.org/wp-content/uploads/2021/11/FINAL-Ship-it-Zero-Campaign-Report.pdf.

Rojo, Cristina. (2021). El impacto ambiental de que Amazon te entregue un paquete en 24 horas. *Ballena Blanca*. https://ballenablanca.es/impacto-ambiental-amazon-te-entregue-paquete-24-horas-2/.

Rondinelli, Dennis A. (2002). Transnational Corporations: International Citizens or New Sovereigns? *Business and Society Review* 107, no. 4: 391–413.

Ross, Andrew. (2021). Is Care Work Already the Future? *New Labor Forum* 30, no. 1: 12–18.

Roy, Pierre-Olivier. (2020, August). The Environmental environmental footprint of paper vs. electronic books goes here. *Anthropocene*. https://www.anthropocenemagazine.org/2020/08/the-environmental-footprint-of-paper-vs-electronic-books/?gclid=Cj0KCQiAieWOBhCYARIsANcOw0yUmtKaHmCxEvFdqliknkK0dh6piis0udeJF92OdOkzUV0kVk9P4XwaAsEREALwwcB.

Save the Post Office. (2018, July 29). An Amazon puzzle: How many parcels does it ship, how much does it cost, and who delivers what share? *Save the Post Office*. https://savethepostoffice.com/an-amazon-puzzle-how-many-parcels-does-it-ship-how-much-does-it-cost-and-who-delivers-what-share.

Schaffer, Aaron. (2021, June 22). Biden Administration Full of Officials Who Worked for Prominent Tech Companies. *Washington Post*. https://www.washingtonpost.com/politics/2021/06/22/technology-202-biden-administration-full-officials-who-worked-prominent-tech-companies/.

Schor, Juliet B. (2010). *Plenitude: The New Economics of True Wealth*. New York: Penguin.

Schreiber, Melody. (2021, December 15). AmazonSmile Donated More Than $40,000 to Anti-Vaccine Groups in 2020." *Guardian*. https://www.theguardian.com/technology/2021/dec/15/amazonsmile-donations-anti-vaccine-groups.

Shead, Sam. (2021, August 4). Amazon Plans to Cut Waste Following Backlash Over the Destruction of Unused Products. *CNBC*. https://www.cnbc.com/2021/08/04/amazon-plans-to-cut-waste-following-backlash.html.

Shehabi, Aman, Smith, Sarah, Horner, Nathaniel, Azevedo, Inês, Brown, Richard, Koomey, Jonathan, Masanet, Eric, Sartor, Dale, Herrlin, Magnus, and Lintner, William. (2016). *United States Data Center Energy Usage Report*. Lawrence Berkeley National Laboratory, Berkeley, California. LBNL-1005775. http://eta-publications.lbl.gov/sites/default/files/lbnl-1005775_v2.pdf.

Smith, Kimberly K. (2007). *African American Environmental Thought: Foundations*. Lawrence: University of Kansas Press.

Stone, Brad. (2021). *Amazon Unbound: Jeff Bezos and the Invention of a Global Empire*. New York: Simon & Schuster.

Therborn, Göran. (2020). Dreams and Nightmares of the World's Middle Classes. *New Left Review* 124: 63–87.

Umbers, Lachlan, and Moss, Jeremy. (2021). *Climate Justice Beyond the State*. London: Routledge.

Varoufakis, Yanis. (2021). In Conversation with Yanis Varoufakis: Teresa Turkheimer. *Cambridge Journal of Law, Politics, and Art* 1: 419–25.

WEEE Forum. (2021). International E-Waste Day: 57.4 mm Tonnes Expected in 2021. https://weee-forum.org/ws_news/international-e-waste-day-2021/.

Weise, Elizabeth. (2018, June 8). Blue Bins Overflow with Amazon and Walmart Boxes. But We're Actually Recycling Less." *USA Today*. https://www.usatoday.com/story/tech/news/2018/06/08/cardboard-recycling-rates-drop-shopping-amazon-walmart-surges/630967002/.

Young, Kristen Millares. (2019, February 11). Why Amazon's New streamlined packaging is jamming up recycling centers. *Washington Post*. https://www.washingtonpost.com/technology/2019/02/11/why-amazons-new-streamlined-packaging-is-jamming-up-recycling-centers/.

Zook, Matthew, and Grote, Michael H. (2017). The Microgeographies of Global Finance: High-Frequency Trading and the Construction of Information Inequality. *Environment and Planning A: Economy and Space* 49, no. 1: 121–40.

CHAPTER TWELVE

~

Decoding Amazon's Climate Pledge

Public Relations and the Platformization of Governance

Emily West

In June 2020, Amazon announced that it had secured naming rights for a newly refurbished sports arena in Seattle. The home of the newest National Hockey League franchise, the Seattle Kraken, as well as the Women's National Basketball Association's Seattle Storm, would be named not Amazon Arena or Prime arena, nor even Alexa Arena, but Climate Pledge Arena (Amazon, 2020). Named after a corporate carbon accountability organization that Amazon cofounded with the nonprofit Global Optimism in 2019, this move announced the new centrality of The Climate Pledge and green corporate responsibility to Amazon's public image.

Amazon's need to get out in front of environmental criticisms of its business are clear. Although tech companies like Amazon were long imagined to be almost immaterial due to their digital, and seemingly virtual, nature, the public has rapidly become better informed, and alarmed, about the carbon and therefore climate impacts of big tech. Facts and figures such as that information and communication technology account for between 1 and 4 percent of global electricity usage, and the world's data centers consume more electricity than the majority of countries, have attracted the public's attention and created an "energy techlash" (Conca, 2021; Cunliff, 2020).

Relative to its fellow tech giants, Amazon is coming under even greater scrutiny for its environmental impacts and claims to green credentials. With its original business being e-commerce, the material impacts of Amazon are much more visible to the average consumer. Widely reported guilt about frequent piles of Amazon boxes on one's doorstep speaks to this general sentiment, but there's also growing awareness of the extent of Amazon's distribution footprint. From the massive warehouses to the Amazon-branded delivery vehicles in so many neighborhoods since 2018, when the company started moving away from depending entirely on other companies for the last mile, to the variety of Amazon devices (the Kindle, Fire tablets, Echo smart speakers) that are on their inevitable way to being e-waste, the public has many touchpoints with Amazon that bring to mind the company's environmental impact in a concrete, tangible way.

But there are other sources of Amazon's environmental impacts that are much less visible to the everyday user. As the market leader in cloud services, Amazon Web Services (AWS) provides a significant portion of the world's cloud computing capacity, a networked service that relies on cheap power and copious amounts of water to cool its dozens of data centers worldwide. This core infrastructure for so many online businesses and services, including large, well-known ones like Netflix, Zoom, and Comcast, also undergirds the ever-increasing digital services that consumers get from Amazon, including e-books, streaming video, its app store, and Alexa. Amazon's carbon accounting data show that emissions from Amazon-branded products (including manufacture, use, and end-of-life) constitute somewhere close to a quarter of its estimated 2020 carbon footprint (Amazon, 2021a).

The question of who will govern the climate impacts of Amazon, and the digital economy more broadly, is a pressing one. I raise the question of governance because while Amazon may be following applicable laws and government regulations (as far as we know), the push toward reducing carbon outputs and greening business is playing out as much, if not more, in the realm of nongovernmental organizations, particularly across borders, than among nation-states (Levy and Newell, 2005). This is not an accident. Corporations would prefer to obviate the need for state-based environmental regulation by creating their own environmental goals and standards and accountability organizations. The benefits of this approach are at least threefold: (1) taking the lead on green business practices makes corporations appear responsible and caring in the eyes of the public, which can enhance their brands and customer relations; (2) nongovernmental agreements and accountability organizations can create international standards that simplify business across national borders; and (3) by owning the idea of corporate environmental responsibility, corporations can promote and institutionalize environmental standards that will be more business- and growth-friendly than those advocated by environmental activists, scientists, and perhaps even by politicians. When large corporations succeed in normalizing their preferred standards or regulations, it creates a type of regulatory capture that advantages them against competitors and particularly smaller players in the marketplace.

Due to Amazon's size, dominance in a variety of markets, and the types of businesses that it operates in, it is often observed that it is no longer just a business but has meaningfully become "essential infrastructure" in a variety of respects (Khan, 2017, 803). Or, as small business advocate Stacy Mitchell (2018) puts it, Amazon doesn't just want to compete in the market, "it wants to *become* the market" (emphasis added). Amazon's size and dominance in some markets makes it a de facto setter of standards—another feature of its infrastructural nature. As theorists of infrastructure Susan Leigh Star and Geoffrey Bowker wrote, "Standards undergird our potential for action in the world, both political and scientific; they make the infrastructure possible" (2006, p. 157). Whether packaging specifications, shipping speeds, product prices, wages for warehouse work, or productivity benchmarks for logistics workers, the multiple ways in which Amazon itself sets standards for businesses, local governments, and employers make its influence more akin to governance than merely private activity. In other words, concentrated market power can become de facto regulatory power (Open Markets Institute, 2018, p. 2).

This chapter examines what we know of Amazon's environmental record, and how it is increasingly positioning itself as a leader in green corporate accountability. I place Amazon's efforts at the intersection of public relations capitalism and platform self-regulation in order to explain their strategy and significance. Anne M. Cronin offers the concept of public relations capitalism to describe the "relationship . . . between political culture and commercial culture that is mediated by PR and other promotional industries" (2018, p. 1). In this formulation, public relations is an "active transformational force" that fills the gap in trust and participation that people have in actual democratic politics, promising instead voice and representation via the corporation or brand (Cronin, 2018, p. 3).

While public relations capitalism describes how corporations fill the gap left by a decline in conventional politics, platform self-regulation—or "Regulation.com" as legal scholar Marta Cantero Gamito coins it—points to the ways digital platforms "are developing their own governance frameworks based on self-regulation, trust, and reputation" (Gamito, 2017, p. 53). This includes how these companies set standards and regulate user behavior on their platforms, such as content standards on social media platforms or product health and safety standards on e-commerce platforms, as well as self-regulation of the platform itself, such as internal goals for hiring people of color or veterans, or benchmarks for reducing carbon outputs.

Trust and reputation of the brand are at the heart of both public relations capitalism and platform self-regulation. If citizens and consumers are to accept the corporation representing their political interests by proxy, then they must trust that brand in order to see it as a legitimate political actor. And both politicians and users must have some level of trust in a platform's integrity in order to accept the company setting and enforcing rules for users, as well as for governing itself.

Critical scholars have long observed a migration of governance from the state to corporations in the political-economic context of neoliberalism (Dean, 2010; Gamito, 2017). Melissa Aronczyk and Maria I. Espinoza describe a decades-long history of public relations professionals positioning themselves as "cultural producers of environmental governance," with the goal of offering "corporate environmentalism as an alternative to public policy" (2021, p. 1). These efforts resulted in a shift in United Nations' environmental rhetoric conceptualizing corporations "as a culprit and a threat" at their 1972 environment conference, to including industry and allowing its representatives to significantly shape the agenda at the United Nations' 1992 Earth Summit in Rio (Aronczyk and Espinoza, 2022, p. 128). Based on what we have seen so far of Amazon branding itself as a green corporate citizen, creating its own carbon accountability organization, and setting and endorsing consumer-facing environmental product standards, I ask: what are the emergent benefits and risks to environmental self-regulation by platforms, as exemplified by Amazon?

Amazon's Record: From Climate Laggard to Self-Styled Green Corporate Citizen

Climate Pledge Arena would have been hard to predict in 2016 when Greenpeace USA gave Amazon a grade of "C" in its Clicking Clean scorecard, well behind the "A" grades awarded to US tech giants Apple, Google, and Facebook, and still behind other competitors Microsoft, eBay, and Etsy who earned a "B" (Cook et al., 2017, p. 8). In 2016, AWS' Greenpeace Clean Energy Index—an estimate of the "dirty" versus renewable energy mix powering its data centers—was only 17 percent compared to Apple's 83 percent. Greenpeace judged Amazon favorably on its advocacy for green energy (a B); moderately for its procurement of renewable energy sources, energy efficiency and mitigation, and renewable energy commitment and siting policy (Cs); and terribly on energy transparency (F) (Cook et al., 2017, p. 43). At least in 2016, Greenpeace judged Amazon to be too vague on the nature of the renewable energy purchases powering its data centers, as well as on what the company meant by "Carbon Neutral" which it was claiming for certain AWS regions.

The specifics matter, given the creative carbon accounting practices that have emerged as corporations have come under increasing pressure to green their energy consumption (Pasek, 2019). One example of a carbon "shortcut" is unbundled clean energy certificates, known as renewable energy certificates in the United States, which can be purchased to claim an offset from carbon-based energy that a company has actually used. As critics point out, these financial instruments have little real-world impact on the use of fossil fuels, as they fail to push the energy utilities in the locations where companies are actually using power to switch to renewables. More meaningful is when corporations create their own clean energy sources, contract locally with clean energy providers, or work with utilities to incentivize the construction of new sources of clean energy (Naik, 2021). As Anastasia O'Rourke of Yale University's Carbon Containment Lab has put it, there's unlikely to be a large enough supply of "quality" carbon offset products to meet the demands of corporations who would like to solve their emissions balance sheets this way; reducing emissions and directly using renewables have to be big parts of the mix (Scheimer and Chakrabarti, 2021).

Amazon has also been judged much less transparent than its big tech competitors by the international nongovernmental organization the Carbon Disclosure Project (2021), which runs a "global disclosure system for investors, companies, cities, states and regions to manage their environmental impacts." Amazon declined to respond to the Carbon Disclosure Project's carbon questionnaires from at least 2010 until 2021, when they responded for the first time, leading the company to be awarded the default grade of F by this carbon accounting organization for many years.

Amazon, then, was long known to be slow, relative to its big tech competitors, in prioritizing sustainability, and consistently less transparent with independent accounting organizations about its energy footprint and the evidence for its renewable energy claims. This is not to say that Amazon hasn't had sustainability programs. Amazon made a pledge in 2014 to eventually run all its data centers on 100 percent renewable energy (Finley, 2014), an ambitious goal given the rapid rate at which its cloud services business was growing. Nevertheless, the admittedly vague pledge (at the time) was a number of years after similar pledges from tech competitors Apple, Google, and Facebook (Finley, 2014). In service of this goal, Amazon started building its own solar and wind farms in 2015 (Amazon, 2015), and putting solar arrays on the roofs of its fulfillment centers in 2017 (Clark, 2017).

Of course, tech companies' environmental impacts don't always end with data centers, although their energy and cooling needs are substantial and too often fall outside of public consciousness. Amazon in particular must consider the environmental impacts of its e-commerce operations and electronic devices. Top of mind for its customers, of course, are the ubiquitous Amazon packages that adorn their doorsteps. In 2008 Amazon started the Frustration-Free Packaging program. With its name and promotional framing, the program emphasizes making it "frustration-free" for end-consumers to open their packages, but another goal of the program is to make packaging 100 percent recyclable and to reduce excess packaging in goods designed to be sold online (Amazon, 2021e). Amazon boasts that the program so far has eliminated one million tons of packaging material, features special eco-designs for products like Tide laundry detergent, and describes the company's development of all-paper mailers, among other initiatives. While packaging is one focus, Amazon has also made promises about the carbon impacts of product shipping, announcing in 2019 its Shipment Zero plan, a program with an arguably misleading name that aims to make 50 percent of its shipments "net zero carbon" by 2030 (Clark, 2021).

As Amazon's delivery vehicles—the semis with the Amazon smile on the highways as well as the dark blue delivery vehicles in people's neighborhoods—become increasingly visible, Amazon has turned its attention to reducing its carbon impacts by not just seeking out electric vehicles, but investing in a company that will manufacture them. Amazon has been the lead investor in Rivian, an American electric vehicle manufacturer seeking to compete with Tesla. Amazon's investment capital has been accompanied by an advance order of one hundred thousand electric delivery vans that Rivian has designed specifically for the needs of Amazon drivers (Amazon, 2021a). Already being beta-tested in some markets, including Los Angeles, Amazon is ramping up expectations about a broad rollout of electric vehicles, which will be mobile ads for Amazon's commitment to reducing the carbon outputs of its fulfillment and delivery operations. Here we see how the sheer scale of Amazon—its deep pockets for investment, the extent of its logistics operation—put it in the position to make an environmental difference with both its own business practices, and with the way these visibly set a new standard which competitors, in this case delivery companies like FedEx and UPS, will feel pressured to meet.

Despite not having been a leader at least among big tech in sustainability, and being relatively secretive with independent carbon accounting organizations, Amazon has not been shy about presenting itself as a good green corporate citizen. In addition to the specific sustainability initiatives it has pursued, and publicized, for a number of years, Amazon has symbolically styled itself as an environmental leader. The Seattle Spheres—two glass domes that are part of Amazon's headquarters in Seattle—feature hydroponic plants throughout its interior. Although mostly reserved for employees to meet and work, the Spheres are an attraction and public-facing "green" initiative that visitors can learn more about in a gallery below or on a prescheduled tour (Amazon, 2018). Part innovative workspace, part symbolic gesture aimed at its Seattle neighbors and the broader public, the Spheres celebrate biodiversity with the inclusion of forty thousand plants from thirty different countries, focusing especially on plants from cloud forest ecosystems (Amazon, 2021a). Perhaps a coincidence, but "cloud" and "ecosystem" are two of the most prevalent metaphors from the natural world that Amazon uses to describe its business, with the cloud referring to its data storage, databases, software, and analytics provided via offsite networked servers, and ecosystem describing the array of connected products and services that Amazon provides (West, 2022). The Spheres' plants bring Amazon's favored natural metaphors for its technologies to life—an argument in architectural form. A similarly spectacular eco-building is planned for HQ2 in Arlington, Virginia. Called The Helix, the building spirals upwards and "interweaves manicured gardens and native plants and trees," inspired by "the natural world, where the double helix geometry can be found in many forms, including plants, seashells, DNA strands, and even our galaxy," according to its lead architect (Fedderly, 2021).

Amazon has also called publicly for greater government regulation of the energy industry. In 2016, Amazon joined Apple, Google, and Microsoft in a joint *amicus curie* brief supporting President Obama's US Clean Power Plan, advocating for more stringent emissions standards for American power plants. Amazon has engaged in similar advocacy efforts at the state level and in the European Union (Amazon, 2021a). Amazon is vocal about governments reducing the energy industry's emissions and dependence on fossil fuels in part because it is competing for renewables so that it can continue its tremendous rate of growth while still setting and achieving ambitious goals for greening its business. Whether direct access to renewable forms of energy or access to quality carbon offsets, there's not currently enough to support the energy needs of the rapidly growing and energy-intensive tech sector, let alone the rest of the economy.

"All In": The Climate Pledge

After being widely considered a climate laggard, especially relative to its big tech brethren, and focusing mainly on projects like Frustration-Free Packaging which are noticeable to the end-consumer's day-to-day interactions with the brand, in 2019 Amazon suddenly embraced leadership in corporate climate responsibility. It went "All In," as the title of its 2019 Sustainability Report, released to coincide with The Climate Pledge, announced. Amazon joined forces with a nonprofit organization called Global Optimism to create The Climate Pledge, a set of promises on the part of corporations, the highlight of which is to run their businesses on net-zero carbon by 2040, ten years earlier than the goal of the Paris Agreement, the international treaty on climate change brokered by the United Nations in 2015. Since Amazon's own credentials in the climate action space were not necessarily top notch, the collaboration with Global Optimism was key; the organization was cofounded by Christiana Figueres, former Executive Secretary of the UN Framework Convention on Climate Change, and a key leader of the Paris Agreement. The Climate Pledge commits its signatories to (1) "measure and report greenhouse gas emissions [verified by a third-party auditor] on a regular basis"; (2) "implement decarbonization strategies . . . including efficiency improvements, renewable energy, materials reductions, and other carbon emission elimination strategies"; and (3) use credible renewable energy certificates to offset any nonrenewable energies that cannot be eliminated or replaced (Amazon, 2021a).

Amazon announced The Climate Pledge in September 2019, and less than two years later said that it was on track to have its own operations powered by renewables by 2025, and to achieve net-zero carbon across the whole business by 2040. The latter goal takes into account the broader supply chains in which Amazon is embedded, including manufacture of its devices and packaging, customer transportation to its physical stores, manufacture of its capital goods such as equipment and buildings, and emissions from across the delivery and fulfillment processes (Amazon, 2021f). Shipment Zero, originally announced before The Climate Pledge, is part of decarbonizing its activities, as is greater efficiency in its buildings, led symbolically by Climate Pledge Arena, which aims to be the first net-zero carbon certified events arena in the world (Amazon, 2020). Amazon had already been installing solar panels and built a wind farm, but creation of its own sources of renewable energy as well as purchasing it have accelerated since the announcement of The Climate Pledge. Amazon had a total of 232 wind and solar projects with a capacity of twenty-seven million megawatt hours annually by 2021 (Amazon, 2021a). And Amazon reports that, "in 2020, we became the world's largest corporate purchaser of renewable energy, reaching 65%

renewable energy across our business" (Amazon, 2021a, p. 26). Complementary activities include its "Right Now Climate Fund" that invests in "reforestation projects and climate mitigation solutions" around the world (Amazon, 2021a, p. 21–22), and its much bigger Climate Pledge Fund, a two billion dollar fund that invests in "climate tech"—the development of technologies and data-driven approaches to reduce the impact of human activity on greenhouse gases and climate change (Dillon, 2021; The Collider, 2019). These investments include the aforementioned electric vehicle company Rivian, as well as companies developing cleaner fuels and low-carbon construction materials, among other projects.

All of a sudden in 2019, Amazon hit the accelerator with its efforts to decarbonize its business. In its sustainability reports, Amazon does caution that it will take time for these efforts to pay off, in part because the company is growing at a breakneck pace. This is certainly true of AWS, the leading provider of cloud computing which is increasingly a central infrastructure for the broader internet, but also for the e-commerce and streaming sides of Amazon, both of which exploded in terms of demand during 2020 especially during the COVID-19 lockdowns. Amazon's revenue grew 38 percent from 2019 to 2020, and its net profit was up 84 percent (Kohan, 2021). In order to manage expectations about the immediate impacts of its new climate initiatives, Amazon distinguishes between "carbon intensity" and "carbon reduction," as demonstrated in Figure 12.1, which shows how carbon intensity—or grams of carbon dioxide equivalent per dollar of gross merchandise sales—has declined since 2018 even while total carbon emissions have actually grown considerably (Amazon, 2021a, p. 15).

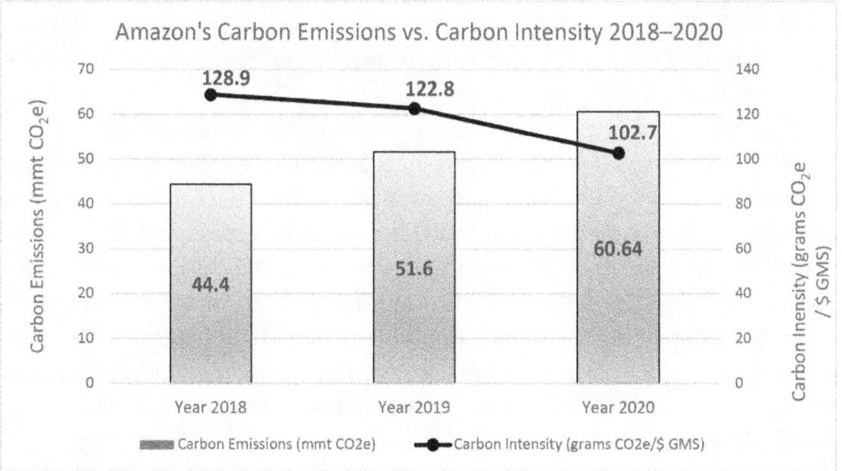

Figure 12.1. Amazon's Carbon Emissions vs. Carbon Intensity 2018-2020. Data sourced from Amazon, 2021a, p.15.
Emily West

Why did Amazon amp up its focus on climate so dramatically? Did they suddenly believe in the climate science that was decades in the making, or feel newly alarmed at the rate of climate change? Were they responding to a groundswell of demand among their customers for more progress on climate issues? There's little evidence for these reasons, and strong circumstantial evidence that rising employee and shareholder unhappiness, and pressure from these constituencies starting to spill into public view, were contributors to the shift to climate. In 2018 the organization Amazon Employees for Climate Justice was formed by Amazon workers who wanted to see Amazon do more, much more, with their considerable market power about the climate crisis. The organization, composed of high-skilled salaried workers who hold stock in the company, filed a shareholders' resolution with the Board demanding a company-wide climate plan (Conger, 2018). Not long afterwards, Amazon announced the Shipment Zero program. Finding the promise to reduce carbon impacts of just shipping too modest, the employees continued their pressure campaign and reported very little response from company leadership, and even retaliation against some of the leading activists. Yet on the eve of a planned employee walkout to protest Amazon's lack of action, the company announced the formation of The Climate Pledge (Scheimer and Chakrabarti, 2021). Although Amazon denies that it was influenced by this internal organizing, it's fair to speculate that it was one thing for the Carbon Disclosure Project and Greenpeace to make noise about Amazon's environmental record, and another for there to be large walkouts from its white-collar workers and public letters circulating at shareholders' meetings. Amazon, for many years one of the most valuable, trusted, and even loved brands in the United States, needed to become proactive about climate criticism, and what better way than to not just respond to the carbon accounting of others, but start their own bigger, better, more influential climate initiative.

Amazon hasn't just made strides toward carbon transparency and efficiency (and eventually, they have pledged, reduction), but has positioned itself as a market leader that sets the standards for other large corporations to follow. While Amazon cofounded The Climate Pledge and was its first signatory, there have now been more than two hundred companies who have joined the Pledge, and Amazon can, and does, claim some credit for all of them as its cofounder. As large corporations like IBM, Unilever, PepsiCo, and Microsoft join, as highlighted in Amazon press releases and ensuing news coverage, the achievement is symbolically connected to Amazon's brand (Amazon, 2021b).

While there are public relations reasons to be more proactive than reactive in relation to corporate carbon accountability, there is also a compelling strategic reason, which is to preempt government regulation. The tagline of The Climate Pledge—"Paris . . . 10 Years Early"—makes the argument that if you want fast and meaningful change on climate, you should look not to your elected representatives or intergovernmental organizations, but to corporations. With The Climate Pledge Amazon aimed to flip the script from climate laggard to leader, displaying more ambition and competence (it argues) than the governments in the countries in which it does business. It's a bold play for the reputational capital and trust that would be needed for voters to cede environmental goal-setting and accountability to corporations and the auditing organizations that they themselves identify to monitor them.

Given the unpredictability in federal environmental governance in the United States, featuring wide swings in environmental and energy policy positions among administrations with very different positions on climate, it is understandable that citizens and even some climate change activists might see corporate America has a surer bet for achieving results and consistent focus on carbon reduction and mitigation than lawmakers. Indeed, in its Clicking Clean report, Greenpeace highlighted the leadership role that the tech industry plays for the rest of the business community, arguing in 2016 that "major internet companies' leadership [particularly Apple and Google at that time] has been a catalyst in driving a broader set of corporations to adopt 100% renewable goals, contributing to a dramatic increase in renewable deals in the U.S. signed directly by corporations" (Cook et al., 2017, p. 7). Similarly Tom Rivett-Carnac, the other cofounder of Global Optimism, and a longtime climate activist who, like Figueres, formerly worked at the United Nations on climate issues as well as at the Carbon Disclosure Project, also looks to corporations to move the needle on climate change because of his self-described pragmatism. As he told Meghna Chakrabarti on National Public Radio's *On Point*, "the modern corporation is the most powerful actor in the world, along with investors. They can drive demand . . . and they can absolutely influence policy as well" (Scheimer and Chakrabarti, 2021).

Policy observers are commonly concerned about the issue of regulatory capture, where regulators are unduly influenced by large market players through some combination of lobbying, campaign contributions, and a revolving door of personnel between regulatory agencies and the industries they oversee. What we see here instead is regulatory preemption. The perceived need for government oversight of industry will be greatly reduced if tech companies like Amazon appear to successfully regulate themselves, and especially if they can demonstrate even greater boldness than elected officials and the regulatory agencies they oversee.

But Amazon is not just a large, famous company—it is a platform. And as a platform business it achieves de facto market regulation not just through its size, or by visibly setting standards that competitors then feel pressured to meet, but by actually being a marketplace, a "critical intermediary" for business (Khan, 2017, p. 803). Environmental governance is a relatively new development in a longer history of platform governance, more commonly associated with content moderation, product safety, and user privacy. Amazon is now using its position as a dominant platform business to enhance its profile as a corporate regulator of green accountability, at least in e-commerce. As part of its launch of The Climate Pledge agreement for corporations, Amazon created a Climate Pledge Friendly designation for products sold on its site. The Climate Pledge Friendly designation "recognizes products with improvements in at least one aspect of sustainability" (Amazon, 2021c). In practice, this means that products must be certified by one of thirty organizations, ranging in focus from animal welfare to product safety to organic ingredients to reduced carbon footprint. Or products can qualify for Amazon's own Compact by Design Certification, which calculates which products within a given category have the best "unit efficiency," meaning they can be shipped with the least amount of volume and weight, and therefore with a less carbon-intensive shipping footprint than competing products (Amazon, 2021d). Amazon has, then, assigned itself the role of clearinghouse for the proliferating labels and designations for product safety and green credentials that critics of greenwashing have argued confuse consumers and can lead to deception or misleading claims (Dahl, 2010). While US federal agencies have their own particular product certifications, such as US EPA Safer Choice and Energy Star, Amazon seeks to enhance its climate credibility with consumers by creating its own seemingly authoritative Climate Pledge Friendly umbrella certification, thereby becoming a gatekeeper for product sellers on its e-commerce site, which controls more than half of US online retail (Pymnts, 2021).

What are the benefits and risks of Amazon, one of the most powerful and well-resourced corporations in the world, assuming the mantle of corporate climate leadership and hastening the path to net-zero carbon? Certainly, once Amazon turned its mind to making real change in its carbon emissions, it had tremendously deep pockets, energy, and human resources to devote to it. Despite having slow-walked climate responsiveness for most of its corporate history, in 2019 it leaped ahead, perhaps not as far as its internal and external critics would have liked, but decisively in the right direction.

Amazon is famous for making new initiatives, such as the Kindle and the Alexa artificial intelligence voice assistant, happen very quickly and effectively, and finally that type of urgency and know-how appears to be targeted toward the climate crisis. While the tech sector is well known for moving fast and breaking things, as Facebook founder Mark Zuckerberg famously coined it, if pointed in the right direction, perhaps it can "move fast and fix things."

But the Regulation.com approach to the governance of carbon reduction also has its drawbacks. While Amazon is an enormous company with large distribution footprints and long reach throughout its supply chains, its regulatory influence will never extend across the entire economy as government regulation would. Amazon's approach to climate change is riven through with "technological solutionism" (Morozov, 2013). Through its Climate Pledge Fund investments, it hopes not just to fund the climate tech breakthroughs of the future, but profit from them when more countries and industries need these technologies to achieve their carbon reduction goals, due to the Paris agreement or some other pressure point. Finally, Amazon's approach to greening its business is inherently limited by its need to protect business growth and consumer satisfaction. Both have been key to Amazon's success since the earliest days—Amazon has always sought to become bigger and "delight" more people with ever more products and services. Amazon's number one leadership principle has always been "customer obsession," and as suggested by its soft-pedaled, often hard-to-find engagements with customers on issues of carbon reduction so far (even information about Climate Pledge Friendly designations is hard to find on the website), it's unlikely to start disrupting the ease and convenience of the user. It leaves the question of how effective even ambitious corporate self-regulation on the environment can be if it won't touch the third rails of constant growth and customer ease.

As Amazon touts its ambitious goals and eventually, one hopes, progress in carbon reduction, the question also arises whether urgency from citizens to demand more stringent and far-reaching environmental government regulation will be diminished. As Cronin argues, corporations seek to fill the void left by government and offer trust in their brands in lieu of the trust that people have lost in their political leaders. If The Climate Pledge puts more pressure on the business community and on government to keep up and apply the standards set by Amazon more broadly, then its positive impact will exceed the program itself. However, if the prominence of The Pledge eases environmental scrutiny and pressure on other actors, because the goals it sets and perhaps achieves are comforting to consumers and citizens, then even while the program itself is successful, the net impact may well not be.

Conclusion

Before The Climate Pledge, Amazon was already in a powerful position of platform governance. By setting standards and *being* the market for many products and services, it had already become infrastructural in a variety of respects, be it in the realms of product search and information, cloud computing, or online retail logistics. With The Climate Pledge, Amazon has indicated a desire to keep up with its big tech counterparts like Apple and Google, and even aims to outdo them in its net-zero carbon ambitions, all the more challenging given how much of its business involves moving physical stuff across space. But as a company that sets the conditions for so many businesses that use its various platforms (e.g., the Amazon retail website, AWS, Alexa), as well as those that contribute to its operations, it is in a powerful position to dictate terms for what carbon reduction and accounting will look like. Just as its standards for shipping speeds and packaging specifications have driven industry-wide standards, so will its climate benchmarks.

At this particular juncture, Amazon's self-regulation is more stringent than what governments are requiring of it, and political attempts to rein in fossil fuel emissions are, in the United States at least, in disarray. But should citizens hand over trust and leadership on climate action to a corporation beholden only to its shareholders and the stock market? Should we welcome The Climate Pledge because of its commitment to speed, so important given the clear urgency for action on reducing the emissions that warm the planet, communicated with increasing frequency by climate scientists? Or should we remain mindful of the risks inherent in preemptive self-regulation? The fact that Amazon is in a position to be so influential in its climate policies creates a circular argument that justifies and normalizes the company's size and monopolistic nature of its platform businesses.

References

Amazon. (2015, June 10). Amazon Web Services Announces New Renewable Energy Project in Virginia. *Amazon Press Archive*. https://press.aboutamazon.com/news-releases/news-release-details/amazon-web-services-announces-new-renewable-energy-project.

———. (2018, January 29). The Spheres Blossom at Amazon's Urban HQ in Seattle. *Amazon Press Center*. https://press.aboutamazon.com/news-releases/news-release-details/spheres-blossom-amazons-urban-hq-seattle.

———. (2020, June 25). Amazon Secures Naming Rights for Future Home of Seattle's New NHL Franchise, and Calls It Climate Pledge Arena. *Amazon Press*

Center. https://press.aboutamazon.com/news-releases/news-release-details/amazon-secures-naming-rights-future-home-seattles-new-nhl.

———. (2021a, June). Amazon 2020 Sustainability Report: Further and Faster, Together. *Amazon Sustainability*. https://sustainability.aboutamazon.com/about/report-builder.

———. (2021b, June 23). Amazon Becomes Largest Corporate Buyer of Renewable Energy in the U.S. *Amazon Press Center*. https://press.aboutamazon.com/news-releases/news-release-details/amazon-becomes-largest-corporate-buyer-renewable-energy-us.

———. (2021c). Amazon: Climate Pledge Friendly. https://www.amazon.com/b?ie=UTF8&node=21221607011.

———. (2021d). Amazon: Compact by Design. https://www.amazon.com/b?node=21221609011.

———. (2021e). Improving Our Packing. https://sustainability.aboutamazon.com/environment/circular-economy/packaging.

———. (2021f). Reaching Net-Zero Carbon by 2040: Measuring, Mapping, and Reducing Carbon the Amazonian Way. *Amazon Sustainability*. https://sustainability.aboutamazon.com/carbon-methodology.pdf.

Aronczyk, Melissa, and Espinoza, Maria I. (2021). Big Data for Climate Action or Climate Action for Big Data? *Big Data & Society* 8, no. 1: 1–15.

———. (2022). *A Strategic Nature: Public Relations and the Politics of American Environmentalism*. New York, NY: Oxford University Press.

Carbon Disclosure Project. (2021). https://www.cdp.net/en.

Clark, Dave. (2017, March 2). Solar power delivers a win-win-win. *Amazon*. https://www.aboutamazon.com/news/sustainability/solar-power-delivers-a-win-win-win.

———. (2021, February 18). Delivering Shipment Zero, a Vision for Net Zero Carbon Shipments. https://www.aboutamazon.com/news/sustainability/delivering-shipment-zero-a-vision-for-net-zero-carbon-shipments.

The Collider. (2019, March 1). What the Heck is Climate Tech? *The Collider*. https://thecollider.org/what-the-heck-is-climate-tech/.

Conca, James. (2021, May 24). Big Tech Companies Look to Clean Energy to Slake Their Enormous Thirst. *Forbes*. https://www.forbes.com/sites/jamesconca/2021/05/24/big-tech-companies-look-to-clean-energy-to-slake-their-enormous-thirst/?sh=699215575615&utm_source=pocket_mylist.

Conger, Kate. (2018, December 16). Tech Workers Got Paid in Company Stock. They Used It to Agitate for Change. *The New York Times*. https://www.nytimes.com/2018/12/16/technology/tech-workers-company-stock-shareholder-activism.html.

Cook, Gary, Lee, Jude, Tsai, Tamina, Kong, Ada, Deans, John, Johnson, Brian, and Jardim, Elizabeth J. (2017). Clicking Clean: Who Is Winning the Race to Build a Green Internet?" *Greenpeace Inc., Washington, DC* 5: 1–102.

Cronin, Anne M. (2018). *Public Relations Capitalism: Promotional Culture, Publics and Commercial Democracy*. Cham, Switzerland: Palgrave Macmillan.

Cunliff, Colin. (2020, July 6). Beyond the Energy Techlash: The Real Climate Impacts of Information Technology. *Information Technology & Innovation Foundation*. https://itif.org/publications/2020/07/06/beyond-energy-techlash-real-climate-impacts-information-technology?utm_source=pocket_mylist.

Dahl, Richard. (2010). Greenwashing: Do You Know What You're Buying? *Environmental Health Perspectives* 118, no. 6: A246–52.

Dean, Mitchell. (2010). *Governmentality: Power and Rule in Modern Society*. Second edition. Los Angeles, CA: Sage Publications.

Dillon, Ted. (2021, January 20). Climate Tech Vs. Cleantech: What's the Difference? *Clean Energy Ventures*. https://cleanenergyventures.com/clean-energy-venture-capital/climatetech-is-cleantech-in-need-of-a-rebrand/.

Fedderly, Eva. (2021, February 3). Amazon Unveils Nature-Infused HQ2 Design that Includes "The Helix." *Architectural Digest*. https://www.architecturaldigest.com/story/amazon-unveils-nature-infused-hq2-design-includes-helix.

Finley, Klint. (2014, November 19). Amazon Vows to Run on 100 Percent Renewable Energy. *Wired*. https://www.wired.com/2014/11/amazon-vows-run-100-renewable-energy/.

Gamito, Marta Cantero. (2017). Regulation.com: Self-Regulation and Contract Governance in the Platform Economy: A Research Agenda. *European Journal of Legal Studies* 9, no. 2: 53–68.

Khan, Lina M. (2017). Amazon's Antitrust Paradox. *Yale Law Journal* 126: 710–805.

Kohan, Shelley E. (2021, February 2). Amazon's Net Profit Soars 84% with Sales Hitting $386 Billion. *Forbes*. https://www.forbes.com/sites/shelleykohan/2021/02/02/amazons-net-profit-soars-84-with-sales-hitting-386-billion/?sh=ce5ecf813349.

Levy, David L., and Newell, Peter J. (2005). Introduction: The Business of Global Environmental Governance. In *The Business of Global Environmental Governance*, edited by David L. Levy and Peter J. Newell, 1–17. Cambridge, MA: The MIT Press.

Mitchell, Stacy. (2018, February 15). Amazon Doesn't Just Want to Dominate the Market—It Wants to Become the Market." *The Nation*. https://www.thenation.com/article/archive/amazon-doesnt-just-want-to-dominate-the-market-it-wants-to-become-the-market/.

Morozov, Evgeny. (2013). *To Save Everything, Click Here: The Folly of Technological Solutionism*. New York, NY: Public Affairs.

Naik, Gautam. (2021, May 25). Problematic Corporate Purchases of Clean Energy Credits Threaten Net Zero Goals. *S&P Global*. https://www.spglobal.com/esg/insights/problematic-corporate-purchases-of-clean-energy-credits-threaten-net-zero-goals?utm_source=pocket_mylist.

Open Markets Institute. (2018, May 30). Public Comments of the Open Markets Institute Submitted to the Antitrust Division Roundtable Examining "Consumers Costs of Anticompetitive Regulation." https://www.openmarketsinstitute.org/publications/public-comments-open-markets-institute-submitted-antitrust-division-roundtable-examining-consumer-costs-anticompetitive-regulations.

Pasek, Anne. (2019). Managing Carbon and Data Flows: Fungible Forms of Mediation in the Cloud. *Culture Machine* 16: 1–15.

Pymnts. (2021, March 11). Amazon and Wal-mart Are Nearly Tied in Full-Year Share of Retail Sales. *Pymnts.com*. https://www.pymnts.com/news/retail/2021/amazon-walmart-nearly-tied-in-full-year-share-of-retail-sales/.

Scheimer, Dorey, and Chakrabarti, Meghna. (2021, July 9). The Prime Effect: The Environmental Footprint Behind the World's Largest Online Retailer. *On Point* [Radio/Podcast]. https://www.wbur.org/onpoint/2021/07/09/the-prime-effect-amazons-environmental-impact.

Star, Susan Leigh, and Bowker, Geoffrey C. (2006). How to Infrastructure. In *Handbook of New Media: Social Shaping and Social Consequences of ICTs*, edited by Leah A. Lievrouw and Sonia Livingstone, 230–45. Thousand Oaks, CA: Sage.

West, Emily. (2022). *Buy Now: How Amazon Branded Convenience and Normalized Monopoly*. Cambridge, MA: The MIT Press.

CHAPTER THIRTEEN

~

Confronting the Regionalism of Amazon Web Services

Patrick Brodie and Paul O'Neill

From its origins as an online bookstore to becoming a global logistics giant, Amazon has expanded its reach into increasingly disparate regions of the world, integrating and entrenching itself within the global economy, whilst determining and influencing people's habits and modes of consumption. As a pioneer of the "just-in-time" models of networked logistics and management (see Stone, 2013), the company's business models are adept at optimizing value fulfilment through their vast fleet of warehouse workers, delivery drivers, and, more recently, technological supply chains. Calling to mind early geographies of globalization and the conquest of "space by time" via what geographer David Harvey called "time-space compression" (see Harvey, 1989), Amazon's ability to secure near instantaneous delivery of goods and information across its territories has required astute geographical manoeuvring that erodes spatial and political barriers to continuous flow.

Aside from general e-commerce services and consumer-oriented goods, Amazon generates significant revenue streams from its subsidiary Amazon Web Services (AWS), a company that provides 'cloud' computing services and online storage space to individual customers and businesses such as AirBnB, Netflix, and Twitch. Furthermore, AWS works extensively with the US government, providing services to federal agencies intelligence services. In 2021, AWS accounted for approximately 13 percent of Amazon's total revenue (Novet, 2021). The company has been embroiled in a legal battle with Microsoft over a cloud computing contract with the US Department of Defense; however, following extensive litigation, the DoD has terminated the contract. Amazon founder Jeff Bezos has also provoked the ire of political leaders such as US President Donald Trump and Saudi Arabian Crown Prince Mohammed bin Salman, largely through the tech mogul's ownership of *The Washington Post* and its criticism of their regimes. AWS specifically has been embroiled in industrial disputes with the People's Republic of China, where the company hosts two infrastructure regions (in Ningxia and Beijing, as well as another in Hong Kong) but also faces serious and scrutinous regulation as a US multi-national due to ongoing geopolitical tensions between the two powers. As a corporate actor on the world stage, Amazon—and AWS especially—seems to be gaining and exerting significant geopolitical influence.

This chapter will interrogate the territorial politics of AWS through what we call the "regionalism" of its global infrastructures. The global infrastructural apparatus of AWS is demarcated across regions and availability zones. AWS regions are located either in or within close proximity to major urban centres including Beijing, Hong Kong, Ningxia, Osaka, Seoul, Singapore, Sydney, Tokyo—and those are just its "Asia-Pacific" (another, larger regional designation) operations (AWS, n.d.-b). There are currently twenty-five AWS regions globally, each assigned a unique coded reference specific to their geographical location, such as eu-west-1 (Dublin), us-east-1 (Northern Virginia), me-south-1 (Middle East - Bahrain), ap-northeast-1 (Asia Pacific - Tokyo), ca-central (Canada - Montréal), and so on. As of early 2022, there were plans for seven more, including one in Israel. Each AWS region operates in isolation from the others, ensuring stability and robust fault tolerance. Within each region are "availability zones," clusters of individual data centres located in proximity to each other. AWS Edge locations are also data centres but are primarily used for the caching of data offering lower latency in contrast to the hyperscale availability zone centres which are utilised for resource-intensive operations including server hosting, data processing, and data analytics. Other related services offered within the AWS infrastructure see the company encroach even further within localised spaces—their 'outposts' place AWS servers onsite at various commercial enterprises, allowing secure and direct access back to a larger-scale availability zone. Across all these locations, AWS servers host government assets and business and consumer data, and act as computing hubs for a number of industries.

While Amazon publicises its global infrastructures of regions and availability zones at a broad geographical level, the exact locations of their data centres remain intentionally hidden. The placement of the clusters is in many ways determined by state incentives and data privacy/sovereignty rules in different territories, such as tax breaks or low levels of data regulation.

Even identifying the exact locations of AWS data centres can be problematic, often requiring a diverse range of open-source intelligence techniques (see Burrington, 2016). These conceptions of territories and regions rewrite geographies of data use and storage in the image of AWS—determining where certain services are needed, what regulations require compliance and which need to be avoided entirely. They also use enormous amounts of infrastructural resources—from energy and water to run and cool the servers, to fibre optic connections, to new road and transport links to support them. Furthermore, Amazon and AWS specifically are not only availing of state and local infrastructural resources, they are also becoming crucial in providing them—from the privatization of delivery services (Amazon may be the United States' largest private employer soon [Villegas and Beachy, 2021]) to storage for government documents and data.

But logistics and digital media companies like Amazon do not simply obliterate space and existing regimes of governance in the process of becoming a crucial infrastructure for global circulation; rather, they employ savvy spatial and territorial mechanisms to increase their influence and grow and secure profits. One way in which they do so is through what we call "regionalism," following key geographical discourses about the governing and management of particular clusters of people, places, and resources based on dynamics which include infrastructure, politics, culture, environments, atmospheres, and geology. John Tomaney defines "regionalism" within the context of human geography as "the identification and mobilization of divisions formed in relation to subnational, socioeconomic, cultural, or political territories. . . . If regions are social constructions, regionalism is how they are fabricated by administrators, intellectuals, and politicians" (2017). While people can self-identify regionally, and there are definite cultural claims toward regional difference and identity, regionalism "tends to imply a territorial understanding of the production of space" and "the persistence of regionalism as a cultural and political form reaffirms the importance of the making (and unmaking) of territorial boundaries" (2017). Thus Amazon's mobilization of regionalism, intentionally or not, speaks to a longer history of regional construction via state (or state-like) formations which mobilize territory for particular socio-economic, political, or cultural purposes, carrying or enacting particular forms of sovereignty, whether for governance or capital accumulation.

In this chapter, we make a wider argument about the politics of "regionalism" as determined and administered by tech companies. The territorial strategies of AWS operate with the full partnership of states and often without the explicit consent of local populations whose data is being used/

serviced or whose public resources and tax money are being funnelled into data centre locations. To illustrate this point, we will look specifically at two AWS "infrastructure regions," eu-west-1 (suburban Dublin) and ca-central (Québec, Canada), which are illustrative of AWS strategies more broadly. It is unlikely that Amazon expects users in its regions to identify according to how the company does. However, what is important is how Amazon mobilizes regional constructions of territory to further its corporate strategies—for example, in "eu-west," "ca-central," or the "Secret Region" of its state contracts with the United States. The territorialization of data geographies within AWS infrastructure presents problems for researchers focusing on Amazon's global operations. There is certainly a strategic and adaptive template by which AWS plans, builds, and operates their data infrastructures in certain places, by which the company must dissolve certain existing orders upon placing data infrastructure—and its assemblage of energy, cable, and water systems—in a certain place. However, unexpected and place-specific frictions necessarily arise and must be dealt with as the infrastructure is developed and built. While, as Anna Tsing argues, "friction" is not only resistance but also "where the rubber hits the road" for the global operations of capital (2004), propelling it forwards to new spaces and avenues of accumulation, it may be useful to look at how Amazon is expanding its territory beyond obvious points of friction—like where they build their data centres—to include places beyond the urban "regions" they promote. To press against this "frictionless" idea of Amazon's global reach and expansion, we will conclude this chapter on a more speculative note by looking at how conceptions of "eco-regions" and other more environmentally attuned conceptions of space and ecology may disrupt Amazon's top-down territorial delineations.

Regionalism and Geopolitics

Scholars of territorial governance focus on the ways that territory is entangled with various forms of sovereignty, classification, and strategy concerning the governance and administration of land. Amazon, like Walmart and other companies who operate via the management policies of logistics (see Lecavalier, 2017), see space similarly to the way a state does: as new territory that must be repurposed and made profitable, as places conquered to forge new routes of accumulation. Scholars of logistics like Jesse Lecavalier (2017) and Deborah Cowen (2014) trace the histories of these forms of management to their military origins. Sam Walton of Walmart, a pioneer of logistical business management, was a military enthusiast and an amateur pilot who would often visualize new territories for Walmart stores in the US south and Midwest by flying a private plane over them. Amazon similarly operates by forging new "frontiers" for their operations across the world, globalizing their operations by breaking into new markets and working across (and transforming) preexisting logistical infrastructure. In doing so, the company creates a map of the world that mirrors its own strategic interests. As Mattias Borg Rasmussen and Christian Lund argue in terms of what they call "colonial territorialization," new "frontiers" were crucial in "dissolv[ing] existing social orders—property systems, political jurisdictions, rights, and social contracts—whereas territorialization is shorthand for all the dynamics that establish them and re-order space anew" (2018, 388). States manage territories by classifying and drawing boundaries which strategically divide up resources by "governing access, policing boundaries, and defining space" (Rasmussen and Lund, 2018, 388). Examples of such state-led management can be found in the cultivation of territories for strategic development zones such as those found in Ireland or as nature reserves/special areas of conservation (e.g., certain forests and boglands). Amazon may not quite have the power of a state to govern in this way, but its modes of defining and managing territory "regionally" impose boundaries upon the digital systems that make up their cloud infrastructure. These forms of territorialization determine what we can access, where it is stored, who governs and regulates it, and what businesses and governments pay to use it.

The sheer scale and economic power of companies such as Amazon raises interesting questions surrounding how they can be regulated at the state level. An obvious example of this is Ireland, which aside from being an AWS region is also the Europe, Middle East, and Africa headquarters of many of the US multinationals that have come to define the concept of "Big Tech," including Apple, Facebook, and Google. This means that the regulation of these companies falls under the jurisdiction of the Irish Data Protection Commissioner. In 2021, the budget of the IDPC was twenty-one million euros, a rather small amount that underlines the "David against Goliath" battle faced by nation states in regulating these companies (see O'Neill, 2021). Recent proposals to give companies like Amazon a seat at the United Nations due to their ever-growing infrastructural power point to the changing landscape of the geopolitics of communication technology (Schott, 2021).

Hardt and Negri (2000) asserted years ago that nation-state sovereignty has been largely supplanted by the global sovereignty of deterritorialized capital, compelling state and state-like formations to fall into line to ensure competitiveness. The circulations of capital appear to exist everywhere and yet nowhere—Amazon is enormously influential in the everyday lives of many people around the world and accumulates capital and influence at an alarming rate, but it is hard to pinpoint why and where their material operations have the most power and leverage. Years ago, before it was clear to many in the critical humanities and social sciences how integrated into our everyday lives AWS is, a colleague of one of this study's authors who worked in the tech industry joked to them that it would be easier to just give in—Amazon had already won and were dictating global systems of data and digital infrastructure even more than it appeared on the surface. According to this view, AWS was already *everywhere*, and national and other borders scarcely mattered. The deterritorialized world of capital was already here; Hardt and Negri's worst fears were realized through the expansionary operations of AWS, and it was time to start living with it.

But this statement by the author's colleague was perhaps premature. Amazon's operations are actually *highly* spatialized by zoning, border mechanisms, and infrastructures of residual state power and multinational corporate sovereignty. As scholars like Sandro Mezzadra and Brett Neilson (2013), Keller Easterling (2014), and Aihwa Ong (2006) have shown, power relations on a global scale are reproduced through localized forms of spatial development, multiplied across sequestered zones, and given the appearance of a seamless neoliberal utopia. Keller Easterling calls this "extrastatecraft": "As a site of multiple, overlapping, or nested forms of sovereignty, where domestic and transnational jurisdictions collide, infrastructure space becomes a medium of what might be called extrastatecraft—a portmanteau describing the often-undisclosed activities outside of, in addition to, and sometimes even in partnership with statecraft" (2014, 15). The spaces of global capital are thus circulated by conflicting sovereignties. These form part of mechanized systems of rule that nonetheless rely on the biopower of geographically distributed, but highly policed labour pools, which are often strategically divided along class, ethnic, and gender lines to weaken claims to rights and citizenship (Ong, 2006). Amazon is adept at this, hiring mostly migrant and poor workforces in their warehouse logistics operations and actually encouraging short turnover by essentially wringing workers dry before throwing them away (Villegas and Beach, 2021). AWS is also increasingly embedded in the very governance of territories. Its contracts with state departments and agencies mean that an increasing amount of public information is now hosted on the private cloud servers of Amazon, stored in business and technology parks in different suburbs around the world. But how do they decide where to place these operations in the first place? What makes a "region" attractive for one of these manufactured "infrastructure regions"?

The answer may, unsurprisingly, lie in regionalism, and how Amazon and other tech companies leverage regional economic strategies for their own benefit. Rather than flattening out regional and national borders, "globalization can be seen as the process of the integration and differentiation of multiple, alternative, and competing capitalisms, each subject to specific local, regional, and historical contingencies" (Lee and LiPuma, 2002, 205). Following the decline of Bretton Woods in the 1970s, global markets became effectively naturalized by the growth of financial speculation and algorithmic trading. Now the dictates of markets drive local and regional economies, eroding the power of state and other formations to regulate powerful companies. Under these specific conditions of neoliberal capitalism, the formation, ideology, and policy of nation-states is often mobilized for continued intensification of the global system itself. As David Harvey notes, "the neoliberal state needs nationalism of a certain sort to survive. Forced to operate as a competitive agent in the world market and seeking to establish the best possible business climate, it mobilizes nationalism in its effort to succeed. Competition produces ephemeral winners and losers in the global struggle for position" (2005, 85).

Thus, in a globalized world, national policies of industrial growth are dictated by global financial trends, supranational intervention, and the availability and attraction of private finance on an open global market. Often, these dynamics result in regional formations *across* borders to generate particular advantages evident in Nordic cooperation models, trade agreements like the North American Free Trade Agreement, and even UK-wide strategic policies as opposed to policies pursued by individual devolved governments. As Ong argues, discussions of regionalism dominated many early debates about globalization, in that the regional construction of administrative units in places like Southeast Asia (e.g. "Greater China") and the European Union (2004, 69–70) seemed to form emerging state-like responses to the deterritorializing thrusts of financial globalization. Within these new regimes of trade and rule, regional partnerships and designations, along with particular forms of zoning, became increasingly important for administering rapid production and exchange, yet politics and culture proved to be more complex to rein in. Individual nation-states, as well as municipalities within individual nation-states, must similarly compete for investment even within these apparently harmonious, macroeconomic regional constructions. Drawing from Harvey's (2005) argument referenced earlier, the competitive drive that stimulates economic nationalism may also operate as a cultural nationalism animated by financial arrangements.

In Ireland, for example, companies have taken advantage of a European-low 12.5 percent corporation tax rate, a planning system which favors foreign direct investment over local objection, and lapses in environmental protections and a history of facilitating extractive industries. An official at an influential semistate company in Ireland told one of the authors that data centre companies effectively shop across different regions to receive different bids for locations, energy prices, and tax incentives, pitting offers from one state or locality against another. In Québec, one official for semistate energy company Hydro Québec told us the same thing, that they had put together an entire team for data centre proposals, complete with templates for energy usage, pricing, metrics, incentives, and the like, because it was becoming too much work to continually put together packages for companies that were only shopping, without necessarily buying. As high-profile cases in Athenry, Ireland (Brodie, 2020b), and Vaudreuil-Dorion, Québec (Brodie and Velkova, 2021) demonstrate, the policies and practices of speculation often leave behind ruins of global market volatility, in the form of vacant land and local resentment, or abandoned large-scale infrastructures which consumed significant tax benefits and local energy—only to be switched off at the first sign of market fluctuation.

As the Québec instance shows, competitive energy prices are becoming crucial for states in attracting data centres, although energy supply is a looming problem in places attempting to transition from fossil fuel to renewable-powered grids. Places like Québec and some jurisdictions in Europe are in much better shape in terms of renewable supply—Québec's grid, for example, is powered by nearly 100 percent renewables. This means that electricity drawn for data centres is difficult to criticize through a mainstream climate change lens, as long as the supply remains adequate to the demand. However, as we will discuss in the following, even these potential positives are necessarily embedded within the extractive geographic frameworks of growth shared by AWS and all global tech companies and extending *across* colonially defined boundaries to ensure function.

AWS seizes upon the regional competition strategies required by contemporary global capitalism, including competitive tax incentives, low electricity prices, infrastructural availability (including fibre), workforces, and other territorial factors, while in themselves remaking the map in their image—by creating their own sense of "infrastructure regions" divided across availability zones, edge nodes, and smaller infrastructural formations like "edge sites" and "wavelength zones."

Amazon Web Services Policy and Operations

Within the global infrastructure of AWS the continuities of imperial regionalism are palpable—Africa and South America have only one "region" apiece, centred in Cape Town, South Africa and São Paolo, Brazil, respectively. If AWS represents the industry standard of cloud technology and connectivity, the ongoing uneven development of digital industries is crystallized in the colonial geographical distribution and regional conception of AWS—"Africa" as a unitary continental formation, for example, despite its vast heterogeneity and significant proportion of the global population. The operations of AWS similarly follow existing routes and barriers between the former colonial metropoles and the colonized world, crystallizing existing and uneven formations of infrastructural power within its private data storage and distribution apparatus. The entire continent of Africa has only one infrastructure region, in Cape Town, South Africa, and two edge locations, also in South Africa. Invoices from the rest of the African continent are mostly rerouted through the European Union (AWS, n.d.-a). The dynamic by which capital from emerging data systems funnels back from the global south to the global north is often referred to as "data colonialism" (Couldry and Mejias, 2019; Thatcher et al., 2016). This term has been employed by scholars, especially geographers and critical data researchers, to map the asymmetries and expose the unevenness of the extractive systems that drive contemporary data economies. As Jim Thatcher et al. (2016) note, so-called big data is based on a model of perpetual growth: more and more data will lead to more and more profit, centralized through the operations of a few enormously powerful companies, mostly in the Global North. Incorporating "new" and "emerging" regions into this growth machine involves connecting and building infrastructure in places in order to incorporate them into the system that feeds the wealth of these companies.

This is not to unproblematically apply global geopolitics to Amazon or the operations of other Big Tech companies as though they have already inherited the earth and its global dynamics of imperial extraction, however state-like (and aligned with state formations) they have become. After all, Amazon is not singularly accepted everywhere it goes, and states continue to maneuver around the company with their own geopolitical interests and strategies. Take the case of a rumoured expansion into Buenos Aires, Argentina, which put the country in competition with Brazil, who hosted their lone South American infrastructure region (AWS ended up only opting for an edge location in Buenos Aires, instead expanding their availability zone in São Paolo; see Goodison, 2020); or the disputes between AWS and the People's Republic of China.

The operations of AWS also function differently *within* different territories. But this does not mean that the dynamics of imperial expansion do not apply; as Couldry and Mejias note, "data colonialism" entails not only the geographical *expansion* of digital systems of data collection, but also the intensification of activities in more localized places or in our social lives (2019). The infrastructural apparatus of AWS, as mentioned in the introduction, embodies a variety of different scales, much of which operates across different sites of social organization and the everyday logistics of Amazon's activities. It is the dynamic across these scales that drives the continual expansion of AWS—the more people are online, the more data they collect, the more profit can eventually be made from on- and offline activities. This leads, in turn, to requirements for more data centres, availability zones, edge sites, and "wavelength zones." Thus the regional expansion and distribution of AWS is not only about where it goes and why, but about what happens once the company has established itself in a new location, and the ways in which it asserts its dominance through business practices, consumer relations, environmental procedures, and other processes associated with operating large scale industrial infrastructures. In Ireland, AWS funds data centre training programs at universities like Technological University Dublin and enters into fifteen-year contracts with renewable energy providers like wind farms, dictating the flows of knowledge and energy into particular forms of Amazon-approved managerial and technical acumen into the foreseeable future. Relations between local culture, society, and politics change when a company is located somewhere for a long time, coming to affect the outcomes of governance in more complex ways than competition and coercion (see Brodie, 2021).

Despite how embedded Amazon is in people's lives on- and off-line, it is hard to track down its data centres without being privy to their corporate location strategies. For example, in Québec, the sites were never publicly revealed; much speculation occurred on online forums, including the idea that a former Ericsson data centre in Vaudreuil-Dorion (just off the island of Montréal) would be bought by the company for their new operations (see Brodie and Velkova, 2021). Some suspected the data centres would be as secure as the gambling servers that host the city's robust casino economy; others would not even dare speculate for fear of security repercussions (personal requests by the authors to any planners or company officials were stonewalled). The closest estimates are similarly regional. Montréal's "South Shore," for example, is rumoured to be one location amongst an estimated three data centres in the metropolitan area. ROOT, a Canadian colocation data centre provider, announced in 2017 (soon after the AWS announcement) that they had landed an "anchor tenant" employing a large proportion of their data centre capacity in their facilities in the Montréal suburbs. However, the anchor company could not be named because of the potential involvement of AWS or one of the other hyperscale tech companies (Miller, 2017). One reason for Amazon's expansion into Montréal as opposed to Toronto or Vancouver, beyond cheap energy prices, was most likely land, as the real estate market is much friendlier in Québec than the other provinces (Immen, 2021). Another possible reason is in relation to concerns over data sovereignty (Rastello, 2021). This is characteristic of the cloud services ecosystem—a supply chain of companies, sectors, and policy arrangements with blurred distinctions between one another, an "industry" that sustains itself via the diverse supply chains required to support it and which include data services, real estate, construction, and so on (see Brodie, 2020a, 2021; Hogan, 2021; Johnson, 2019). It would seem that much like their non-descript, quick-build sheds in Dublin, their Montréal facility is thus also under-the-radar and purely functional. This contrasts with the large-scale, spectacular infrastructures made more publicly by Facebook, Google, and Microsoft, who strategically visualize and mediate the "cloud" image as green (see Carruth, 2014) and as a beneficial and natural development within communities and landscapes. AWS drops this act, seemingly admitting to industrial scale and pure functionality in its placement and construction of new infrastructures.

Eco-/Bioregions and the Political Ecology of Amazon Web Services

The ecologies through which the "regionalism" of AWS operates are disrupted and are far more complex than the basic and self-serving geographical conceptualisation offered by AWS. As scholars in the environmental humanities have long emphasized, capitalism's destructive and transformative timescales affect violence on human and more-than-human levels (Nixon, 2011; Tsing, 2015), traversing boundaries and networks dictated by colonial histories of movement and exploitation. Whether through "data colonialism" or more outright forms of neocolonial extraction, whether critical mineral mining for computer components or fracking for natural gas reserves, the operations of AWS work within and affect a greater political ecology that extends far beyond its often-featureless suburban warehouses.

Much has been written about the climatic implications of data centres, especially in terms of their environmental impact and their effect on water (Hogan, 2015) and energy systems (Bresnihan and Brodie, 2021; Velkova, 2021). Like other server farms, AWS facilities require the maintenance of a controlled microclimate that efficiently cools overheated servers as well as dealing with waste heat and other atmospheric externalities. The company's facilities in the Dublin suburb of Tallaght, for example, will use their waste heat as part of a district heating scheme for the local area (Lally, 2019), a practice already institutionalized across much of northern Europe (Velkova, 2016). One of the primary reasons companies located their facilities in Ireland, according to their own corporate framing, is to avail of the country's normally cool climate (see Brodie, 2020a) and its water supply, since these features reduce the astronomical amount of energy required for cooling in warmer climates. However, that is only a fraction of the story: despite these "natural" advantages, Ireland's total energy use is growing steadily, primarily due to the demands of data centres, and by 2030 they are expected to be using 30 percent of the country's electricity supply on a daily basis. AWS will make up a significant portion of this due to the sheer scale of its multiple facilities in the country, each of which uses as much daily energy as a small Irish town.

In Ireland, Amazon's infrastructure necessarily spans different eco-regions, biomes, and "physiographic units" (biogeographical distinctions that are mapped via certain classifications of ecological characteristics). For example, Ireland's two eco-regions are "north Atlantic moist mixed forests" (unique to the country's western regions, shared with far northwest Scotland) and "Celtic broadleaf forests." While AWS data centers are as yet built only in a heavily urbanized corridor surrounding Dublin, the political ecology of the company extends across the island. Water supply to cool the data farms is provided by any number of water sources that feed into Dublin, whether from the nearby Wicklow Mountains or elsewhere in the surrounding area. Wind farms built on the unique biomes of peat blanket bogs, which make up much of the "north Atlantic moist mixed forests" eco-region in the west, provide energy exclusively to AWS data centres in Dublin. These wind farms make use of the blustery climate in the west of Ireland, and, like other wind farms, will need to become increasingly "datafied" in order to manage the intermittency of wind sources via meteorological forecasting, thus adding another link to the data supply chain (Bresnihan and Brodie, 2021). These wind farms have led to significant local objections and caused peat landslides due to the scale of land transformation required to make these landscapes stable for large-scale wind turbine construction (including to build access roads). In addition, the cables that supply data traffic to and from North America traverse the Atlantic seafloor and reach the west coast on remote beaches (see Starosielski, 2015). These ecological entanglements are often only seen by the Irish state and Amazon as "resources" and managed as such, meaning that there are few checks on how they are used.

In Quebec, these energy ecologies are even more entangled, even if on the surface they are less controversial. Ninety-five percent of the province's energy generation is supplied by hydroelectric dams spanning the vast province, with another 4 percent provided by wind (Canada Energy Regulator, 2021). When AWS draws from the grid in Quebec, it is directly benefiting from this abundant renewable energy array, meaning that arguments about energy supply tend to be cut short. However, beneath the surface lies a wealth of controversy: the scale of Hydro Québec's power generation necessarily disrupts the multiple ecologies of the bioregions all across the vast province of Quebec. In addition, Hydro Québec, as an institution of the settler colonial government, operates on unceded or stolen Indigenous land and often comes into friction with Indigenous communities and lifeways. This enactment of colonial territorial sovereignty and its disruptive, large-scale energy culture directly benefits AWS through its Canada Central infrastructure region.

We are not necessarily trying to develop a comprehensive map of different ecological regions and conceptions that might disrupt the territory-generating ambitions of AWS. Rather, we wish to look at how the very ecologies that support and define its global networks point to various links in the supply chain that can be observed, studied, and broken. After all, the supply chain does not end even within the demarcated territories that we have been taking as our example. The minerals and materials for the servers and computer components used by AWS in its data centres in Dublin do not come from other parts of Ireland; rather, they are mined and manufactured in the Global South in places like the Democratic Republic of the Congo and the People's Republic of China. Lithium for the backup batteries in Amazon's Montréal data facilities was shipped in, from elsewhere in Canada or from Bolivia or Afghanistan or elsewhere. These toxic components are then disposed of and recycled in other locations far from the facilities where they are utilised (see Gabrys, 2011). The waste economies and obsolescence of digital infrastructures like AWS data centres (see Taylor, 2021) demand that we pay close attention to the resources, ecologies, and supply chains necessary to sustain their operations. We can perhaps learn from the supply chain approaches to environmental politics advocated by Thea Riofrancos (2019) and Martín Arboleda (2020), in that we need to map and conceive of the global scale of Big Tech's operations before being able to truly form a global movement to curtail their power. Workers and activists, including the Make Amazon Pay campaign, are already finding ways to connect struggles across Amazon's sites of operation worldwide, and scholars of Amazon are following suit by identifying how worker and climate justice are necessarily intertwined (Vgontzas, 2021). These struggles will benefit from better understanding the way that Amazon's various corporate operations promote themselves regionally, and part of that will come from activists and scholars animating regional connections and disruptive ecologies across the territories and the boundaries enforced by the state and by corporations like Amazon.

Conclusion

This short chapter can only begin to point out how the dynamics of AWS' regional imaginations of the world have been operationalized across different geographies, speculating upon geographical dynamics that may continue to emerge as Amazon continues to cement its influence in the global cloud infrastructure. We must remember that these regions, and the policies and strategies that define them, are not fixed. After all, states and regional governments *can* in fact regulate against data centre development, however difficult it appears to counter the sheer capital power of these companies. Regional competition via tax rates may hopefully be on the decline due to comprehensive regulatory legislation and agreements proposed by the Organisation for Economic Co-operation and Development for a more standardized global corporate tax regime. US multi-nationals have recently pressured the Irish government to sign up to proposals by the OECD for a global corporate tax rate of 15 percent, whilst there is increased rancour in Europe at Ireland's failure to adequately regulate the tech companies based in the country. However, much as Ireland resisted this reform for so long, individual states or territories can act as a barrier to regulation (see, for example, Ireland's struggles with data protection due to the overbearing power of Big Tech companies in their state business strategies [Murgia and Espinoza, 2021]). It is ultimately to the benefit of these industries to be seen as compliant; reform will come largely through measures designed to sustain rather than curb these companies.

In some ways, then, even the remaining regulatory power of the state only affirms the power of these companies in enforcing *governments* to comply with public relations measures that are impossible to ignore. And in this environment, when tax rates may become less of a factor, the availability of resources like energy, land, and water becomes even more important. See, for example, Singapore and Amsterdam, both of which "paused" data centre development in 2019 over concerns for energy supply and land availability. In winter 2022, Ireland followed suit for similar reasons, with the state grid operator enacting a de facto moratorium on data centres in the Dublin region for the next few years. The declining availability of energy had already influenced AWS to locate a new data cluster in Drogheda, its first outside the immediate Dublin region. But beyond Drogheda, the side effect of this "pause" has been to encourage proposals and development of data centres in

Ireland's rural regions, closer to untapped renewable electricity supply. Thus these types of regulation introduce new geographical and regional formations. The availability of energy generation could become an increasingly pressing issue of regional competition, both within countries and between them.

Looking at the operations of AWS, it becomes clear that we need to foreground different ways of imagining regions beyond the normative geographies of development and capitalism. Part of this will come from refusing to draw additional boundaries on landscapes that necessarily thwart them or define their own fluid environments. Colonialism and capitalism have long drawn boundaries that do not account for what's actually there, based more on the division of resources and an infrastructural "view from nowhere" that only accounts for avenues of accumulation and not alternative lifeways (see Spice, 2018). Other epistemologies of "regions" and space in general might counter the forced boundaries and regionalisms of AWS and other cloud providers. If our collective lives and well-being are increasingly being migrated to the "cloud" (as Couldry and Mejias suggest is key to the dynamic of "data colonialism" and its implications for political subjectivity), we need to continue to be mindful of the material territoriality of these companies and their use and imaginations of regions and the boundaries enforced by states and capitalist designations. This is true whether we are thinking through the state's reliance on these companies, our consumer activity, or the administration of the systems we use to live. By understanding existing ecologies and how both human and more-than-human existence thrives through them, we can form a better politics of dissent against the manufactured regionalism of Big Tech.

References

Arboleda, Martín. (2020). *Planetary Mine: Territories of Extraction under Late Capitalism*. Brooklyn: Verso.

AWS. (n.d.-a). AWS Europe Countries and Territories. https://aws.amazon.com/legal/aws-emea-countries/.

———. (n.d.-b). Regions and Availability Zones. https://aws.amazon.com/about-aws/global-infrastructure/regions_az/.

Bresnihan, Patrick, and Brodie, Patrick. (2021). New Extractive Frontiers in Ireland and the Moebius Strip of Wind/Data." *Environment and Planning E: Nature and Space* 4, no. 4: 1645–64.

Brodie, Patrick. (2020a). Climate Extraction and Supply Chains of Data. *Media, Culture and Society* 42, no. 7-8: 1095–114.

Brodie, Patrick. (2020b). "Stuck in Mud in the Fields of Athenry': Apple, Territory, and Popular Politics. *Culture Machine* 19: 1–34.

Brodie, Patrick. (2021). Hosting Cultures: Placing the Global Data Centre "Industry." *Canadian Journal of Communication* 46, no. 2: 151–76.

Brodie, Patrick, and Velkova, Julia. (2021). Cloud ruins: Ericsson's Vaudreuil-Dorion data centre and infrastructural abandonment. *Information, Communication & Society* 24, no. 6: 869–85.

Burrington, Ingrid. (2016, November 8). Why Amazon's Data Centers Are Hidden in Spy Country. *The Atlantic*. https://www.theatlantic.com/technology/archive/2016/01/amazon-web-services-data-center/423147/.

Canada Energy Regulator. (2021, July 19). Provincial and Territorial Energy Profiles —Quebec. *Canada Energy Regulator*. https://www.cer-rec.gc.ca/en/data-analysis/energy-markets/provincial-territorial-energy-profiles/provincial-territorial-energy-profiles-quebec.html.

Carruth, Allison. (2014). The Digital Cloud and the Micropolitics of Energy. *Public Culture* 26, no. 2: 339–64.

Couldry, Nick, and Mejias, Ulises A. (2019). Data Colonialism: Rethinking Big Data's Relation to the Contemporary Subject. *Television and New Media* 20, no. 4: 336–49.

Cowen, Deborah. (2014). *The Deadly Life of Logistics: Mapping Violence in Global Trade*. Minneapolis, MN: University of Minnesota Press.

Easterling, Keller. (2014). *Extrastatecraft: The Power of Infrastructure Space*. Brooklyn, NY: Verso.

Gabrys, Jennifer. (2011). *Digital Rubbish: A Natural History of Electronics*. Ann Arbor, MI: University of Michigan Press.

Goodison, Donna. (2020, February 5). AWS Plans Data Center Expansion In Brazil. *CRN*. https://www.crn.com/news/cloud/aws-plans-data-center-expansion-in-brazil.

Hardt, Michael, and Negri, Antonio. (2000). *Empire*. Cambridge, MA: Harvard University Press.

Harvey, David. (1989). *The Condition of Postmodernity: An Enquiry into the Origin of Cultural Change*. Blackwell.

Harvey, David. (2005). *A Brief History of Neoliberalism*. Oxford University Press.

Hogan, Mél. (2015). Data flows and water woes: The Utah Data Center. *Big Data and Society* 2, no. 2: 1–12.

Hogan, Mél. (2021). The Data Center Industrial Complex. In *Saturation*, edited by Melody Jue and Rafico Ruiz. Durham, NC: Duke University Press.

Immen, Wallace. (2021, May 25). Demand for storage space in the cloud creates a land rush. *The Globe and Mail*. https://www.theglobeandmail.com/business/industry-news/property-report/article-demand-for-storage-space-in-the-cloud-creates-a-land-rush/.

Johnson, Alix. (2019). Data centers as infrastructural in-betweens: Expanding connections and enduring marginalities in Iceland. *American Ethnologist* 46, no. 1: 75–88.

Lally, Donal. (2019, October 2). The Sacred Fire of a Data Centre. *Strelka Magazine*. https://strelkamag.com/en/article/the-sacred-fire-of-a-data-center.

Lecavalier, Jesse. (2017). *The Rule of Logistics*. Minneapolis, MN: University of Minnesota Press.

Lee, Benjamin, and LiPuma, Edward. (2002). Cultures of Circulation: The Imaginations of Modernity. *Public Culture* 14, no. 1: 191–213.

Miller, Rich. (2017, October 17). ROOT Data Center Puts Montreal on the Hyperscale Map. https://datacenterfrontier.com/root-data-centers/.

Murgia, Madhumita, and Espinoza, Javier. (2021, September 13). Ireland is "worst bottleneck" for enforcing EU data privacy law —ICCL. *The Irish Times*. https://www.irishtimes.com/business/technology/ireland-is-worst-bottleneck-for-enforcing-eu-data-privacy-law-iccl-1.4672480.

Rasmussen, Mattias Borg, and Lund, Christian. (2018). Reconfiguring Frontier Spaces: The territorialization of resource control. *World Development* 101: 388–99.

Rastello, Sandrine. (2021, 30 March). Buyers target Canada's data centre market, lured by cheap power. *BNN Bloomberg*. https://www.bnnbloomberg.ca/buyers-target-canada-s-data-centre-market-lured-by-cheap-power-1.1584122.

Nixon, Rob. (2011). *Slow Violence and the Environmentalism of the Poor*. Cambridge, MA: Harvard University Press.

Novet, Jordan. (2021, July 29). Amazon cloud revenue growth accelerates to 37% in Q2. *CNBC*. https://www.cnbc.com/2021/07/29/aws-earnings-q2-2021.html.

O'Neill, Paul. (2021). Networked States: A Tour of Dublin's Digital Ecosystem. In *States of Entanglement: Data in the Irish Landscape*. New York: Actar Publishers.

Ong, Aihwa. (2004). The Chinese Axis: Zoning Technologies and Variegated Sovereignty. *Journal of East Asian Studies* 4: 69–96.

Ong, Aihwa. (2006). *Neoliberalism as Exception: Mutations in Citizenship and Sovereignty*. Durham, NC: Duke University Press.

Riofrancos, Thea. (2019, December 7). What Green Costs. *Logic*. https://logicmag.io/nature/what-green-costs/.

Schott, Ben. (2021, October 3). Give Amazon and Facebook a Seat at the United Nations. *Bloomberg*. https://www.bloomberg.com/opinion/articles/2021-10-03/give-amazon-and-facebook-a-seat-at-the-united-nations.

Spice, Anne. (2018). Fighting Invasive Infrastructures: Indigenous Relations against Pipelines. *Environment and Society* 9: 40–56.

Starosielski, Nicole. (2015). *The Undersea Network*. Durham, NC: Duke University Press.

Stone, Brad. (2013). *The Everything Store: Jeff Bezos and the Age of Amazon*. Little, Brown, and Company.

Taylor, A.R.E. (2021). Standing by for data loss: Failure, preparedness and the cloud. *ephemera: theory and politics in organization* 21, no. 1: 59–93.

Thatcher, Jim, O'Sullivan, David, and Mahmoudi, Dillon. (2016). Data Colonialism through Accumulation by Dispossession: New Metaphors for Daily Data. *Environment and Planning D: Society and Space* 34, no. 6: 990–1006.

Tomaney, John. (2017). Regionalism. In *The International Encyclopedia of Geography: People, the Earth, Environment, and Technology*, edited by Douglas Richardson,

Noel Castree, Michael F. Goodchild, Audrey Kobayashi, Weidong Liu, and Richard A. Marston. Hoboken, NJ: Wiley.

Tsing, Anna. (2004). *Friction: An Ethnography of Global Connection*. Princeton, NJ: Princeton University Press.

Tsing, Anna. (2015). *Mushroom at the End of the World: On the Possibility of Life in Capitalist Ruins*. Princeton, NJ: Princeton University Press.

Velkova, Julia. (2016). Data that warms: Waste heat, infrastructural convergence and the computation traffic commodity. *Big Data and Society* 3, no. 2: 1–10.

Velkova, Julia. (2021). Thermopolitics of data: cloud infrastructures and energy futures. *Cultural Studies* 35, no. 4-5: 663–83.

Vgontzas, Nantina. (Forthcoming). Toward Degrowth: Worker Power, Surveillance Abolition, and Climate Justice at Amazon. *New Global Studies*. http://ssrn.com/abstract=3981869.

Villegas, Alexander, and Beachy, Susan C. (2021). Inside Amazon's Employment Machine. *The New York Times*. https://www.nytimes.com/interactive/2021/06/15/us/amazon-workers.html.

PART V

APPENDIX

APPENDIX

~

Art and Action

Hiba Ali and Nina Sarnelle

Gig Economy and Automation

These projects investigate the ongoing transformation of the labor economy toward part-time and low-wage forms of work. Powered by platforms like Amazon's Mechanical Turk (mTurk), these "jobs" are typically paid incrementally by the task, and often utilize the worker's own personal space or equipment, reducing overhead and increasing flexibility for companies as they avoid long-term contracts and employee benefits, while building a workforce that is unstable, undervalued and disposable.

Danielle Dean, *Amazon (Proxy)* (2021)

Four live actors interact with videos of Amazon mTurk workers in a hybrid reality that imaginatively conflates contemporary working conditions with the 1934 worker's revolt at Fordlandia, a city developed in the Amazon to produce rubber for the Ford Motor Company.

https://hyperallergic.com/687741/danielle-dean-wades-through-two-hollow-utopias/

Liz Magic Laser, *In Real Life* (2019)

A multi-channel video installation that documents the lives of gig-workers around the world who support themselves on platforms like PeoplePerHour, Upwork, and Fiverr. The workers are also employed to create this "reality show," contributing voiceover, animation, and other production services.

https://lizmagiclaser.berta.me/in-real-life_/

Sebastian Schmieg, *I Will Say Whatever You Want In Front of a Pizza*, 2017

A video in the form of a Prezi presentation given by a cloudworker employed to train or impersonate bots. They are employed first by a pizza delivery service, then Amazon mTurk, and begin to think critically about their labor.

http://i-will-say-whatever-you-want-in-front-of-a-pizza.schloss-post.com/

Michael Mandiberg, *Workflow* (2017)

This body of work includes *Quantified Self Portrait (Rhythms)*, an audio work composed from the artist's heartrate data and email alert sounds; *Quantified Self Portrait (One Year Performance)*, a video created from images captured from the artist's computer and phone every fifteen minutes for a year, using the same process that is employed to surveil online workers; and *Postmodern Times*, a recreation of Charlie Chaplin's *Modern Times* produced by different workers on Fiverr.com.

https://www.lacma.org/art/exhibition/michael-mandiberg-workflow

Elisa Giardina Papa, *Technologies of Care* (2016)

A collaged video project that engages an invisible workforce of online caregivers: an ASMR artist, an online dating coach, a fetish video performer

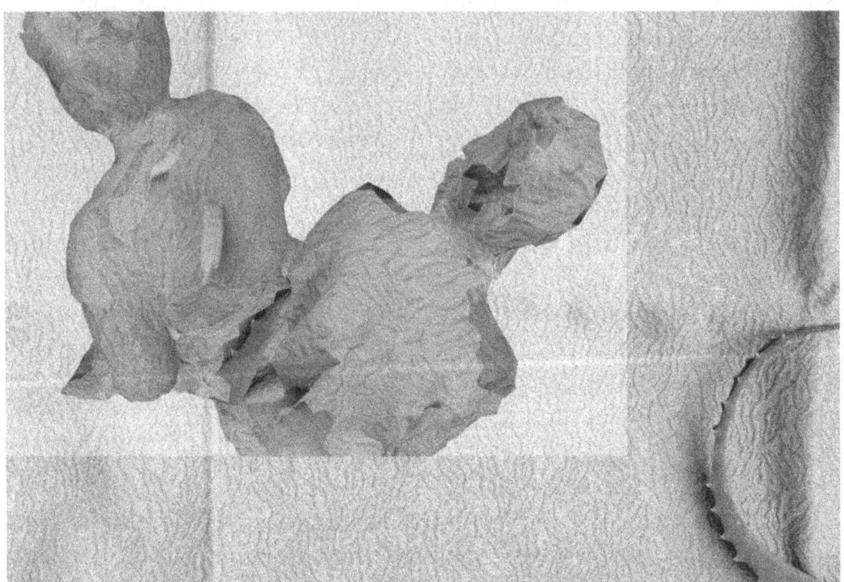

Figure 14.1. Elisa Giardina Papa, *Technologies of Care*, 2016. Still frame from video. Commissioned by Rhizome.org.

and fairytale author, a social media fan-for-hire, a nail wrap designer, and a customer service operator, based in Brazil, Greece, the Philippines, Venezuela, and the United States.

https://rhizome.org/editorial/2016/oct/04/the-download-technologies-of-care/

Anxious to Make (Liat Berdugo and Emily Martinez), *The Future of Work: Testimonials* (2016)

A video commissioned from "testimonial actors" on Fiverr.com. The actors hired were not given a script. Instead, they were presented with a series of questions about jobs, the sharing economy, and the future of work. To the artists' knowledge, the following responses reflect the personal views and experiences of these workers.

https://anxioustomake.ga/futureofwork

Further Information

Precarity Lab, *Technoprecarious* (2020)
Domenico Quaranta and Janez Janša (editors), *Hyperemployment: Post-work, Online Labour and Automation* (2020)
Mary L. Gray and Siddharth Suri, *Ghost Work: How to Stop Silicon Valley from Building a New Global Underclass* (2019)
Virginia Eubanks, *Automating Inequality: How High-Tech Tools Profile, Police, and Punish the Poor* (2018)
Astra Taylor, *The Automation Charade* (2018)
Nick Srnicek, *Platform Capitalism* (2016)
Trebor Scholz, editor, *Digital Labor: The Internet as Playground and Factory* (2013)

Precarious Labor and Resistance

This section addresses labor issues and organizing in the workplace, with specific attention paid to the ways in which certain types of underpaid and under-regulated jobs are racialized, gendered, and designed to exploit migrant workers' citizenship status. In warehouses and delivery trucks across the country, Amazon is known for using contract-based employment to withhold benefits, surveilling workers to enforce inhumane productivity standards, union busting, and failing to keep workers safe during COVID-19. This list includes organizations who have collectivized and unionized for worker dignity and rights.

Simon Denny, *Amazon Worker Cage* (2019)

A full-size creation of Amazon's 2016 patent for a "worker cage" designed to protect humans from the heavy machinery operating in a warehouse. Amazon itself never made the cage, but it remains in the public imagination as a portrait of labor alienation and the shifting relationship between humans and machines.

https://vimeo.com/426808612

Cat Bluemke, *Gigco: Escape the Gig Economy* (2019)

A mobile game that critiques the gamification of labor through tech-infused gig work. "Defend your minimum-wage job against impending automation in quick-paced, casual gameplay. If you make it to the end of your shift, you rack up points after-hours by using the company's social media app."

http://catbluemke.com/gigco.html

Hiba Ali, *Abra* (2018)

A five-minute video which places Ali in conversation with Amazon's customer-obsessed so-called mascot, Peccy. Their discussion about working-class labor, surveillance, and bubbles (economic, social, and soap filled) literally paints the video orange. They contend that orange is the contemporary color of labor and surveillance; it is racialized and classed.

https://hibaali.info/projects/abra

Figure 14.2. Hiba Ali, *Abra*, 2018. Still frame from video.

Cao Fei, *Asia One* (2018)

A sprawling sixty-three-minute fictional film shot in some of China's most advanced industrial facilities. With sparse dialogue, the narrative follows the only two employees wandering through an enormous automated sorting center, weaving together dreamlike sequences including a large inflatable octopus, a grapefruit spill, and a Cultural Revolution–era dance interlude.

http://www.caofei.com/works.aspx?id=79&year=2018&wtid=3

Jen Liu, *Pink Slime Caesar Shift* (2018)

A stylized twenty-four-minute video that presents proposals to alter the DNA of mass-produced in vitro hamburgers to carry secret messages of labor insurrection on behalf of Special Economic Zone female factory workers in China.

https://vimeo.com/256398759

Sanela Jahic, *The Factory* (2018)

Filmed in the context of local manufacturing plants, this longform video presents a series of dialogues between the machine, work, worker, owner, and c/Capital.

http://sanelajahic.com/works/the-factory/

Rodrigo Valenzuela, *Prole* (2015)

A nine-minute video that weaves among a group of Spanish-speaking laborers playing soccer in an unfinished building. This ethereal, intimate footage is collaged with voiceover in which they describe their working conditions and debate whether to unionize, instigating broader discussions about individualism, collectivity, and what it means to "work like an American."

http://www.rodrigovalenzuela.com/prole-1

Thảo Nguyên Phan, *Mekong Mechanical* (2012)

A hypnotic eighteen-minute video that depicts the night shift of a young female worker processing catfish in a factory in the Mekong Delta of southern Vietnam.

https://www.thaonguyenphan.com/mekong-mechanical

Organizations

Amazonians United

A movement of workers fighting for dignity. Together they identify workplace issues among Amazon workers internationally and take action to gain control over their work and collective future.

https://www.amazoniansunited.org/

Athena

A broad coalition of organizations taking on Amazon because they believe that control over our lives, our communities, and our democracy should be in our hands.

https://athenaforall.org/

The Awood Center

A worker-led organization of recent immigrants developing the next generation of leaders in Minnesota's diverse East African communities. This group made national news organizing Somali Amazon employees in protests, making some of the biggest labor gains against Amazon in the United States so far.

http://www.awoodcenter.org/

Justdue.it

A website made in response to Amazon's antiunion propaganda website "justdo.it" to support unionization efforts in Bessemer, Alabama.

https://www.vice.com/en/article/5dpkad/amazon-launches-anti-union-website-to-derail-alabama-union-drive

Make Amazon Pay

A network of global warehouse workers, climate activists, and citizens pushing back against Amazon.

https://makeamazonpay.com/

Support Amazon Workers

A website created to promote protests and actions held internationally.

https://supportamazonworkers.org/

Further Information

Alec MacGillis, *Fulfillment: Winning and Losing in One-Click America* (2021)

Sarah Jaffe, *Work Won't Love You Back* (2021)

Kyle Lewis and Will Stronge, *Overtime: Why We Need a Shorter Working Week* (2021)

Heike Geissler, *Seasonal Associate* (2018)

Sandro Mezzadra and Brett Neilson, *Border as Method, or, the Multiplication of Labor* (2013)

David R. Roediger, *The Wages of Whiteness: Race and the Making of the American Working Class* (2007)

Kim Moody, *US Labor in Trouble and Transition: The Failure of Reform from Above, the Promise of Revival from Below* (2007)

Sleep and Rest

In a culture of ever-expanding work hours, competitive hiring practices, and tracked performance metrics, the act of sleeping, resting, or abstaining from work (by choice or necessity) becomes an act of defiance. The following projects address accelerating pressures to perform and begin to reclaim the body as more than just a site of production. They explore the many ways that a cultural work "ethic" is constructed and reproduced.

Riar Rizaldi, *The Right To Do Nothing* (2021)

A forty-eight-minute atmospheric audio work with illustrations by Rega Ayundya Putri that tells the story of an Indonesian migrant domestic worker in Hong Kong who is trapped (or blessed) inside an ultraterrestrial world where the idea of work does not exist.

https://rizaldiriar.com/malas.html

Sašo Sedlaček, *Oblomo: Busy Being Lazy* (2020)

An art installation, digital platform, and custom software that uses biometric data to turn "inactivity, motionlessness, laziness into an economic value." Using its own cryptocurrency, the app rewards user inactivity by depositing Oblomo coins into their electronic wallet.

https://sasosedlacek.com/oblomo/

Beatriz Colomina, *Bed-In* (2018)

A recreation of John Lennon and Yoko Ono's 1969 "Bed-In." In the bed, Colomina holds interviews with architects, curators, and critics in pajamas, exploring the contemporary bed as a site of both work and sleep.

https://troika.uk.com/article/recent-bed-in-conversation-with-beatriz-colomina/

Danilo Correale, *No More Sleep No More* (2015)

A 240-minute video created from conversations with sleep experts and academics discussing "the condition of wakefulness in postmodernity."

http://www.danilocorreale.com/no-more-sleep-no-more

Yoojin Lee, *sleeping (in 'a city that never sleeps')* (2015)

A two-part video in which the artist sleeps on an air mattress in public spaces, raising questions about societal ideologies around work and rest, as well as who is allowed to sleep in public.

https://www.nijooy.com/sleepinginacity/

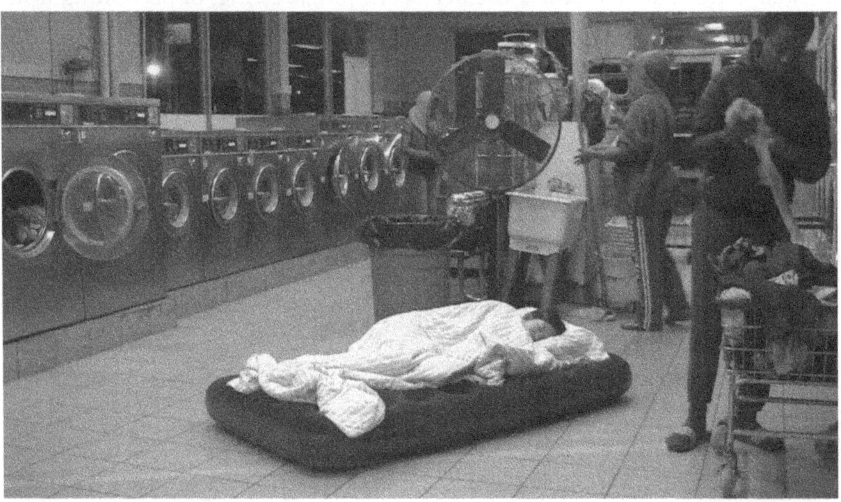

Figure 14.3. Yoojin Lee, *sleeping (in 'a city that never sleeps')*, 2015. Still frame from video.

Rodrigo Valenzuela, *Sisifo* (2015)

A two-channel video that layers audio from a sports coach and a former athlete preaching about "work ethic," "ability," and "success," over footage of janitors cleaning up a stadium after a game, carrying hundreds of black trash bags up the endless flights of stairs.

http://www.rodrigovalenzuela.com/el-sisifo

Further Information

Helen Hester and Nick Srnicek, *After Work: What is Left?* (lecture, 2019)
Silvio Lorusso, *Entreprecariat* (2019)
James Bridle, *New Dark Age: Technology and the End of the Future* (2018)
Jonathan Crary, *24/7: Late Capitalism and the Ends of Sleep* (2014)
Kathi Weeks, *The Problem with Work: Feminism, Marxism, Antiwork Politics, and Postwork Imaginaries* (2011)
André Gorz, *Reclaiming Work: Beyond the Wage-Based Society* (1999)
Mladen Stilinović, *In Praise of Laziness* (1993)

Dataveillance

The works featured in this section highlight ways in which information is used as a tool for subjugation and control, and explore actions that communities can take to protect themselves, obscure their data, and undermine the surveillance regime. Amazon harvests data from our online purchases, as well as through devices like the Echo, Ring camera, Fire products, and Kindle. This section is organized in two parts: one consists of art projects, and the other features organizations tackling issues of surveillance and privacy rights locally, many of them working in Black, brown, and working-class communities to resist the white supremacist data infrastructure.

Lauren McCarthy, *LAUREN* (2020)

A durational performance in which the artist plays the role of Amazon's "Alexa," installing networked smart devices and watching/interacting with participants in their own home. This work explores tensions between intimacy and privacy, convenience and agency, human labor and automation.

https://lauren-mccarthy.com/LAUREN

Shalini Kantayya, *Coded Bias* (2020)

A documentary following researcher Joy Buolamwini's discovery that facial recognition software is failing to accurately identify dark-skinned faces. As Buolamwini goes on to uncover widespread algorithmic bias, the film reveals threats artificial intelligence poses to civil rights and democracy.

https://www.codedbias.com/

Noah Levenson, *Stealing Ur Feelings* (2019)

A six-minute augmented reality experience that analyzes the viewer's face in real-time, revealing how popular apps like Snapchat use facial recognition technology to collect emotional data, make consequential decisions, and promote inequalities.

https://stealingurfeelin.gs/

Mandy Harris Williams, *Brown Up Your Feed* (2018)

A hashtag (#BrownUpYourFeed), lecture series, social media campaign, and challenge to think critically about who is "followed" and why. Created to push back against algorithm bias, this project encourages us to "reclaim their space online and rebuke the racism, misogyny and homophobia that often fill up our feeds."

https://youtu.be/SzpFH_lvwb8

Caroline Sinders, *Feminist Data Set* (2017–ongoing)

A set of workshops and toolkits created to interrogate every step of the artificial intelligence creation process from a critical feminist perspective. How might data set creation, training, and building a chatbot be repurposed to protest the Big Data industry?

https://carolinesinders.com/feminist-data-set/

Maryam Monalisa Gharavi, *Face/Less: Human, Inhuman, Abhuman* (2017)

A lecture that explores the political importance of the face in an age of surveillance and facial recognition. How is the "faceless" or covered face constructed as a threat, rendered inhuman or abhuman?

https://www.youtube.com/watch?v=EGihvChXzQM

Tabita Rezaire, *Deep Down Tidal* (2017)

A video essay that connects deep ocean fiberoptic cable lines to the Transatlantic slave trade routes, investigating water as an interface for communication that can also be used in the service of capitalist domination.

https://vimeo.com/248887185

Figure 14.4. Tabita Rezaire, *Deep Down Tidal*, 2017. Still frame from video.

Zach Blas, *Face Cages* (2014–2016)

A series of metal masks/wearable sculptures based on the intersecting diagrams imposed by facial recognition software. Worn for the camera by four queer artists, these biometric wireframes render the violence of data collection and computational abstraction as a literal "cage of information."

https://zachblas.info/works/face-cages/

Organizations

Algorithmic Justice League

An organization that combines art and research to illuminate the social implications and harms of artificial intelligence.

https://www.ajl.org/

Data 4 Black Lives

A movement of activists, organizers, and mathematicians committed to using data science to create concrete and measurable change in the lives of Black people. Tools like statistical modeling, data visualization, and crowd-sourcing, in the right hands, are powerful instruments for fighting bias, building progressive movements, and promoting civic engagement.

https://d4bl.org/

Ida B. Wells Just Data Lab

A Princeton Lab that rethinks and retools the relationship between stories and statistics, power and technology, data and justice.

https://www.thejustdatalab.com/

Our Data Bodies

A five-person team concerned about the ways our communities' digital information is collected, stored, and shared by government and corporations and how different data systems impact re-entry, fair housing, public assistance, and community development.

https://www.odbproject.org/

Stop LAPD Spying

A Los Angeles organization committed to dismantling government-sanctioned spying and intelligence gathering. They reject all forms of police oppression and any policy that makes people into suspects in the eyes of the state.

https://stoplapdspying.org

Theater of the Techno-Oppressed

A workshop adapting Augusto Boal's Theater of the Oppressed to explore power dynamics of contemporary techno-oppression, staging confrontations between characters engaged in digital interaction.

http://fredvanamstel.com/outreach/theater-of-the-techno-oppressed

Watching the Watchers

A toolkit that demystifies surveillance technologies in Seattle within the context of US structural inequities.

https://coveillance.org/

Further Information

Neema Githere, *What is Data Healing?* (2020)

Vladan Joler and Matteo Pasquinelli, *Nooscape* (2020)

Wendy Liu, *Abolish Silicon Valley: How to Liberate Technology from Capitalism* (2020)

Jessa Lingel and Kate Crawford, *Alexa, Tell Me About Your Mother: The History of the Secretary and the End of Secrecy* (2020)

Thao Phan, *Amazon Echo and the Aesthetics of Whiteness* (2019)

Kate Crawford and Trevor Paglen, *Excavating AI: The Politics of Images in Machine Learning Training Sets* (2019)

Joy Buolamwini, *Response: Racial and Gender bias in Amazon Rekognition—Commercial AI System for Analyzing Faces* (2019)
Safiya Umoja Noble, *Algorithms of Oppression* (2018)
Lisa Nakamura, *Indigneous Circuits* (2014)

Amazonification

Amazonification is a term used by financial analysts to refer to the company's rapid expansion—often with a celebratory or reverent tone—and the sheer force with which it gobbled up market share and reorganized and decimated existing industries. From its earliest days as the online bookseller that shuttered bookstores large and small, to the corporation's restructuring of distribution and logistics infrastructure and the enormous reach of Amazon Web Services, a strategy of disruption, domination, and monopolization forms the core of the corporation's business practices. The following projects address the rise of Amazon ubiquity, watching its myriad products and services inflate to governmental proportions and creep into every part of our lives.

Center for Land Use Interpretation, *Going with the Flow: Amazon in the Southland* (2021)

An exhibition documenting the current state of Amazon retail distribution facilities in Southern California, where fulfillment centers, warehouses, and delivery stations have been rapidly expanding in recent years.

http://clui.org/section/going-flow-amazon-southland

Mungo Thomson, *Snowman* (2020)

A series of bronze cast sculptures that perfectly simulate the ubiquitous stack of Amazon boxes left on a doorstep. These quotidian monuments to consumption were installed on the fake streets of the Paramount backlot in Los Angeles, like a plaything for zoomers in a place where it never snows.

http://mungothomson.com/work/snowman/

Nina Sarnelle, *Big Opening Event* (2019)

Five hundred Amazon boxes collected from all over the country are dropped from the ceiling of a new "fulfillment center" in an opening ceremony modeled after the balloon releases of public celebrations and political rallies. A thirty-minute video essay connects this celebratory spectacle to the misguided fanfare around mass commercial development projects.

https://vimeo.com/398862225/8cc8ee7e43

Figure 14.5. Nina Sarnelle, *Big Opening Event,* 2019. Commissioned by Black Cube Nomadic Museum.

Gottfried Haider, *Box with the air of its own making* (2019)

A series of air cushions collected from Amazon boxes and sent off for air quality analysis. Air cushions are inflated inside Amazon facilities using the warehouse's ambient air, creating a capsule of the worker's immediate environment that circulates anonymously around the world with every package.

https://gottfriedhaider.com/Box-with-the-air-of-its-own-making

Cao Fei, *11.11* (2018)

A sixty-minute documentary capturing the labor of JD.com logistics (the largest e-commerce site and largest retailer in China) before and after the Double Eleven Shopping Day (equivalent to Black Friday). The film travels from a distribution center in the outskirts of Beijing to JD.com headquarters, to the delivery network and couriers working at online shopping terminals.

http://www.caofei.com/works.aspx?id=78&year=2018&wtid=3

Roger Beebe, *Amazonia* (2017)

A twenty-five-minute film that explores the people and places "at the other end of the internet." The piece visits each of the four original Amazon fulfillment centers in Delaware, Nevada, Kansas, and Kentucky to reveal ways that e-commerce is transforming real space and labor practices.

http://www.rogerbeebe.com/films/amazonia.php

Excerpt: https://vimeo.com/351213988/e7ea8c312f

Further Information

Cory Doctorow, *Urban Broadband Deserts: Digital Redlining is a Policy, not an Accident* (2021)

Jake Alimahomed-Wilson; Ellen Reese, editors, *The Cost of Free Shipping* (2020)

Mark Graham, Rob Kitchin, Shannon Mattern, and Joe Shaw, editors, *How to Run a City Like Amazon, and Other Fables* (2019)

Danielle Child, *Working Aesthetics: Labour, Art and Capitalism* (2019)

Charmaine Chua, *"Indurable" Monstrosities: Megaships, Megaports, and Transpacific Infrastructures of Violence* (lecture, 2018)

Jesse Le Cavalier, *The Rule of Logistics: Walmart and the Architecture of Fulfillment* (2016)

Deborah Cowen, *The Deadly Life of Logistics: Mapping Violence in Global Trade* (2014)

Brad Stone, *The Everything Store: Jeff Bezos and the Age of Amazon* (2013)

~

Index

Abra (Ali), 310, *310*
acquisitions, 51–52, 211–13, 217–21, 228–29
activism: artists and, xix; Black Lives Matter movement, 234–35, 238; for climate justice, 247–48; human labor and, 259; against Mturk, 191n2; on streaming services, 235–36; virtuous viewing as, 227–28
Adorno, Theodor, 198
advertising, 235–40, *236–39*
Affordable Care Act, 214–15
Africa, 234–35, 258, 291, 294–95, 299
Agger, Ben, 197–98, 201
Alexa, 204, 281
Algorithmic Justice League, 317
algorithms: algorithmic logistical media, 117–18, *119*, 120; algorithmic management, 138–39; for business, 184–85; data and, 183–84; with FBA, 109; management of, 187; with 1-click button, 102, 107–9; recommendations from, 120–26; software and, 117–18; for technology companies, xiv
Ali, Hiba, 310, *310*
Alibaba, x, 105–6
allocative efficiency, 8
Amazon: Alexa, 204; Alibaba compared to, 105–6; Apple and, 81n242; automation at, 109–10; climate justice at, 255–60, 269–72, 276–82, *277*; Compact by Design Certification, 280; competition to, 27–28, 79n227, 80n235; consumption for, 202–7; in COVID-19, xi–xii, 150–51, 254–55; cross-subsidization schemes at, 85n288; culture and, xvi–xvii, 4–5; Dash Button, 203–4; deliveries from, 39–42; Diapers.com to, 87n311; DoD and, 287–88; DOJ and, 35, 83n276; Echo, 217, 232, 270, 315; e-commerce on, 77n203; electricity consumption at, 253–54; employees, 27, 92n373; environmental impact of, xvii–xix; in Europe, 259; FBA, 28, 39–42, 109; FCs, 131–34, 138–39, 141–42, 143; female employees at, 177, *178–79*,

179; Frustration-Free Packaging program, 274; "Gazelle Project," 4; in globalization, 291–92; Google and, 88n320, 282; Greenpeace on, 272–73, 278; The Helix building by, 275; history of, ix–x, 200–202, 272–75; infrastructure at, 125–26; investing by, 6; labor at, 133–35; market shares by, 87n312; in media, 3, 32; as monopolies, xiii–xiv; Netflix and, 228–31; patents at, 116; philosophy at, 132–33; politics at, 207–8; power of, 62n19; pricing at, 80n240, 83n272; profits at, 3, 24–27; public relations at, 272–76; public utilities and, 56–57; publishing at, 29–30, 81n253; Quidsi acquisition, 36–39; reputation of, 61n15, 159, 250–52; resistance and, xv–xvi; Ring doorbell and, 231–32; sales tax on, 77n204; scholarship on, xii–xv; to SEC, 78; Shipment Zero program, 278; shipping at, 89n331, 203; stock, 61n12, 206n77; strategy at, x–xi, xiii–xiv, 24–28, 60n8; structural dominance of, 28; third-party sellers on, 105–6; Uber and, 56, 250–51; virtuous viewing and, 234–40, *236–39*; to Wall Street, 80n232; Walmart and, 36–37, 87n319, 88n324, 290–91. *See also specific topics*

Amazon (Proxy) (Dean, D.), 307

AmazonBasics, 44

Amazon Empire (PBS), 218

Amazon Flex, 126

Amazon Fresh, 220–21

Amazon Go, 218

Amazonia (Beebe), 320

Amazonians United, 312

Amazonification, 319–21, *320*

Amazon Labor Union, 216

Amazon Marketplace, 28, 43–45, 57, 103–5, 109–12, 118

Amazon Mom program, 37–38

Amazon Prime: Amazon Studios and, 228–31, *230*; consumption for, 196–200, 207–8; in culture, 195–96; deliveries by, 90n346; food delivery on, 156; history of, 202–7; Hollywood compared to, 229; labor and, 252–53; loyalty program, 25; Netflix and, 253; pricing of, 26–27; Prime Now hubs, 41; Prime Reading, 201; Prime Video Library, 205–8; profits from, 26; shipping, 36; strategy at, 195–96; in US, xvi–xvii; Whole Foods on, 212

Amazon Standard Identification Number (ASIN), 108

Amazon Studios: Amazon Prime and, 228–31, *230*; politics at, 234–40, *236–39*; strategy of, xvii; streaming services from, 217–18; virtuous viewing and, 227–28, 231–34, 241–42

Amazon Technology Academy, 232

Amazon Web Services (AWS): carbon emissions at, 273; cloud business at, 231, 252–54, 277; cyberattacks against, 53; e-commerce on, 231; essential-facilities for, 58; infrastructure at, 270, 296; Mturk and, 149, 183; platforms with, 153–56; policy, 294–97; political ecology of, 297–300; power of, 44–45; profits from, 60n8; regionalism of, 287–90, 300–301; reputation of, 252–54; strategy of, xii–xiii, 290–94; streaming services and, 217–18; territorial politics of, xix; to Wall Street, 91n351

Amazon Worker Cage (Denny), 310

Amazon Workers and Supporters, 149

Amobi, Tuna, 71n144

AMT. *See* Mechanical Turk

anticipatory shipping, 115–18, *119*, 120–26

antitrust laws: anticompetitive conduct, 45–49; to Chicago School, 6–9; for competition, 17–23, 75n187; conduct remedies in, 71n141; Congress on, 62n21; consumer welfare and, 64n37, 65n43, 74n174; in democracy, 74n177; for e-books, 31; enforcement of, 68n106, 70n138; in Europe, 92n376; philosophy of, 59–60; politics of, 73n167, 98n459; against predatory pricing, 9–14, 50–51; against private power, 74n178; with public utilities, 54–55; regulation and, 49–50; in US, 3–6; vertical integration and, 14–17, 51–54, 71n140

The Antitrust Paradox, 8, 12–13, 37, 69n128

APIs. *See* application program interfaces

Apple: Amazon and, 81n242; Apple Pay, 217; competition with, 282; digital music to, 29; Google and, x, 82n261, 273; iTunes Store, 201

application program interfaces (APIs), 188

applied predictive analytics, 126

Arbery, Ahmaud, 227

Arlington, Virginia, xi

Arnold, Thurman, 14–15

art, about Mturk, 165–68, *167–79*, 170–71, 173–77, 179–80, *181*

artificial intelligence, 127n3

artists, xix

Aschoff, Nicole, 214

Asia, 288

Asia One (Fei), 311

ASIN. *See* Amazon Standard Identification Number

Athena, 312

The Atwood Center, 312

augmented despotism, 131–33, 135, 139–43

automation: at Amazon, 109–10; with barcodes, 133–34; of consumption, 204; in Europe, 156–57; of food delivery, 154–56; gig economy and, xix, 307–9, *308*; human labor and, 136–37, 152; humans compared to, 136–37; of labor, xiv–xv; of management, 186; philosophy of, 134–35; software for, 133; in US, xv–xvi

AWS. *See* Amazon Web Services

Baer, Bill, 62n21, 72n145

Bank Holding Company Act (1956), 52

banking, 52–53, 96n428

barcodes, 133–34, 137, 139

bargaining power, 50

Barnes & Noble, 32, 34, 82n260, 200

Bazaarvoice network, 94n403

BeautyBar.com, 36

Bed-In (Colomina), 314

Beebe, Roger, 320

below-cost pricing, 29–36, 48, 56, 81n255, 84n279

Berdugo, Liat, 309

Best Buy, 202

Bezos, Jeff: acquisitions by, 228–29; on competition, 221; with Congress, 110; during COVID-19, 166; on creative content, 238; culture to, 242; to employees, 176–77, *176–78*; to investors, 61n13; to Justice Department, 5; leadership of, 165, 240; Mackey and, 213–14, 216; net worth of, 158–59, 233; pricing by, 29; Quidsi to, 86n303; reputation of, 183–84; Salke and, 228; in space, 257–58; strategy of, ix–x, 25, 200; to Wall Street, 3

Big Opening Event (Sarnelle), 319, *320*

Big Tech, 291, 295, 301

billionaire biodiversity, 247–50

Bing, 88n320

Bingo Hell (film), 238–39, *238–39*, 241
bin Salman, Mohammed, 288
bioregions, 297–300
BIPOC community, 227–28
Black Friday, 259
Black Lives Matter movement, 234–35, 238
Black voices advertising campaign, 227–28, 235–41, *236–39*
Blas, Zach, 317
Blog Theory (Dean, J.), 198
Blood Sugar Sex Magic (Red Hot Chili Peppers), 200
Bluemke, Cat, 310
Blue Yonder, 127n3
Books-A-Million, 200
Bork, Robert, 8, 11–13, 16–17, 37–39, 64n38, 69n128, 70n133
Bowker, Geoffrey, 271
Bowman, Ward, 11–12
Box with the air of its own making (Haider), 320
Braverman, Harry, 134
Brazil, 295
brick-and-mortar stores, 33, 39, 44, 79n225
Brooke Group Ltd. v. Brown & Williamson Tobacco Corp., 13–14, 33, 48
Brown Shoe v. United States, 15
Brown Up Your Feed (Williams), 316
Brown & Williamson, 13–14
browser extensions, 104–5
Burke, Edmund, 258
burrough, xtine, *167*, *169*, *171–72*, *174*
business: algorithms for, 184–85; in China, 47; climate justice in, 272–75; cloud, 44–45, 153–54, 191n1, 231, 252–54, 275–77, 287–88; collusion in, 6–7; competition in, 62n20; consumer welfare in, 51; coupons for, 83n275; dominance in, 24–27; expansion in, 27–28; with FBA, 102; in globalization, 98n458; in Hollywood, 234–35; mergers, 8–9; microwork software for, 184–85, 188–90; monopolies in, 319; multiple business lines, 23, 27–28; philosophy, 25; power in, 59–60; private label, 110; profits, 3–4; prophylactic approaches to, 52, 57; in public relations, 269–72; scale in, 49; social planning in, 257; software companies, 189–90; strategy, 23; structure, 5–6

calculation centers, 123
Canada, 294, 296–99
capitalism: capital in, 104, 134–35; colonialism and, 301; commodities in, 199; communicative, 198; competition in, 201–2, 293; Conscious Capitalism movement, 212, 214–15, 217; consumers in, 196–97; data in, 143; despotism in, 135; with e-commerce, 153–54; fast, 197–98; issues in, 196; to Mackey, xvii; platform, 158; politics of, 102; production in, 140; race in, 241; scholarship on, xviii; surveillance, 131–32, 142–43, 242; venture, 47–48, 189–90
capital markets, 45–49
carbon emissions, 254–55, 273, 277, *277*
Carter, Jimmy, 237
Center for Land Use Interpretation, 319
Chakrabarti, Meghna, 279
The Chi (film), 240
Chicago School: antitrust laws to, 6–9; on competition, 18; consumer welfare to, 22; economics of, 11–12; history of, 63n29; market efficiencies in, 19; mergers in, 70n139; philosophy of, 75n182; on predatory pricing, 35, 67n82; on rational

actors, 24; scholarship from, 21, 33–34; Supreme Court and, 12; theory, 16; on vertical integration, 17, 42
China, x, 47, 52, 251, 299
Clay, Dorothy, *172*
Clayton Act, 9–10, 14–15, 66n56, 66nn56–57, 84n285, 86n305
Clean Power Plan, US, 275
Clicking Clean report, 279
climate justice: activism for, 247–48; at Amazon, 255–60, 269–72, 276–82, *277*; in business, 272–75; carbon emissions and, 254–55; employees for, xviii, 247–48, 255–57; in environmental humanities, 297–98; Greenpeace on, 253; recycling in, 251–52
Clinton, Hillary, 59
cloud business, 44–45, 153–54, 191n1, 231, 252–54, 275–77, 287–88. *See also* Amazon Web Services
clustering, data, 122
Coded Bias (Kantayya), 316
collusion, 6–7
Colomina, Beatriz, 314
colonialism, 301
Comcast, 17, 270
commerce, 52–53
commodities, 101–2, 136, 199, 202–3, 206–7
communicative capitalism, 198
Compact by Design Certification, 280
competition: to Amazon, 27–28, 79n227, 80n235; antitrust laws for, 17–23, 75n187; with Apple, 282; with Barnes & Noble, 82n260; with Bazaarvoice network, 94n403; Bezos on, 221; in business, 62n20; in capitalism, 201–2, 293; in cloud business, 287–88; Congress on, 23; consumer welfare and, 5–6, 99n464; for deliveries, 274; in e-books, 82n259, 83n267; to Google, 38–39; in markets, 6–9, 18–19, 41; in online platform markets, 50–54; predatory pricing and, 48–49; profits and, 59; regulation of, 66n67, 72n145, 75n188; in Robinson-Patman Act, 66n71; scholarship on, 63n29; between streaming services, 234–35; Supreme Court on, 10–11; between third-party sellers, 106–7, *107*; UK Competition and Markets Authority, 155; for UPS, 88n330; in US, 7
computer programming, 183–91
conduct remedies, 71n141
confidential information, 110–11
conflict, on platforms, 156–58
Congress: on antitrust laws, 62n21; Bezos with, 110; on competition, 23; consumer welfare to, 18; on economics, 20–21; monopolies to, 8; regulation by, 57–58; Robinson-Patman Act (1936) to, 89n311; scholarship on, 16; Sherman Act in, 20; Supreme Court and, 9–10
Conscious Capitalism movement, 212, 214–15, 217
consumer *dividuals*, 122
consumer electronics, 248, 259
consumer habits, 79n222, 106–8
consumer welfare: allocative efficiency and, 8; antitrust laws and, 64n37, 65n43, 74n174; in business, 51; to Chicago School, 22; competition and, 5–6, 99n464; to Congress, 18; data and, 46; economics of, 19–22; media on, 24; with monopolies, 64n38; politics of, 18–19, 59–60, 272; scholarship on, 19; technology and, 62n20; in US, 26
consumption: for Amazon, 202–7; for Amazon Prime, 196–200, 207–8; automation of, 204; of e-books, 200–202; electricity, 253–54; energy, 275; media, 199–200; politics of, 195–96;

production and, 121; of streaming services, 195–96
contemporary logistics, 159
content producers, 198–99
control, of employees, 138–39
Correale, Danilo, 314
costs, 39
Cote, Denise, 30–31
Coulson, Grover, 239
coupons, 83n275
COVID-19: Amazon in, xi–xii, 150–51, 254–55; Bezos during, 166; deliveries after, 218–19; for Deliveroo, 156; economics during, 252; for employees, 177, 179; employees during, 309–13, *310*; hiring during, 232–33; in US, x, 251; for Whole Foods, 214–15, 217
Cowen, Deborah, 290–91
creative content. *See specific topics*
creative resistance, 179
Cronin, Anne M., 271, 281
cross-subsidization schemes, 85n288
crowdsourcing, 187
Cultural Studies, xi–xii
culture: Amazon and, xvi–xvii, 4–5; Amazon Prime in, 195–96; to Bezos, 242; disruption in, 200–202; e-books in, 29–36; materiality paradox in, 249–50; technology and, 248–49; vertical integration in, 22; violence and, 250–60
customer history, 123–24
customer service, 212–13
cyberattacks, 53
cybertarianism, 249–50

Dallas Museum of Art Center for Creative Connections, *174*
Dash Cart, 220
Dashmart, 219
data: algorithms and, 183–84; in barcodes, 137; at brick-and-mortar stores, 44; from browser extensions, 104–5; in capitalism, 143; centers, 253–54, 298, 300–301; in cloud business, 191n1; clustering, 122; colonialism, 295–96; on consumer habits, 106–8; consumer welfare and, 46; controllers, 111; dataveillance, 315–19, *317*; from deliveries, 118; exploitation of, 34, 43–45; generation, 132–33; hyperscale data centers, 253–54; from mergers, 51; patents with, 123–24; personal, 87n316; power of, 48–49; from private label business, 110; on product niches, 104–5; purchase, 120; regulation, 288–89; researchers, 295; science, 92n373, 115–16; in surveillance capitalism, 142; from Target, 53; to technology companies, xvii–xviii; transaction, 115–16
Data 4 Black Lives, 317
Davis, Mike, 250–51
Dean, Danielle, 307
Dean, Jodi, 198
Deep Down Tidal (Rezaire), 316, *317*
Deleuze, Gilles, 134–35
deliveries: from Amazon, 39–42; by Amazon Prime, 90n346; competition for, 274; after COVID-19, 218–19; data from, 118; food delivery, 154–58; politics of, 231–32; Whole Foods, 259
Deliveroo, 154–58
demand, 63n30, 121, 125–26, 127n3
democracy, 74n177
Denny, Simon, 310
Department of Defense (DoD), 287–88
Department of Justice (DOJ): on acquisitions, 48; Amazon and, 35, 83n276; FTC and, 45–46, 49, 62n21, 70n138; on media, 74n180, 85n292; monopolies to, 72n147; predatory pricing to, 29–30; US, 5, 17

Diapers.com, 36, 87n311
Didi Chuxing, 52
digital labor, xvi, 168, *169–70*, 170, 183–91
digital media, 289
digital music, 29
digital warehouses, 137
discriminatory pricing, 32–33
Disney+, 195, 229
disruption, 165–66, 200–202
distribution, xiv, 8, 69n130, 117–18, 198–99, 269–70
diversity, of markets, 19–20
dividuals, 122
DoD. *See* Department of Defense
DOJ. *See* Department of Justice
dominance: in business, 24–27; dominant platforms, 54–58; in infrastructure, 43; leveraging, 39–42; market, 24–27, 76n191, 271; structural, 28; of Uber, 47; from vertical integration, 44
Door-Dash, 154–55, 219
Douglas, William O., 21

Easterling, Keller, 292
e-commerce: on Amazon, 77n203; on AWS, 231; brick-and-mortar stores and, 33; capitalism with, 153–54; distribution footprint in, 269–70; e-books, 29–36, 48, 80n240, 82n259, 83n267, 200–202; economics of, 38; employees in, 28; independent sellers in, 41–45; infrastructure of, 27–28, 45, 55, 58, 133–35; Internet for, 58–60; in markets, 4–5; media on, 59; nondiscrimination in, 56–57; platforms for, 124–25; profits in, 46–47; success, ix–x; warehouses for, 152–53
economics: of Chicago School Revolution, 11–12; Congress on, 20–21; of consumer habits, 79n222; of consumer welfare, 19–22; during COVID-19, 252; of creative content, xvii; of e-commerce, 38; economic structuralism, 6–8; of globalization, 98n458, 292–93; in Global South, 254; of Internet, xii–xiii, 48–49; of libertarian technologists, x; markets and, 24–27; of monopolies, 3–6; politics and, 53–54; of predatory pricing, 58–59; of pricing, xiii–xiv; of profits, xiv; of purchasing, 91n352; rational actors in, 24; scholarship on, 45–46, 63n25; service economy, 141; of stocks, 61n12; structure in, 17–18; of taxes, x–xi; of UPCs, 108; of value realization, 101–2; violence and, 247–50; of warehouses, 40–41. *See also specific topics*
ecoregions, 297–300
Edison, Thomas, 189
efficient market hypothesis (EMH), 48
electricity consumption, 253–54
11.11 (Fei), 320
Emergency (film), *230*
emerging markets, 115–16
EMH. *See* efficient market hypothesis
employees: Amazon, 27, 92n373; augmented despotism with, 139–43; Bezos to, 176–77, *176–78*; for climate justice, xviii, 247–48, 255–57; control of, 138–39; during COVID-19, 309–13, *310*; COVID-19 for, 177, 179; dehumanization of, 233–34; at Deliveroo, 154–55; digital labor for, 183–91; in e-commerce, 28; female, 177, 179, *179*; of gig economy, 155–56; HITs for, 176–77, *176–77*; in "Illuminated Voices" exhibit, *175*, 175–76; in *The Laboring Self* exhibition, 173–77, *174*, *174–77*; machinic dispossession of, 135–37; in *Mechanical Olympics*, 166–68, *167–68*, 180; in *Mediations*

on Digital Labor, 168, *169–70*, 170; at Mturk, 156, 179–80, *181*, 191n3; race of, 241–42; resistance by, 150–52, 158–59; in "Return to Sender" exhibit, 176–77, *176–77*; strikes by, 156–57; Team Member Healthy Discount Incentive Program for, 215–16; in US, 259–60; *Vigil for Some Bodies* by, 170–71, *171–73*, 173, 180; in warehouses, 62n17, 131–35, 143, 248; Whole Foods, xv, 216–17, 222n7
energy consumption, 275
Engles, Friedrich, 258
environmental humanities, 297–98
environmental impact, xvii–xix
Environmental Protection Agency (EPA), 280
Escape the Gig Economy (Bluemke), 310
essential facilities doctrine, 57–58
ethnic studies, 190–91
Europe, 92n376, 137, 156–57, 259, 293–94
The Expanse (TV show), 159
expansion, 27–28, 47
exploitation, of data, 34, 43–45
Extinction Rebellion, 259
extrastatecraft, 292

Facebook, x, 47, 51–52, 140, 273, 281
Face Cages (Blas), 317
Face/Less (Gharavi), 316
The Factory (Jahic), 311
fair returns, 98n445
fair trade, 66n58
Fandango, 195
Fast Capitalism (Agger), 197–98
FBA. *See* Fulfillment-by-Amazon
FCs. *See* fulfillment centers
Federal Trade Commission (FTC): Clayton Act for, 86n305; DOJ and, 45–46, 49, 62n21, 70n138; Federal Trade Commission Act, 14, 21; history of, xiv; on mergers, 17, 37; monopolies to, 8–9; politics of, 12; predatory pricing to, 67n82; Supreme Court and, 16; vertical integration to, 69n116
FedEx, 40–42, 89n337, 126, 274
Fei, Cao, 311, 320
female employees, 177, 179, *179*
Feminist Data Set (Sinders), 316
Figueres, Christiana, 276
Fishwick, Adam, 254
Floyd, George, 227
food delivery, 154–58
Ford Motor Company, 16
free markets, 54
Friedman, Milton, 75n189
Frith, Simon, 197
Frustration-Free Packaging program, 274
FTC. *See* Federal Trade Commission
Fulfillment-by-Amazon (FBA), 28, 39–42, 102, 109, *172*
fulfillment centers (FCs), 131–34, 138–39, 141–43, 171, 173
fulfillment logistics, 135–36
full-time work, 141–42
The Future of Work (Berdugo and Martinez), 309

Galbraith, John Kenneth, 21, 73n173
Gamito, Marta Cantero, 271
"Gazelle Project," 4
geopolitics, 288–94
George, James, 20–21
Gharavi, Maryam Monalisa, 316
Ghosh, Shamik, 167, *168*
Ghosh, Soham, 167, *168*
gig economy, xix, 155–56, 307–9, *308*
Glenn, Evelyn Nakano, 191
globalization: in Africa, 234–35, 258, 291, 294–95, 299; Amazon in, 291–92; business in, 98n458; economics of, 99n458, 292–93; in Europe, 137; Ireland in, 291, 293–94, 296, 298–

301; labor in, 185–86; regionalism in, 294–97; Whole Foods in, 211–12; after World War II, 115
Global North, 254, 295
Global Optimism, xviii–xix, 276
Global South, 250, 254, 299
Going with the Flow (Center for Land Use Interpretation), 319
Goldman, Emma, 173–74
Goldman Sachs, 254
Google: Amazon and, 88n320, 282; Apple and, x, 82n261, 273; competition to, 38–39; Facebook and, 140; to FTC, 46; Microsoft and, 253; Uber and, 53, 143
Go Set a Watchman (Lee, H.), 31
Great Depression, 14–15
Greenpeace, 253, 272–73, 278, 279
grocery shopping. *See* Whole Foods
growth, 47
Grubhub, 154–55
Guattari, Félix, 134–35
Guerrero, Gigi Saul, 238–39, *239*

Hachette, 4
Haider, Gottfried, 320
Hammond, Stig, 187–88
Harvey, David, 287, 293
Harvey, Martin, 151–52
HBO Max, 195
health care, 214–15
Heidegger, Martin, 102
The Helix building, 275
Hesse, Renata, 98n459, 99n464
"Hired Hands" display, *174*, 175–76
A History of Standard Oil Company (Tarbell), 9
HITs. *See* human intelligence tasks
Hoar, George, 20
Holland, John, 151
Hollywood, 229, 234–35
homogeneous markets, 121
horizontal mergers, 8–9, 37–39
Horkheimer, Max, 198
Howe, Jeff, 187
human intelligence tasks (HITs), xvi, 165–67, *167–68*, *170*, 176–77, *176–77*
human labor, 136–37, 139–40, 143, 152, 188, 259
Huws, Ursula, 134
hyperscale data centers, 253–54

IBM, 278
Ida B. Wells Just Data Lab, 318
"Illuminated Voices" exhibit, *175*, 175–76
independent sellers, 41–45
Independent Workers Union, 157–58
India, 185–86
Industrial Revolution, 103
industry, 7, 40–41, 95n417, 95n419
information, 104–5, 110–11
infrastructure: at Amazon, 125–26; at AWS, 270, 296; dominance in, 43; of e-commerce, 27–28, 45, 55, 58, 133–35; logistics of, 116–17, 120; for 1-click button, 101–3, 111–12; of warehouses, 109–10
initial public offerings (IPOs), 157–58
innovation, 8–9
In Real Life (Laser), 307
Instagram, 51–52
International Digital Media and Arts Association, 173
International Energy Agency, 253
Internet: cybertarianism, 249–50; for e-commerce, 58–60; economics of, xii–xiii, 48–49; net neutrality, 97n444; public utilities compared to, 56; spam, 186. *See also specific topics*
Interstate Commerce Commission, 54
investing, 6, 47–48, 92n381, 94n399, 189–90
IPOs. *See* initial public offerings
Irani, Lilly, 153

Ireland, 291, 293–94, 296, 298–301
iTunes Store, 201
I Will Say Whatever You Want In Front of a Pizza (Schmieg), 308

Jahic, Sanela, 311
James Bond franchise, 207
Jana Partners, 211
Japan, 248–49
Jenkins, Barry, 240
Jobs, Steve, 189
job-sharing platforms, 189–90
Jungle Scout, 105
jurisprudence, 13
Justdue.it, 312
just-in-case concept, 103–5
Just Walk Out, 219–21

Kant, Immanuel, 258
Kantayya, Shalini, 316
Katz, Miranda, 180
Kelly-Rae, Chanin, 233–34
Kennedy, Anthony, 13–14
Kiersey, Nicholas, 254
Kindle, 29–36, 82n259, 200–202, 206, 251, 259, 281
Kleiner Perkins, ix
knowledge machines, 126
Kroger, 220

labor: at Amazon, 133–35; Amazon Labor Union, 216; Amazon Prime and, 252–53; automation of, xiv–xv; digital, xvi, 168, *169–70*, 170, 183–91; full-time work, 141–42; in globalization, 185–86; history of, 159; human, 136–37, 139–40, 143, 152, 188, 259; management and, 132–33; with Mturk, 307–9, *308*; organization of, 136; precarious, xix, 309–13, *310*; production and, 109–10, 132, 159; regulation of, 292; from sweatshops, 173–74; temp workers, 141–42
Laser, Liz Magic, 307
LAUREN (McCarthy), 315
Lee, Harper, 31
Lee, Yoojin, 314, *314*
Levenson, Noah, 316
leveraging dominance, 39–42
libertarian technologists, x
Ligget, 13–14
LinkedIn, 92n376
lithium, 299
Liu, Jen, 311
LiveNation, 17, 71n143
logistics: algorithmic logistical media, 117–18, *119*, 120; contemporary, 159; of digital media, 289; fulfillment, 135–36; of infrastructure, 116–17, 120; media, 127n2; operations, 131; of platforms, 158–59; of probability, 115–18, *119*, 120–26; race and, 231–34; of suppliers, 158
Lord of the Rings franchise, 207
loss-leading, 30–31
Lund, Christian, 291
Luxemburg, Rosa, 258
Lyft, 52

machinic dispossession, 131–37, 143
Mackey, John, xvii, 211–17, 219, 221, 222n7
Macy's, 25
Make Amazon Pay, 312
management, 132–33, 138–43, 186–87, 216
Manchester By the Sea (film), 229–30
Mandiberg, Michael, 308
The Man in the High Castle (TV show), 235
manufacturing, 250
Marcuse, Herbert, 258–59

markets: barriers in, 36–39; capital, 45–49; competition in, 6–9, 18–19, 41; diversity of, 19–20; e-commerce in, 4–5; economics and, 24–27; emerging, 115–16; EMH, 48; free, 54; homogeneous, 121; market dominance, 24–27, 76n191, 271; market efficiencies, 16–17, 19; market power, 22, 24, 46; monopolies in, 11; online platform, 50–54; open, 73n173; production of, 115–17, 121–26; profits and, 24–27; structure of, 6; UK Competition and Markets Authority, 155; US, 12
Martinez, Emily, 309
The Marvelous Mrs. Maisel (TV show), 238
Marx, Karl, 103–4, 109, 134–35, 140–41, 143
Master (film), *230*
materiality paradox, 249–50
Matsushita Electric Industrial Co. v. Zenith Radio Corp, 12–13, 33, 48
McCarthy, Lauren, 315
MCI Communications Corp. v. American Telephone & Telegraph Co., 57–58
McQueen, Steve, 240
McSweeny, Terrell, 49
Mechanical Turk (Mturk): activism against, 191n2; AWS and, 149, 183; disruption with, 165–66; employees at, 156, 179–80, *181*, 191n3; HITs at, xvi, 165–66; "Illuminated Voices" exhibit about, *175*, 175–76; *The Laboring Self* exhibition about, 173–77, *174*, *174–77*; labor with, 307–9, *308*; *Mechanical Olympics*, 166–68, *167–68*, 180; *Mediations on Digital Labor* and, 168, *169–70*, 170; microtasks on, xv; platforms with, 152–53; politics of, 183–91; reputation of, 158–59; "Return to Sender" exhibit about, 176–77, *176–77*; *Vigil for Some Bodies*, 170–71, *171–73*, 173, 180; warehouses and, 150; in *Women's Work is (Screen) Saved*, 177, 179, *179*
media: algorithmic logistical, 117–18, *119*, 120; Amazon in, 3, 32; on consumer welfare, 24; consumption, 199–200; digital, 289; DOJ on, 74n180, 85n292; on e-commerce, 59; logistics, 127n2; print, 197; speculation in, 4; after World War II, 197
Mediations on Digital Labor, 168, *169–70*, 170
Mekong Mechanical (Phan), 311
mergers: in Chicago School, 70n139; in Clayton Act, 15; data from, 51; FTC on, 17, 37; horizontal, 8–9, 37–39; review of, 65n47; structure in, 65n41; in telecommunications, 71n143; vertical, 16–17
Meta. *See* Facebook
Method and System for Anticipatory Package Shipping (patent), 116
Mezzadra, Sandro, 292
MGM Studios, 207
Microsoft, 45–46, 92n376, 253, 278
microtasks, xv
microwork, 184–85, 188–90
migration, 152
Miller-Tydings Act, 10
Mitchell, Sara, xiii
Mitchell, Stacy, 271
monopolies: Amazon as, xiii–xiv; in business, 319; to Congress, 8; consumer welfare with, 64n38; distribution by, 69n130; to DOJ, 72n147; dominant platforms as, 54–58; economics of, 3–6; to FTC, 8–9; in markets, 11; oligopolies and, 6–7, 46, 59; Standard Oil, 9–10
Montréal, Canada, 296–97
Mosco, Vincent, 204

Mturk. *See* Mechanical Turk
multiple business lines, 23, 27–28
Munn v. Illinois, 54–55
Musk, Elon, 234

Nader, Ralph, 21
NAFTA. *See* North American Free Trade Agreement
National Retail Federation, 32–33
NBC, 17
Neilson, Brett, 292
neoliberalism, 272
Netflix, 53, 195, 228–31, 253, 270
net neutrality, 97n444
networking, ix
1984 (Orwell), 199, 206
no alternative sellers, 106–7, *107*
No More Sleep No More (Correale), 314
nondiscrimination, 55–57
nonprice effects, 8–9
Nook, 32, 200
North American Free Trade Agreement (NAFTA), 293
Notes from Below, 150–52, 155–56
The Nutty Professor series, *236*, 237

Obamacare, 214–15
Oblomo (Sedlaček), 313
OECD. *See* Organisation for Economic Co-operation and Development
oligopolies, 6–7, 46, 59, 256–57
on-demand streaming video, 204–5
1-click button: algorithms with, 102, 107–9; infrastructure for, 101–3, 111–12; no alternative sellers and, 106–7, *107*; ready-to-hand concept with, 103–5; supply chain arbitrage with, 105–6; value realization with, 109–11
Ong, Aihwa, 292
online behavior, 79n225
online platform markets, 50–54
open markets, 73n173
opportunity scores, 105
organic food. *See* Whole Foods
Organisation for Economic Co-operation and Development (OECD), 300
organization, 149–52, 154
O'Rourke, Anastasia, 273
Orwell, George, 199, 206
Our Data Bodies, 318
outcomes, 22
output, 18–19

Pallot, Richard, 247
Papa, Elisa Giardina, *308*, 308–9
parasitic management, 143
Paris Agreement, 276
patents, 116, 123–24
personal data, 87n316
personalized pricing, 32–33
Perzanowski, Aaron, 198–99
Peters, John D., 117, 127n2
Phan, Thảo Nguyên, 311
philosophy: at Amazon, 132–33; of antitrust laws, 59–60; of augmented despotism, 135; of automation, 134–35; business, 25; of Chicago School, 75n182; of consumer electronics, 259; of fair returns, 98n445; investing, 94n399; of machinic dispossession, 134; of private power, 75n186; social change and, 180; of Whole Foods, xvii
pick, in warehouses, 138–39
Pick-and-Shovel play, 154
Pink Slime Caesar Shift (Liu), 311
platforms: with AWS, 153–56; capitalism, 158; capital markets and, 45–49; for cloud business, 153–54; conflict on, 156–58; dominant, 54–58; in e-commerce, 124–25; job-sharing, 189–90; logistics of, 158–59; with Mturk, 152–53; online platform markets, 50–54;

platform governance, 281; power on, 49–58, 96n432; regulation of, 54–60; Rekognition, 232; scholarship on, 149–50; of vectorialists, 103–4
politics: at Amazon, 207–8; at Amazon Studios, 234–40, *236–39*; of antitrust laws, 73n167, 98n459; of capitalism, 102; of consumer welfare, 18–19, 59–60, 272; of consumption, 195–96; of creative resistance, 179; of customer service, 212–13; of deliveries, 231–32; of digital labor, xvi; economics and, 53–54; of FTC, 12; geopolitics, 288–94; of Mturk, 183–91; of nondiscrimination, 55; political ecology, 297–300; of regulation, 96n432, 270–71; of Sherman Act, 8–10, 20, 75n186; territorial, xix; of "too-big-to-fail" policy, 53; of virtuous viewing, 228–31, *230*
Posner, Richard, 7
Postmates, 154–55
Powell, Walter, 154
power: abuse of, 19–20, 59; of Amazon, 62n19; of AWS, 44–45; bargaining, 50; in business, 59–60; of companies, 22; of data, 48–49; of information, 104; market, 22, 24, 46; of market dominance, 24–27; of oligopolies, 256–57; on platforms, 49–58, 96n432; private, 21, 74n178, 75n186; for profits, 111–12; structural dominance, 28; of third-party sellers, 111–12
precarious labor, xix, 309–13, *310*
predatory pricing: antitrust laws against, 9–14, 50–51; Chicago School on, 35, 67n82; competition and, 48–49; to DOJ, 29–30; economics of, 58–59; to FTC, 67n82; loss-leading and, 30–31; recoupment test and, 32
prediction, 125–26, 127n3
pricing: at Amazon, 80n240, 83n272; of Amazon Prime, 26–27; below-cost, 29–36, 48, 56, 81n255, 84n279; by Bezos, 29; in Clayton Act, 66n57; of commodities, 202–3; discriminatory, 32–33; economics of, xiii–xiv; effects, 65n47; investing and, 92n381; nonprice effects, 8–9; output and, 18–19; personalized, 32–33; price-cutting, 66n71, 67n93; price-fixing, 6–7; price theory, 6–8, 63n30; rate settings for, 55–56; in recoupment test, 33–34, 68n105; resale price maintenance, 10; in Sherman Act, 63n24; Supreme Court on, 50–51; at Uber, 93n391; at Walmart, 31, 81n255. *See also* predatory pricing
print media, 197
private label business, 110
private power, 21, 74n178, 75n186
probability, 115–18, *119*, 120–26
process, 22–23
production: in capitalism, 140; consumption and, 121; distribution and, xiv, 8; labor and, 109–10, 132, 159; of markets, 115–17, 121–26; from suppliers, 21–22
product niches, 104–5
profits: at Amazon, 3, 24–27; from Amazon Prime, 26; from AWS, 60n8; business, 3–4; competition and, 59; in e-commerce, 46–47; economics of, xiv; at Facebook, 47; markets and, 24–27; power for, 111–12
Progressive movement, in US, 54
Prole (Valenzuela), 311
prophylactic approaches, 52, 57, 95n419
public relations, 269–76
public utilities, 54–57, 98n445

publishing, 29–30, 32, 34–36, 80n240, 81n253. *See also specific topics*
purchase data, 120

Québec, Canada, 294, 296–99
Queen & Slim (film), 240
Quidsi, 36–39, 86n303

race, 227–28, 231–42, *236–39*. *See also* virtuous viewing
Ramirez, Edith, 62n21
Ranciere, Jacques, 180
Rasmussen, Mattias Borg, 291
rate settings, 55–56
rational actors, 24
ready-to-hand concept, 103–5
Reagan, Ronald, 17
recommendations, from algorithms, 120–26
recoupment test, 14, 29–36, 68n105, 68n107
recycling, 251–52
Redbox, 195
Red Hot Chili Peppers, 200
Reed, James, 21
regionalism: of AWS, 287–90, 300–301; ecoregions, 297–300; geopolitics and, 290–94; in globalization, 294–97
regulation: antitrust laws and, 49–50; in banking, 96n428; of competition, 66n67, 72n145, 75n188; by Congress, 57–58; data, 288–89; Global Optimism for, xviii–xix; of labor, 292; Marx on, 140–41; of platforms, 54–60; politics of, 96n432, 270–71; of public utilities, 54–56; self-regulation, 279–80, 282; social, 140–41; Supreme Court on, 54–55; in US, xii
Rekognition, 232
Reputation Institute, 4
requests for proposals (RFPs), x–xi
resale price maintenance, 10
resistance, xv–xvi, xix, 149–52, 158–59, 179, 309–13, *310*
resources, 63n30
rest, 313–15, *314*
retail, 81n255, 118
"Return to Sender" exhibit, 176–77, *176–77*
Rezaire, Tabita, 316, *317*
RFPs. *See* requests for proposals
The Right To Do Nothing (Rizaldi), 313
Ring doorbell, 231–32
Rivett-Carnac, Tom, 279
Rizaldi, Riar, 313
Robinson-Patman Act (1936), 10–12, 66n64, 66n71, 89n311
Rolnik, Guy, 63n29
Roosevelt, Franklin, 75n188
Rosenfeld, Morris, 173–74
Rossiter, Ned, 117

SaferWay, 214
sales tax, 77n204
Salke, Jennifer, 228
Sam Goody, 202
Sarnelle, Nina, 319, *320*
Saudi Arabia, 288
scale, 49
Schmieg, Sebastian, 308
Schultz, Jason, 198–99
science, 92n373, 115–16, 277, *277*
Scotland, 150
Scott, MacKenzie, ix
Searle, John, 115
Sears, 25
Seattle, Washington, x, xi
Seattle Kraken, 269
Securities and Exchange Commission (SEC), 78
Sedlaček, Sašo, 313
self-regulation, 279–80, 282
Separations Principle, 95n417
service economy, 141

Sherman, John, 20
Sherman Act: Clayton Act and, 14, 84n285; in Congress, 20; jurisprudence in, 13; for Microsoft, 45–46; politics of, 8–10, 20, 75n186; pricing in, 63n24
shipping: at Amazon, 89n331, 203; Amazon Prime, 36; anticipatory, 115–18, *119*, 120–26; for retail, 118; Shipment Zero program, 278
Silberman, Six, 153
Sinders, Caroline, 316
Sisifo (Valenzuela), 315
sleep, 313–15, *314*
sleeping (Lee, Y.), 314, *314*
Small Axe films, 240
Smalls, Christian, 234
smartphones, 157
Smith, Paul, 197
Snowman (Thomson), 319
social change, 180
social media. *See specific platforms*
social planning, 257
social regulation, 140–41
social systems, 125–26
software, 117–18, 133, 143, 184–85, 188–90
Sony Pictures, 229
SoundCloud, 199, 231
South Africa, 295
spam (Internet), 186
speculation, 4
sports, 252–53, 269
Spotify, 199
Standard Oil, 9–10
Standard & Poor's 500, 4
Starbucks, 216
Starnaman, Sabrina, 173–74, *174*
Star Wars franchise, 207
Stealing Ur Feelings (Levenson), 316
stocks, 61n12, 76n195, 157–58, 206n77, 254
Stop LAPD Spying, 318
stow, in warehouses, 135–37
Strategic Organizing Center, 102
streaming services: activism on, 235–36; advertising on, 235–40, *236–39*; from Amazon Studios, 217–18; AWS and, 217–18; choices for, 227–28; competition between, 234–35; consumption of, 195–96; on-demand streaming video, 204–5; options, 206–7; sports on, 252–53. *See also* Amazon Prime
strikes, 156–57
structure: of anticompetitive conduct, 45–49; business, 5–6; in economics, 17–18; economic structuralism, 6–8; of markets, 6; in mergers, 65n41; process and, 22–23; structural concerns, 23; structural dominance, 28
subscription models, 195–96, 205–6
subsidies, 34–35, 85n288
Sundance Film Festival, 229–30
suppliers, 21–22, 105–6, 121, 158, 251
Support Amazon Workers, 312
Supreme Court: Bork on, 12–13; Chicago School and, 12; Clayton Act and, 15; on competition, 10–11; Congress and, 9–10; essential facilities doctrine for, 57–58; FTC and, 16; on pricing, 50–51; recoupment test from, 14; on regulation, 54–55; scholarship to, 68n106; on Sherman Act, 8
surveillance, in warehouses, 171, *172*
surveillance capitalism, 131–32, 142–43, 242
sweatshops, 173–74

Tamir, Dahn, 187–88
Tarbell, Ida, 3, 9
Target, 26, 39, 53, 87n312, 203
taxes, x–xi, 77n204, 293–94
Taylor, Breonna, 227

Team Member Healthy Discount Incentive Program (Whole Foods), 215–16
Technologies of Care (Papa), *308*, 308–9
technology: Big Tech, 291, 295, 301; companies, xii–xiv, xvii–xviii; consumer electronics, 248; consumer welfare and, 62n20; culture and, 248–49; human labor and, 139–40; Just Walk Out, 219–21; libertarian technologists, x; technological solutionism, 281
telecommunications, 71n143
temp workers, 141–42
Tencent, x
Tesla, 234, 274
Thatcher, Jim, 295
Theater of the Techno-Oppressed, 318
third-party sellers, 105–7, *107*, 110–12, 154
Thomson, Mungo, 319
Thrift, Nigel, 122
Ticketmaster, 17, 71n143
Tomaney, John, 289
"too-big-to-fail" policy, 53
Tower Records, 202
transaction data, 115–16
Transnational Couriers Federation, 157
Trump, Donald, 288
Tryon, Chuck, 204–5
Turkopticon, 153
Tyler Perry productions, 237

Uber, 47, 52–53, 56, 93n391, 134, 143, 154–55, 250–51
Underground Railroad series, 240
United Kingdom, 150–51, 154–58
United Parcel Service (UPS), 39–42, 88n330, 89n337, 126, 274
United States (US): Affordable Care Act in, 214–15; Amazon Prime in, xvi–xvii; antitrust laws in, 3–6; automation in, xv–xvi; Bank Holding Company Act in, 52; Black Friday in, 259; Black Lives Matter movement in, 234–35, 238; Clean Power Plan, 275; competition in, 7; consumer welfare in, 26; COVID-19 in, x, 251; DoD, 287–88; DOJ, 5, 17; employees in, 259–60; EPA, 280; in geopolitics, 288–90; India and, 185–86; markets, 12; multinationals, 291; organic food in, 221; Progressive movement in, 54; race in, 227–28; regulation in, xii; RFPs in, x–xi; Saudi Arabia and, 288; technology companies in, xii–xiii; warehouses in, 151, 242. *See also specific topics*
universal product codes (UPCs), 106, 108
UPS. *See* United Parcel Service
US. *See* United States
Utah Pie, 11–12
Utah Pie Co. v. Continental Baking Co., 11

Vaheesan, Sandeep, 57
Valenzuela, Rodrigo, 311, 315
value realization, 101–2, 109–11
Varney, Christine, 70n139
vectorialists, 103–4
venture capitalism, 47–48, 189–90
vertical integration, 14–17, 22, 42–44, 51–54, 69n116, 69n128, 71n140
Vigil for Some Bodies, 170–71, *171–73*, 173, 180
violence: culture and, 250–60; economics and, 247–50
virtuous viewing: Amazon and, 234–40, *236–39*; Amazon Studios and, 227–28, 231–34, 241–42; politics of, 228–31, *230*

Waite, Morrison, 55
Waithe, Lena, 240
The Walking Dead (TV show), 206

Wall Street, ix, 3, 76n195, 80n232, 91n351
Walmart: Amazon and, 36–37, 87n319, 88n324, 290–91; Best Buy and, 202; distribution centers, 118; fulfillment logistics at, 135–36; Kroger and, 220; pricing at, 31, 81n255; strategy at, 25–26, 38–39; Target and, 87n312
Walt Disney Company, 229
Walton, Sam, 290–91
warehouses: digital, 137; for e-commerce, 152–53; employees in, 62n17, 131–35, 143, 248; in industry, 40–41; infrastructure of, 109–10; management of, 139–43; Mturk and, 150; pick in, 138–39; in Scotland, 150; stow in, 135–37; surveillance in, 171, *172*; in US, 151, 242
Warner Bros., 229
Washington Post, 217–18
Watching the Watchers, 318
waterbed effect, 89n333
Wayans Brothers films, 237
West, Emily, 212–13
WhatsApp, 51–52, 157
Whole Foods: acquisition of, 211–13, 217–21; deliveries, 259; employees, xv, 216–17, 222n7; history of, 213–17; philosophy of, xvii
Williams, Mandy Harris, 316
Women's Work is (Screen) Saved, 177, 179, *179*
Workflow (Mandiberg), 308
World War II, 115, 197, 248–49
Wozniak, Steve, 189
Wu, Tim, 95n417

Yahoo, 88n320
YouTube, 166, *167–68*

Zenith Radio Corp., 12–13
Zingales, Luigi, 63n29
Zoom, 270
Zuboff, Shoshana, 131–32
Zuckerberg, Mark, 281

~

List of Contributors

Hiba Ali is an assistant professor at the college of design in the art and technology program at the University of Oregon. They are a digital artist, educator, scholar, DJ, experimental music producer, and curator based across Chicago, Illinois, Austin, Texas, and Toronto, Ontario. Their performances and videos concern surveillance, womxn/womyn of color, and labor.

David Arditi is an associate professor of sociology at the University of Texas at Arlington. He also serves as the director of the Center for Theory. Arditi has published several books including *Streaming Culture: Subscription Platforms and the Unending Consumption*, *iTake-Over: The Recording Industry in the Streaming Era*, and *Getting Signed: Record Contracts, Musicians and Power in Society*.

Patrick Brodie completed an FRQSC postdoctoral fellowship in the Department of Art History and Communication Studies at McGill University in Montréal. He is currently an assistant professor (ad astra fellow) in the School of Information and Communication Studies at University College Dublin. His research focuses on the environmental politics of digital media infrastructure, with a particular interest in the connections between energy and data. He has published and forthcoming writing in journals including *Media, Culture and Society*, *New Media and Society*, *Information, Communication, and Society*, and *Culture Machine*, among other venues. He is a member of the Grierson Research Group and the Global Emergent Media Lab.

xtine burrough (x/x or she/her) is a media artist recognized with commissions or grant funding from the Photographers' Gallery, London; Puffin Foundation West; Humanities Texas; The National Lottery (United Kingdom); and California Humanities. A professor in the School of Arts, Technology, and Emerging Communication at UT Dallas, burrough directs LabSynthE.

Callum Cant is a postdoctoral researcher at the Oxford Internet Institute on the Global Partnership for AI's "Fair Work for AI" project focusing on regulatory frameworks for artificial intelligence in the workplace. His first book, *Riding for Deliveroo*, is an investigation of class conflict in platform capitalism.

Lisa Daily works and teaches at New York University as Director of Community Engagement and Associate Faculty at the Gallatin School. Daily's research interests center on visual media, capitalist formations, humanitarianism, labor, and consumer/commodity cultures with a focus on issues of inequality and power regarding race, gender, class politics, and geopolitical divides. She holds a PhD in cultural studies from George Mason University.

Alessandro Delfanti is an associate professor at the University of Toronto, where he researches the politics of digital technology. He is the author of *The Warehouse: Workers and Robots at Amazon.*

Brett Hutchins is professor of media and communications and Head of the School of Media, Film and Journalism at Monash University. His books include *Environmental Conflict and Media* (co-editor), *Sport Beyond Television: The Internet, Digital Media & the Rise of Networked Media Sport* (co-author), and *Digital Media Sport: Technology, Culture & Power in the Network Society* (co-editor). His most recent articles appear in *International Journal of Communication, Telematics and Informatics*, *Media, Culture & Society*, and *Communication & Sport.*

Lilly Irani is an associate professor of communication and science studies at the University of California, San Diego. She co-founded digital worker advocacy organization and software project Turkopticon, now a worker-run organization. She is author of *Chasing Innovation: Making Entrepreneurial Citizens in Modern India* (2019) and *Redacted* (with Jesse Marx) (2021).

Lina Khan is associate professor of law at Columbia University and in 2021 was named chair of the Federal Trade Commission in the Biden administration. Khan teaches and writes about antitrust law, infrastructure industries law, the antimonopoly tradition, and law and political economy.

Libby Lester is director of the Institute for Social Change and UNESCO Chair in Communication, Environment and Heritage at the University of Tasmania. Her publications include *Global Trade and Mediatised Environmental Protest*, *Media and Environment*, and *Transnational Protests and the Media* (co-author).

Richard Maxwell is professor of media studies at Queens College, City University of New York. His publications include *The Spectacle of Democracy*, *Culture Works: The Political Economy of Culture*, *Herbert Schiller*, *Global Hollywood* (co-author), *Greening the Media* (co-author), *The Routledge Companion to Labor and Media*, *Media and the Ecological Crisis* (co-editor), and *How Green is Your Smartphone?* (co-author).

Toby Miller is profesor visitante, Universidad Complutense Madrid and Research Professor of the Graduate Division, University of California, Riverside. His most recent books are *A COVID Charter, a Better World*, *Violence*, *The Persistence of Violence: Colombian Popular Culture*, and *How Green is Your Smartphone?*

Whitney Monaghan is a lecturer in communications and media studies at Monash University. Her publications include *Queer Girls, Temporality and Screen Media: Not Just a Phase*, and *Queer Theory Now: From Foundations to Futures* (co-author).

Eva-Maria Nyckel is a PhD candidate at the Humboldt University of Berlin. She has been working on the investigation of digital process management systems such as Salesforce and their influence on work processes and organizational environments. Central questions in her research are how the implementation of management algorithms transforms our notion of work itself as something that is programmable, and how these systems affect the idea of separating different forms of labor.

Paul O'Neill is a postdoctoral research fellow in the ADAPT centre for AI-Driven Digital Content Technology at University College Dublin. His research is concerned with the implications of our collective dependency on networked technology. As an artist-researcher, Paul has exhibited and presented his work at various cultural institutions and events including Science Gallery (Dublin), Ars Electronica festival (Linz) and Inspace (Edinburgh) and has writing for publications including the Institute of Network Cultures (Amsterdam) and ANNEX—Ireland's representative at the 2021 Venice Architecture Biennale.

Ulysses Pascal is a researcher in information studies. Their research focuses on market infrastructure and the role of information technologies in the global production and reproduction of market logics. Specifically, they ask how interfaces, protocols, metadata schema, and communication technologies structure power relations embedded in multi-sided market platforms.

Nikolaus Poechhacker is a postdoctoral researcher at the Digital Age Research Center (D!ARC), University of Klagenfurt. In his work he is researching the relationship between democratic institutions, law, social order, and algorithmic systems in various domains, bringing together perspectives from media theory, STS, computer science, and sociology.

Nina Sarnelle is an artist and musician living on stolen Tongva/Kizh/Chumash land that is often referred to as Los Angeles. She earned a bachelor of arts from Oberlin College and a master of fine arts from Carnegie Mellon University in 2012. A founding member of artist collectives Institute for New Feeling and dadpranks, her artwork includes intimate participatory performances, large public events, music composition, video, and sculpture.

Emily West is professor of communication at the University of Massachusetts Amherst, with research interests in the areas of platform studies, consumer culture, and digital media. She is the author of *Buy Now: How Amazon Branded Convenience and Normalized Monopoly* (2022) and co-editor of *The Routledge Companion to Advertising and Promotional Culture* (2013).

Jamie Woodcock is a senior lecturer at the Open University and a researcher based in London. He is the author of *The Fight Against Platform Capitalism* (2021), *The Gig Economy* (2019), *Marx at the Arcade* (2019), and *Working the Phones* (2017).

~

About the Editors

Paul Smith is professor of cultural studies and global affairs at George Mason University. Between 1999 and 2002, he was chaired professor and department head of Media and Cultural Studies at the University of Sussex. At George Mason he has been director of the Center for the Study of the Americas and currently teaches mostly in the cultural studies PhD program, but also for global affairs. He was elected president of the national Cultural Studies Association (2016–2018). He is the author of *Pound Revised*, *Discerning the Subject*, *Clint Eastwood: A Cultural Production*, *Millennial Dreams: Culture and Capital in the North*, and *Primitive America: The Ideology of Capitalist Democracy*. He has edited *Men in Feminism* (with Alice Jardine), *Madonnarama* (with Lisa Frank), and *Boys*, and has published a book of translations from Jean Louis Schefer, *The Enigmatic Body*. His essays and articles have appeared in scores of journals and collections in the United States and overseas. His most recent edited volume is *The Renewal of Cultural Studies*, and he is currently completing a book on COVID vaccines.

Alexander Monea is an assistant professor in the English department and cultural studies program at George Mason University. He researches the history and cultural impacts of computers and digital media. He is the author of *The Digital Closet: How the Internet Became Straight* and co-author of *The Prisonhouse of the Circuit: Politics of Control from Analog to Digital*. He is also an editor for the journal *Data & Policy* focusing on the area of ethics, equity, and trust. He received his PhD in Communication, Rhetoric, and Digital Media from North Carolina State University.

Maillim Santiago is a media and culture scholar pursuing a cultural studies doctoral track at George Mason University. She has contributed work to *MAI: Feminism & Visual Culture* and Final Girls Film Festival. She received her master of fine arts in entrepreneurial digital cinema from the University of Central Florida. Her work has screened across the country, including the Brooklyn Women's Film Festival, Tampa Bay Comic Con, Florida's Undergraduate Research Conference, Orlando Film Festival, Final Girls Film Festival, and more.

www.ingramcontent.com/pod-product-compliance
Lightning Source LLC
Chambersburg PA
CBHW021105270326
41929CB00009B/742

* 9 7 8 1 5 3 8 1 7 5 5 8 3 *